A MATTER OF DISPUTE

A MATTER OF DISPUTE

MORALITY, DEMOCRACY, AND LAW

CHRISTOPHER J. PETERS

OXFORD
UNIVERSITY PRESS

Oxford University Press, Inc., publishes works that further Oxford University's objective
of excellence in research, scholarship, and education.

Oxford   New York
Auckland   Cape Town   Dar es Salaam   Hong Kong   Karachi   Kuala Lumpur   Madrid   Melbourne
Mexico City   Nairobi   New Delhi   Shanghai   Taipei   Toronto

With offices in
Argentina   Austria   Brazil   Chile   Czech Republic   France   Greece   Guatemala   Hungary   Italy
Japan   Poland   Portugal   Singapore   South Korea   Switzerland   Thailand   Turkey   Ukraine
Vietnam

Copyright © 2011 by Oxford University Press, Inc.

Published by Oxford University Press, Inc.
198 Madison Avenue, New York, New York 10016

Oxford is a registered trademark of Oxford University Press
Oxford University Press is a registered trademark of Oxford University Press, Inc.

Library of Congress Cataloging-in-Publication Data

Peters, Christopher J.
 A matter of dispute : morality, democracy, and law / Christopher J. Peters.
   p. cm.
 Includes bibliographical references and index.
 ISBN 978-0-19-538722-3 ((hardback) : alk. paper)
 1. Rule of law—Philosophy. 2. Law—Moral and ethical aspects. 3. Law—Methodology.
 I. Title.
 K3171.P669 2011
 340'.112—dc22

                                                             2010031839

 2 3 4 5 6 7 8 9

Printed in the United States of America on acid-free paper

Note to Readers
This publication is designed to provide accurate and authoritative information in regard to the subject matter
covered. It is based upon sources believed to be accurate and reliable and is intended to be current as of
thetime it was written. It is sold with the understanding that the publisher is not engaged in rendering legal,
accounting, or other professional services. If legal advice or other expert assistance is required, the services of
a competent professional person should be sought. Also, to confirm that the information has not been
affected or changed by recent developments, traditional legal research techniques should be used, including
checking primary sources where appropriate.

*(Based on the Declaration of Principles jointly adopted by a Committee of the
American Bar Association and a Committee of Publishers and Associations.)*

You may order this or any other Oxford University Press publication by
visiting the Oxford University Press website at www.oup.com

For Trish,
who knows there are three words that can never be replaced with new ones

CONTENTS

The Price of Law

Suppose you have the misfortune of being President of the United States on September 11, 2001, the day al-Qaeda terrorists hijack four jet airliners, crashing two into the New York World Trade Center towers, a third into the Pentagon building outside Washington, D.C., and a fourth (after passengers mount resistance) into a field in Pennsylvania, thus killing almost 3000 people within the space of about an hour and forty-five minutes.

In the days, weeks, and months after September 11, you will have many horribly difficult decisions to make. One of them, let's suppose, is whether to authorize the National Security Agency (NSA), a clandestine organization charged with gathering intelligence in foreign countries, to secretly wiretap phone calls and intercept e-mails between people in the United States and people abroad suspected of al-Qaeda ties. The decision seems at first like a no-brainer. The 9/11 attacks were devastating to the country, not just in terms of lost life, but economically and, perhaps worse, psychologically; you view your chief responsibility as President to be the prevention of similar attacks on your watch. Al-Qaeda is a far-flung international terrorist organization with a declared agenda of bringing mayhem to the United States and its allies, domestically and abroad. The surveillance would be employed only against people identified by the NSA's highly trained professionals as likely al-Qaeda contacts or affiliates. None of the information gathered would be used for any purpose other than the prevention of future terrorist acts—which it might very well accomplish.

But there is a problem. Your legal advisers tell you that the surveillance you contemplate, if conducted without a judicially granted warrant, probably would be illegal. There is a federal statute on the books—enacted in the mid-1970s in the wake of the Watergate scandal—that requires a warrant before the communications of people within the United States can be monitored or intercepted. Because some of the parties to the conversations the NSA wants to monitor would be located within the United States, the surveillance technically falls within the scope of this statute. And it is out of the question to seek a warrant every time the NSA wants to place a wiretap; time and secrecy are too much of the essence.

So you have a choice. You can do what you think is appropriate, perhaps even necessary, to protect the country and its citizens from further catastrophic terrorist attacks. Or you can obey the law—not just the statute requiring a warrant for electronic surveillance, but Article II of the Constitution, which imposes upon you, the President and thus the nation's highest-ranking law-enforcement official, a duty to "take Care that the Laws be faithfully executed."

The question is not just which you should choose. The question is why, with so much at stake, you should think there is any good reason to obey the law at all—to follow the rules on paper rather than do what you believe is morally right.

It is that remarkably difficult question that this book attempts to answer.

* * *

The central ideas advanced in this book, and indeed the book itself, have occupied what is, on reflection, a startlingly large portion of my career in the legal academy, and I could not have reached this point of rough comfort with the state of those ideas and their treatment here without the help and support of a great many people.

Substantive comments in various forums and formats were offered generously by Larry Alexander, Neal Devins, Tony Dillof, Michael Dorf, Rob Kar, Michael Moore, Ofer Raban, Brad Roth, Larry Solum, Jeremy Waldron, Wil Waluchow, Vince Wellman, and participants in workshops at the law schools of the University of Baltimore, the University of Chicago, the University of Florida, Loyola Marymount University, the University of Michigan, the University of Minnesota, the University of Oregon, the University of Toledo, and Wayne State University. Many friends and colleagues went beyond the call of duty to help me with this project and, more generally, with my development as a scholar, including Larry Alexander, Neal Devins, Fred Schauer, Larry Solum, Cass Sunstein, and Wil Waluchow. Extraordinary collegiality and moral support came from Phil Closius, Tony Dillof, Paul Dubinsky, Garrett Epps, Janet Findlater, Greg Fox, Lance Gable, Peter Henning, Freddie Lombard, Joan Mahoney, Brad Roth, Elizabeth Samuels, Jon Weinberg, Vince Wellman, and Steve Winter. Erica Beecher-Monas, John Bessler, Ellen Dannin, Greg Fox, Brad Roth, and Wil Waluchow shared with me their experiences of the publishing process. Deans Victor Gold at Loyola; Jim Robinson, Joan Mahoney, Freddie Lombard, Frank Wu, and Bob Ackerman at Wayne State; and Phil Closius at Toledo and Baltimore all provided financial and administrative support for the project, as did Walter Edwards and the Humanities Center at Wayne State and, in the form of a Career Development Chair, the Provost's Office at that university. Associate Deans Freddie Lombard, David Moran, and John Rothchild at Wayne State and Jane Murphy at Baltimore contributed invaluable administrative coordination and guidance. Special mention, with a heavy heart, is owed to the late David Leonard, my colleague for a short time at Loyola Los Angeles and the former Associate Dean for Research there, whose generosity and kindness I will always remember. I am profoundly grateful to all these colleagues.

My students, just as much as my colleagues, have helped shape this project over the years. Michelle Chaudhuri, Doug Salzenstein, Steve Cappellino, and

Todd Stuart at Wayne State, Rosannah Mah and Dominique Nasr at Loyola, and Anastasia Albright at Baltimore all provided excellent research assistance. Adam Geffen and Todd Stuart deserve particular credit for prodding Vince Wellman and me to join them as the "Hamburger Philosophers," a quartet that met faithfully, if irregularly, for several years around Detroit to discuss legal philosophy over burgers and beers. Many students in my constitutional law and civil procedure courses, and particularly in my various theory seminars, have asked seemingly innocuous questions that, because I had no good answers for them, prompted me to think much more carefully about some persistent issues in those subjects and thus to develop and refine the arguments in this book. My deepest thanks go to all of them for their enthusiasm, energy, and tolerance.

I owe much as well to the secretaries and administrative assistants who have made my copies, formatted my letters, kept my files, sent out my reprints, generally bolstered my confidence, and performed many other seemingly thankless tasks on my behalf during the past decade and a half. They include Betty Maltz, Lois Cowan, and Olive Hyman at Wayne State, Janis Weston at Michigan, Peggye Cummings at Toledo, Marina Castaneda at Loyola, and Barb Fischer and Laurie Schnitzer at Baltimore. Though it is small reward for their efforts, they have my heartfelt gratitude.

My most profound thanks are due to the family members whose companionship, good cheer, patience, and love have sustained me, sometimes in the face of flagging enthusiasm, as an eighteen-month project became a five- (or six- or seven-) year marathon, depending on how one counts. My uncle Steve Tigner lent both his philosophical insight and portions of his enormous library to the project. My father Tim Peters, and my father-in-law Chuck Webster, each (presumably unbeknownst to the other) played the appropriately paternal and entirely necessary role of gentle but persistent prodder; my mother Pat Peters and my mother-in-law Helen Webster performed the appropriately maternal, and equally necessary, functions of tactfully changing the subject. My brother Andy, his wife Karen, and my sister Emily, all of them familiar with the motivational and other challenges of academia, cheered me on unfailingly, and their wonderful children provided both pleasant diversion and crucial perspective. My sister-in-law Mary Beth, her husband Dave, and their boys, as well as my brother-in-law Mike and his wife Sarah, all mercifully tolerated the strange absent-minded habits of the law professor in their midst and leavened them frequently with welcome talk of sports and other more important matters. Various aunts, uncles, and cousins in both families showed a charitable interest in my efforts. My maternal grandparents Don and Ruth Anderson, both now well into their nineties, and my paternal grandparents John and Emma Peters, both now gone, set a standard of forthright principle and regard for honest effort to which I can only aspire in vain.

And then, finally, there is the deepest debt of all, the one I owe to my wife Trish, who has endured (by choice!) for well over a decade the arrhythmic hours of her academic spouse, the half-conversations at dinner while his mind was on legal theory, the flirtations with potential employers from Tucson to Tallahassee, the sudden declaration when the book was supposedly nearing completion that he had decided "to replace all the current words with new ones." Trish has been my cheerleader, my conscience, my common sense, my confidant, my companion; and while the day I finished this book might have been the happiest of her life, the day I married her will always be the happiest of mine.

Baltimore, Maryland
August 2010

1. INTRODUCTION
A Government of Laws

In 1780 John Adams authored, almost singlehandedly, the constitution of the Commonwealth of Massachusetts, now the world's oldest continually enforced written charter of government. Adams included in the document what is, on reflection, a striking aspiration: that the Commonwealth would become "a government of laws and not of men."[1]

The phrase "a government of laws and not of men" (which Adams cribbed, as it happens, from the seventeenth-century English philosopher James Harrington[2]) has since become familiar, even commonplace, as shorthand for the ideal of constitutional democracy, of democracy under law. It suggests in part the salient distinction between a democratic system and the European monarchies and oligarchies from which Adams and his fellow Founders sought to break. In a democracy the laws are made by the people themselves, not some cadre of privileged elites, and so no single individual is somehow above the law. The laws of the many, in a democratic polity, override the will of the few.

Even this familiar notion—that democratically enacted laws trump individual will—turns out, as we will see, to be fraught with difficulty. Democratically enacted laws, indeed laws in general, typically purport to supersede not just the individual's will, but also the individual's *judgment*; they purport to prohibit (or require) action even when the actor believes, in all good faith, that the action is

---

1. Mass. Const. part 1, art. XXX.

2. In his *Oceana*, Harrington bemoaned what he saw as the slow historical degradation of government, from the "ancient" understanding that governance is "an art wher[e]by a civil society of men is instituted and preserv'd upon the foundation of common right or interest"—an "empire of laws, and not of men"—to the "modern" pathology of government as "an art wher[e]by som[e] man, or som[e] few men, subject a city or a nation, and rule it according to his or their privat[e] interest"—an "empire of men, and not of laws." James Harrington, The Oceana and Other Works 31–56 (John Toland ed., 1771) (1656), *available at* http://oll.libertyfund.org/EBooks/Harrington_0050.pdf. Harrington's characterization of the "ancient" view drew in part upon Aristotle, who wrote in the *Politics* that "[t]he true forms of government... are those in which the one, or the few, or the many, govern with a view to the common interest; but governments which rule with a view to the private interest, whether of the one, or of the few, or of the many, are perversions." Aristotle, *Politics, in* The Basic Works of Aristotle 1127, book III, at 1185 (Benjamin Jowett trans., Richard McKeon ed., 1941) [hereinafter *Politics*]. Both Aristotle and Harrington thus anticipated James Madison's definition in *Federalist No.* 10 of a "faction" as "a number of citizens, whether amounting to a majority or minority of the whole, who are united and actuated by some common impulse of passion, or of interest, adverse to the rights of other citizens, or to the permanent and aggregate interests of the community." The Federalist No. 10, at 123 (James Madison) (Isaac Kramnick ed., 1987).

the right (or wrong) thing to do. Law, that is, asserts the capacity to override or alter an individual's own moral reasoning in some sense—to require a person to act in a way she otherwise thinks is wrong—and it is far from clear what, if anything, might justify this extraordinary claim.

But Adams's "government of laws" suggests something more than simply a description of popular government—something that in fact seems opposed to the very notion of rule by the people. Adams and his colleagues were establishing a *constitutional* democracy: The Massachusetts constitution that Adams framed in 1780, and its national counterpart ratified less than a decade later, contained (and still contain) provisions binding, or purporting to bind, democratic government itself. In the constitutional democracy fashioned by Adams and his fellows, "a government of laws" really was a system of democratic government *under* law. Adams thus claimed for law, not just the capacity to trump individual judgment, but the authority to supersede even the collective judgment of the democratic people themselves.

The idea of "a government of laws and not of men" thus embodies something akin to what Winston Churchill saw in Soviet Russia: "a riddle, wrapped in a mystery, inside an enigma." The riddle is just what it might be about democracy, as distinct from other forms of government, that gives it the authority Adams proclaims on its behalf. The mystery is how democracy, given its special qualities (whatever those might be), somehow can itself be overridden by a higher source of law. And the enigma that surrounds them both is what I will call *the problem of legal authority*: How can law, whatever its source, claim the capacity to require people, individually or collectively, to do things they otherwise think are wrong?

These three conundrums—democracy, constitutional law, and legal authority generally—and their interlocking relationship with each other are the central subjects of this book. I hope here to give meaning to Adams's comfortable but quaint belief in a government of laws—to explain how such a thing might be possible despite the implausibly ambitious nature of its claims. I hope also to infuse that notion with continuing value, to make a persuasive case that a government of laws remains an aspiration worth having. I hope, in short, to defend Adams's ideal against what will turn out to be rather powerful attacks from a variety of directions.

But first it will help to get a sense of what those attacks might look like—of why the familiar notion of a government of laws needs defending in the first place.

1. THE PROBLEM OF EXCEPTIONS

We can begin to understand the precarious position in which Adams's ideal finds itself by examining a phenomenon I will call the *Problem of Exceptions*. Consider the following hypothetical cases.

- *The Case of the Sick Child*. A mother is driving her urgently sick child to the hospital. May she exceed the legal speed limit in doing so?

- *The Case of the Unjust Statute.* A judge believes that a faithful application of a democratically enacted statute would, in the particular case she must decide, produce a deeply unjust result. May she use her legal skills to distort the law in order to avoid that outcome?
- *The Case of the Obstructionist Constitution.* A majority of the citizens of a democratic nation believe that constitutional restrictions on the treatment of criminal suspects unnecessarily impede the government's efforts to protect against terrorist attacks. Amending the constitution would be difficult and time-consuming. May the government, with the majority's tacit approval, exceed those restrictions?

Notice, first of all, that despite John Adams's law-trumps-men hierarchy, it is not immediately clear in any of these examples that the law should control individual judgment. In the Case of the Sick Child, for instance, it seems at least plausible that the imperative of getting the child to the hospital in time outweighs whatever values might be served by obeying the speed limit. If so, then obeying the law would seem to produce a morally suboptimal result; it would seem to be the morally wrong thing to do, all things considered. It seems possible, in other words, that the mother would be doing the morally right thing by following her own individual judgment, not the law's, about how fast to drive in those circumstances.

To recognize this possibility is not to say that the speed limit law is always, or even often, morally counterproductive, or that widespread violation of it is justified. It may well be that in nine cases out of ten, or ninety-nine out of a hundred, obeying the speed limit is the right thing to do. But the problem—a fundamental problem, it turns out, in legal and political theory generally, and in this book specifically—is that all general rules, even good ones, have exceptions. In some cases—perhaps very few, but *some*—the circumstances will be such that a person will do the morally right thing by *not* following the rule. And, crucially, *any* case might turn out to be one of those exceptions.

This is how Aristotle put the point in his *Nicomachean Ethics*:

> [A]ll law is universal but about some things it is not possible to make a universal statement which shall be correct. In those cases, then, in which it is necessary to speak universally, but not possible to do so correctly, the law takes the usual case, though it is not ignorant of the possibility of error. And it is none the less correct; for the error is not in the law nor in the legislator but in the nature of the thing, since the matter of practical affairs is of this kind from the start.[3]

---

3. Aristotle, *Nicomachean Ethics,* in THE BASIC WORKS OF ARISTOTLE 935, book V, at 1020 (W. D. Ross trans., Richard McKeon ed., 1941) [hereinafter *Nicomachean Ethics*].

It seems possible that, as applied in the Case of the Sick Child, the "universal statement" represented by the speed limit law would be incorrect—that the case is an exception to that general law, and therefore that following the law would constitute an "error" in that case. Of course, there are other facts we would like to know before deciding this: How serious is the child's illness? How good a driver is the mother? What are the driving conditions? By how much does she propose to exceed the speed limit? And so on. Aristotle's point, though, is that these ad hoc factors can never comprehensively be embedded into the general rule itself. There is no way for a legislature in the real world to anticipate every particular circumstance in which someone might be tempted to violate the speed limit, and thus every possible instance in which violation might be justified. And even if the legislature magically could anticipate the infinite variety of future circumstances in which the law might apply, there is no way it could draft an intelligible "universal statement," or general rule, to account for all of them. This is no fault of the legislature's, as Aristotle was careful to point out. The problem—which I will call the *Problem of Exceptions*—is simply "in the nature of the thing."

A. Can the Problem Be Solved with Rules?
Note that if, "in the nature of the thing," every general rule has exceptions, then any given instance of a rule's application may itself *be* such an exception. After all, there is no general rule we can use to determine when a particular case qualifies as an exception to another general rule. Suppose, for instance, that the speed limit law forbids exceeding a certain maximum speed "unless circumstances warrant." The additional, exception-recognizing provision of the rule would not tell the mother in the Case of the Sick Child anything very useful; she still would have to determine for herself whether the circumstances at hand *do* warrant an exception, which is precisely what she would have had to decide absent the exception-recognizing language.

It is true that the existence of this exception provision may give the mother some hope that she will not be punished if she is caught exceeding the speed limit, and that hope might be enough to tip her assessment of the moral balance in favor of taking that risk. But the mother still will have to guess, in essence, whether the legal authorities—the police officer who stops her for speeding, the judge who hears the resulting case—will agree with her own assessment of what "circumstances warrant" in that particular instance. This element of ad hoc guesswork suggests that the "unless circumstances warrant" exception is not really a *rule* at all; it is at most what legal theorists would call a "standard," a norm that leaves a good deal—perhaps all that is important—open to individual judgment.[4] Such an amorphous standard cannot eliminate the sense in which the

---

4. An injunction to act in a certain way "unless circumstances warrant" may not even qualify as a standard, as it seems to provide almost no guidance or constraint to a legal

Case of the Sick Child is governed by an individual's judgment rather than by a general legal rule.

Suppose, though, that the permissible exceptions to the speed limit law are codified in a more stringently rule-like form. Perhaps the legislature has included in the statute an explicit list of circumstances under which exceeding the posted limit is appropriate; or perhaps the courts have accomplished the same thing by deciding a series of cases interpreting the meaning of "unless circumstances warrant" on particular sets of facts.

Notice, of course, that the more exceptions there are written in, legislatively or judicially, to the rule, the more complex the rule becomes, and thus the more difficult it becomes for those subject to the rule to identify and obey its requirements. (Is the mother supposed to phone her lawyer before driving her sick child to the hospital?) But for present purposes the more important point is this: A rule specifying exceptions may *itself* have exceptions. Suppose the mother is familiar with this exception-laden speed limit law and believes her circumstances do not fall within any of the listed exceptions. She still will have to decide whether her circumstances *should* be an exception to the rule—whether the morally correct thing for her to do would be to exceed the speed limit despite the absence of some formal legal exception allowing her to do so.

There is, in other words, no way to use rules to solve the Problem of Exceptions. That problem is endemic to all general rules, including rules that attempt to specify exceptions to themselves or to other rules. Every rule may have an exception; and any given case may turn out to be an exception to the rule.

B. The Necessity of Ad Hoc Decisionmaking

Is there no other way to avoid the Problem of Exceptions? The only alternative to deciding things by general rules is deciding them by specific ad hoc decisions: by allowing someone to determine whether a given instance is an exception to an applicable general rule. Again, such ad hoc determinations themselves cannot be dictated by general rules, because those rules themselves may have

---

subject at all, even assuming the subject elects to "obey" the standard. The label "standard" typically is used to describe a sort of loose, highly indeterminate rule, a norm that provides some, albeit minimal, constraint; Cass Sunstein, for example, cites the examples of a ban on "excessive" speeds on the highway and a requirement that airplane pilots be "competent." *See* Cass R. Sunstein, Legal Reasoning and Political Conflict 27 (1996) [hereinafter Sunstein, Legal Reasoning]. These examples constrain at least in the sense that they imply a set of considerations by which compliance with their dictates might be judged: considerations of safety in the former example and of aviation skill in the latter. I'm not sure "unless circumstances warrant" constrains even to this degree. In any event, Sunstein includes a taxonomy of different types of norms in Chapter 1 of *Legal Reasoning and Political Conflict. See also* Kathleen M. Sullivan, *Foreword: The Justices of Rules and Standards*, 106 Harv. L. Rev. 22, 57–61 (1992) (providing definitions of rules and standards as well as other legal directives).

exceptions. Any decision whether a general rule should be followed or disobeyed in the name of reaching the morally optimal result necessarily will be made by means of a particularistic judgment based on the facts of a single case. And barring a science-fiction world in which people cede their moral agency to machines, such judgments necessarily will be made by individuals—by flesh-and-blood men and women, like the mother in the Case of the Sick Child.[5]

But must these ad hoc decisions about whether to follow rules be made by those subject to the rules themselves? Must we rely on the mother to decide for herself whether to disobey the speed limit in driving her sick child to the hospital—or can we assign that decision to someone else, perhaps some more-objective and thus more-trustworthy third party? In a sense, of course, we typically *do* assign such decisions to individuals other than the person whose conduct is in question. If a police officer clocks the mother doing seventy in a fifty-mile-per-hour zone, the officer must decide whether to pull her over and, if he does, whether to issue a speeding ticket. If the officer issues a ticket and the mother contests it, a judge must decide whether to convict her of a misdemeanor and force her to pay a fine.

But the possibility that others—legal officials—will make their own decisions about the propriety of the mother's conduct does not relieve the mother of having to make her own decision. As with many instances involving legal rules, the likelihood that the mother would be caught and punished for violating the speed limit may be relatively small; as any driver knows, police cruisers are relatively few and far between on even the busiest roads (and are never around when another driver cuts you off or speeds past you doing ninety). The mother, then, cannot simply throw up her hands and violate the law, confident that the supposedly more objective mind of a police officer or a judge eventually will sort out the permissibility of her conduct. And in any event, as I will suggest at greater length below, the possibility of being caught and sanctioned for violating the law, even if it is considerable—even if it rises to the level of a certainty—is likely to be only one of many factors that will come into play in the mother's process of deciding how to act. She must throw that possibility into the mix alongside other factors weighing against exceeding the speed limit—danger to herself, to her child, to other drivers—and factors weighing in favor of exceeding the limit—the urgency of her child's illness, the good weather conditions, the relatively empty roads. The chance that legal officials or others might themselves assess her conduct, then, can hardly relieve the mother of her own moral responsibility to decide what to do.

In fact that possibility—that legal officials will sit in judgment of others' disobedience of the law—only magnifies the impact of the Problem of Exceptions.

---

5. Even in such a world, people would, presumably, have to decide on a case-by-case basis whether to accept or reject the machine's judgment. The rule "Obey the machine" might itself have exceptions.

Consider the position of the judge who must decide whether to convict the mother after she is caught and ticketed for speeding. The judge may believe a conviction would be unjust; but she may believe, at the same time, that the law requires conviction. (This is one iteration of the Case of the Unjust Statute.) The judge now is in a position analogous to the mother's in deciding whether to disobey the law in the first place: She too must decide whether this particular circumstance constitutes a moral exception to a general legal rule. And, like the mother in the first instance, the judge cannot make that decision in any way other than by exercising her own moral judgment on the matter. She cannot simply follow the law blindly, for to decide to follow the law is to make a decision with moral consequences. The judge, like the speeding mother, is a flesh-and-blood person, not an automaton, and flesh-and-blood persons have a choice whether to obey laws or not; they are not irrevocably hard-wired to do so. The same goes for the citizens of a democracy who, in the Case of the Obstructionist Constitution, must decide whether to insist on obedience to constitutional principles or to look the other way; they too cannot avoid deciding for themselves, each of them as individual voters and thus all of them collectively, what to do.

The Problem of Exceptions reveals, then, a sense in which the idea of "a government of laws and not of men" is simply incoherent. *Of course* men, and women, and sometimes groups of men and women, ultimately must rule, at least to the extent of deciding whether to obey legal commands in particular cases. The mother cannot somehow avoid the necessity of deciding whether to obey the speed limit in the Case of the Sick Child; she cannot somehow abandon her individual judgment entirely in deference to the law. Nor can the judge abandon judgment in the Case of the Unjust Statute, or the members of the democratic majority in the Case of the Obstructionist Constitution. Men and women—from ordinary people going about their everyday tasks against a backdrop of law, to judges and other government officials interpreting, enforcing, and applying the law, to each of us as a democratic citizen deciding whether to honor constitutional limits on our collective power as a majority—must "govern" in the final analysis; the laws cannot magically apply (or recognize exceptions to) themselves.

Which leaves us with the following troublesome question: Does the Problem of Exceptions render nonsensical Adams's time-honored and comforting notion of "a government of laws and not of men"?

2. ARISTOTLE'S CHALLENGE

I think not; for we need not understand Adams as having demanded the impossibility of government, or life, without human judgment.

Adams's point was not that law should replace human judgment, but rather that human judgment—in particular, the judgment of those humans who hold political power—should, in some way, be meaningfully *constrained* by law. In "a government of laws," individual legal subjects, mindful of the imperfection of legal rules and of their own ultimate responsibility for their decisions, would nonetheless attribute considerable normative force to law's claims upon those decisions; they would consider their decisionmaking authority to be limited by law in some meaningful sense, even if some space for individual judgment remains. Judges and other government officials would acknowledge some real duty to uphold the law rather than simply to implement their own unfettered judgments about justice or good policy. Democratic majorities would recognize and respect the existence of constitutional principles as real, substantial counterweights to the demands of momentary exigencies.

"A government of laws," in other words, might be understood as a system in which legal rules and commands strongly influence the normative decisionmaking of individuals, ordinary as well as powerful, given that they cannot displace individual decisionmaking altogether. (I will discuss the nature of that influence in greater depth in the next chapter.) This account is more plausible than one that denies Aristotle's insight about the Problem of Exceptions or the inevitable role for individual judgment that insight entails.

But there remains an Aristotelian threat to Adams's rule-of-law ideal. Suppose we acknowledge that every general rule has exceptions—circumstances in which the morally best thing to do is something other than what the general rule prescribes. And suppose we further acknowledge that ultimately it is up to each of us as individuals to determine whether a particular circumstance in which we find ourselves qualifies as such an exception. We might then suspect, not just that law's demands ultimately are subject to our own judgment, but that law has little of normative substance to offer us in reaching that judgment. We might find it difficult, that is, to understand why law ought to motivate our decisionmaking at all, much less bind or obligate or constrain or "govern" it.

Consider again the Case of the Sick Child. Suppose the mother, in deciding whether to violate the speed limit, takes into account all the relevant factors known to her, including the Problem of Exceptions. As we have already noted, she might conclude that her case *is* an exception—one in which it would be morally better, all things considered, to disobey the law's command. But given that her decision ultimately will be based on her own moral judgment, why should she take any account whatsoever of the speed limit law in exercising that judgment? The legislature that enacted the speed limit, after all, could not have anticipated and considered the precise combination of circumstances in which she finds herself: a child with just this particular serious illness; road conditions that are just so; the exact set of driving skills that she possesses; and so on. Surely she is in a better position to know how fast to drive, *under these particular circumstances*, than the legislature was when it enacted the law.

The question for the mother then becomes, not whether she should consider herself bound by the legislature's (apparently inferior) judgment, but whether that judgment is relevant to her decisionmaking at all. Why not simply consider all of these particularistic factors directly, without pausing to consider the legislature's obviously imperfect resolution of the question? Perhaps more to the point, why think of the legislature's dictate as somehow *dominant* in her decisional process—as influential in a strong enough way to make sense of the idea that law somehow "governs" or "rules"?

One possibility is that the legislature's judgment, though seemingly inferior to her own particularistic one, nonetheless might constitute a sort of general expert *advice*—an admonition that driving faster than a certain speed is, under many or most circumstances, unsafe. The legislature, after all, may have enjoyed certain qualitative decisionmaking advantages despite its ignorance of the particular circumstances the mother now faces. As a multimember body, it presumably incorporated a diversity of talents, viewpoints, and knowledge, as well as a need for deliberation, into its decisional process; it had the time and resources to research its decision thoroughly; and its distance from the particulars of the situation may actually have lent valuable objectivity to its conclusions. The mother thus might have reason to strongly consider the speed limit law on the ground that knowledge of the legislature's judgment might improve her own.

As I will discuss at some length in Chapter 2, this basic idea—that law has some authority by virtue of its capacity to help legal subjects reach better moral decisions—lies at the heart of an influential defense of legal authority and, by extension, of the rule of law. For present purposes, however, it will suffice to notice that an account of law as *advice* hardly can be described as an account of "a government of laws." To take advice from the law is not in any meaningful sense to be "governed" by the law, any more than taking advice from a friend means being governed by that friend. For law to have any real meaning as *law*, it must involve some normative force that is stronger than mere advice. The Problem of Exceptions shows that law cannot completely foreclose individual human judgment, but law must have the capacity to affect that judgment in a more substantial way than mere advice can.

There is another salient possibility here, one to which I alluded earlier: The mother, in deciding whether to obey the speed limit law, might take into account the chance of being caught and punished for violating it. The threat of sanctions may well play a larger motivational role than mere advice; and indeed there seems to be an intuitive connection between the ideas of "government" or "rule" or "constraint" and that of official sanctions for disobedience. Can the notion of "a government of laws" be given meaning simply by referring to the likelihood that people often figure the threat of sanctions into their moral deliberations about whether to obey the law?

Not satisfactorily, no, for two related reasons. The first is that the threat of sanctions cannot be a phenomenon that *distinguishes* a government of laws from a government of men, or from any other kind of government, for that matter. Oligarchs and dictators typically back their edicts with the threat of force, sometimes with the threat of greater force than a system governed by law would bring to bear for the same transgression. The threat of force—or rather the capacity of such a threat to meaningfully alter people's reasoning about how to behave—cannot then be a reason to prefer a government of laws to a government of men.

Another way to put this point is to notice that a government's moral capacity to enforce its rules or commands by force seems to follow from its legitimacy—from the moral justifiability of those rules or commands on other grounds—rather than the other way around. If we think government is morally desirable, it is not because we need an excuse for the use of force; there is plenty of occasion for that absent government. Indeed, governments typically claim a monopoly (or near-monopoly) on the use of force, and the idea of government under law implies that the government's use of force will be subject to legal constraints. We can hardly justify those constraints by reference to the very thing they are supposed to be constraining.

The second reason why the threat of sanctions cannot support the idea of a government of laws is that the threat is likely to be weakest when the need for it is strongest. Considering our other two hypothetical cases underscores this point. Suppose again that the statute at issue in the Case of the Unjust Statute is the speed limit law as applied to the mother in the Case of the Sick Child. The threat of sanctions for disobedience is unlikely to play a significant role in the moral calculations of the judge deciding whether to convict the mother; the judge, if she is a skilled lawyer, probably can find a way (a procedural formality, a creative legal interpretation) to avoid a conviction without herself being "caught" violating the law and "punished" for it (and in any event her "punishment" most likely would be no worse than the reversal of her decision by an appellate court). And yet legal officials like the judge are precisely the kinds of individuals Adams had most squarely in mind when he called for a government of laws and not of men; for they are the people directly charged with making the decisions of governance. The threat of sanctions hardly can support a government of laws if it is unlikely to motivate obedience to the law by government officials.

This point is even more salient in circumstances like the Case of the Obstructionist Constitution, where the decisionmakers in question—a majority of the citizenry itself—are those who hold the ultimate political power. There are no formal sanctions in store for a political majority that chooses to ignore constitutional limitations; there is no threat of being "caught" and "punished" for violating the law. If the majority treats its constitution as binding law, it does so for reasons other than the fear of official punishment for disobedience. But of course it was constitutional law—legal restraints imposed, ultimately, on the political majority—that Adams and his fellow Founders envisioned as the primary tool of "a government of laws." The threat of sanctions is wholly incapable of explaining that vision.

What is needed to justify the idea of a government of laws is an account of why law *should* have normative force—of why, morally speaking, those deciding how to act *should* be strongly influenced by applicable legal rules, in a way that makes sense of law's claims to "obedience" rather than mere acknowledgment or attention. Such an account might lead to an understanding of how sanctions justifiably may be imposed for disobedience; but the account cannot itself be driven by the possibility of sanctions. Without an account like this, Adams's notion of a government of laws appears to dissolve; all decisions, even those supposedly subject to law, take on the appearance of ad hoc moral judgments by individual men and women, and it is these individual men and women, not the law, that truly govern. The law becomes mere window dressing.

Aristotle's Problem of Exceptions therefore engenders, after all, a very powerful challenge to the idea of the rule of law. Aristotle recognized this when, in his *Politics*, he posed "the vexed question whether the best law or the best man should rule."[6] This was the same question that Adams implicitly answered with his demand for a government of laws rather than men; but Aristotle gave the opposite answer. Because even the best laws are subject to exceptions, Aristotle argued, good government consists of wise and virtuous men capable of making sound particularistic decisions—including decisions regarding whether, in any given case, to obey the law. The best government, he concluded, is a government of men and not of laws, because only individual moral judgment has the capacity to generate the right answer in every case.[7]

---

6. *Politics, supra* note 2, book III, at 1203.

7. Aristotle built his case for an enlightened monarchy or aristocracy in the *Politics* upon his observation of the Problem of Exceptions in the *Nicomachean Ethics*. In the *Ethics*, Aristotle asserted that judges and others applying general rules should use "equitable" powers to recognize implicit exceptions to those rules where appropriate:

> When the law speaks universally,... and a case arises on it which is not covered by the universal statement, then it is right... to say what the legislator himself would have said had he been present, and would have put into his law if he had known. Hence the equitable is just, and better than one kind of justice—not better than absolute justice but better than the error that arises from the absoluteness of the statement.

Nicomachean Ethics, supra note 3, book V, at 1020; *see also* Aristotle, *Rhetoric, in* THE BASIC WORKS OF ARISTOTLE 1325, book I, at 1371–72 (W. Rhys Roberts trans., Richard McKeon ed., 1941) [hereinafter *Rhetoric*] (explaining equity as "the sort of justice which goes beyond written law"). The need to recognize appropriate exceptions to general rules implied a government run by a small handful of wise and virtuous men capable of making those decisions in a way that served the general interest. *See generally Politics, supra* note 2, book III, at 1176–1205. For a description of Aristotle's view that individual virtue must trump legality and a comparison of that view to Locke's, see Ross J. Corbett, *Locke and Aristotle on the Limits of Law*, 2006, http://www.allacademic.com//meta/p_mla_apa_research_citation/1/5/0/6/5/pages150657/p150657-1.php (presented at the 2006 Annual Meeting of the American Political Science Association).

Aristotle thus questioned perhaps the central premise upon which Adams and his fellow Founders built the constitutional democracy that Americans still live under today, more than 200 years later—a system that, in one of modern history's most compelling tales, has spread and continues to spread in its basic form to countries around the world. The premise is that the rule of law is morally valuable—that even those holding political power (indeed, even democratic majorities) should be subject to legal constraints. In furtherance of that premise, the Founders designed the prototype of a system of majoritarian democracy, in which ultimate political power is wielded by the people, and of constitutionalism, in which even the people themselves are bound by fundamental law. Aristotle's dispute with that premise—we can call it *Aristotle's Challenge*—is simply that the rule of law is not as attractive as all that; that the rule of men and women, provided they are wise and virtuous enough, is better still.

3. THE PLAN OF THE BOOK

This book is, in essence, a type of response to Aristotle's Challenge. Its core thesis is that the rule of law—Adams's "government of laws and not of men"—can be understood as morally justified despite Aristotle's skepticism about it. One ancillary thesis is that the central legal and political institutions of constitutional democratic government—majoritarian democracy, participatory adjudication, and constitutional law—can be defended as ways of implementing the rule of law. Another is that understanding the connections among the rule of law, democracy, adjudication, and constitutionalism can shed light on some persistent theoretical problems that afflict each of these phenomena.

In the chapters that follow, I will answer Aristotle's Challenge by developing what I will call a *Dispute-Resolution*, or *DR*, account of law. The DR account is intended as a way of explaining, and morally justifying, the considerable normative force that law exerts over individuals, from people going about their everyday lives, to judges, to other government officials, to democratic citizens deciding momentous questions of principle and policy. As its name suggests, the DR account justifies obedience to law as a way of resolving, or mitigating or avoiding, otherwise-costly disputes about what should be done. Although it is not the only plausible account of legal authority, I will suggest that it constitutes a better response to Aristotle's Challenge than its major rivals—and also, not incidentally, that it supports a particularly satisfying and illuminating understanding of the fundamental legal and political institutions that characterize the American system of constitutional democracy (as well as other systems around the world that share key elements of the American system).

I begin building the DR account in Chapter 2 by discussing at greater length the problem at the core of Aristotle's Challenge: the problem of legal authority, that is, of how to justify obedience to law in a suitably strong sense, given that law sometimes (perhaps often) prescribes morally suboptimal actions. I will describe three influential accounts of legal authority—accounts based, respectively, on law's capacity to provide epistemic guidance; on its derivation from the consent of the governed; and on its ability to solve coordination problems—and will argue that none of them provides a satisfactory answer to Aristotle's Challenge. As an alternative, I will offer the DR account, sketching its basic outlines and suggesting how it might support a better response to Aristotle than its competitors.

Chapter 3 adds flesh to the bare bones of the DR account. I begin there with a simple, bipartite model of dispute resolution, and I use that model to illustrate three core aspects of the DR account. First, the basic model demonstrates how people might be motivated to develop procedures to avoid or resolve disputes. Second, it illustrates the essential qualities that suitable dispute-resolution procedures would possess, namely reasonable competence and impartiality in the eyes of the disputants. Third, it explains why a losing disputant—one who is dissatisfied with the substantive result of the procedure—nonetheless might have a powerful moral reason to accept that result. The basic model of dispute resolution in Chapter 3 thus illustrates, in straightforward form, the normative mechanisms by which legal authority operates on the DR account.

Chapter 4 extends this basic model of dispute resolution to a system in which general legal rules play an important role. General legal rules are advantageous, probably even necessary, in a modern society for a number of familiar reasons. But while the basic bipartite model of dispute resolution—essentially an adjudicative paradigm—illustrates how general rules can be applied authoritatively to particular cases, explaining the authority of the rules themselves requires a more sophisticated model. In Chapter 4, I envision majoritarian democracy as a reasonably competent and impartial way to resolve *ex ante* disputes about the content of general legal rules and thus to make those rules authoritative. In essence, I contend that a DR account of law leads to a democratic account of lawmaking, that is, of legislation and politics.

Chapters 5 and 6 address the paradigmatic form of dispute resolution—adjudication—in light of the DR account of law generally and of majoritarian democracy in particular. Democratic statutes cannot by themselves resolve every controversy; facts often will be disputed and, crucially, statutes often will themselves be indeterminate. I contend in Chapter 5 that adjudication—that is, adjudication structured in a certain way—can be a "democratic" means of interpreting and applying democratic statutes. The so-called adversary system brings meaningful participation to the adjudicative process, and the common-law method avoids binding those whose interests are not represented in the process. I contend as well that courts, operating democratically, can plausibly apply even indeterminate statutes, thus extending the authority of democratic legislation beyond those cases clearly resolved by the legislature. In Chapter 6, I use this democratic model of adjudication to assess some current questions about the interplay among judges, litigants, and democratic legislation.

Chapters 7 and 8 focus on the context in which the two fundamental dispute-resolving institutions justified by the DR account—majoritarian democracy and participatory adjudication—intersect most saliently: constitutional law. Constitutional law often is seen as deeply in tension with the idea of democracy; but in chapters 7 and 8 I contend that the DR account in fact supports constitutional law on the same grounds that it supports democracy, namely as a reasonably competent and impartial way to avoid or resolve certain kinds of disputes. The analysis in Chapter 7 envisions constitutional law as a means of preventing certain kinds of failure of democratic authority and resolving disputes about whether these failures have occurred. It suggests as well that (most of) the substance of actual American constitutional practice can be understood in this dysfunction-avoiding and dispute-resolving light.

In Chapter 8, I examine the procedures of American constitutional law: the enactment of general, relatively abstract constitutional rules by an extraordinarily deliberative supermajoritarian process, and the interpretation and application of those rules by procedures of adjudication that are simultaneously participatory and separate from ordinary politics. I explain how those procedures serve the constitutional function of preventing, and resolving disputes about, breaches of democratic authority. By externalizing the creation and application of constitutional rules—subjecting them to written, relatively obdurate norms interpreted through a politically insulated process—constitutional law resolves disputes about those rules with relative impartiality. At the same time, the process keeps contact with long-term trends in popular values by incorporating meaningful participation and political influence in both the making and the applying of constitutional rules. The result, I suggest, is a set of constitutional procedures that acceptably balances the desire for impartiality with the perception of competence.

I also address, in Chapter 8, perhaps the greatest topic of ongoing controversy in both constitutional theory and constitutional practice: the methodology of constitutional interpretation. Contemporary debates about constitutional interpretation typically pit relatively formalist approaches ("originalism" and "textualism") that emphasize the Constitution's status as law against relatively pragmatic approaches (variants of "living constitutionalism") that emphasize the need for flexibility and judicial discretion. As such, they recapitulate, in a sense, the battle between Adams's "government of laws" and Aristotle's government by virtuous men. In Chapter 8, I use the DR account to explain how the search for impartiality animates the desire for constitutional formalism, while the desire for competence motivates the drive toward pragmatic flexibility. I argue that each polar approach, taken to its extreme, sacrifices too much of the quality that underwrites its opposite: Pure formalism (even if it were possible—which, I explain, it is not) buys impartiality at the expense of competence, while pure pragmatism purchases competence at the cost of impartiality. The best interpretive method, I conclude, lies somewhere in between the two extremes: It preserves impartiality by grounding constitutional decisions in justifications that reasonably can be attributed to the Constitution, and it enhances competence by developing and applying these justifications over time through the common-law method.

4. THEORY (LEGAL, POLITICAL, ADJUDICATIVE, CONSTITUTIONAL)

In addition to this book's substantive aims—defending the rule of law, and connecting it to democracy, participatory adjudication, and constitutionalism—the book has what might be called a methodological goal: demonstrating the relationship among seemingly discrete problems across a number of different theoretical disciplines. (Those readers with no particular interest in the relationships among different branches of academic theory should feel free to skip this discussion and go straight to section 5, below.)

A. Analytic Legal Philosophy and the Problem of Legal Authority

The DR account at the center of this book is developed initially as a response to a problem of legal authority—how can law require us to do things we think are morally suboptimal?—and that problem has been most fully explored by theorists writing in an area known as *analytic legal philosophy*.[8] It seems natural to think that the authority of the law should relate somehow to the legitimacy of the institutions that make and apply the law; but for various reasons, analytic legal philosophers have pursued that connection only sparingly.

Probably the biggest reason for this has to do with the particular methodology of analytic legal philosophy. Since the germinal work of H.L.A. Hart in the mid-twentieth century,[9] analytic legal philosophers typically have seen their project as conceptual rather than practical (focused on ideas and their interrelationships

---

8. The most influential treatment of the conceptual problems raised by the idea of legal authority is that of Joseph Raz. *See* Joseph Raz, The Authority of Law: Essays on Law and Morality 3–33 (1979) [hereinafter Raz, Authority of Law]; Joseph Raz, The Morality of Freedom 23–105 (1986) [hereinafter Raz, Morality of Freedom]; *see also* Scott J. Shapiro, *Authority, in* The Oxford Handbook of Jurisprudence & Philosophy of Law 382, 402–08 (Jules Coleman & Scott Shapiro eds., 2002). Other analytic legal philosophers' writings on authority typically have been responsive in some way to Raz's work. *See* Leslie Green, The Authority of the State (1988); Shapiro, *supra*; Larry Alexander, *Law and Exclusionary Reasons,* 7 Phil. Topics 18 (1990); Heidi Hurd, *Challenging Authority,* 100 Yale L.J. 1611 (1991); Michael Moore, *Authority, Law, and Razian Reasons,* 62 S. Cal. L. Rev. 827 (1989); Stephen Perry, *Second-Order Reasons, Uncertainty, and Legal Theory,* 62 S. Cal. L. Rev. 913 (1989).

9. Hart's classic 1961 book *The Concept of Law* remains the foundational text of contemporary analytic legal philosophy. *See* H.L.A. Hart, The Concept of Law (2d ed. 1994) (1961); *see also* Robin Bradley Kar, *Hart's Response to Exclusive Legal Positivism,* 95 Geo. L.J. 393, 394–405 (2007) (describing Hart's influence).

rather than persons, things, or events in the real world); descriptive rather than normative (seeking to describe and explain phenomena rather than to evaluate them); and general rather than specific (offering insights that apply to law always and everywhere rather than in a certain time and place). This type of methodology is not well-suited to assessing particular legal institutions or practices (democratic legislatures, common-law courts, constitutional adjudication) or to doing so normatively. In studying problems of legal authority, then, analytic legal philosophers usually have been content to explore the formal structural mechanics of authority without examining its substantive underpinnings.[10]

A second, related reason is that the interest of analytic legal philosophy in legal authority came about almost by accident. The discipline's central concern has always been to understand the relationship between law and morality, and in his major work *The Concept of Law*, Hart advanced that project in a number of ways. Hart was heir to a "positivist" philosophical tradition that understood law as a social rather than a divine or natural phenomenon: Law was *posited* by human practices and institutions, not handed down by God or inherent in the nature of things.[11] Unlike many of his positivist predecessors, however, Hart saw that law consisted of more than yes-or-no commands; instead, Hart asserted, law was best understood as a system of rules, including primary rules directly regulating people's conduct, secondary rules governing the creation, application, and alteration of the primary rules, and a foundational "rule of recognition" specifying the conditions for the validity of all other legal rules in the system. The rule of recognition—and thus the system of legal rules it made possible—was a social creation, the product of agreement (explicit or tacit) among a sufficient number of those wielding power within the society; in this way law was distinct from morality, which was a natural rather than a social phenomenon (or perhaps a social phenomenon of a very different type).

At the same time, law resembled morality in its normativity—in the fact that those subject to it (lawyers, judges, other legal officials, ordinary citizens) typically felt themselves obligated in some sense to obey legal rules. This "internal point of view" toward the law, Hart theorized, was the product of a certain kind of psychological state shared by most members of the society, a "critical

---

10. The work of Joseph Raz is a salient exception. Raz, whose reputation initially was forged firmly within the territory of analytic legal philosophy, has sought to connect his formal account of legal authority to a normative account of political legitimacy. This is the task of the "service conception" described below. *See* RAZ, MORALITY OF FREEDOM, *supra* note 8, at 38–105.

11. Previous influential thinkers in the legal positivist tradition included Thomas Hobbes, Jeremy Bentham, John Austin, and Hans Kelsen. *See* THOMAS HOBBES, LEVIATHAN part II, at 311–35 (C. B. Macpherson ed., 1968) (1651); JEREMY BENTHAM, A FRAGMENT ON GOVERNMENT (F. C. Montague ed., 1891) (1776); JOHN AUSTIN, THE PROVINCE OF JURISPRUDENCE DETERMINED (Wilfred E. Rumble ed., 1995) (1832); HANS KELSEN, PURE THEORY OF LAW (Max Knight trans., 2002) (1934).

reflective attitude to certain patterns of behavior as a common standard";[12] earlier positivist theorists had neglected this attitude in describing law as merely orders backed by threats or predictions of what legal officials would do.[13] And Hart believed that while law and morality were distinct, law was capable of incorporating aspects of morality, of making moral principles legally relevant; indeed he thought such incorporation was necessary to explain the pervasive use of what seem like moral standards ("due care," the "reasonable man," and the like) in adjudication and elsewhere in the law.[14]

The problem of legal authority became important to analytic legal philosophy as followers of Hart began examining and testing the implications of some of these central tenets. Noticing that Hart's account of the internal point of view lacked sufficient detail to explain the special sense of obligation that law imposes, Joseph Raz proposed a more sophisticated explanation of how law affects the moral reasoning of those subject to it. Raz suggested that law creates "exclusionary reasons"—second-order reasons for a person not to act on certain first-order moral reasons that otherwise would apply.[15] A legal rule that people must perform their contracts, for example, might eliminate certain valid moral reasons that a person otherwise might have for failing to perform, thus changing the moral calculus and requiring the person to perform the contract. Analytically this approach made good sense of the mechanics of legal obligation. Normatively, however, it raised the question of why we might think law has the capacity to alter the existing moral calculus in this way. Why should someone pay attention to the law's exclusionary reasons rather than simply acting on the balance of first-order moral reasons as she sees them?

This was the problem of legal authority that lies at the heart of Aristotle's Challenge; and Raz offered an answer to it. He asserted that legal authority— law's provision of exclusionary reasons—was "legitimate," or morally justified, to the extent a person is more likely to take the morally correct action by considering those exclusionary reasons than by assessing, and acting on, the full panoply of full-order moral reasons herself, without the benefit of law.[16] In shorthand, law's authority is legitimate when the law knows better than the individual legal

---

12. HART, *supra* note 9, at 57.

13. *See id.* 82–91. Hart cited Austin for the view that law was simply orders backed by threats. *Id.* at 18–25; AUSTIN, *supra* note 11, at xxi, 117–19. Hart cited Oliver Wendell Holmes for the view that law consisted merely of predictions of official behavior. HART, *supra* note 9, at 1 n.2; Oliver Wendell Holmes, *The Path of the Law*, 10 HARV. L. REV. 457 (1897).

14. *See* HART, *supra* note 9, at 204; *see also* Kar, *supra* note 9, at 399 (describing Hart's "Incorporation Thesis").

15. RAZ, AUTHORITY OF LAW, *supra* note 8, at 3–33. In later work, Raz refers to such reasons as "pre-emptive" reasons. *See* RAZ, MORALITY OF FREEDOM, *supra* note 8, at 38–69.

16. *See* RAZ, MORALITY OF FREEDOM, *supra* note 8, at 53–80.

subject how to behave in a particular instance. This is Raz's "service conception" of legal authority: Law performs the moral service of mediating between the individual legal subject and the first-order moral reasons that apply to her, thus enhancing the likelihood that the individual will do the morally right thing.[17]

Raz's service conception is the most prominent example of what I will refer to, in Chapter 2, as an Epistemic-Guidance (EG) account of legal authority. I will argue in that chapter that EG accounts suffer from a debilitating, if not fatal, flaw that undermines the response they offer to Aristotle's Challenge. For present purposes, the point is simply that analytic legal philosophy's attention to the problem of legal authority derives not from an interest in that subject for its own sake, but rather from the discipline's primary occupation with more conceptual issues. Raz's service conception is a normative account of law's authority, but there has been relatively little interest within analytic legal philosophy in connecting the conceptual mechanics of legal authority to the normative questions of how law should be created and applied. For example, Raz himself acknowledges that the service conception would not always justify legal authority—that legal authority depends on the contingent empirical question of whether the law, in any given instance, can in fact improve the moral decisionmaking of individuals subject to it.[18] Answering that question would seem to require examining the processes of lawmaking themselves; but analytic legal philosophers generally have preferred to leave this project to the realms of political science and political philosophy.[19]

B. Political Theory and the Problem of Political Legitimacy

For their part, the denizens of these realms—practitioners of *political theory*—have not, also for understandable reasons, been particularly attentive to questions about law.[20] The most interesting problems in political theory, for our purposes in this book, are those relating to whether, and how, democratic government can be justified as opposed to its alternatives, and to how democratic government should be structured in order to best fulfill its justifications. On the

---

17. Raz uses the label "service conception" in Joseph Raz, *Authority and Justification, in* AUTHORITY 115, 131–32 (Joseph Raz ed., 1990). He outlines the conception without that particular label in RAZ, MORALITY OF FREEDOM, *supra* note 8, at 70–88.

18. RAZ, MORALITY OF FREEDOM, *supra* note 8, at 70–80.

19. A notable exception is Jeremy Waldron, who recently has attempted to connect the concerns of analytic legal philosophy with those of political theory. *See* JEREMY WALDRON, LAW AND DISAGREEMENT (1999); Jeremy Waldron, *Legal and Political Philosophy, in* OXFORD HANDBOOK OF JURISPRUDENCE & PHILOSOPHY OF LAW, *supra* note 8, at 352.

20. Here too, Jeremy Waldron is a salient exception. *See supra* note 19. Another is Richard Posner, a prominent federal judge with diverse and influential intellectual interests, including in political philosophy. Posner has sought to unite issues of political legitimacy, judicial duties, and legal interpretation under the umbrella of philosophical pragmatism. *See, e.g.,* RICHARD A. POSNER, LAW, PRAGMATISM, AND DEMOCRACY (2003).

former set of issues, democratic theorists tend to divide into two camps: those who think democracy is justifiable at least partly because it tends to produce good (or in some way effective) decisions, and those who think democracy is justifiable solely because its processes are valuable, quite apart from the decisions it produces.[21]

The potential connection between this debate and the problem of legal authority seems obvious. Raz's service conception, for example, becomes more (or less) plausible to the extent government is more (or less) capable of generating morally optimal decisions; conversely, one who accepts the service conception should be more (or less) inclined to support democracy to the extent that form of government is more (or less) able to fulfill the conception's requirements. But political theorists typically have not sought to link questions of democratic legitimacy to problems of legal authority. Indeed many participants in debates about democracy—with the notable exception of some members of the legal academy[22]—indulge a caricaturized picture of the law and legal institutions.

---

21. The former, instrumentalist camp includes John Stuart Mill, John Dewey, some modern deliberative democratic theorists like Cass Sunstein, and the political philosopher David Estlund, to name just a few. See JOHN STUART MILL, CONSIDERATIONS ON REPRESENTATIVE GOVERNMENT (1861), reprinted in JOHN STUART MILL, UTILITARIANISM, ON LIBERTY, AND CONSIDERATIONS ON REPRESENTATIVE GOVERNMENT 187 (H. B. Acton ed., J. M. Dent & Sons 1972); JOHN DEWEY, Intelligence and Morals, in JOHN DEWEY: THE POLITICAL WRITINGS 66 (Debra Morris & Ian Shapiro eds., Hackett Publ'g Co. 1993) (1908); John Dewey, The Ethics of Democracy, in THE EARLY WORKS 227 (1967), reprinted in JOHN DEWEY: THE POLITICAL WRITINGS 59 (Debra Morris & Ian Shapiro eds., Hackett Publ'g Co. 1993); John Dewey, The Public and Its Problems, reprinted in 2 JOHN DEWEY: THE LATER WORKS 1925–1953 at 235 (Jo Ann Boydston ed., S. Ill. Univ. Press 1984) (1927); CASS R. SUNSTEIN, THE PARTIAL CONSTITUTION (1993) [hereinafter SUNSTEIN, PARTIAL CONSTITUTION]; DAVID M. ESTLUND, DEMOCRATIC AUTHORITY: A PHILOSOPHICAL FRAMEWORK (2008).

The latter, noninstrumentalist camp includes John Locke, Immanuel Kant, John Rawls, other modern deliberative democratic theorists like Jürgen Habermas and Joshua Cohen, and Jeremy Waldron. See JOHN LOCKE, Second Treatise of Government, in TWO TREATISES OF GOVERNMENT 305, § 95–99 at 374–77 (Peter Laslett ed., 1960); Immanuel Kant, On the Common Saying: "This May Be True in Theory, But It Does Not Apply in Practice," reprinted in KANT: POLITICAL WRITINGS 61 at 74 (Hans Reiss ed., H. B. Nisbet trans., 2d ed. 1991) (1793); JOHN RAWLS, A THEORY OF JUSTICE (1971); JOHN RAWLS, POLITICAL LIBERALISM (1993) [hereinafter RAWLS, POLITICAL LIBERALISM]; JÜRGEN HABERMAS, BETWEEN FACTS AND NORMS: CONTRIBUTIONS TO A DISCOURSE THEORY OF LAW AND DEMOCRACY (William Rehg trans., 1996); Joshua Cohen, Deliberation and Democratic Legitimacy, in DELIBERATIVE DEMOCRACY: ESSAYS ON REASON AND POLITICS 67 (James Bohman & William Rehg eds., 1997); WALDRON, supra note 19, at 232–54.

22. Cass Sunstein, for example, has been scrupulously attentive to institutional differences among courts, administrative agencies, and legislatures in detailing his vision of deliberative democracy. See generally CASS R. SUNSTEIN, DEMOCRACY AND THE PROBLEM OF FREE SPEECH (1995) [hereinafter SUNSTEIN, FREE SPEECH]; SUNSTEIN, LEGAL

John Rawls, for example, held up the Supreme Court as an "exemplar" of the "public reason" according to which, he believed, political deliberation generally should occur;[23] Ronald Dworkin takes a similar perspective.[24] At the opposite extreme, many political scientists hold a jaundiced view of judges as simply "politicians in robes," denying any meaningful distinction between law and politics.[25]

C. Adjudicative Theory and the Problem of Judicial Duty

Not surprisingly, lawyers and judges themselves tend to understand the activities of courts in ways that are more nuanced (though not without their own pathologies). There is a long American tradition of more-or-less theoretical writing about the role of judges and the place of adjudication within the larger system of democratic government, which we might loosely group together under the label *adjudicative theory*. Putting aside perhaps the most prominent subset of this category—work in the special context of constitutional law, which I will discuss separately below—most adjudicative theory has focused, in a variety of ways, on the questions of how judges in particular ought to act, and how adjudication more generally ought to be structured, in order to maximize competence and maintain legitimacy.

For present purposes, a central dichotomy appearing in this diverse body of work has been a tension between competing ideas of the primary function of judges and courts: as resolvers of disputes, charged with applying existing legal norms to particular sets of facts; or as makers of policy, tasked with the development of new legal norms to be applied prospectively. In practice, of course, courts tend to do a fair amount of both dispute-resolving and policy-making; the question is which should dominate when these roles conflict. The more traditional dispute-resolving view appears, in various forms, in the work of the mid-century Legal Process theorist Lon Fuller, who argued that courts' competence decreases as the issues for decision become more multifaceted;[26]

REASONING, *supra* note 4; CASS R. SUNSTEIN, ONE CASE AT A TIME: JUDICIAL MINIMALISM ON THE SUPREME COURT (1999) [hereinafter SUNSTEIN, ONE CASE AT A TIME]; SUNSTEIN, PARTIAL CONSTITUTION, *supra* note 21.

23. RAWLS, POLITICAL LIBERALISM, *supra* note 21, at 231–40.

24. *See* RONALD DWORKIN, FREEDOM'S LAW: THE MORAL READING OF THE AMERICAN CONSTITUTION 1–38 (1996) [hereinafter DWORKIN, FREEDOM'S LAW].

25. *See, e.g.,* JEFFREY A. SEGAL & HAROLD J. SPAETH, THE SUPREME COURT AND THE ATTITUDINAL MODEL (1993); *see also* Barry Friedman, *The Politics of Judicial Review*, 84 TEX. L. REV. 257 (2005) (describing the "attitudinal model" of judicial behavior). Not that political scientists are the only scholars to believe this of judges; Critical Legal Studies theorists within the legal academy hold similar views. *See, e.g.,* DUNCAN KENNEDY, A CRITIQUE OF ADJUDICATION (Fin de siècle) (1998); Girardeau A. Spann, *Pure Politics*, 88 MICH. L. REV. 1971 (1990).

26. *See* Lon L. Fuller, *The Forms and Limits of Adjudication*, 92 HARV. L. REV. 353 (1978).

of legal philosopher Ronald Dworkin, who contends that judges have a duty to decide based on principle;[27] and of public-law theorist Cass Sunstein, who espouses "judicial minimalism" as a way of avoiding error and deferring to the political branches.[28] The policy-making position has been espoused, again in diverse ways, by Fuller's Legal Process colleagues Henry M. Hart and Albert Sacks, who saw courts as important vehicles of public policy;[29] by contemporary proponents of "dynamic statutory interpretation" like William Eskridge;[30] by theorists who, like Abram Chayes and Owen Fiss, argue that adjudication must adapt to the necessities of public-interest litigation;[31] and by self-described "legal pragmatist" Richard Posner, who contends that judges should use every means at their disposal to achieve all-things-considered good results.[32]

These adjudicative theorists are, typically, explicitly normative (unlike analytic legal philosophers) and attentive to the connection between the activities of courts and the overall legitimacy of the political system (unlike many political theorists). But, with the arguable exceptions of Dworkin and Fuller,[33] they have

---

27. *See generally* RONALD DWORKIN, LAW'S EMPIRE 176–275 (1986) [hereinafter DWORKIN, LAW'S EMPIRE] (describing the principle of political "integrity" and the concept of law as integrity).

28. *See* SUNSTEIN, ONE CASE AT A TIME, *supra* note 22, at 6, 38, 136. Sunstein's minimalism owes much to that of Alexander Bickel, a constitutional theorist associated with the Legal Process school. *See* ALEXANDER M. BICKEL, THE LEAST DANGEROUS BRANCH: THE SUPREME COURT AT THE BAR OF POLITICS (2d ed., Yale Univ. Press 1986) (1962).

29. Hart and Sacks saw the common law, at least historically, as "the basic instrument of official regulation in the legal systems of... the American states." HENRY M. HART, JR. & ALBERT M. SACKS, THE LEGAL PROCESS: BASIC PROBLEMS IN THE MAKING AND APPLICATION OF LAW 341 (William N. Eskridge, Jr. & Philip P. Frickey eds., 1994). They also endorsed a relatively expansive judicial role in the interpretation of statutes. *See id.* at 1111–1380.

30. *See* WILLIAM N. ESKRIDGE, JR., DYNAMIC STATUTORY INTERPRETATION (1994). Not coincidentally, Eskridge is partly responsible for rejuvenating interest in the Hart and Sacks teaching materials by coediting them, with Philip Frickey, in a 1994 hardcover edition. *See* HART & SACKS, *supra* note 29.

31. *See* Abram Chayes, *The Role of the Judge in Public Law Litigation*, 89 HARV. L. REV. 1281 (1976); Owen M. Fiss, *Foreword: The Forms of Justice*, 93 HARV. L. REV. 1, 25–27 (1979).

32. *See* POSNER, *supra* note 20, at 94–96 (advocating pragmatism among American judges). In the generally pragmatic tenor of his views, Posner is heir to a tradition that includes Oliver Wendell Holmes and Benjamin Cardozo—both of whom also were judges. *See* Holmes, *supra* note 13; BENJAMIN N. CARDOZO, THE NATURE OF THE JUDICIAL PROCESS (1921).

33. Dworkin presents the normative element of his theory of adjudication—the existence of a principle of political morality he calls "integrity"—as an explanation of how a state might be "legitimate," by which Dworkin means that "its constitutional structure and practices are such that its citizens have a general obligation to obey political decisions that purport to impose duties on them." DWORKIN, LAW'S EMPIRE, *supra* note 27, at 191.

not sought to understand the judicial role in the context of concerns for legal authority more generally; indeed some, in particular Posner, have expressly decried such efforts at "grand theory."[34]

D. Constitutional Theory and the Countermajoritarian Difficulty

As I suggested above, adjudicative theory overlaps substantially with *constitutional theory*, a discipline concerned with understanding, typically in normative terms, the grounds, structure, and methodology of constitutionalism and judicial review. It is the latter topic—judicial review, or the authority of courts to declare government actions invalid for violation of constitutional limitations—that has preoccupied American constitutional theory for much of its history.[35] Judicial review confers substantial power on judges, and yet judges—in particular American federal judges, who are never subject to popular election and serve for life (assuming "good behavior")[36]—are relatively insulated from democratic political incentives. Judicial review thus presents what the constitutional theorist Alexander Bickel called a "countermajoritarian difficulty":[37] It is a puzzlingly prominent antidemocratic force in what is supposed to be a democratic system of government.

Most of the major works in American constitutional theory have sought to justify, to define the limits of, or occasionally to critique judicial review's

---

This sounds very much like the concept of legal authority as I use it here, although Dworkin's actual explication of "law as integrity" reads more like an interpretation of legal practice than a normative account of legal authority. For his part, Fuller argued that certain procedural features of law (including some features of adjudication) are morally required; from these arguments one might infer a connection between adjudicative theory and a general theory of legal authority, although Fuller himself never made this connection explicit. *See* LON L. FULLER, THE MORALITY OF LAW (rev. ed. 1969) (1964).

34. *See* RICHARD A. POSNER, THE PROBLEMATICS OF MORAL AND LEGAL THEORY (1999) [hereinafter POSNER, THE PROBLEMATICS]; *see also* SUNSTEIN, LEGAL REASONING, *supra* note 4, at 194–96.

35. For a historical overview of this preoccupation, see Barry Friedman, *The Birth of an Academic Obsession: The History of the Countermajoritarian Difficulty, Part Five*, 112 YALE L.J. 153 (2002).

36. The appointment of federal judges is governed in the first instance by Article II, § 2 of the Constitution, which confers upon the president the power to "nominate, and by and with the Advice and Consent of the Senate, [to] appoint... Judges of the supreme Court, and all other Officers of the United States, whose Appointments are not herein otherwise provided for." U.S. CONST. art. II, § 2. Judicial tenure and compensation is subject to the provisions of Article III, § 1, which provides that "Judges, both of the supreme and inferior Courts, shall hold their Offices during good Behaviour, and shall, at stated Times, receive for their Services a Compensation, which shall not be diminished during their Continuance in Office." *Id.* art. III, § 1.

37. *See* BICKEL, *supra* note 28, at 16.

countermajoritarian status.[38] Only recently have constitutional theorists seriously begun to ask similar questions about constitutionalism itself—the imposition of legal limits, typically with a textual basis, upon the authority of democratic government—which, after all, is a precondition of judicial review and is at least as countermajoritarian. (Judicial review involves subjecting majoritarian decisions to the approval of contemporary judges; constitutionalism involves subjecting majoritarian decisions to rules or principles laid down by long-dead Framers.)[39]

Constitutional theory frequently makes contact not only with adjudicative theory, but also, not surprisingly, with the theory of democracy. (Constitutional law, after all, seems to involve a clash between the two institutions, majoritarian democracy on the one hand and adjudication on the other.) Defenders of constitutionalism and judicial review, for instance, typically argue that those practices are in fact compatible with democracy, properly understood, because something about judicial decisionmaking captures an aspect of democracy that majoritarian politics lacks (a commitment to principle, perhaps)[40] or improves the democratic process by eliminating antidemocratic pathologies (such as irrational biases and political entrenchment).[41] Interestingly, however, with a few exceptions, constitutional theorists have not tried to examine constitutional law

---

38. The list of worthy examples is long, but it certainly would include at least the following: BRUCE ACKERMAN, 1 WE THE PEOPLE: FOUNDATIONS (1991); BRUCE ACKERMAN, 2 WE THE PEOPLE: TRANSFORMATIONS (1998); BICKEL, supra note 28; ROBERT BORK, THE TEMPTING OF AMERICA: THE POLITICAL SEDUCTION OF THE LAW (1990); DWORKIN, FREEDOM'S LAW, supra note 24; LEARNED HAND, THE BILL OF RIGHTS (1958); JOHN HART ELY, DEMOCRACY AND DISTRUST: A THEORY OF JUDICIAL REVIEW (1980); James Bradley Thayer, The Origin and Scope of the American Doctrine of Constitutional Law, 7 HARV. L. REV. 129 (1893); Herbert Wechsler, Toward Neutral Principles of Constitutional Law, 73 HARV. L. REV. 1 (1959).

39. Recent challenges to the legitimacy of constitutionalism include LARRY D. KRAMER, THE PEOPLE THEMSELVES: POPULAR CONSTITUTIONALISM AND JUDICIAL REVIEW (2004); MARK TUSHNET, TAKING THE CONSTITUTION AWAY FROM THE COURTS (1999); WALDRON, supra note 19, at 209–312. Kramer and Tushnet style their projects as critiques of judicial review or "judicial supremacy"—a slippery term that typically means judicial review that is broadly binding on parties other than litigants in a particular court case—but in fact many of their arguments are attacks on the notion of constitutionalism itself. Recent defenses of constitutionalism include CHRISTOPHER L. EISGRUBER, CONSTITUTIONAL SELF-GOVERNMENT (2001); LAWRENCE G. SAGER, JUSTICE IN PLAINCLOTHES: A THEORY OF AMERICAN CONSTITUTIONAL PRACTICE (2004); W. J. WALUCHOW, A COMMON LAW THEORY OF JUDICIAL REVIEW: THE LIVING TREE (2007), and many of the essays in CONSTITUTIONALISM: PHILOSOPHICAL FOUNDATIONS (Larry Alexander ed., 1998).

40. The leading examples of this type of view are BICKEL, supra note 28, and DWORKIN, FREEDOM'S LAW, supra note 24.

41. John Hart Ely pioneered this approach. See ELY, supra note 38.

through the larger lens of legal authority.[42] This lacuna is remarkable, given that constitutional law appears to exemplify the problem of legal authority in especially salient terms. As the Case of the Obstructionist Constitution suggests, ultimately there are no real sanctions against a political majority for violating constitutional limitations; and in practice there are no real sanctions against (lifetime-tenured) Supreme Court justices for doing so. In the final analysis, all that exists of constitutional law is whatever moral authority those subject to it choose to give it; and so the question of what that moral authority might be—of where it might come from—looms particularly large.

The methodological aim of this book is, in essence, to unite these seemingly disparate problems in distinct fields of study under a single analytical framework. Each problem, I will argue, presents an aspect of Aristotle's Challenge; questions of legal authority, of the relative roles of law and morality in individual judgment, course through all of them. And each problem can be better understood, I will claim, by focusing on the imperative to resolve disputes and the methodology of resolving them acceptably.

5. ASSUMPTIONS AND CAVEATS

My project, then, is to develop a response to Aristotle's Challenge that focuses on dispute resolution—the DR account—and to build from that response a basic understanding of the central institutions of constitutional democratic government: majoritarian democracy; adversary, common-law adjudication; and constitutional law. In articulating and applying the DR account, I hope to illuminate some central and persistent problems across various theoretical disciplines: analytic legal philosophy, democratic political theory, theory of adjudication, and constitutional theory.

The nature of the project requires that I indulge certain assumptions going forward; it also calls for certain caveats. The assumptions have to do with the perspective adopted for the book's analysis, the caveats with its strength and scope.

A. The First Assumption: The Subject-Specific Perspective
In responding to Aristotle's Challenge and developing the DR account, I typically will adopt a *subject-specific perspective*; that is, I will focus on the perspective of a legal subject, a person (or, in some cases, an institution or group of people)

---

42. Some exceptions are Jeremy Waldron, *The Core of the Case Against Judicial Review*, 115 YALE L.J. 1346 (2006); Larry Alexander, *Introduction, in* CONSTITUTIONALISM: PHILOSOPHICAL FOUNDATIONS, *supra* note 40, at 1, 1–15; and Joseph Raz, *On the Authority and Interpretation of Constitutions: Some Preliminaries, in* CONSTITUTIONALISM: PHILOSOPHICAL FOUNDATIONS, *supra* note 40, at 152, 152–93.

trying to decide how to act in light of a legal rule, command, or other norm that purports to require or forbid certain conduct. The subject-specific perspective is in contrast to other possible perspectives one might take with respect to the law: the perspective of society as a whole; of the person or institution that makes the law; or of an outsider observing, in anthropological fashion, how the participants in a legal system behave.

Why focus on the subject-specific perspective? Simply because I think it constitutes the lowest common denominator, as it were, of the various aspects of Aristotle's Challenge; first-person individual choice is the basic unit of legal authority and obligation.[43] As I explained earlier in this chapter, the question of

---

43. It is worth pausing a moment to relate my assumption of the first-person perspective of a disputant or legal subject to an issue that has recently emerged in analytic legal philosophy, namely whether recognition of a "second-person standpoint" is helpful to understanding the obligatory nature of law. Robin Kar, building on the work of moral philosopher Stephen Darwall, has argued that contemporary accounts of legal authority erroneously ignore the second-person standpoint, and that correcting this oversight resolves some important problems with those accounts. By "the second-person standpoint," Kar means a moral perspective that recognizes interpersonal moral claims—claims arising from duties owed to a particular person by another particular person, by virtue of the relationship between them. Kar argues that law can be understood as conferring second-personal duties and obligations, and thus as supporting second-personal claims, that are distinct from the duties, obligations, and resulting claims conferred by morality. In this way, Kar concludes, law—even law that incorporates aspects of morality—makes a "practical difference" in people's moral reasoning; it carries authority, and imposes obligations, that morality does not. *See* Kar, *supra note* 9, at 424, 428–30 (citing STEPHEN DARWALL, THE SECOND-PERSON STANDPOINT: MORALITY, RESPECT, AND ACCOUNTABILITY (2006)).

By adopting what I term the subject-specific perspective in my arguments here, I do not mean to foreclose Kar's second-person moral standpoint, or indeed to take any position on the conceptual or normative validity of that standpoint or its relevance to law. I believe the second-person standpoint could be accommodated within the subject-specific perspective I am assuming, in the following way: In deciding how to act in light of some legal rule or other legal norm, an individual legal subject might take account of second-personal claims as well as other types of reasons (including "first-personal" reasons—reasons that apply without regard to particular interpersonal relationships—and "third-personal" reasons— reasons that apply without regard to the identity of the person to whom they apply). The subject-specific perspective relates not to the types of reasons that are relevant to a person in deliberating about how to act (unlike the "standpoints" discussed by Kar), but rather to the position of that person with respect to the law, that is, to the capacity of law to contribute some reasons (whatever their type) to that person's moral deliberations.

I do think, however, that it is possible that the DR account of legal authority I will develop in this book might itself be understood as an account of second-personal reasons for action. I will contend that the imperative of avoiding, mitigating, or resolving disputes about what to do creates powerful reasons to obey the law even when one disagrees (morally) with the law's commands. Disputes seem, virtually by definition, to be interpersonal in the sense captured by Kar's and Darwall's concept of the second-person standpoint: There is no such thing as an abstract or universal dispute (or, for that matter, a unilateral

how persons—ultimately individual persons—who are subject to the law should act in light of the law is at the heart of Aristotle's Challenge, and of the idea of the rule of law to which the Challenge is directed. Individual legal subjects (like the mother in the Case of the Sick Child) must decide in the first instance whether to obey the primary rules of law that govern day-to-day conduct. Even in a (fanciful) system where everyone, or almost everyone, who chooses to disobey the law can be caught and punished, individual legal officials (like the judge in the Case of the Unjust Statute) must decide whether to impose the legally required punishment. And ultimately it is up to whichever collection of individuals holds power in a given society (like the democratic majority in the Case of the Obstructionist Constitution) to decide whether to observe the society's fundamental laws. The rule of law is, at bottom, a matter of individual choice. It makes sense, then, to build an account of the rule of law around the choices that individual legal subjects must make.

At certain stages of my arguments, I will alter this subject-specific perspective a bit to focus, not on persons purportedly bound by existing legal commands or other norms, but on parties trying to resolve or avoid disputes. In Chapter 3, for instance, I will articulate a simple bipartite model of dispute resolution by imagining what might motivate two members of a pre-legal society who find themselves in conflict with one another. In Chapter 4, I will extend that simple model to a complex society seeking to avoid and resolve inevitable disputes by means of legal rules. And in Chapters 7 and 8, I will consider whether, and why, a democratic society might choose to adopt constitutional law and judicial review

---

dispute); disputes only occur between or among two or more particular people or groups of people. The imperative of avoiding, mitigating, or resolving a dispute, therefore, might be seen as a kind of second-personal obligation owed by the disputants or potential disputants to each other (or, possibly, to others—friends, family, members of the community— who stand to be harmed by an unresolved dispute). This obligation presumably would be a moral, not a legal, one; but the legal obligations that flow from it might be seen as *distinctively* legal rather than moral, as they might require a person to take or refrain from particular actions that she would not otherwise (without the law) choose to take or refrain from taking. And those obligations might be second-personal in the sense meant by Kar and Darwall—flowing from some particular interpersonal relationship to which the legal subject is a party.

I suspect that the question of whether the DR account I offer here is a type of second-personal account will turn on whether we think our moral reasons to avoid or resolve disputes are "agent-centered," that is, whether they impose nontransferable, nonfungible obligations on (or to) particular people. On the connection between agent-centered obligations and the second-person standpoint, see Kar, *supra* note 9, at 429–30. I do not want, or need, to take a position on this issue for my purposes here; I don't believe anything about the DR account turns on whether the dispute-resolving imperative that animates it is agent-centered. Thus I think one can assess my arguments in this book quite independently of one's agreement or disagreement with Kar's or Darwall's analyses of the second-person standpoint.

as mechanisms of dispute-avoidance and dispute-resolution. In each of these contexts the focal question will be, not the retrospective one of whether to follow a disagreeable existing legal norm, but the prospective one of whether to adopt certain procedures and institutions for creating legal norms. Even here, though, the ultimate conundrum with which I will be concerned revolves around the problem of legal authority: In suggesting that people in these circumstances have reason to submit their disputes to law, I will be suggesting as well that people have reason to honor and obey the results once their disputes have been resolved according to law.

B. The Second Assumption: Persons as Good-Faith Moral Reasoners

I also will assume, for most purposes, that the individual legal subjects whose choices I discuss are *good-faith moral reasoners*—that in deciding how to act, each person wants, and tries, to do the morally right thing. This assumption precludes the possibility that a legal subject will, like Oliver Wendell Holmes's famous "bad man,"[44] decide what to do based solely on his own personal advantage. It is of course possible that the dictates of morality will coincide with the personal advantage of a legal subject; it also is possible that the fact that a given course of action would be personally advantageous to the legal subject is relevant to how that person, morally, ought to act. And so it is possible that a given legal subject, in reasoning morally about how to act, will take his own self-interest into account. But I will assume that if a legal subject decides to act in a way that furthers his own advantage, he does so because, and only because, he believes that is what morality requires.

This assumption obviously does not correspond exactly, or even remotely, to the state of affairs in the real world. As such, it would be manifestly inappropriate if my project here were largely descriptive. But my project is substantially, though not entirely, normative: I want to articulate a case for why people (citizens, judges, democratic majorities) *should* respect the law, so long as certain conditions are satisfied. Thus I will assume that the legal subjects whom I use as examples are trying to behave as they, morally, should behave.

It is important to note, however, that my assumption that people are good-faith moral reasoners is almost entirely formal rather than substantive. I recognize, of course, that there is substantial room for disagreement about what morality in fact requires, and for the most part I will not take, much less assume, a position within that debate. I will assume that people want and try to do the right thing, but (with one exception) I will not assume any particular view

---

44. "If you want to know the law and nothing else, you must look at it as a bad man, who cares only for the material consequences which such knowledge enables him to predict, not as a good one, who finds his reasons for conduct, whether inside the law or outside of it, in the vaguer sanctions of conscience." Holmes, *supra* note 13, at 459.

about what the right thing entails or about the nature or source of the moral considerations relevant to answering that question.[45]

The exception will arise in Chapter 3, when I indulge the assumption that most people will, as a matter of morality, be strongly motivated to avoid, mitigate, or resolve certain disputes. I will not go to great lengths to defend that proposition, either normatively (as a statement about what people should want to do) or descriptively (as a statement about what people in fact want to do). Instead I will allow the DR account that flows from this assumption, and my applications of that account to various political and legal practices over the course of the book, to serve as their own evidence of the assumption's normative and descriptive validity. If the DR account and its applications to actual practices seem normatively attractive, then the dispute-resolving imperative at the heart of that account might seem attractive as well; if the DR account seems descriptively plausible, so might the dispute-resolving imperative as an understanding of how people actually behave.

In the final two chapters of the book, I will articulate a defense of constitutionalism and judicial review that turns on the possibility that the decisions of certain political actors—legislators, other government officials, political majorities—sometimes will be distorted by self-interest or other forms of partiality. This might seem to contradict my premise that legal subjects are good-faith moral reasoners, but that perception would be mistaken. For one thing, people acting in complete good faith might still, thanks to the unperceived influence of self-interest, get it wrong; their decisions might be distorted by self-interest without their knowing it. More to the point, however, I will suggest in those chapters

---

45. I should note the fact that there is room for disagreement, not only about the substantive requirements of morality, but also about the metaphysics of morality—about whether morality really exists in an objective sense, as opposed to being, say, nothing more than the product of an individual's state of mind. While I will assume a moral realist position on this issue—that is, I'll assume that morality has some objective existence, that statements about the requirements of morality can in fact be objectively true—I believe my arguments here can be accepted even by someone who rejects or is skeptical about moral realism. Aristotle's Challenge, the core problem to which I'm responding, assumes only that there is the potential for conflict, within the reasoning of individual legal subjects, between the perceived dictates of law and the perceived dictates of some source of norms that is hierarchically superior to law; it does not assume that this superior nonlegal source of norms—which I will refer to as "morality" in shorthand—has actual objective existence. If we suppose for a moment that moral realism is false, Aristotle's Challenge would retain its bite so long as legal subjects believe, however falsely, that there is an applicable source of norms that is hierarchically superior to law and with whose demands those of law sometimes conflict. Legal subjects still would have to decide whether to obey the dictates of law or of this conflicting perceived source of norms. And the DR account I will present in this book still would offer legal subjects a reason to obey the dictates of law, so long as those subjects perceive (however falsely) that the imperative to resolve disputes flows from the (falsely perceived) superior source of norms.

that the danger of political self-interest creates a reason, not for the self-interested officials and others *themselves* to institute and obey rules of constitutional law, but rather for the potential subjects of their decisions—the democratic citizens who will be bound by them—to establish rules of constitutional law as a way of avoiding official self-interest and the challenges to authority it might inspire. My case for constitutional law will depend not on the danger that legal subjects will act out of self-interest, but on the danger that those claiming legal authority will act out of self-interest. I will touch on this point again in those final chapters.

C. The Third Assumption: The Irrelevance of Formal Sanctions

For reasons I've suggested already, I will assume as well that legal subjects do not consider the possibility of formal sanctions for disobedience as part of their reasoning about whether to obey the law. Of course this assumption is probably at least as unrealistic in a descriptive sense as the assumption that persons are good-faith moral reasoners. While research in psychology suggests that fear of sanctions is only one among many motives for obedience to the law,[46] surely the threat of sanctions frequently plays at least some role in people's calculations.

For my purposes, however, I will assume away the threat of formal sanctions because, as I explained earlier, sanctions ultimately must follow law rather than the other way around. Individuals may be motivated by sanctions to obey the law, but legal officials (like the judge in the Case of the Unjust Statute) typically will require some other motivation; and, in a democratic system, individuals ultimately *are* the relevant legal officials (as the Case of the Obstructionist Constitution demonstrates). Since I am concerned with developing a general account of legal authority, not an account that applies only where the threat of sanctions is meaningfully present, I need to articulate reasons to obey law even absent that threat. Assuming the threat away is my methodology for identifying those reasons.[47]

---

46. *See* TOM R. TYLER, WHY PEOPLE OBEY THE LAW (rev. ed. 2006).

47. Some analytic legal philosophers believe that, in order for a primary legal rule to possess authority, ordinary citizens need not be motivated to obey it by anything other than the threat of formal sanctions; legal authority requires only that a sufficient number of legal officials be motivated to enforce that rule—that is, to obey the secondary rules requiring that it be enforced—by something other than the threat of formal sanctions. *See, e.g.*, Kar, *supra* note 9, at 416–17 (citing Scott Shapiro, *On Hart's Way Out*, in HART'S POSTSCRIPT 100, 175 (Jules Coleman ed., 2001)). But this argument assumes too sharp a distinction between primary and secondary rules on the one hand, and between ordinary citizens and legal officials on the other.

Consider again the Case of the Obstructionist Constitution. In a sense, the constitutional restrictions in question—requiring that criminal suspects be afforded certain rights—are secondary rules, as they govern the validity of the primary rules that legal officials may impose upon criminal suspects. But in another sense they are themselves primary rules, as they directly regulate the conduct of ordinary citizens by preventing

D. The First Caveat: An Account, Not a Comprehensive Theory

The DR account I will develop here is just that: an account—or, if you prefer, a model—rather than a comprehensive theory of legal authority. Its aim is to supply a general justification of legal authority that is both normatively and descriptively plausible, in part because it persuasively explains the central

---

them from demanding that their government treat criminal suspects in a certain way. If a majority of citizens chooses to obey (or to allow or cause their representatives in government to obey) a constitutional rule, the explanation must lie in something other than the threat of formal sanctions for disobedience, which are minimal or nonexistent in such a case. Constitutional rules thus seem to possess authority over ordinary citizens quite apart from the threat of sanctions.

While constitutional rules might seem at first glance to be anomalous in this respect, I think that appearance is misleading. The sanctionless authority of constitutional rules reveals that for some purposes—in a modern constitutional democracy, for some very salient and important purposes—ordinary citizens in effect *are* legal officials. Democratic citizens, for example, possess the power to vote, which influences how formal legal officials behave, including whether and to what extent they obey constitutional (and other legal) rules. Democratic citizens may exercise their power to vote in a way that communicates their respect for the law, and thus motivates a similar respect in legal officials; and it is hard to see how the virtually nonexistent threat of formal legal sanctions against the voters for "disobedience" could explain such behavior. (If anything, it is the legal officials, fearful of losing their jobs at the hands of the voters, whose obedience to the law is likely to be motivated by the threat of sanctions.)

More broadly, there are of course many historical examples of the subjects even of nondemocratic regimes asserting their power, through resistance passive or violent, to punish or change official conduct they find objectionable. On a Lockeian view, this "right of revolution" is an appropriate response to official abuses of power—that is, conduct by legal officials that is itself contrary to the fundamental law of the land. *See* LOCKE, *supra* note 21, § 199–243, at 446–77. Thomas Jefferson and his fellow American revolutionaries explained their actions in Lockeian terms, not as a rejection of law but as a necessary corrective against official lawlessness. (Compare the second paragraph of the Declaration of Independence ("a long train of abuses and usurpations") with section 225 of Locke's *Second Treatise* ("a long train of Abuses, Prevarications, and Artifices").) To revolt or resist the law *in the name of* law is to pursue the law despite, not because of, the threat of formal sanctions. Such behavior on the part of ordinary citizens or subjects must involve respect for law on non-sanction-related grounds.

Of course, it may be the case that a given act of popular rebellion or resistance is motivated not by a desire to reassert the law against official abuses, but by a contempt for the legal system itself. On the Hartian view accepted by most contemporary legal positivists, a legal system is built upon a fundamental "rule of recognition" whose authority is accepted by a sufficient number of those in power. To overthrow an existing legal system is, then, to overthrow its rule of recognition; it is to shatter the previous agreement regarding the authority of that rule. The history of violent resistance and revolution in nondemocratic regimes suggests that a rule of recognition ultimately must gain some acceptance among ordinary citizens or subjects, not just among legal officials, in order to effectively support a legal system.

features of many of our real-world legal institutions and practices. I will not claim that the DR account adequately explains every aspect of legal authority. (For instance, I will punt on the questions of the exact strength of the duty of legal obedience that the DR account justifies, and of the precise mechanics by which that duty operates in practical reasoning.) I will assert, rather, that the DR account does a better job in most circumstances than its chief competitors of explaining the core feature of legal authority, namely its capacity to provide strong reasons to take actions one believes to be morally suboptimal. Even this claim, however, will not be absolute; I will not assert that the DR account is the only plausible way to explain the specially obligatory nature of law, and indeed I suspect that no single account can provide a completely satisfactory explanation of that feature. I will try to note the areas in which the DR account falls short during the course of my arguments.

E. The Second Caveat: Sufficient, Not Necessary

Nor, relatedly, will I claim that the DR account is the only account that fits our actual legal institutions and practices. I do tend to believe the DR account fits better than the alternatives with the central legal institutions and practices I discuss in this book, but I will make that case piecemeal rather than systematically; my goal will be to persuade readers that the DR account plausibly explains those practices and institutions and helps us think productively about some of their important features, not that they cannot adequately be understood without that account. I will claim, in essence, that the DR account is sufficient for a persuasive basic understanding of many of our central legal institutions and practices; I will not claim the account is necessary for such an understanding.

By the same token, I will focus on a particular set of legal institutions and practices (albeit at a fairly abstract level), namely those of the contemporary American legal system. (It is these phenomena to which I sometimes refer, perhaps somewhat presumptuously, as "our" practices and institutions.) To the extent the DR account helps us understand these particular American phenomena, it may help us also to understand similar phenomena in other systems. But I am not claiming universal applicability for my arguments here, at least not at the level of application to features of particular systems. Admittedly there is a

---

Which brings us back to the context of constitutional rules. For a democratic majority to ignore, or to allow its representatives to ignore, applicable constitutional limitations may very well be for that society's rule of recognition, in Hartian terms, to change—from a rule by which the constitution's limitations are strictly binding to a rule by which they are not. It may in essence be a revolution without violence. If so, then the post-Hartian distinction between legal officials (who must be motivated to obey secondary legal rules, including the rule of recognition, for reasons other than the fear of sanctions) and ordinary citizens (who must be motivated to obey only the primary rules and may be motivated solely by sanctions) degrades even further.

universal aspect to my claims about the DR account: I will develop that account, initially, in a way that is abstracted from particular legal practices, institutions, or systems. But I do not intend to assert that the general roots of the account must always produce exactly the same kind of tree. There may well be legal and political institutions of widely different forms that would be compatible with the basic outlines of the DR account (and remember that I am not claiming that the DR account is the only plausible account of legal authority in any event). Nor, as I will point out periodically and emphasize in the Epilogue, is it clear that the DR account will "work"—will justify legal authority—under all conditions; some fundamental level of social agreement is necessary for the account, and institutions and practices built upon it, to function.

F. The Third Caveat: The Persistent Possibility of Morally Justified Disobedience

Finally, allow me to presage here a point I will elaborate in the next chapter: Nothing in my arguments in this book will support the conclusion that legal disobedience is *never* morally justified. I think this would be a highly implausible position to take; it seems clear to me that disobedience to the law, even to legitimately authoritative law, sometimes will be morally justifiable. Otherwise we would not admire civilly disobedient figures like Gandhi and Martin Luther King. The claim I will make for the relationship between the DR account and legal authority is this: The DR account justifies a *prima facie* moral duty to obey legitimate legal norms. I will acknowledge, as I think anyone must, that this *prima facie* duty sometimes can be overcome by countervailing moral considerations.

Of course, such an admission concedes a good deal to Aristotle; it grants the point that the judgment of men sometimes trumps the rule of law. But it does not concede everything, or even most of what matters. It still allows for an account upon which legal authority, and thus the idea of a government of laws, has real meaning. I begin to explain how in the next chapter.

2. THE PROBLEM OF LAW'S AUTHORITY

Aristotle's Challenge is in essence a challenge to the idea of *legal authority*—to law's capacity to motivate us, morally speaking, to take or refrain from certain actions. But legal authority turns out to be a somewhat mysterious concept. Law purports to *command* us, not merely to give suggestions or advice. It commands us, moreover, to behave in certain ways without regard to whether we believe doing so is morally correct. And yet there are instances in which it seems right to disobey law's supposed commands. How then should we understand the normative claims law asserts upon us through its commands, rules, and other norms?

Providing a basic answer to that question is the first task of this chapter. I contend below that law is best seen as conferring a *prima facie*, but not an absolute, moral duty of obedience upon its subjects. As I explain, that *prima facie* duty must be separate and independent from the moral duty that would exist without the law; the law, that is, must give rise to *content-independent* reasons for action, reasons that do not rely on what it is the law tells its subjects to do. And it is this content-independent aspect of legal authority that opens the door to Aristotle's Challenge.

The second task of this chapter is to sketch and evaluate four prominent types of attempt to resolve the problem of legal authority. I will argue that three of them, while informative, ultimately are unsatisfactory, each for its own reasons. The fourth is a basic form of the Dispute-Resolution (DR) account that will structure the remainder of this book. I will briefly explain here how the DR account might avoid the problems that afflict its three rivals, before developing that account more comprehensively in the ensuing chapters.

1. THE NORMATIVE STRENGTH OF LEGAL AUTHORITY

In Chapter 1, I suggested that the moral reason to act provided by authoritative legal commands would have to be special or especially strong in some way in order to make sense of the notion that law "governs" or "rules" us. Law must provide something other than an ordinary reason for action. Consider the decision process that the mother in the Case of the Sick Child might work her way through. She will have many morally relevant reasons to drive faster than fifty-five miles per hour (which is, let us say, the posted speed limit) in taking her child to the hospital: the child's urgent need for medical attention; her own sobriety, experience, and skill as a driver; the presence of clear, dry weather; the relative lack of other cars on the streets at that time of day.[1] She also will have many reasons not to drive faster than fifty-five: the possibility of injuring herself, her child, or others; the risk of causing property damage; the chance that she will get to the hospital in time even if she drives more slowly; and so on. (Remember: For purposes of my arguments going forward, I will assume away the threat of sanctions as a morally relevant reason for action.)

For the mother to take the reason provided by the existence of a legal rule against driving faster than fifty-five—whatever the nature of that reason—and simply throw it in the hopper with all these other reasons would be to misunderstand what she owes the law, or at least what the law claims of her. The law—more precisely, the legislature or whoever created the law; the legal officials charged with enforcing it; and the society on whose behalf the legislature and other legal officials are acting—will not be satisfied if the mother considers the law's command as merely one reason among many that are relevant to her decision of how fast to drive. Suppose, for example, that the mother is caught and charged with speeding. Her proving in court that she *considered* the speed limit in deciding how to act will hardly be enough to relieve her of legal liability. The law demands, or purports to demand, not mere consideration, but *obedience*.

Whatever the law purports to demand, however, it is implausible to think that legal authority actually implies an absolute requirement of obedience. Such an understanding would allow no room for the possibility of morally justifiable disobedience to the law, and that possibility seems too deeply ingrained in our collective consciousness to be dismissed so easily. An absolutist understanding of legal obligation would forbid all civil disobedience, for example—Martin Luther King's violation of trespass and disturbing-the-peace laws while leading civil rights protests in the South, Gandhi's nonviolent (but often illegal) resistance to British rule in India—and it seems likely that any reasonably accurate account of legal authority should allow for instances like these. Indeed, it seems likely that even less-momentous examples of disobedience to law—speeding to the hospital with a sick child, perhaps—need to be accommodated within a viable theory of legal authority. The possibility of rightful disobedience to law supposes that, in some cases at least, other reasons besides those embodied in a legal command will exist, will be eligible for consideration, and will in fact

---

1. For our purposes, we can classify any factor that is morally relevant to a legal subject's decisionmaking as a "reason" for or against a particular action. Decision theorists often further subclassify what I will call "reasons" into *beliefs* about the world—that the child is sick, that the roads are clear, and so on—and *preferences* for various states of affairs—a healthy child. *See* Robin Bradley Kar, *Hart's Response to Exclusive Legal Positivism*, 95 Geo. L.J. 393, 430–31 (2007) (describing these categories of reasons). It will be sufficient for my arguments here to describe both types of phenomena—beliefs and preferences—simply as "reasons."

outweigh the reason or reasons embodied in the command. It supposes, that is, a nonabsolutist conception of legal authority.

One source of potential confusion about the normative force of legal authority is the fact that the law itself typically speaks in absolutist terms—purporting to "prohibit" or "require" certain actions, using the language of "shall" and "must" and "shall not" and the like—and that it often doles out punishments in a way that seems to follow automatically from disobedience. Legal rules and commands typically do not present themselves as simply one reason or set of reasons for action that should be thrown into the mix with a bunch of other applicable reasons, potentially to be outweighed or trumped by them. But the fact that law demands (or purports to demand) absolute obedience does not mean that absolute obedience is what we owe the law; more to the point, it does not mean that the concept of legal authority is best understood to carry absolute normative force. There may be sound strategic reasons for law to misrepresent itself as absolutely binding. If there is a high risk that people will underestimate the strength of their reasons to obey the law relative to their reasons not to, the law might try to mitigate this risk by forbidding (or purporting to forbid) people from engaging in that calculus in the first place. It may be that the harm flowing from erroneous obedience to the law (thanks to a belief that the law demands absolute obedience) is, on the whole, less than the harm that would be caused by erroneous disobedience to the law (thanks to a recognition that legal authority is not absolute).[2]

Nor is it clear that the law's claim to absoluteness often is consummated in practice. The criminal law, for example—seemingly the paradigm of absolutist legal authority—is in fact riddled with opportunities for leniency to justified offenders. Law enforcement officers can (and surely often do) look the other way; prosecutors can (and often do) decline to prosecute; judges can (and sometimes do) exercise their discretion to admit questionable exculpatory evidence; juries can (and often do) refuse to convict; governors and presidents can (and occasionally do) commute sentences and issue pardons. Most of these decisions are effectively unreviewable for error. Their presence and prominence suggest that the law, when push comes to shove, is not as absolutist as it purports to be.

It is highly implausible, then, that the concept of legal authority really implies an absolute moral duty of obedience, even if those who participate in the legal system act as though it does; and in fact it is far from clear that legal officials really *do* always act as though legal authority is absolute. On the other hand, as we have seen, it is just as implausible to think that legal authority provides

---

2. On the "moral gap" between the justification of strict enforcement of legal rules and the justification of disobedience of rules in particular cases, see LARRY ALEXANDER & EMILY SHERWIN, THE RULE OF RULES: MORALITY, RULES, & THE DILEMMAS OF LAW 53–95 (2001); on the impossibility of closing the gap by strictly sanctioning disobedience, see *id*. at 77–86.

nothing more than an ordinary moral reason for action, one on an equal footing with all the other applicable moral reasons. Clearly there is something special about authoritative legal commands that makes disobedience, if not absolutely impermissible, then at least presumptively so. Most legal philosophers agree that legal commands create reasons that differ *somehow* from ordinary reasons for action, either in their special strength, their special effect on other reasons, or both.[3] They disagree widely, however, about just *how* the reasons created by legal commands are special. Some argue that a legal command creates a reason for action that preempts other reasons or excludes our consideration of them;[4] others contend that a legal command creates a presumption of action in accordance with it;[5] still others argue that it changes the weight of other applicable reasons for action.[6]

These issues regarding the strength of law's authority are important as well as difficult. Thankfully, we need not resolve them in order to provide a satisfactory response to Aristotle's Challenge. Aristotle's Challenge goes, not to the precise conceptual mechanics by which legal authority operates, but to the basic idea that law can motivate us to act in ways we believe to be morally suboptimal. That idea can be captured by assuming that legal authority, if it is a valid concept at all, entails at least a *prima facie* duty of obedience to authoritative legal commands— that is, a presumption of considerable (if indeterminate) strength that a legal command should be obeyed, but one that might in some instances be overcome by countervailing reasons favoring disobedience. For our purposes, we need not specify exactly how strong this *prima facie* duty is or what kinds of countervailing reasons might be sufficient to overcome it.

---

3. Scott Shapiro is an exception; he takes the position that legal commands are best understood not as reasons for action at all, but as *constraints* on action that preclude reasoning about how to act. *See* Scott J. Shapiro, *Authority*, *in* THE OXFORD HANDBOOK OF JURISPRUDENCE & PHILOSOPHY OF LAW 382, 415–30 (Jules Coleman & Scott Shapiro eds., 2002). To be precise, Shapiro argues that legal commands must be understood as constraints if legal authority is justified by what I will refer to later in this chapter as an Epistemic-Guidance function. Shapiro also offers an alternative justification of legal authority, a version of what I will refer to as a Dispute-Resolution justification; on that justification, Shapiro contends, legal commands may in fact be understood as reasons (or as providing reasons) for action. *See id.* at 431–39.

4. *See, e.g.,* JOSEPH RAZ, THE MORALITY OF FREEDOM 57–62 (1986) [hereinafter RAZ, MORALITY OF FREEDOM].

5. *See, e.g.,* Stephen Perry, *Second Order Reasons, Uncertainty, and Legal Theory*, 62 S. CAL. L. REV. 913 (1989) [hereinafter Perry, *Second Order Reasons*].

6. *See, e.g.,* Stephen Perry, *Judicial Obligation, Precedent and the Common Law*, 7 OXFORD J. LEG. STUD. 215 (1987); Perry, *Second Order Reasons, supra* note 5, at 932–36. For a survey of the various views on the nature and force of legal commands, see Shapiro, *supra* note 3, at 402–15.

2. THE CONCEPTUAL NATURE OF LEGAL AUTHORITY

Whatever the strength of the reason or duty supplied by legal authority, that reason or duty must, as a conceptual matter, be *content-independent*. A reason is content-independent if its validity does not depend on the rightness or value of *what* it tells us to do, that is, on the quality of its substantive content. A reason is content-*dependent* if its validity does turn on the rightness or value of what it tells us to do.[7] To adapt an example from Scott Shapiro,[8] suppose I have two good reasons for taking out the garbage. Reason R_1 is that the garbage is stinking up my kitchen, and taking it out would make my wife and me happier by removing the offensive smell. Reason R_2 is that my wife, whose authority I recognize in matters of housekeeping, has ordered me to take out the garbage. R_1 is a content-dependent reason; its validity depends on the value of what it tells me to do, namely the obvious advantages of removing odorous garbage from our kitchen. R_2 is a content-independent reason; its validity depends not at all on the value of the action it supports and entirely on the *source* of the command or other directive that embodies it, namely my wife, whose authority in these matters I acknowledge.[9]

The very notion of legal authority depends on the existence of content-independent reasons to obey the law. To say that a legal command possesses authority is to say that there is at least a *prima facie* duty to obey that command, *even if one disagrees with its substantive content*. If the concept of legal authority entailed "obedience" only to legal commands with which one agreed in substance, it would be either entirely superfluous or entirely toothless. It would be superfluous when a person agrees with the command's substantive content, because in such a case that person would choose the same course of action without the command. And it would be toothless when a person disagrees with the command's content, because in such a case that person would have no reason to obey the command. The idea of legal authority thus supposes that people have reasons to obey legal commands with which they disagree in substance; and such reasons must, by definition, be content-independent reasons.

---

7. *See, e.g.*, H.L.A. Hart, The Concept of Law 253–55 (2d ed. 1994) (1961); Shapiro, *supra* note 3, at 389.

8. *See* Shapiro, *supra* note 3, at 389.

9. Must a content-independent reason turn on the *source* of the directive that embodies it? Not necessarily. It is conceivable, for example, that the *form* of a directive might create a content-independent reason to act. A gentle suggestion from my wife that I take out the garbage might be more effective than a curt command (or vice versa). More generally, there are contexts, such as international diplomacy and military operations, in which directives or requests are required by etiquette or protocol to take a certain form. But most content-independent reasons—certainly the vast majority of those relevant to the authority of law—will turn on the source of a directive.

3. ARISTOTLE'S CHALLENGE REVISITED

Going forward, then, we can assume that legal authority claims to impose on legal subjects a moral duty to act (or to refrain from acting) that is both *prima facie* (rather than absolute) and *content-independent*. This conceptual structure of legal authority, however, leaves unresolved our question-in-chief, namely whether legal authority, so construed, can be normatively justified.

Aristotle, remember, believed that rule by virtuous men is superior to rule by law. We can understand this position as a partial (but dangerous) challenge to the concept of legal authority as we have defined it. If virtuous men are the ultimate rulers, they need not obey the law; they have nothing like a *prima facie* duty to do so. Their only duty is to act according to their all-things-considered judgments about what is right. In doing so, a virtuous ruler might decide to do what the law commands, but not because he recognizes the law's authority over him; he would do so only if he agrees with the substance of that command, that is, only if the balance of the content-dependent reasons tells him to. A virtuous ruler might consider the law in deciding what to do, but only for its content; he would treat the law as providing, not authoritative commands, but rather a sort of advice about how to act, advice that he would be free to ignore if it seems outweighed by the balance of content-dependent reasons. And as we saw in Chapter 1, treating legal commands as advice is not the same as being governed by law.

Of course, Aristotle did not want to completely deny the existence of legal authority. Virtuous rulers need not be bound by law, but they do need to *rule*, meaning that others in society must feel themselves bound by the commands they issue. The rulers' commands must themselves possess authority. So legal authority must be justified even on an Aristotelian account. But Aristotle's notion of legal authority does not extend to the rulers themselves, who are bound only by their own judgment. Aristotle's government is a government *by* law, but not a government *under* law. In this respect Aristotle's views were a precursor to those of Thomas Hobbes, as we will see.

It also is true that the conception of legal authority I am assuming here, which envisions law as imposing only a *prima facie* duty and not an absolute one, opens the door in a certain respect to Aristotle's rule by virtuous men. A *prima facie* duty might be overcome in some circumstances, which means that the concept of legal authority leaves on the table the possibility of justifiable disobedience to law. So long as that possibility remains, we would rather have good on-the-spot decisionmakers—virtuous (and smart, and knowledgeable, and experienced, etc.) men and women—to determine whether disobedience *is* justifiable in any given case. To this extent Aristotle is correct that the "best man" should rule, that "[e]nlightened statesmen [should] be at the helm," to paraphrase James Madison.[10]

---

10. THE FEDERALIST No. 10, at 123, 125 (James Madison) (Isaac Kramnick ed., 1987) [hereinafter Madison, FEDERALIST No. 10].

But Aristotle's challenge, understood in its broadest sense, does more than raise the possibility of rightful disobedience to the law; it calls into question the validity of even a *prima facie* duty of obedience. If men and women can be sufficiently virtuous and enlightened to decide for themselves when the presumption of obedience has been overcome, what is the value of the presumption? Doesn't it make more sense to allow these virtuous, enlightened men and women to directly assess all the relevant reasons for action, without the meddling (and inevitably imperfect) interference of the law?

A defense of the idea of law's authority—of Adams's "government of laws"—against the full brunt of Aristotle's Challenge requires a justification of the special (if not absolute) force that legal commands possess, the *prima facie* duty they create. It requires an explanation of why even virtuous and enlightened men and women, including virtuous and enlightened men and women who happen to be public officials, cannot simply ignore or disobey the law when they disagree with it, but must at least presumptively adhere to its requirements absent some especially compelling case against doing so.

4. THE EPISTEMIC-GUIDANCE ACCOUNT

One type of explanation was suggested by Aristotle's teacher Plato. In his *Republic,* Plato outlined the form of an ideal city-state, one that would be ruled by "guardians" schooled in both warfare and philosophy and painstakingly raised and educated to serve only the public interest. Plato asserted that "by reason. . . of the knowledge which resides in this presiding and ruling part of itself"—that is, in the Guardians—"the whole State. . . [would] be wise":[11] All the citizens of the Republic would be made better off—wiser, happier, more virtuous—by obeying the Guardians than by acting according to their own inferior moral judgments.

In Plato's ideal republic lie the seeds of a seemingly powerful response to Aristotle's challenge. If it turns out that the lawmakers in a society are considerably wiser than their legal subjects, then obeying the lawmakers' commands might make sense even when a legal subject disagrees with them. By hypothesis the lawmakers, after all, are more likely to know what is best than are ordinary legal subjects, and so an ordinary legal subject who disagrees with a legal command is likely to be wrong. A subject then acts correctly by obeying a law with which she disagrees, because she is more likely to get it right—to act in the way that is morally best—by obeying than by following her own unalloyed judgment.

Of course, it's not immediately clear that this Platonic answer to Aristotle (if we can indulge an anachronism for the moment) gives legal officials themselves, as opposed to private citizens, a reason to obey the law. A philosophically trained, ideally virtuous Guardian may justifiably believe that she can improve

---

11. PLATO, REPUBLIC book IV, at 127 (Benjamin Jowett trans., Barnes & Noble 2004).

on a general legal rule in a particular instance, even if an ordinary legal subject would not be justified in such a belief. Plato, however, thought that even Guardians (in their individual capacities) should obey general laws.[12] The explanation for this might lie in the idea that the wisdom and virtue of the Guardians as a collective body far exceeds the wisdom and virtue of any particular Guardian, placing an individual Guardian in almost (if not quite) the same position as an ordinary citizen with respect to the duty to obey a general law.

As this possibility of collective wisdom suggests, the scope of the Platonic response is not limited to elitist views of governing competence like Plato's own. Many defenses of democratic government turn at least in part on the notion that the collective wisdom of the masses—of a conglomeration of people of diverse education, wealth, experience, tastes, etc.—greatly surpasses the wisdom of any individual or small group within society and thus forms the best foundation for government.[13] John Stuart Mill, for example, believed that "the general prosperity attains a greater height, and is more widely diffused, in proportion to the amount and variety of the personal energies enlisted in promoting it."[14] When applied to the problem of legal authority posed by Aristotle, this populist version of the Platonic response holds that individuals should obey legal commands with which they disagree because (and to the extent that) those commands issue from a democratic process whose collective ability to determine and declare what

---

12. *See id.* book V, at 160 ("the guardians themselves must obey the laws, and they must also imitate the spirit of them in any details which are intrusted to their care").

13. Cass Sunstein refers to this general proposition as a "many minds" argument. *See* CASS R. SUNSTEIN, A CONSTITUTION OF MANY MINDS (2009). Sunstein parses the various potential grounds of many minds arguments in his preface. *Id.* at ix–xi.

14. JOHN STUART MILL, CONSIDERATIONS ON REPRESENTATIVE GOVERNMENT (1861), *reprinted in* JOHN STUART MILL, UTILITARIANISM, ON LIBERTY, AND CONSIDERATIONS ON REPRESENTATIVE GOVERNMENT 187, 224 (H. B. Acton ed., J. M. Dent & Sons 1972). The idea that broader participation in government gives it more expertise also was a major theme of the early twentieth-century philosopher John Dewey. *See* JOHN DEWEY, *Intelligence and Morals, in* JOHN DEWEY: THE POLITICAL WRITINGS 66 (Debra Morris & Ian Shapiro eds., 1993) (1908) [hereinafter DEWEY, WRITINGS]; JOHN DEWEY, *The Ethics of Democracy, in* THE EARLY WORKS (1967), *reprinted in* DEWEY, WRITINGS, *supra*, at 59; JOHN DEWEY, *The Public and Its Problems, in* 2 JOHN DEWEY: THE LATER WORKS 1925–1953 235 (Jo Ann Boyston ed., 1984) (1927); JOHN DEWEY, *Creative Democracy: The Task Before Us, in* DEWEY: WRITINGS, *supra*, at 77; JOHN DEWEY, *Liberalism and Social Action, in* 11 JOHN DEWEY: THE LATER WORKS 1925–1953 1 (Jo Ann Boydston ed., 1987) (1935); JOHN DEWEY, *The Economic Basis of the New Society, in* DEWEY: WRITINGS, *supra*, at 169.

For an interpretive overview of Dewey's views on democracy, see Chapter 3 of RICHARD POSNER, LAW, PRAGMATISM, AND DEMOCRACY (2003). As Posner puts it, "Dewey turned Plato on his head by accepting the linkage between knowledge and politics but arguing that knowledge is democratic and so should politics be. . ." *Id.* at 104. Mill should be credited with having made this move at least half a century before Dewey made it.

is right far outweighs the individual's personal capacity to do so. It holds, in short, that many heads are better than one.

As we saw in Chapter 1, the legal and political philosopher Joseph Raz offers a contemporary (and more formal) version of the Platonic account. On Raz's "service conception" of legal authority, valid law serves those subject to it by assisting them with their reasoning. By offering legal commands as content-independent reasons for action that exclude otherwise applicable content-dependent reasons, the law (according to Raz) makes it more likely that legal subjects will act rightly than if those subjects attempt to directly assess the balance of content-dependent reasons by themselves. Like Plato and Mill, Raz of course recognizes that legal commands must issue from some specially competent process in order to perform this epistemic-guidance function and claim *legitimate* authority.[15]

I will refer generally to this Platonic response, in its many possible versions, as an *Epistemic-Guidance* (EG) account of legal authority.[16] An EG account holds in essence that legal authority is justified by (and to the extent of) law's greater capacity than unalloyed individual judgment to get things right, to prescribe morally correct action; it asserts that the recognition, by legal subjects, of (at least) a *prima facie* content-independent duty to obey legitimate law produces morally better results than legal subjects' direct assessment of the content-dependent reasons for action. To Aristotle's question of why virtuous actors should obey the law, Plato, Mill, and Raz answer that, thanks to the law's considerably superior wisdom (at least so long as the law is legitimate—that is, generated by an appropriate process), even virtuous actors are more likely to act rightly by doing so.

A. Epistemic Guidance, Substance, and Authority

There is, as we will see, a considerable grain of truth in the EG account of legal authority. (Each account I will canvass in this chapter rings true in at least one

---

15. *See* RAZ, MORALITY OF FREEDOM, *supra* note 4, at 21–105. I am indebted to Scott Shapiro's clear and pithy explication of Raz's theory. *See* Shapiro, *supra* note 3, at 402–08.

16. Here I'm afraid I risk confusion with legal philosopher Scott Shapiro's use of the term "epistemic guidance" to describe a different phenomenon. Shapiro has distinguished between the law's provision of "motivational" guidance, by which he means reason to obey the law by virtue of law's authority, and "epistemic" guidance, by which he means the use of legal commands as evidence about what one ought to do. *See* Scott Shapiro, *On Hart's Way Out, in* HART'S POSTSCRIPT 149, 173 (Jules Coleman ed., 2001) [hereinafter *On Hart's Way Out*]; *see also* Kar, *supra* note 1, at 416. I use the term "Epistemic-Guidance account" here to describe a justification of legal authority that turns on law's capacity to improve legal subjects' moral reasoning about how to act, such as Raz's service conception; on this view, an EG account of legal authority seeks to explain what Shapiro calls "motivational" guidance rather than what he calls "epistemic" guidance. I've decided to use the term regardless of this potential for confusion, however, because I think it best captures the normative essence of this type of explanation of legal authority.

important way; this is of course what explains their appeal.) But there is a debilitating flaw in the EG account as well, one revealed by the nonabsolutist conception of legal authority I offered earlier in this chapter.

I suggested earlier that law cannot demand our blind obedience, but rather
creates a *prima facie* duty to act in accordance with its commands—a duty that
might, in a special case, be overridden by the balance of other applicable reasons.
We might think of this *prima facie* conception of legal authority as in essence a
general rule that people ought to obey the law—a rule that, like all general rules,
is subject to exceptions, as we saw in Chapter 1. What the notion of a *prima facie*
duty accomplishes is simply to make the instance of exceptions relatively rare,
by creating a reason to obey the law that can be overcome in relatively few
instances; in this way it makes sense of the special obligatory character of the
law. But, as we also saw in Chapter 1, it will of course be up to the individual legal
subject in every instance to decide whether that case *is* such an exception, that is,
whether the reasons against obeying the law are, in that instance, so strong as to
overwhelm the *prima facie* duty created by a legal command. There simply is no
way around this inevitable element of ad hoc individual judgment.

Note that the Problem of Exceptions applies not only to the question of the
law's *substance*—of what it tells legal subjects to do—but also to the question of
the law's *authority*—of its capacity to impose a *prima facie* duty to do that thing.
Any given instance might be an exception to an applicable legal rule, in the sense
that the reasons to disobey the law overcome the *prima facie* duty to obey it. But
by the same token, any given instance might be an exception to the *authority* of
a legal rule, in the sense that the justification for that rule's authority does not
apply in that instance. Suppose, for example, that the mother in the Case of the
Sick Child generally treats legal rules as imposing a *prima facie* duty of obedience. Consistent with this general view, she may decide that the reasons to
exceed the speed limit outweigh this *prima facie* duty in that particular case, and
that the morally correct thing to do (even acknowledging the law's authority)
therefore is to exceed the speed limit.

But the mother also might conclude that, in her particular case, the usual
prima facie duty of obedience does not even apply—that the law in fact *lacks
authority* over her in that case. The rule that the law generally creates a *prima
facie* duty of obedience, after all, is just that—a general rule; and as Aristotle
reminds us, all general rules have exceptions. So it is conceivable for the mother
to conclude that her case is an exception to the general rule that law imposes a
prima facie duty, and thus that the law in fact possesses no authority over her
whatsoever in that case.

And note that if she does reach this conclusion, it will be all the easier to reach
a second conclusion as well, namely that the morally correct thing for her to
do, all things considered, is to disobey the applicable legal command in that particular instance. Having concluded that the law lacks authority in her case, she
will not, as a result, have to overcome any *prima facie* duty of obedience to the

applicable legal rule; and the reasons to disobey that rule (that is, to act contrary to what the rule requires) will not need to be as strong as they otherwise would. It thus will become more likely that she will decide to disobey the legal rule.

The Problem of Exceptions thus requires that both the question of whether to obey the law *and* the question of whether the law has authority ultimately be subjected to the ad hoc judgment of individual legal subjects. There is no way around this conclusion, either—not even to jettison the notion of a *prima facie* duty of obedience in favor of an absolute one, as I explain below—and it is a conclusion that will apply regardless of the particular account of legal authority one adopts. It turns out, however, that this aspect of the Problem of Exceptions spells special trouble for the EG account of legal authority.

The problem for the EG account is that it makes the law's *substance*, or content, directly relevant to the question of the law's *authority*. Suppose the mother in the Case of the Sick Child accepts the EG account as a justification of law's general capacity to impose upon her a *prima facie* duty of obedience. Suppose further that in this particular instance, she believes that the reasons to act contrary to what the law commands—to exceed the posted speed limit—are strong enough to outweigh the *prima facie* duty the law imposes. Her conclusion to this effect must be based on a belief that the speed limit law dictates a morally incorrect course of action in that case (coupled, most likely, with a belief that the consequences of taking this morally incorrect action would, in that case, be especially severe). Recall, however, that the EG account turns on the idea that the law is better able than the individual legal subject to identify morally correct actions. For the mother to conclude that, in her case, the law dictates a morally *incorrect* action is for her to deny the basis of the law's authority in that case; it is to conclude that, at least in that particular instance, the law is *not* better able than the individual legal subject to identify the morally correct action.

Of course, the mother still might believe that the law is *generally*—over the majority of cases—better able than she is to determine how best, morally, to act. But, again, this is a general rule, and general rules always have exceptions. The mother's conclusion that the law is (substantively) wrong in the Case of the Sick Child amounts, in essence, to a conclusion that her particular case is an exception to the general, EG-based authority of the law.

By making the question of law's substantive correctness relevant to the question of law's authority in this way, the EG account stumbles badly as a convincing justification of true legal authority. In order for law to have true authority, remember, it must provide a content-independent reason for action, a reason unrelated to the substance of what the law commands. But the EG account lets content-dependent reasons in through the back door. Conceptually, it is true that the law's EG function gives a legal subject, like the mother in the Case of the Sick Child, a content-independent reason for action, namely the law's superior capacity to decide how best to act. In practice, however, the legal subject's perception of the existence and strength of that content-independent reason will depend on her assessment of the content-dependent reasons for action; it will depend on whether she agrees or disagrees with the substance of what the law commands. We can refer to this as the *Encroachment Flaw* in the EG account: Content-dependent reasons encroach onto the supposedly content-independent territory of legal authority.

Thanks to the Encroachment Flaw, the EG account thus fails to provide a persuasive account of legal authority when one is needed most. To have true authority, law must be able to motivate legal subjects to take actions they otherwise would think morally suboptimal. But it's not clear that law can do this on the EG account. Whenever a legal subject disagrees with the law's commands—especially where that disagreement is strong, and where the subject believes the costs of acting incorrectly are high—that subject will, if she adopts the EG account, have reason to reject the authority of the law altogether.

B. The *Prima Facie* Duty Revisited

Is it possible that the Encroachment Flaw in the EG account—its failure adequately to segregate content-dependent from content-independent reasons, and thus substance from authority—is merely an artifact of the nonabsolutist conception of legal authority I have adopted, by which law creates a *prima facie* but not an absolute duty? This possibility is suggested by the apparent fact that a person who is subject to an absolute duty to obey the law is, by virtue of that duty, forbidden to disobey the law's commands under any circumstances. Would not such a person thus be forbidden to disobey the law on the ground that he disagrees with the law's authority in a particular case?

The answer is no. Even an absolutist conception of legal authority must depend on the *legitimacy* of that authority, that is, on whether the law really possesses the authority it claims. And it is precisely the legitimacy of law's authority that the EG account allows a person to question on content-dependent grounds.

Consider for a moment a common nonlegal example of authority apparently justified by the EG function: A patient recognizes his doctor's authority to prescribe drugs and other treatments for his medical problems and obeys the doctor's orders without question. And suppose the patient acknowledges that his doctor's authority is absolute: He is under an absolute duty, not merely a *prima facie* one, to obey his doctor's commands regarding his health.

Now imagine the doctor begins extending her (supposed) absolute authority into other, arguably nonmedical spheres of the patient's life, ordering him to quit his stressful job, for example, or to break off a troubled personal relationship, or to watch only lighthearted romantic comedies on television. At some point the patient is likely to think the doctor's orders are straying so far from what is reasonably necessary to protect his health that they no longer are authoritative—not because the doctor's authority is less than absolute within its sphere, but because these ancillary matters do not seem to fall within her sphere of authority at all. The fact that the doctor is an authority on certain matters does not mean the doctor is an authority on *everything*; nor does it mean she is an authority on the question of which matters she is an authority about. And the patient is unlikely simply to take the doctor's word for it that the jurisdiction of her authority, as it were, extends to these seemingly far-flung questions; her merely claiming such authority does not make it so. Inevitably the patient will have to exercise his own independent judgment to assess the legitimacy of the doctor's supposed authority on these matters.

In exercising his own judgment regarding the legitimacy of the doctor's authority, however, the patient no longer is simply offering blind obedience to the doctor's orders. The absolute nature of the doctor's authority within its proper sphere does not preclude—cannot preclude—the patient from making his own all-things-considered decisions about the extent of that sphere, and thus the legitimacy of the authority.

For analogous reasons, even absolute legal authority cannot preclude people from making judgments about the legitimacy of that authority, judgments that must be made from outside the binding scope of the authority itself. It is plausible to think that the scope of law's legitimate authority extents far more broadly than the scope of a doctor's legitimate authority; but it is highly implausible to think the scope of law's authority is infinite. Certainly it is implausible to believe, following an EG account, that law is an epistemic authority on everything.[17] At the very least the extent of law's authority seems reasonably open to question. Legal subjects, then, cannot escape the need to exercise their own judgments regarding the scope of law's legitimate authority. And on an EG account, those judgments cannot help but be influenced, perhaps driven, by considerations of substance—by an assessment of whether law is in fact getting the right answers to particular kinds of questions. The less frequently we think the law is answering a certain kind of question correctly, the less likely we are (on the EG account) to conclude that the law's authority over that kind of question is legitimate.

So we must sometimes question the legitimacy of law's supposed authority, even if we assume that authority, when legitimate, to be absolute. But if the legitimacy of legal authority is sometimes open to question, it is always open to question. *Any* instance may, again, be an exception to the general rule of law's legitimate authority. The same factors that can make us reject the law's authority over a type or set of cases can make us reject it in any particular case. Suppose we conclude that law lacks authority over issues stemming from close personal relationships because individuals are more likely than the law to resolve those issues correctly. Having concluded this with respect to a family or genre of cases, we cannot now deny that this possibility—that the individual is a better decision-maker than the law, and thus that the EG justification of legal authority fails—in

---

17. Raz recognizes the possibility that legal authority will exist with respect to some areas of regulation but not others. *See* Raz, MORALITY OF FREEDOM, *supra* note 4, at 70–80.

fact exists in *every* case. The law lacks legitimate authority over close personal relationships because the EG rationale fails in most cases in that category; but surely the EG rationale will fail in at least *some* cases in *most* (if not all) categories. And we cannot know which cases those are, or even how to draw lines between the various categories of cases, without assessing the legitimacy of the law's authority on a case-by-case basis (here again the specter of the Problem of Exceptions). Doing so, of course, will require us to assess whether the law's epistemic authority is justified in each case, and surely our belief about whether the law is substantively correct—about whether its command aligns with the content-dependent reasons for action—will be relevant in that assessment. Thus the Encroachment Flaw in the EG account reappears.

Note, finally, that even if we assume an extremely implausible world in which law is a legitimate epistemic authority on absolutely everything, we still would need to exercise our own independent judgment to determine whether a particular directive really qualifies as *law*. To indulge again a medical analogy, imagine a stranger appearing at your hospital bedside and purporting, without offering credentials, to be a "doctor" with authority to direct your medical treatment; or imagine two different doctors disagreeing about what the appropriate treatment should be; or imagine being treated by a "doctor" whose "medical degree," hung on her office wall, was conferred by Joe's School of Medicine and Auto-Body Repair. When a question arises about whether someone claiming authority really possesses it, we have no choice but to exercise our own independent judgment in answering that question, and thus in deciding whether to obey the putative authority's commands. And, on an EG account, surely our own views about the substantive correctness of what the (supposed) authority is commanding us to do should be considered relevant to the question whether that supposed authority really *is* an authority that we must obey. The stronger our disagreement with the substance of a command, the less likely we are to treat that command as having issued from a legitimate authority and thus as possessing authority over us. (An order from a self-proclaimed "doctor" to treat your cancerous tumor by standing on your head and singing the lyrics to *Pippin* is likely to cause you to question the "doctor's" credentials.)

These observations, I think, strongly affirm the initial case against an absolutist conception of legal authority by demonstrating that, short of expressions of divine will, there really cannot be such a thing as blind obedience to a supposedly authoritative command. (Even expressions of divine will might not qualify; for how are we supposed to determine whether a command that purports to be from God really *is* from God without exercising our own judgment on the matter?) Perhaps more importantly for present purposes, they demonstrate that the EG justification of legal authority fails to compellingly answer Aristotle's Challenge, regardless of how absolutist one thinks such an answer must be. While the EG account can, as a conceptual matter, provide a content-independent reason to obey the law, as a practical matter that reason inevitably will be compromised by a person's direct assessment of content-dependent reasons for action, calling its status as content-independent—and thus its ability to support true legal authority—into doubt. The EG account thus has trouble explaining why Aristotle's "best" men and women—those whose judgment is especially deserving of confidence—presumptively should obey even the best laws in the cases that really matter: cases in which the individual actor strongly disagrees with the substance of the law's commands.

C. The Problem of Disagreement

At the root of the problem of legal authority embodied in Aristotle's Challenge, and of the shortcomings of the EG response to that challenge, is the fact of *moral disagreement.*

If the right thing to do in any particular case always were crystal clear to everyone—if there were no possibility of disagreement about it—then law itself would be largely unnecessary, or rather it would be necessary only to control those who know the right thing to do but still refuse to do it. Cultivating virtuous men and women to live in and run a society (an idea that has captivated idealist political thinkers from Plato to Mill to Marx) would be all that was required. And the answer to Aristotle's Challenge would be so obvious that the challenge would lose its meaning: *Of course* we would prefer the best men and women to the best laws; in a world of morally omniscient, perfectly virtuous men and women, laws would be superfluous.[18]

The very existence of law, then, can be understood largely as a response to the problem of moral disagreement. And moral disagreement—disagreement caused by the divergent results of different people's attempts to reason, in good faith, about what reason or morality requires—will be endemic in a society of any complexity and diversity. Political philosopher John Rawls coined a term— "the burdens of judgment"—to describe the source of inevitable disagreement "between reasonable persons."[19] The burdens of judgment are "the many hazards involved in the correct (and conscientious) exercise of our powers of reason and judgment in the ordinary course of. . . life," hazards including the complexity of the facts we have to work with, the vagueness of the moral and

---

18. Well, laws would be *mostly* superfluous in such a world. We probably still would need some of them to help us coordinate our behavior. Consider many traffic regulations, such as the rule that everyone traveling in the same direction must drive on a particular side of the road. There is no independently "right" or "wrong" answer—not even a "best" answer—to the question of which side of the road to drive on; the only "right" answer is one that is the same for everyone. So even morally omniscient, perfectly virtuous citizens would need rules telling them on which side of the road to drive. But most laws are not of this purely coordinating type. On this point, see my discussion of coordination later in the chapter.

19. John Rawls, A Theory of Justice 54–58 (1971) [hereinafter Rawls, Theory].

political principles we must apply to those facts, and the influence of our divergent life experiences on the way each of us assesses facts, recognizes and interprets principles, and applies the latter to the former.[20] The inexorability and universality of the burdens of judgment mean that disagreement—not just disagreement motivated by narrow self-interests that conflict, but good-faith, *reasonable* disagreement—will be rampant in all but the simplest and most homogeneous communities.[21]

Legality is a strategy for deciding how to act in the face of disagreement—for allowing people to do things when they disagree about the merits of doing them. Seen in this light, the problem with the EG account is that it fails to make adequate sense of law as a strategy for resolving disagreement. In order to resolve disagreement, law must provide some powerful reason for people who disagree with its commands nonetheless to obey them. But the reason offered by the EG account—that the law's judgment is epistemically superior to its subjects' judgments, is more likely than its subjects' judgments to be morally correct—often proves to be a weak reason indeed. Someone who strongly disagrees with the substance of a legal command also thereby has reason to disagree with the authority of that command—with the EG justification for obeying it. "The law is right and you are wrong" simply is not a very convincing argument for obedience to legal commands one finds objectionable.

One would think that a compelling justification of law's authority would be grounded in the fact of disagreement, not embarrassed by it. If law would be largely unnecessary without disagreement, then a response to disagreement must be at the very core of law. The EG account comes up short in this respect, but the EG account is hardly the only account available to us.

---

20. *See id.* at 56–57. For an application of Rawls's burdens of judgment to the narrower context of politics, see JEREMY WALDRON, LAW AND DISAGREEMENT 111–18, 149–63 (1999).

21. During the American Founding, fear of this kind of disagreement was one important ground of Anti-Federalist objection to the proposed national Constitution. The Anti-Federalist writer "Brutus" asserted that "[i]n a republic, the manners, sentiments, and interests of the people should be similar. If this be not the case, there will be a constant clashing of opinions; and the representatives of one part will be continually striving against those of the other." 2 THE COMPLETE ANTIFEDERALIST 369 (Herbert Storing ed., 1980). The Anti-Federalists thus opposed the proposed Constitution's shift of substantial power from the governments of the (then) relatively small and cohesive states to the national government. Such objections prompted James Madison's famous rejoinder, in *Federalist No. 10*, that a national system of representation, by virtue of its capacity to govern a large and diverse populace, would mitigate the danger of self-interested majority "factions," a danger that was acute in a small and relatively homogeneous republic. *See* Madison, FEDERALIST NO. 10, *supra* note 10, at 126–28.

5. THE CONSENSUALIST ACCOUNT

Consider another potential response to Aristotle's Challenge, popular with political thinkers as diverse as Hobbes and Abraham Lincoln: the idea that legal authority can be grounded in the fact of *consent*.

Here is how consent might justify legal authority. Imagine a dispute between two people, Alice and Barney. Suppose Alice and Barney agree with each other to allow Calvin to resolve their dispute. If Calvin then resolves the dispute in favor of Alice, Barney has a content-independent reason to honor that decision: namely his *ex ante* consent to allowing Calvin to resolve the dispute. We might even think Barney's consent imposes on Barney a duty, at least a *prima facie* duty, to honor Calvin's decision. We might think, that is, that by virtue of Barney's consent to be bound by Calvin's decision, that decision has authority over Barney.

Now suppose that Alice and Barney anticipate that additional disputes between them might arise in the future. Suppose they agree to allow Calvin to resolve all of these future disputes. If Calvin, pursuant to this agreement, resolves a future dispute against Barney, Barney again has a content-independent reason—perhaps even a *prima facie* duty—to honor Calvin's decision (as would Alice if Calvin resolves a dispute against her). Indeed, we might say that Calvin has general authority to resolve disputes between Alice and Barney, that is, authority over Alice and Barney with respect to his resolution of their disputes.

Finally, imagine that instead of two individuals agreeing on a procedure for resolving future disputes, we have an entire community of people agreeing on such a procedure. If every member of that community consents to a procedure—"Let Calvin decide"—then every member of the community has a content-independent reason, perhaps a *prima facie* duty, to adhere to the results of that procedure. And if we replace "Let Calvin decide" with a more complex set of agreed-upon procedures and institutions—a legislature to enact general laws, an executive to enforce those laws, a judiciary to interpret and apply them in particular cases, and so forth—we might be able to say that every member of the community has a *prima facie* duty to obey the results of these procedures and institutions. We might be able to say, in other words, that every member of the community has a *prima facie* duty to obey the law—that the law in that community possesses authority over all the community's members—by virtue of their consent.

A. Legal Authority and Actual Consent

Is the idea of consent capable of providing a justification of the general authority of the law, as this line of reasoning suggests? It is not, at least not without substantial help from other types of normative arguments.

Consider first the kind of moral grounding that consent must have in order to create anything like a *prima facie* duty to act. If an act of consent carries the normative power that the examples above assume, that power must flow from a certain understanding of the value of human autonomy. On this understanding, commonly associated with Kant,[22] autonomy exists, and has inherent value, to the extent an individual has the capacity to play a meaningful part in shaping the conditions of her own life; and to shape the conditions of one's own life is to make decisions that have consequences for that life. A decision to *consent* to be bound by a procedure or institution, even if one disagrees with the substance generated by it, thus is a manifestation of human autonomy, and the value of autonomy necessitates the attribution of some binding effect to that decision. Not to do so, after all, would be to deny the individual the capacity to shape her own life by, among other things, giving her consent.[23]

It turns out to be difficult, however, to identify anything like an autonomous act of consent behind the demands the law typically makes on a person in the conditions of modern society. Most residents of any real-world society will not have given their *express* consent to be bound by that society's laws. (In the United States, only non-native-born citizens must swear an oath to "support and defend the Constitution and laws of the United States of America" and "bear true faith and allegiance to the same.") Nor is it clear that even the giving of express "consent" would, in most cases, do the trick. Legal theorist Randy Barnett asks us to imagine the U.S. government's requiring every person residing within the country to take an oath promising to obey the country's laws:

> Suppose one refused to take the oath. Would one then not be bound by the laws of the United States? Or would one then be expelled from the country? The latter prospect presupposes that the person who is demanding we take an oath is an "authority" who has the right to expel us if we refuse, but it is his authority that is at issue in the first place and that supposedly depends on our consent. All this is quite circular.[24]

True "consent," in other words, cannot be given under penalty of suffering precisely that thing one supposedly is consenting to. As Barnett puts it, "[f]or consent to bind a person, there must be a way to say 'no' as well as 'yes.'"[25]

---

22. *See generally* IMMANUEL KANT, GROUNDWORK OF THE METAPHYSIC OF MORALS (H. J. Paton trans. 1964).

23. *See* Joseph Raz, *On the Authority and Interpretation of Constitutions: Some Preliminaries, in* CONSTITUTIONALISM: PHILOSOPHICAL FOUNDATIONS 152, 162–63 (Larry Alexander ed., 1998) [hereinafter Raz, *Authority and Interpretation*]:

> There is some normative force to the fact that one gives one's free and informed consent to an arrangement affecting oneself. . . Consent, whether wise or foolish, expresses the will of the agent concerning the conduct of his own life. Whatever mess results from his consent is, in part at least, of his own making. Since his life is his own, it is relevant whether it is under his control or not, and consent shows that it is.

24. RANDY E. BARNETT, RESTORING THE LOST CONSTITUTION 17 (2004).

25. *Id.* at 21.

This fact also undercuts two popular arguments tying legal authority to consent: the arguments from *continued residence* within a legal community and from *democratic participation*. The former argument holds, in the words of Jean-Jacques Rousseau, that "[t]o reside within the state after its actual establishment. . . is to consent to it,"[26] or in John Locke's words that "tacit Consent" to the state's authority arises from a person's "Possession, or Enjoyment, of any part of the Dominions of. . . Government."[27] The problem here is that the barriers to answering "no" to the question of consent will, for many or most people, be insurmountably high. Ceasing to "reside within the state" in order to withhold one's consent to that state's laws often would mean sacrificing homes, friends, jobs, perhaps families. In essence, the community seeking to impose its laws typically is in a much stronger bargaining position than the individual upon whom they would be imposed, and it is difficult to say that the individual has freely—autonomously—consented to live under the community's laws.

Nor will there always be an alternative community in which to reside whose laws are preferable (much less an alternative community that *has* no existing body of law). The contractarian political theories of Locke, Rousseau, and Hobbes posited a group of people's consenting to law as an alternative to a lawless "state of nature," and in so doing creating an ideal legal system more or less from scratch. Inhabitants of the real world, however, typically cannot create legal systems from scratch; at best they can choose from an array of decidedly imperfect extant legal systems, assuming they can choose at all. Inferring "tacit consent" to general legal authority under such conditions is akin to offering a prisoner the "choice" between the bastinado or the rack and then inferring his "consent" to be tortured as a result of the choice. As political philosopher David Estlund puts it, this would "make hash out of the idea of consent."[28]

It might be argued, though, that in a particular type of legal system—a participatory democracy, in which each citizen has an equal and meaningful opportunity, through voting and other means, to influence the content of the laws—consent to legal authority can be inferred from a citizen's exercise of that participatory right.[29] Abraham Lincoln famously identified "the sheet anchor of American republicanism" as the principle "that no man is good enough to govern another man, without that other's consent," and by "consent" Lincoln

---

26. JEAN JACQUES ROUSSEAU, THE SOCIAL CONTRACT book IV, at 168 (Willmoore Kendall trans., 1954).

27. JOHN LOCKE, *The Second Treatise of Government*, in TWO TREATISES OF GOVERNMENT 305, § 199 at 392 (Peter Laslett ed., 1960) (emphasis altered).

28. DAVID M. ESTLUND, DEMOCRATIC AUTHORITY: A PHILOSOPHICAL FRAMEWORK 9 (2008).

29. My refutation of this argument follows that of BARNETT, *supra* note 24, at 14–17.

meant "[a]llow[ing] ALL the governed an equal voice in the government."[30] But here, too, the problem in equating democratic participation with true consent is an absence of some effective means of *refusing* consent, of saying "no." Democratic citizens are held to be bound by *all* the laws promulgated by democratic means, whether they voted for those laws—or for the legislators who voted for them—or not. A contrary vote, or a refusal to vote at all, has no capacity to release one from the law's authority. (Nor does being a noncitizen who lacks the right to vote altogether.) The situation is well described by Barnett:

> If we vote *for* a candidate and she wins, we have consented to the laws she votes for, but we have also consented to the laws she has voted against.
>
> If we vote *against* the candidate and she wins, we have consented to the laws she votes for or against.
>
> And if we *do not vote at all*, we have consented to the outcome of the process, whatever it may be.[31]

"This," Barnett rightly notes, "is simply not consent."[32]

Actual consent, then, cannot plausibly serve as the basis for an account of general legal authority. As we will see in the next chapter, there is a sense, nonetheless, in which something like actual consent plays an important role in a more satisfactory account of legal authority. The socially contingent nature of actual consent—the fact that its existence, and thus the existence of legal authority, depends in some way on the particular circumstances of the society in question—will be reflected in the DR account; on that account, the legitimacy of law's authority over a legal subject will depend in part on whether others within a society also recognize its legitimacy. But an adequate account of legal authority cannot turn solely on the presence of actual consent.

B. Legal Authority and Constructive Consent

Is there a way to take advantage of the normative power of consent without imposing the impossible burden of actual consent? Some political theorists have attempted essentially this task using the idea of *constructive consent*. The most prominent example is John Rawls, who argued that "principles of justice" are valid to the extent they would be agreed to by individuals in a hypothetical "original position" of absolute equality and complete ignorance about how each participant in particular would be affected by the principles agreed upon.[33]

---

30. Abraham Lincoln, The Repeal of the Missouri Compromise and the Propriety of Its Restoration: Speech at Peoria, Illinois, in Reply to Senator Douglas (October 16, 1854), *in* ABRAHAM LINCOLN: HIS SPEECHES AND WRITINGS 283, 304 (Roy P. Basler ed., 1946) (emphasis altered).

31. BARNETT, *supra* note 24, at 16.

32. *Id.* at 17.

33. *See* RAWLS, THEORY, *supra* note 19.

Jürgen Habermas pursues a similar line, holding that "norms of action" (including legal norms) are valid if (and only if) "all possibly affected persons could agree [to them] as participants in rational discourses," that is, under idealized conditions of democratic debate.[34] Rawls and Habermas suggest that normative force can flow from the fact that a person *would* have consented to a procedure under certain idealized conditions, even if that person did not actually do so. Perhaps this idea of constructive consent can be used to justify legal authority: A person might have a content-independent *prima facie* duty to obey a law generated by a procedure to which that person would have consented under the right circumstances.

In assessing this possibility, we first need to notice how the normative mechanics of constructive consent differ from those of actual consent. The power of actual consent lies precisely in its actuality: A person has a reason to abide by his own consent just because he has given it. It is a person's real act of consenting that effectuates his autonomy, which is the ultimate normative basis for treating consent as binding. The reason for action provided by actual consent does not depend on the act of consent's having been wise or even morally justifiable (although its lack of wisdom or morality might provide countervailing reasons *against* abiding by that act, that is, in favor of overriding whatever duty the act of consent has created). So long as consent was given under sufficient conditions of autonomy (e.g., knowledge of what is being consented to, intent to consent to it, and an absence of coercion or duress), the act of consenting carries some normative force.

Constructive consent is quite different. The point of constructive consent as a normative device usually is understood to be the epistemic one of identifying norms—e.g., Rawls's "principles of justice"—that can be seen as having a certain substantive moral quality by virtue of having been generated by idealized procedures. One's reason to obey a norm that is the product of constructive consent is *not* that one actually has autonomously consented to the norm, but rather that the norm can be trusted in some way (as substantively just, for example) because of its pedigree. True, the idea of constructive consent probably is best understood as incorporating the value of autonomy in a certain way: It holds that norms can be seen as just (or otherwise trustworthy) precisely because someone *would* have (autonomously) consented to them under the appropriate conditions. But consent itself is not its driving normative force. That force flows, instead, from the substantive quality of whatever norms we can attribute to hypothetical consent.[35]

---

34. *See* JÜRGEN HABERMAS, BETWEEN FACTS AND NORMS: CONTRIBUTIONS TO A DISCOURSE THEORY OF LAW AND DEMOCRACY 107, 447–50 (William Rehg trans., 1996).

35. As legal theorist Frank Michelman puts it, "hypothetical consent based on correct reasoning is a substantive, not a procedural, test for the justified character of a set

This means that a theory of constructive consent is incomplete without some account of the substantive norms that the appropriate idealized conditions would generate. The constructive-consent theorist must offer reasons to believe that persons acting autonomously under the appropriate conditions would consent to a particular norm or set of norms. And those reasons inevitably will be moral reasons, going to the substantive quality (the rightness, the goodness, the justice, the beneficial nature) of the norms in question. The constructive-consent theorist will have to explain why a person acting under the appropriate conditions *should* consent to those norms, that is, would have moral reasons to consent, reasons that outweigh the countervailing reasons. Irrational or unjustifiable consent, therefore, is off the table on constructive-consent accounts.

Constructive consent is, in this sense, a merely formal account of legal authority rather than a substantive one. It must be filled in with some morally plausible substantive account—some reason or set of reasons justifying consent—in order to justify legal authority. And this means that the capacity of constructive consent to solve the problem of legal authority ultimately will depend entirely on the capacity of this independent substantive account to do so.

Suppose, for example, that we attempt to justify legal authority, not by directly relying on the problematic EG account, but by piggybacking that account onto a constructive consent approach. As we have seen, the content-independent duty to obey the law that the EG account purports to provide is undermined by the Encroachment Flaw—the likelihood that a legal subject will use her disagreement with the law's substance as a reason to question the law's authority. Perhaps, however, we can resuscitate that content-independent duty by asserting that the legal subject has constructively consented to it. Suppose it is the case that legal subjects in this particular legal system are in fact much more likely, over the run of cases, to act morally correctly by obeying the law than by directly assessing the content-based reasons for action. (Suppose, in other words, that the EG account assumes a descriptively accurate general picture of law within that system.) We might then be able to say that any legal subject within that system *should* consent to obey all that system's laws, on the ground that he or she will do better, in the long run, by obeying the law than by acting on his or her own unalloyed moral judgment. We might be able to say, in other words, that each legal subject has *constructively consented* to obey the law. Can we then assert that this constructive consent itself imposes a content-independent duty for any given legal subject—say, the mother in the Case of the Sick Child—to obey the law in a particular instance?

I think not; for importing the EG account through the mechanism of constructive consent imports the Encroachment Flaw along with it. Here is how.

---

of [norms]." Frank I. Michelman, *Constitutional Authorship*, in CONSTITUTIONALISM: PHILOSOPHICAL FOUNDATIONS, *supra* note 23, at 64, 88.

Suppose the mother in the Case of the Sick Child must decide whether to obey the speed limit by virtue of the constructive consent argument outlined in the previous paragraph. In order to make that decision (and remember again that the decision whether to obey must, in the final analysis, rest with the individual legal subject), the mother will have to determine whether she can be said to have constructively consented to obey that legal rule.

If the question were whether the mother had *actually* consented to obey the rule, the answer would itself be content-independent; it would turn, not on whether the mother now thinks the rule is substantively right or wrong, but rather on external descriptive facts regarding her state of mind (did she intend to be bound by the rule), her decisional manifestation of that state (did she affirmatively commit herself to be bound by the rule), and the like. But the relevant question for purposes of *constructive* consent is whether the mother *should* have consented to obey the rule. And if the normative justification for constructive consent is supplied by the EG account, then the answer to this question will be content-*dependent*. The mother will determine that she should have consented to obey the rule *if*, and only if, obeying the rule will increase the likelihood that she will act morally correctly as compared with not obeying it. And the fact that the mother now disagrees with the substance of the rule will support a negative answer to this question. Just as the mother would have little reason to recognize the law's superior epistemic capacity on a direct application of the EG account, she will have little reason to conclude that she should have consented to the law by virtue of its superior epistemic capacity. *relating to Knowledge or to the degree of its validation*

But mightn't the mother recognize a duty to obey the law, not by virtue of constructive consent to *that particular legal command*, but by virtue of constructive consent to obey the law *generally*? To put this another way: Mightn't the mother have constructively consented to *refrain* from a case-by-case evaluation of whether to obey the law—to commit to *always* obeying the law—for the reasons suggested by the EG account? Again, I think not; or rather, to be precise, I think the possibility of this sort of general constructive consent cannot solve the problem of legal authority in a particular case like the one the mother faces. Consider the nature of the general constructive consent that the mother would have to recognize in order to consider herself bound: She would have to conclude that she should have consented to be bound by the law in *every* case, including those in which the law dictates the morally incorrect result. But why should she have consented to be bound by the law in cases where the law is in error?

The EG answer is that individual legal subjects cannot be trusted to correctly identify cases in which the law is in error (that is, exceptions to the general rule that law is an epistemic authority). Under close inspection, the EG account turns out to make two separate, if related, claims about the capacity of law as compared to that of the individual legal subject. The first claim is that law generally does a better job of determining how, substantively, a legal subject ought to act. The second claim is that law generally does a better job of identifying exceptions to the first claim—of determining whether, in a given instance, the law in fact has superior epistemic capacity to that of the legal subject. The first claim, as we have seen, cannot support an argument that legal subjects should consent—and thus should be held to have constructively consented—to be bound by law in cases in which they believe the law is substantively wrong. But the second claim might be thought to support such an argument—on the ground that individual legal subjects are likely to be wrong in assessing whether the *law* is substantively wrong in a given case.

Note, however, that from the perspective of the individual legal subject—the mother trying to decide whether to obey the speed limit in the Case of the Sick Child—a rejection of the first claim also leads to a rejection of the second. If the mother believes following the speed limit law would produce the morally incorrect result in that case, then she also must believe she is *correct* in this judgment. One cannot simultaneously believe that proposition P is true, and that one's belief that proposition P is true is itself false. So in rejecting the first claim of the EG account—that the law knows best how substantively to act in that case—the mother also, necessarily, is rejecting the second claim: that the law knows best *whether* the law knows best in that case.

And, finally, the mother's rejection of this second claim also implies, or at least supports, a denial of her general constructive consent to obey the law. In assessing the question of constructive consent, the mother will, again, be asking whether she *should* have consented to be bound by the law. And the fact that the mother has rejected both of law's claims to epistemic authority in this particular case points in the direction of a negative answer to this question of constructive consent. The mother should have consented to obey the law only if doing so would produce morally better results than not consenting to obey. But surely it is morally better to disobey the law than to obey it in cases where the law is wrong. The mother believes she now is faced with such a case; she also believes, for the same reason, that her judgment regarding the law's substantive incorrectness is itself correct. She must then believe that it would be morally better to disobey the law than to obey it in that case. And she can hardly conclude that she should have consented to the opposite result.

The same Encroachment Flaw that afflicts the EG account standing alone thus afflicts that account as incorporated through a constructive-consent approach. Content-based reasons—reasons to conclude that the law's commands are morally incorrect in a particular case—compromise the account's capacity to provide a truly content-independent duty to act, which legal authority, properly understood, must possess. More generally, a constructive-consent approach merely recapitulates the strengths and weaknesses of whatever substantive justification of legal authority is incorporated within it. It leaves open the question whether there is a substantive account that actually can justify legal authority standing on its own; and the EG account does not seem to qualify.

This is not to say that the idea of constructive consent will be entirely useless for our purposes. Constructive consent captures the notion that people may have moral reasons, even moral duties, to do what they *should* have agreed to do before the fact, had they been given the opportunity. And as I will explain in Chapter 3, that notion will be an important ingredient in the DR account of legal authority I will offer.

6. THE DISPUTE-RESOLUTION ACCOUNT

The DR account, I will argue, is superior to the EG account—and is capable of providing substance to a constructive-consent approach—as a justification of legal authority. I will develop the account more fully in the next two chapters. Here I will briefly introduce the account and explain why it might be capable of avoiding the Encroachment Flaw.

A compelling justification of law's authority, remember, must not be embarrassed by the fact of disagreement, which is after all at the core of the need for law. Consider in this regard the response (of a sort) to Aristotle's Challenge offered by Thomas Hobbes in his *Leviathan*. Hobbes imagined the conditions under which people might live (or try to live) together without the benefit of law, and his vision was not a pretty one. "In such condition," Hobbes famously wrote,

> there is no place for Industry; because the fruit thereof is uncertain; and consequently no Culture of the Earth; no Navigation, nor use of the commodities that may be imported by Sea; no commodious Building; no Instruments of moving, and removing such things as require much force; no Knowledge of the face of the Earth; not account of Time; no Arts; no Letters; no Society; and which is worst of all, continuall feare, and danger of violent death; And the life of man, solitary, poore, nasty, brutish, and short.[36]

For Hobbes, the cause of all this misery in the state of nature would, of course, be conflict. Hobbes is often cited for his pessimistic view of human nature, of human beings as predators,[37] and there is considerable support for this assessment in *Leviathan*. Certainly Hobbes understood that that people in the real

---

36. THOMAS HOBBES, LEVIATHAN part I, at 186 (C. B. Macpherson ed., 1968) (1651).

37. *See* Alice Ristroph, *Respect and Resistance in Punishment Theory*, 97 CAL. L. REV. 601, 606 (2009) (stating that Hobbes is "often portrayed as a profound pessimist about human nature"); Peter J. Ahrensdorf, *The Fear of Death and the Longing for Immortality: Hobbes and Thucydides on Human Nature and the Problem of Anarchy*, 94 AM. POL. SCI. REV. 579, 580–81 (2000); Douglas W. Kmiec, *The Human Nature of Freedom and Identity—We Hold More than Random Thoughts*, 29 HARV. J.L. & PUB. POL'Y 33, 38 (2005).

world are rather less than perfectly virtuous in the Aristotelian sense, that we are instead subject to "naturall Passions, that carry us to Partiality, Pride, Revenge, and the like";[38] thus a great source of conflict, for Hobbes, would be humans' attempts to take advantage of each other. But Hobbes also recognized that much conflict would arise not from the absence of human virtue, but rather from inevitable moral disagreement even among people acting in good faith—disagreement arising from what Rawls later called "the burdens of judgment." "[D]ivers[e] men," Hobbes wrote, "differ not [only] in their Judgement, on the senses of what is pleasant, and unpleasant to the tast[e], smell, hearing, touch, and sight; but also of what is conformable, or disagreeable to Reason."[39] Reasonable disagreement, and not just lack of virtue, would trigger conflict, and unchecked conflict would generate "a condition of Warre of every one against every one."[40]

The imperative of avoiding unchecked conflict, Hobbes believed, is what justifies government and law. Hobbes drew a particular kind of connection, one of consent (or "contract"), between the avoidance of conflict and the idea of legal authority: People seeking to remove themselves from (or to avoid falling into) the state of nature, Hobbes asserted, would agree among themselves to establish a commonwealth, each surrendering his or her own authority to unilaterally enforce morality (the "laws of nature") to a sovereign who then would protect all of them from aggression by each other and by foreign powers. This agreement, Hobbes thought, would be absolutely binding and irrevocable; having agreed to surrender her authority to the sovereign, each subject was forever barred from questioning the sovereign's commands—even where those commands would mean her own death.[41] Freedom to question the sovereign, after all, would simply reignite the conflict that it was the sovereign's purpose to avoid.

---

38. HOBBES, *supra* note 36, part II, at 223.
39. *Id.* part I, at 216.
40. *Id.* part I, at 189.
41. *See id.* part II, at 264–65:

[N]othing the Soveraign Representative can doe to a Subject, on what pretence soever, can properly be called Injustice, or Injury; because every Subject is Author of every act the Soveraign doth. . . And therefore it may, and doth often happen in Common-wealths, that a Subject may be put to death, by the command of the Soveraign Power; and yet neither doe the other wrong. . .

Hobbes was not entirely consistent on this point, however, for elsewhere in *Leviathan* he holds that "[a] Covenant not to defend my selfe from force, by force, is always voyd":

For. . . no man can transferre, or lay down his Right to save himselfe from Death. . . the avoyding whereof is the onely End of laying down any Right, and therefore the promise of not resisting force, in no Covenant transferreth any right; nor is obliging.

Id. part I, at 199. It's unclear how a sovereign whose authority, for Hobbes, is based on a "covenant" formed by his subjects thus could rightly use that authority to cause the death of one of those subjects.

Hobbes therefore sided with Aristotle on one narrow (if important) question: He too denied that rulers themselves should be subject to law. An attempt to hold the sovereign to legal standards, he thought, would only initiate more conflict. But from the sovereign on down in a Hobbesian regime, the law would be paramount and unquestioned. The sovereign's commands, as supreme law, would be absolutely authoritative. They would have to be; any question about whether to obey the law would awaken again the specter of costly dispute.

Hobbes styled his absolutist theory of legal authority as a consensualist account. While Hobbes illustrated the account using an example of actual consent in the form of an original compact, the account is better understood as resting on the notion of constructive consent. For the reasons canvassed above, actual consent cannot go very far toward justifying general legal authority, even if we indulge the fanciful notion that every member of society might come together in an original act of unanimous agreement. Such an agreement, after all, could bind only those who actually were party to it on a consent theory; binding nonparties would frustrate rather than further the goal of individual autonomy that underwrites consent. This means that even a unanimous original compact would cease to be binding, and thus would lose its authoritative effect, as the original parties to it leave the society or die off. The authority of the law would be short-lived.

Hobbes's account might fare better, however, as one of constructive consent—as a theory about the reasons why people *should* have consented, and thus should be held to have consented, to the authority of the law. His device of a unanimous original compact, on this view, serves the heuristic function of illustrating the powerful moral reason—perhaps the source of a *prima facie* duty or, in Hobbes's view, an absolute one—that people have to submit to law. That reason is the avoidance of costly conflict. The idea of doing things we find distasteful in order to avoid greater harms is, of course, intuitively and experientially familiar, and Hobbes's approach, stripped of its contractarian accoutrements, simply applies that idea to the problem of legal authority. The fact of moral disagreement, according to Hobbes, means that disputes about what to do inevitably will arise within a society. Those disputes must be settled somehow in order to prevent systemic chaos and violence; and law, on Hobbes's view, is the means of settlement, a way of short-circuiting disagreement by telling people what they should do rather than leaving them to fight about it. A person's reason to obey the law, then, is simply that the alternative—disobedience—may lead to conflict and thus to costs that are higher than those of obedience.

As we will see, the particular type of legal response Hobbes offered to the problem of conflict, absolutist government, constitutes a cure that may prove worse than the disease. But the central Hobbesian insight—that the imperative of avoiding disputes may support a strong moral reason to obey even morally suboptimal legal commands—is no less valuable for the misguided implications Hobbes himself drew from it. This dispute-resolving imperative is the germ of what I will refer to as the *Dispute-Resolution*, or DR, account of legal authority.

It will take considerable work to cultivate this Hobbesian seed into a fuller, more persuasive account of legal authority, one capable of explaining the central features of our own democratic legal institutions. That, of course, is the task for the rest of this book. But we can notice three salient features of the DR account at the outset.

First, the DR account offers a content-independent reason for action, as any account of true legal authority must. To obey the law because doing so avoids or resolves a costly dispute is to obey it for a content-independent reason. Whether a dispute should be resolved, and the benefits of resolving it, need not depend on the moral rightness or wrongness of whatever a legal rule or command tells us to do. If we obey a legal command in order to resolve a dispute, we do so regardless of whether we agree with the substance of that command; in most cases, in fact, we will do so despite our disagreement with its substance. This, in fact, is precisely how legal commands might operate to resolve disputes.

Second, the content-independent reason supplied by the DR account might conceivably be strong enough to support a general *prima facie* duty to obey the law. Hobbes certainly believed it had at least this level of strength—in fact he thought his account supported an absolute duty of obedience—although we can reserve our own judgment on this point until we get a better sense, in the ensuing chapters, of just how the DR account might work and apply to real-world legal institutions and problems. Preliminarily, however, we might notice that most of the real-world circumstances in which law applies are circumstances that involve actual or potential conflict—sometimes on a small scale (how fast to drive on the highway), sometimes on a grand one (how to balance individual rights against national security). We might notice, also, that leaving these conflicts, great or small, unresolved would produce obvious and perhaps quite drastic costs, immediately or in the long run. A quick, rough comparison of the normative basis of the DR account with our own experiences and observations of law thus suggests—at least it does not rule out—that the account, unlike one based on actual consent, might be up to the normative ask of providing a general account of legal authority.

Third and finally, the DR account is capable, at least conceptually, of avoiding the Encroachment Flaw that hobbles the EG account. That flaw, remember, is that disagreement with the law's substance inevitably serves as a reason to question the law's epistemic authority. How can the law be an epistemic authority if it is, in our lights, demonstrably wrong? On a DR account, however, the law's substantive wrongness does not, or at least need not, pose any threat to its authority. The point of law on that account is not to cause people to take particular actions that are morally correct; the point of law is to avoid or resolve disputes about which actions *are* morally correct. The fact, then, that a legal command dictates what a legal subject thinks is morally incorrect action does not serve as a reason for that subject to question the authority of the command. Obeying the command can serve law's function—it can avoid or resolve a dispute—even if the command itself is wrong. Again, this is precisely the point of legal authority on the DR account.

Of course, there are many questions to be answered about a DR account before we can endorse it, chief among them the questions of what law would have to look like in order to perform its supposed dispute-resolution function and of whether the law with which we're familiar actually looks like that. Answering these questions is, again, the task of subsequent chapters. Before we tackle those issues, however, there is another potential rival to the DR account worth exploring, one that can I think be more easily assessed now that we have some basic familiarity with the DR account.

7. CONTINUITY, COORDINATION, AND LEGAL AUTHORITY

It sometimes is suggested that a *prima facie* duty of obedience to the law can be justified by reference to values associated with either *continuity* or *coordination*, or both.[42] Continuity captures the notion that there is some instrumental value in adhering to existing norms, even if (we believe) those norms are substantively incorrect: namely the stability and predictability that arise when people are able to rely on the likelihood that legal (and other) norms will not frequently change. Coordination is the idea that, often, there is value in everyone's pursuing the same course of action—including adhering to the same norm—even if that course of action is not everyone's first choice, because the cost of some people's defecting from that course of action is that everyone ends up worse off.

Continuity turns out to be simply a function of dispute resolution, and thus it dissolves, as a justification of legal authority, into the DR account sketched above. Normative continuity within a society, including legal continuity, is valuable for at least two related reasons. First, continuity of norms creates a stable platform on which institutions (public and private) within that society can function. Institutions are to a large extent *constituted* by norms (legal and otherwise), and they can hardly perform the tasks they are intended to perform if the rules governing what the institution is, how it operates, etc. are in constant flux.[43] Second, continuity of norms allows members of a society to predict with reasonable accuracy what the consequences of their actions are likely to be. This promotes efficiency by reducing the costs of uncertainty and of adjustment to changed circumstances; it also promotes individual autonomy in the sense

---

42. *See generally* ALEXANDER & SHERWIN, *supra* note 2, at 12–25.

43. On the idea, within the particular context of constitutions, that some degree of continuity is necessary for institutions to function, see CHRISTOPHER L. EISGRUBER, CONSTITUTIONAL SELF-GOVERNMENT 12–14 (2001).

suggested in the discussion of consent earlier in this chapter, by making it easier for people to plan ahead and thus to shape the conditions of their own lives.[44]

Assuming we put aside the possibility of externally caused social catastrophe—invasions, natural disasters, and so forth—and the science-fiction fantasy of some sort of mass repetitive amnesia, the primary threat to continuity of norms within a society is of course conflict—dispute over what those norms should be. Hobbes's chaotic imagined world without law was a world defined by instability and unpredictability, a world in which "the fruit" of "Industry. . . is uncertain" and the "life of man" is beset by "continuall feare."[45] Lack of normative continuity is a salient cost of conflict; and thus to settle a conflict, to resolve or avoid a dispute, is just to obtain a measure of continuity, to purchase a reasonable assurance that the resulting settlement can be relied upon in planning individual affairs or carrying out social projects. To treat the value of continuity as a reason to obey an otherwise disagreeable legal command, then, is precisely to respect that command as the settlement of some dispute. It is to decline to reignite an extinguished conflict over what the content of the command should be, or should have been.

Continuity, in other words, is simply one of the benefits of dispute resolution, albeit an extremely important one. The relationship between coordination and legal authority is considerably more complicated. The idea of "coordination" through law in fact subsumes a number of different, though related, problems.[46] One is the problem of *signaling*, in which legal norms are needed simply to inform every person within a group which of two or more equally attractive (or equally inoffensive) alternatives to follow. The classic example here is the need for all vehicles traveling in the same direction to use the same side of the road in order to avoid accidents. Nobody cares *which* side of the road is chosen, so long as it's the *same* side of the road for everybody. The law can facilitate this need for uniformity by specifying which course of action, among equally innocuous alternatives, everyone should choose and then signaling that choice to everyone.

In such cases, the benefits of coordination will, of course, provide a reason for a person to adhere to whatever choice has been specified by the law. But this phenomenon is not really one of legal authority, at least not in the sense in which we have been exploring that concept thus far, because it does not involve a choice between obeying the law and doing what a person otherwise believes

---

44. On the relationship between predictability and autonomy, see generally FRIEDRICH A. VON HAYEK, THE CONSTITUTION OF LIBERTY (1960); *see also* Richard S. Kay, *American Constitutionalism, in* CONSTITUTIONALISM: PHILOSOPHICAL FOUNDATIONS, *supra* note 23, at 22–24.

45. HOBBES, *supra* note 36, part I, at 186.

46. *See* WALDRON, *supra* note 20, at 103–05; Raz, *Authority and Interpretation, supra* note 23, at 168; ALEXANDER & SHERWIN, *supra* note 43, at 55–61.

to be *right*. Because a person will not care one way or the other which side of the road she drives on, so long as it's the same side as every other motorist, she will not be faced with some normatively attractive alternative to a legal command that tugs in the opposite direction. She will have no reason *not* to obey the law, and thus Aristotle's Challenge simply will not apply to her.

Some cases, however, combine the signaling function with an *incentivizing* function. The paradigm example of such a case variously goes under the name "the tragedy of the commons," "the race to the bottom," or "the prisoners' dilemma," depending on the particular version in which it is presented. Suppose a manufacturer must decide whether to invest considerable sums of money to reduce polluting emissions from its factories. It does not want to do so unless all its competitors do so as well, because unilaterally reducing its emissions would drive up its (and only its) costs and thus put it at a competitive disadvantage. But if all its competitors reduce their emissions, the manufacturer has an incentive *not* to reduce its own, thus saving costs and creating a competitive advantage. If every manufacturer follows this logic, none of them will reduce their emissions, and the problem of pollution will get worse and worse for everyone. A solution is a legal rule requiring every competing manufacturer to reduce its emissions, thus improving air quality without putting any one of them at a disadvantage.

Here the legal command is to some extent serving a signaling function: It is telling everyone within the group how to act so as to avoid making them all worse off. But it also is serving an incentivizing function—really two related incentivizing functions. First, it is creating an incentive for any purely self-interested manufacturer—that is, a manufacturer who cares only for its own profits and not at all for the common good—nonetheless to act for the common benefit, namely the incentive of avoiding sanctions for noncompliance. Like the signaling function (but for a different reason), this first type of incentivizing function does not really involve legal *authority* in the sense challenged by Aristotle, because it makes compliance with the law turn on a fear of sanctions for noncompliance. As I discussed in Chapter 1, sanctions may follow from legitimate legal authority, but not the other way around: The mere existence or possibility of sanctions cannot itself justify legal authority.

The "race to the bottom" case, however, also displays a second type of incentivizing function which does seem, at first glance, to involve legal authority. The legal command in question—the law requiring manufacturers to reduce their emissions—creates an additional incentive for *virtuous* manufacturers to act for the common benefit, namely the fact that their competitors will be sanctioned if they do not follow suit and thus are unlikely to defect in a way that would put the virtuous manufacturer at a competitive disadvantage. The legal command thus makes it individually rational for the virtuous manufacturer to do the right thing—the thing it wanted to do anyway but, without the law, was deterred from doing by the inevitability of being punished in the market for doing it. It brings individual rationality into alignment with the collective good. In so doing, law gives the virtuous actor a powerful reason to act in a way it otherwise would not have acted. This is the sense in which the goal of coordination might be said to provide an account of true legal authority, one that does not rely on the capacity of the law to resolve disputes.

I think, however, that this sense is illusory. On this second version of the incentivizing account, a legal command is not *really* acting in an authoritative way, because it's not really telling someone to do something other than what she already believes she should do; it is not, that is, providing a truly content-independent reason for action. Consider the fact that the virtuous but deterred manufacturer in my hypothetical is not *completely* virtuous—otherwise it would act unilaterally to reduce its emissions, even knowing that it would suffer in the market for doing so. The hypothetical, after all, assumes general agreement about what is in the common interest, namely coordinated action to reduce emissions. The legal command to reduce emissions, therefore, is not pulling against what our halfheartedly virtuous manufacturer (along with every other manufacturer) knows to be right; it is simply telling the manufacturer to do what it already knows it should do anyway (and backing up that command with the threat of sanctions). The command to reduce emissions thus is coextensive with morality; it is substantively identical to what morality already demands. It thus does not claim true legal authority, because it does not claim to provide a content-independent reason for action.

There are some caveats here. First, even assuming I am correct that the coordination function does not really support an account of legal authority, this fact does not mean that law never serves the goal of coordination. The threat of legal sanctions can provide purely self-interested people (and thus halfheartedly virtuous people as well) with a powerful reason to obey the law in situations where coordination is required. But this is not a phenomenon of legal authority in the sense in which we have been focusing on that concept, any more than the threat of legal sanctions against would-be lawbreakers in noncoordination situations is a phenomenon of legal authority. Law often accomplishes something useful by punishing or threatening to punish bad-faith lawbreakers. The problem of legal authority, though, is the problem of why people acting entirely in *good* faith should recognize a *prima facie* duty to obey the law, and my point here is that the value of coordination does not resolve that problem.

Second, in rejecting coordination as a foundation of legal authority, I might be accused of assuming a problematic, or at least a controversial, account of what it means to act morally rightly or wrongly in a coordination situation. It might be argued that a person acts morally correctly in defecting from a coordinated solution to a problem, at least where that person's defection or participation will not appreciably affect the success or failure of that solution.[47] On this view, a

---

47. This appears to be the view of Larry Alexander and Emily Sherwin. *See* ALEXANDER & SHERWIN, *supra* note 43, at 57–58.

manufacturer has no moral duty to refrain from polluting so long as most other manufacturers are polluting, because its contribution to the overall amount of pollution will be negligible; by the same token, it has no moral duty to refrain from polluting even if most other manufacturers are *not* polluting, because (again) its contribution to the overall amount of pollution will be negligible. In either case, the manufacturer might gain more by polluting than his pollution will cost to society as a whole, and so polluting would be the right, or at least a morally permissible, thing to do. And if so, then a legal rule forbidding pollution *does* tell the manufacturer to do something it would not otherwise be morally required to do, and thus the law does assert authority over the manufacturer. The value of coordination therefore would support something that looks like an account of true legal authority.

It seems to me that this understanding of the morality of coordination problems draws too bright a line between individual and collective action. In some cases, anyway, it may be true that the individual legal subject (e.g., the manufacturer) has no moral duty, perhaps not even a moral reason, to refrain from a harmful behavior (like polluting) if doing so will make no real difference in the world. (I offer some reasons below to think this will *not* typically be the case.) But it may also be true that the individual legal subject *does* have a duty, or at least a good reason, to take steps to increase the likelihood that his actions *will* make a difference in the world. It is hard to believe that no moral wrongs would be committed if every manufacturer simply went on polluting as before, without attempting to coordinate (with or without legal rules) with other manufacturers to reduce the overall levels of pollution being generated. If the moral best thing for society is to reduce overall pollution levels, then it seems reasonable to impose upon each manufacturer some duty, or at least some good moral reason, to work toward that goal. Simply continuing to discharge pollutants on the theory that one's own contribution will make little difference thus seems to reflect a troublingly narrow conception of one's moral duty.

There is good reason, then, to understand legal solutions to coordination problems not as drastically changing the moral landscape, but rather as signaling the existence of applicable moral duties and the likelihood of sanctions for those who violate them. But even if one accepts the atomistic view of moral duties in coordination problems, the situations in which legal solutions to those problems function in a truly authoritative way are likely to be relatively few. In many cases the consequences of an individual legal subject's defection from a coordinated solution will *not* be *de minimis*. The polluting manufacturer might not contribute appreciably to the overall pollution levels in its society, but it still may do considerable harm to the air quality in the smaller geographic area where it is located. It might, moreover, increase the likelihood that other manufactures will continue to pollute, by signaling that polluting is acceptable or that any nonpolluting manufacturer will find itself at a competitive disadvantage. And of course if the manufacturer's operations are large enough, its defection may in fact contribute appreciably to the society's overall pollution levels. Defection from a coordinated solution thus may have harmful effects beyond the narrow consequences of the particular activities in question, and the existence of these effects may create an independent moral duty not to defect. By prohibiting defection in these circumstances, the law would simply be telling the legal subject to do what morality already requires.

This is just another way of making the point that a great many coordination problems in the real world will not be *pure* coordination problems; they also will feature prominent questions regarding the moral rightness or wrongness of a legal subject's behavior, quite apart from how other legal subjects are behaving. They will, in other words, involve disagreements about how people should act. Resolving those disagreements by means of law is not primarily an act of coordination; it is an act of dispute resolution. Even on an atomistic understanding of the morality of coordination, then, an account of legal authority based on the value of coordination will, in many or most real-world contexts, merge into a DR account. And thus it seems highly unlikely that the value of coordination alone can support a general justification of legal authority of the type required to respond to Aristotle's Challenge.[48]

8. THE TASK AHEAD

So here is where we now stand on the path toward an answer to Aristotle's Challenge, one that makes sense of the idea of "a government of laws." We have examined four attempts to justify general legal authority and seen that three of them are not fully satisfactory. EG accounts founder on the Encroachment Flaw—their failure to adequately separate the substance from the authority of legal commands. Consensualist accounts that turn on actual consent face the problem that actual consent almost never exists; as such they fail to supply a good general account of legal authority. And the notion of constructive consent cannot explain legal authority by itself; it is, rather, simply a formal heuristic device for identifying other, normative accounts that are persuasive. Accounts built on the values of continuity or coordination either lack distinctive content, fail to justify authority in a genuine sense, or (at best) justify legal authority only in a relatively small category of cases.

As an alternative to these problematic efforts, I have introduced the DR account, which suggests that legal authority may be justified by the need to avoid or resolve disputes. That account avoids the Encroachment Flaw; it seems plausible as an explanation of a general, *prima facie* duty of legal obedience; and it

---

48. For an argument that most laws cannot be understood as responses to coordination problems, see JOSEPH RAZ, ETHICS IN THE PUBLIC DOMAIN 330–35 (1994).

offers reasons to obey the law that are distinct from those offered by other accounts. Preliminarily, then, the DR account seems promising as a response to Aristotle's Challenge.

The next two chapters add flesh to what is still a skeletal version of the DR account. In Chapter 3, I illustrate the basic normative mechanics of the account using a simple, bipartite model of dispute resolution. In Chapter 4, I expand the basic model to account for the typical features of modern legal systems, namely the presence of legal rules and of a great many diverse people who are subject to them. Then, beginning with the second half of Chapter 4, I will use the DR approach as a template for understanding the basic political and legal institutions of contemporary constitutional democracy: majoritarian democratic politics, participatory common-law adjudication, and constitutional law.

3. A SIMPLE MODEL OF DISPUTE RESOLUTION

In Chapter 2, I sketched the very broad outlines of an account of legal authority, the Dispute-Resolution (DR) account, that turns on the substantial benefits of avoiding or peacefully resolving disputes. On the DR account, a *prima facie* duty to obey a legal command flows from the potential to avoid or resolve some dispute by doing so. At least as a conceptual matter, the DR account can avoid the Encroachment Flaw that plagues Epistemic-Guidance (EG) accounts, because disagreement with the substance of a legal command need not, on the DR account, undermine a legal subject's belief in that command's authority. The DR account thus seems to make sense of the requirement that legal authority provide powerful content-independent reasons for action.

The aim of this chapter is to flesh out the normative mechanics of the DR account in their most basic form, using a simple bipartite model of dispute resolution. The model is intended to illustrate how a dispute-resolution procedure might be structured in order to create a strong moral reason to obey its results, even if one disagrees with those results. As I will explain at the end of the chapter, this reason will turn out not to be entirely content-independent; the Encroachment Flaw will appear in this model, too, and thus in the DR account of legal authority that the model supports. But that Flaw (as I also will explain) will be substantially less threatening to my version of the DR account than to any version of the EG account.

As I think my exposition here will suggest, the (mostly) content-independent reason for obedience generated by the simple dispute-resolution model, and thus the reason at the core of the DR account, might plausibly be strong enough to justify the sort of *prima facie* duty of obedience that the concept of legal authority supposes. Whether the account actually justifies a *prima facie* duty, however, will depend in large part on the normative strength of the dispute-resolution impulse that animates both the simple model outlined in this chapter and the DR account more generally. And I will not attempt to defend here the claim that this dispute-resolution impulse is strong enough to serve that purpose. Instead I will assume the impulse has sufficient strength; my hope is that subsequent chapters will demonstrate the typical strength of that moral impulse in particular contexts involving legal authority, namely democratic legislation, adjudication, and constitutional law.

There will turn out to be no guarantee that the dispute-resolution impulse, and thus the content-independent reason provided by the DR account, will *always* be sufficiently strong to generate a *prima facie* duty of obedience. But that is simply to say that law will not possess authority in every case. The same conclusion applies to rival accounts of legal authority, and so there is no reason to think it is a special weakness of the DR account (or indeed that it necessarily is a weakness at all).

We can begin by imagining a very simple dispute between two roughly equally situated inhabitants of a society without law.

1. ACCEPTABLE DISPUTE RESOLUTION

Suppose a dispute arises between two people, Aaron and Betty, who live in a society without legal rules or legal institutions like courts and legislatures. It does not matter what the dispute is about, but imagine, for the sake of illustration, that it involves the location of a fence between Aaron's and Betty's respective properties. Of course, the idea of "property" would have an uncertain meaning in a society without law; but we can assume that while the community in which Aaron and Betty live has no formal legal rules, its members do typically recognize nonlegal norms of behavior, such as moral norms and norms of etiquette, and that these nonlegal norms include basic property rights. We can assume also that Aaron and Betty are roughly equally situated with respect to their capacity, or lack of it, to force the other to accept a particular result that one of them favors: Neither Aaron nor Betty is appreciably smarter or physically stronger than the other, or has more friends who could be conscripted as allies, or possesses more-powerful weapons, etc.

With this backdrop in place, it seems plausible to suppose, first of all, that Aaron and Betty will recognize an impulse of some normative strength—again, we can leave open for now the question of how much strength—to attempt to settle their dispute peacefully. Thomas Hobbes's parade of horribles* may apply to Aaron and Betty on a small scale: Leaving the dispute unresolved would produce costly uncertainty and lack of cooperation going forward; trying to "resolve" it by violence might impose even greater costs.

Let us suppose, then, that both Aaron and Betty are motivated to attempt a peaceful resolution of their dispute. The question then will be *how* to resolve their dispute peacefully. Note that a peaceful *resolution* of the dispute must involve a result that both parties are willing to accept; a result that one party cannot accept would merely continue the dispute rather than resolving it.

Here there are three possibilities. First, a result might be reached that would satisfy both parties entirely. I want to eliminate this possibility from our consideration, however, not just because such a case would not involve a real *dispute* at all—if both parties can get the result they favor, there isn't really anything to dispute about—but because it is irrelevant for the overall purpose of this discussion, namely the construction of a basic model that can anchor the DR account of legal authority. Legal authority, remember, entails a duty to obey a result with which one disagrees in substance. Accepting a result because one thinks it is substantively correct is not obeying authority.

*Rhetorical device whereby the speaker argues against taking a certain course of action by listing a number of extremely undesirable events which will ostensibly result from the action

The second possibility is a result that fully satisfies neither party, but that both parties find inoffensive enough to accept rather than continue the dispute. We can refer to this as the possibility of *compromise*. One obvious way to reach a compromise is for both parties to agree to it on its merits, perhaps after a period of negotiation between them. Probably most disputes in the real world are resolved in this way, and indeed in the United States, at least, there is a noteworthy trend toward submitting even relatively significant legal disputes to methods of "alternative dispute resolution," or ADR, rather than to formal adjudication.[1] The possibility of an agreed compromise is instructive for our purposes, because it demonstrates the plausibility of the idea that a disputant might sacrifice the substantive result he or she favors in the name of resolving a dispute.

But I want to assume that Aaron and Betty are unable to agree on a compromise resolution of their conflict. Like the possibility of a result that satisfies everybody, the possibility of a negotiated compromise is an ill fit with the problem of legal authority. The instances in which legal subjects have the opportunity to negotiate their behavior with legal authorities are, in the real world, relatively rare. Much more typical is a situation in which a legal subject is faced with a nonnegotiable legal rule or command and must decide whether to obey it. In order to develop a satisfying account of legal authority in that kind of circumstance, we need to suppose that our model disputants cannot agree on a compromise. This does not mean that an acceptable result of a dispute-resolution process cannot fall somewhere in between the substantive positions of the two disputants. It means only that any such result must, for our purposes, be the product of some procedure other than negotiation between the disputing parties.

The third possibility for peaceful dispute resolution is a procedure that somehow generates a result that the dissatisfied party or parties—perhaps one "losing" disputant, or perhaps both disputants if the result fully satisfies neither—is or are willing to accept rather than allowing the dispute to continue or resolving it by violent means. Might such a procedure exist, and if so, what might it look like?

2. DISPUTE RESOLUTION AND ACCURACY

If Aaron and Betty have decided to attempt a peaceful resolution of their dispute, and if they cannot resolve it through negotiated compromise, then they will have

---

1. *See* 9 U.S.C.A. § 2 (West 2010) (providing for the enforcement in federal court of arbitration agreements); 28 U.S.C.A. § 651(b) (West 2010) (requiring federal courts to adopt local rules authorizing the use of alternative dispute resolution); *see also* Thomas J. Stipanowich, *Arbitration: The "New Litigation,"* 2010 U. Ill. L. Rev. 1, 1 ("Provisions for binding arbitration of disputes are now employed in virtually all kinds of contracts, making arbitration a wide-ranging surrogate for civil litigation.").

to settle on a procedure capable of generating results that even the losing party can accept.

For the sake of clarity, we should note initially that mutual agreement on a suitable procedure must come *before* the losing party's decision whether to accept the result of that procedure; until a procedure is agreed upon and actually put into effect, there will be no losing party and no result for that party to reject or accept. Technically, then, Aaron and Betty must agree on a procedure that each *believes*, from an *ex ante* perspective, is capable of producing a result that he or she *could* accept if he or she turns out to be the loser. The initial choice of a suitable procedure therefore must be made by the disputants from behind a version of what John Rawls called a "veil of ignorance":[2] Neither disputant knows what result the chosen procedure actually will deliver. Once the procedure has been agreed upon and has generated a result, *then* the losing party (or parties, plural; remember, again, that it's possible neither party will be completely satisfied with the result) will have to make an *additional* decision whether to accept that result as a resolution of the dispute. We will explore below the considerations that will become relevant to that *ex post* decision. For now, however, the questions are the *ex ante* ones of whether the disputing parties might agree, ahead of time, on a suitable procedure and, if so, what that procedure might look like.

To begin answering these questions, note first that both disputants would be willing to agree to a procedure that each of them believes is perfectly accurate, that is, guaranteed to generate a morally correct result. By *accuracy*, I mean the likelihood that a procedure will produce a morally correct result; a perfectly accurate procedure is one that is guaranteed to produce a morally correct result. Recall from Chapter 1 that we are assuming that each legal subject—or, in the prelegal universe occupied by Aaron and Betty, each disputant—is a good-faith moral reasoner, seeking to achieve not the result that best serves his or her own narrow self-interest, but rather the result that best accords with the true dictates of morality, whatever they may be. In disagreeing with each other about the proper location of their boundary fence, then, Aaron and Betty are disagreeing about what morality requires. Aaron believes, in good faith, that morality requires the fence to be located on one spot, while Betty believes, in good faith, that morality requires it to be located somewhere else. (I mean the concept of "morality" here to be quite broad, including whatever non-legal norms might be thought relevant to the question at hand. If the term seems overly freighted for a dispute involving the location of a fence, we can easily substitute the idea of "norms" for that of "morals"; I do not mean to beg any significant questions in using the latter term.)

---

2. John Rawls, A Theory of Justice 136–37 (1971) [hereinafter Rawls, Theory of Justice].

If each disputant believes his or her position to be morally (normatively) correct, then each disputant would be willing to accept a procedure that is guaranteed to generate the morally (normatively) correct result. Indeed, even if each disputant recognizes the possibility that he or she is mistaken about what morality requires—and thus that a perfectly accurate procedure might produce a result other than the one he or she currently favors—he or she still would agree to submit their dispute to that perfectly accurate procedure. Doing so, after all, would (by definition) produce the morally correct result, and that is what (we are assuming) each disputant wants—even if it turns out that he or she currently is mistaken about what that morally correct result actually is.

If Aaron and Betty can identify a procedure that both of them agree is perfectly accurate—call it P_A—then they will be willing, *ex ante*, to submit their dispute to that procedure, agreeing to be bound by its result. The difficulty, of course, will lie in identifying P_A. Aaron and Betty disagree about what, substantively speaking, *is* the morally correct result (which is another way of stating the fact that they have a dispute that must somehow be resolved). So they will not be able to identify P_A by reference to a particular result P_A might generate. Aaron cannot offer a particular procedure as P_A on the ground that it will, or is likely to, produce the result *he* thinks is correct; that is precisely what he and Betty disagree about. As Jeremy Waldron puts the point:

> [T]he design of a decision-procedure must be independent of the particular disagreement it is supposed to settle; it is no good if it simply reignites it. . . . Given the disagreement, the whole point . . . is to set up a procedure for generating settlements in a way that can be recognized as legitimate on both sides.[3]

And Betty hardly will recognize as legitimate, from an *ex ante* perspective, a procedure whose supposed merit is that it will generate the result Aaron thinks is correct.

Given this difficulty, it is tempting to think either that the parties will not be able to agree on a procedure to resolve their dispute—a counterexperiential conclusion, given the regularity with which disputes actually are resolved in the real world—or that their agreement must be based on grounds other than the procedure's accuracy. Rawls coined the term "pure procedural justice" to describe a procedure that is thought to be "just" for reasons having nothing to do with the outcomes it generates;[4] Waldron similarly envisions "process-based" or "noninstrumental" reasons for endorsing a procedure.[5] Assuming such reasons exist

---

3. Jeremy Waldron, *The Core of the Case Against Judicial Review*, 115 YALE L.J. 1346, 1373 (2006) [hereinafter Waldron, *Core Case*].

4. RAWLS, THEORY OF JUSTICE, *supra* note 2, at 86.

5. *See* JEREMY WALDRON, LAW AND DISAGREEMENT 252–54 (1999) [hereinafter WALDRON, LAW AND DISAGREEMENT]; Waldron, *Core Case, supra* note 3, at 1386–88.

(certainly a debatable question),[6] are they the only available grounds upon which Aaron and Betty might agree to a dispute-resolution procedure?

In fact they are not. As Waldron notes, it might be possible for disputing parties to agree that a given procedure is accurate even if they disagree about what would constitute a morally correct or optimal outcome of their particular dispute:

> Instead of saying (in a question-begging way) that we should choose those . . . procedures that are most likely to yield a particular controversial [result], we might say instead that we should choose . . . procedures that are most likely to get at the truth . . ., whatever that truth turns out to be.[7]

Imagine, for example, that the members of Aaron and Betty's society regularly consult an oracle who, they all believe, directly channels the word of God and thus is infallible. (Perhaps the existence of the oracle is why the society has no need of laws or legal institutions.) Aaron and Betty might agree to submit their dispute to the oracle on the ground of her perfect accuracy—even though they disagree about what a correct result would be in their particular case. Their mutual confidence in the oracle's perfect accuracy would flow from their belief that the oracle speaks with the voice of God, a belief they can share without regard to their disagreement over the substantive issue that forms the basis of their dispute. At the same time, their agreement would go to the substantive accuracy of the procedure—to its capacity to generate correct results—rather than relying on some innate properties of the procedure that have nothing to do with results. The oracle thus is not an example of Rawls's "pure procedural justice," and Aaron and Betty's reasons for agreeing to it are not purely "process-based" or "noninstrumental" reasons.

The idea of an infallible oracle is a helpful thought experiment, because it demonstrates the conceptual possibility of agreement on accurate procedures in the face of disagreement about the substantive issues those procedures would resolve. But of course it will not do to build an account of legal authority designed to apply in the modern world around the premise that everyone can agree on a perfectly accurate procedure. Not many people in the modern world believe in divine oracles or their equivalent anymore, and those who do are likely to disagree about which divine oracle is the true one. The question will have to be whether Aaron and Betty might agree to a procedure that both recognize will be less than perfectly accurate.

---

6. On this point, see the discussion in section 4, below, in which I question the impression that impartiality has value apart from a concern for accuracy (in other words, that impartiality is a purely process-based, noninstrumental reason for obedience to the results of a procedure).

7. Waldron, Core Case, supra note 3, at 1373. Waldron himself has expressed skepticism about the plausibility of this third option. See WALDRON, LAW AND DISAGREEMENT, supra note 5, at 252–54.

This possibility seems more plausible. Rawls used the term "imperfect procedural justice" to describe procedures that aspire to, but do not guarantee, results that are "just" or morally correct according to some substantive criteria.[8] To foreshadow the arguments in Chapter 5, we can borrow Rawls's example of the criminal trial as a type of imperfect procedural justice:

> The desired outcome is that the defendant should be declared guilty if and only if he has committed the offense with which he is charged. The trial procedure is framed to search for and to establish the truth in this regard. But it seems impossible to design the legal rules so that they always lead to the correct result. The theory of trials examines which procedures and rules of evidence, and the like, are best calculated to advance this purpose consistent with the other ends of the law. Different arrangements for hearing cases may reasonably be expected in different circumstances to yield the right results, not always but at least most of the time.[9]

As Rawls's example indicates, disputants might agree on the *general* criteria of "justice" or "truth" or moral correctness to which a procedure aspires—in the context of a criminal trial, conviction of the defendant if and only if he is guilty— even as they disagree about how those general criteria apply in a particular case (e.g., about whether a given defendant is in fact guilty). And thus they might be able to agree on procedures that seem likely "to yield the right results, not always"—real-world procedures are not divine oracles—"but at least most of the time."[10]

What general features would a procedure that is imperfectly accurate in this way—P_I in shorthand—have to possess in order for Aaron and Betty to agree to submit their dispute to it?

3. ACCURACY AND COMPETENCE

First and most obviously, Aaron and Betty would have to agree that P_I has sufficient *competence*. Competence is, if you will, the potential for accuracy; it is a procedure's capacity to produce a correct decision when functioning properly. A coin toss will produce a correct decision (on a yes-or-no question)

---

8. RAWLS, THEORY OF JUSTICE, *supra* note 2, at 85–86.

9. *Id.*

10. *See also* DAVID M. ESTLUND, DEMOCRATIC AUTHORITY: A PHILOSOPHICAL FRAMEWORK 7–9 (2008) (referring to the idea that "laws are legitimate and authoritative because they are produced by a procedure to make correct decisions" as "epistemic proceduralism"); Lawrence B. Solum, *Procedural Justice*, 78 S. CAL. L. REV. 181, 247–48 (2004) (distinguishing between "case accuracy"—the correctness of the result in a particular instance—and "systemic accuracy"—the capacity of a procedure to generate "more or less accurate results for all future cases").

fifty percent of the time, so its competence level is fifty percent. An omniscient decisionmaker—say, our imaginary divine oracle—would produce a correct decision every time; the oracle's competence level would be one hundred percent. In the real world, most decision-procedures aspire to a competence level that is better than that of a coin toss, but none can claim divinely perfect competence. Rawls's example of a criminal trial illustrates a reasonably but not perfectly competent procedure.

Reasonable competence (as we will see) will not be sufficient for accuracy, but it seems necessary for it. Neither Aaron nor Betty would be likely to agree to a procedure, P_I, if he or she thinks the procedure is perfectly incompetent—lacking any capacity to generate a correct result. But the required *degree* of competence—just how competent the parties will require the procedure to be, or to appear to be, before agreeing to it—will depend on the particular circumstances of the dispute. Each disputant will have to weigh the risk and costs of a morally incorrect result against the costs of leaving the dispute unresolved in order to determine whether P_I is sufficiently competent to merit agreement. Where the costs of irresolution would be quite high, and the substantive issue at stake is not perceived by the parties as tremendously important, a lower degree of procedural competence might suffice; the disputants might decide that it is more important to settle the issue than to settle it correctly. The lower the costs of irresolution, or the higher the costs of an incorrect result, the more competence the parties will demand from the procedure. The degree of competence required of P_I, in other words, will turn on the contingent facts of a particular dispute.

The indicia of the competence that Aaron and Betty seek also will turn on contingent facts, namely on the nature of the general criteria of moral correctness they share. If Aaron and Betty both believe the correct resolution of their dispute depends on the will of God, they will look for a procedure they think is reasonably capable of identifying the will of God and applying it to their dispute—perhaps (in the absence of an infallible oracle) decision by the local cleric. If Aaron and Betty both believe, on the other hand, that the correct resolution of their dispute turns on the application of social customs and mores, they will look for a procedure they think is reasonably capable of identifying and applying those norms—perhaps decisionmaking by a village elder. There is a large, perhaps infinite, variety of possible normative criteria that disputants might agree should apply, and thus a large or infinite variety of ways to choose or design a procedure so as to competently identify the morally correct result.

It is important to note that I am assuming here the possibility of *some* substantive agreement between Aaron and Betty, namely agreement on the general criteria of moral correctness that apply to their dispute. It seems likely that this meta-agreement can be very general indeed and still allow agreement on competent procedures. A quite abstract substantive agreement that God's will should govern the dispute might support a procedural agreement to submit the dispute to someone well-versed in divine commands; an abstract agreement that the community's customs should govern might support an agreement to submit the dispute to a person closely familiar with those customs. Agreement on exactly what the relevant norms consist of—what God commands or what qualifies as custom—or on precisely how those norms apply to the particular facts of the dispute is unnecessary. (If it were necessary, few disputes could be resolved.) Even Rawls's fairly specific example of the criminal trial relies only on moral agreement at a rather general level—on the propositions that guilty people should be punished and that innocent people should not be. It is true that if we parse Rawls's example a bit more closely, we are likely to find that it also assumes agreement on some more-specific normative propositions, such as the criteria of guilt (e.g., knowing violation of a relatively clear criminal prohibition). But, as I will suggest in the next chapter, these more-specific points of apparent agreement typically can be understood as themselves settlements of disagreements. (The content of the criminal law, for instance, is determined by a process of resolving disputes about what actions should be prohibited and punished within a society; the standard of criminal guilt is determined by a process of resolving disputes about the level of culpability sufficient to justify punishment.)

Still, lurking in the background of any agreed-upon procedure must be some very basic general agreement about the substantive norms that will apply to a dispute. It will be difficult, for example, for Aaron and Betty to agree on P_I if Aaron believes the dispute is governed by divine will and Betty believes it is governed by the customs of the community. (It might still be *possible* for Aaron and Betty to agree on P_I in these circumstances; perhaps there is someone in the community who Aaron sees as suitably pious, whom Betty believes is suitably familiar with local custom, and whom both disputants trust to resolve the metaquestion of what norms should apply—God's will or custom?—in a competent way.) But as a general matter, it seems that the higher the level of generality at which the disputants face moral disagreement, the more difficult it will be for them to settle on a P_I that both find suitably competent.

There is an important truism revealed here about the DR account I am fashioning: That account will rely on the factual premise that within the relevant legal or political community, moral agreement is achievable at a level that is relatively abstract, but still particular enough to allow consensus on the normative competence of specific procedures. By using the DR account to explain the central features of the American legal system, I hope to suggest in the following chapters that this very basic level of substantive consensus typically exists within that system. But it is easy to imagine circumstances under which it would not exist; indeed, we can find historical and extant real-world examples that do not require imagination. The DR account cannot justify the rule of law where substantive moral consensus at a very fundamental level is absent. (I will return to this point in the book's Epilogue.)

So a mutual agreement on some reasonable level of predicted competence—the degree and indicia of which will vary with the circumstances—will be necessary in order for disputants like Aaron and Betty to accept a procedure to resolve their dispute. But reasonable competence will not be the only necessary ingredient of accuracy.

4. ACCURACY AND IMPARTIALITY

Suppose that, a divine oracle being unavailable, Aaron proposes to Betty that they submit their dispute for binding resolution by Aaron's uncle Ted. And suppose Betty agrees with Aaron that Ted, as a wise and experienced man familiar with the community's customs, would be sufficiently competent to resolve their dispute. Still, Betty is likely to reject "let Ted decide" as a suitably accurate procedure for resolving that dispute, on the ground that the procedure is not sufficiently *impartial*. Betty's worry will be that Ted, as Aaron's uncle, is likely to be biased in Aaron's favor—that Ted's relationship with Aaron will skew his decisionmaking, causing him, consciously or not, to favor Aaron's position for reasons unrelated to the merits of the dispute. Betty will not be willing to submit to a procedure that seems likely to include a thumb on her opponent's side of the scale.

This example reveals that a mutual perception of reasonable impartiality, like a mutual perception of reasonable competence, is necessary in order for disputing parties to agree that a proposed procedure is suitably accurate. *Impartiality*, in the sense in which I am using the concept here, is the absence from a procedure of extrinsic factors favoring one side of the dispute over another; to put it slightly differently, it is the absence of factors that will prevent a procedure from functioning as it should, to the detriment of one of the disputants. Without a suitable degree of impartiality, even a perfectly competent procedure might not produce an accurate result, for the result would be tainted by factors having nothing to do with the merits. Imagine, for example, that Ted is so well-versed in the community's customs and so skilled at applying those customs to particular disputes that he would, absent any partiality, decide the dispute accurately; and suppose that an accurate decision would produce the result that Betty favors. If Ted's affection for his nephew nonetheless is so strong that—consciously or not—he cannot bring himself to decide against Aaron, then his result (a decision for Aaron) will be inaccurate despite his perfect competence. A large enough degree of partiality thus frustrates accuracy; a sufficient degree of impartiality is necessary for accuracy. And so disputants looking for a mutually acceptable procedure will insist on one that each agrees, *ex ante*, is suitably impartial.

Reasonable impartiality thus can be seen as an essential ingredient of imperfect procedural justice (which I am referring to here as reasonable accuracy). Sometimes, however, impartiality is understood as an entirely process-based, noninstrumental value—as an ingredient, that is, of pure procedural justice.[11] While this understanding is plausible, I believe my understanding here—that impartiality is an instrumental value, in the service of accuracy—is more plausible still (although the question ultimately will not make much difference to the arguments of this book).

The idea that impartiality is an entirely noninstrumental value is likely to be grounded in one or both of two related observations. The first is that, in many familiar decisionmaking contexts, impartiality seems to be the only thing that matters, with competence playing no role at all. If impartiality matters but competence does not, then it is hard to see how accuracy can be the goal of a procedure; impartiality must then have some procedural value wholly uncoupled from accuracy.

Consider some hypothetical circumstances in which it seems at first that impartiality stands alone as a reason to accept a decision-procedure:

- Case A: Two bargain-hunters at a garage sale both want to buy the same $5 item; they toss a coin to see who gets it.
- Case B: A small group of passengers on a rapidly sinking ship must determine which of them gets the final remaining place in the lifeboat; they draw straws to decide.
- Case C: A couple disagrees about what type of pizza to order; they toss a coin to resolve the conflict.

In each of these situations, it seems that a procedure that is wholly impartial, but not at all competent, is being agreed upon to resolve a dispute. Tossing a coin and drawing straws are wholly impartial procedures because, although factors extrinsic to the merits (pure chance) will decide the dispute, they will decide it in a way that has no tendency to favor one disputant over the other. And yet neither procedure seems truly competent to assess and apply the merits; a coin-toss or drawing straws generates the morally correct result, if at all, only by chance. These examples therefore might be thought to demonstrate that impartiality really is a noninstrumental value, because it is capable of resolving disputes even where accuracy clearly is not a goal.

What these cases really show, however, is simply that in circumstances where competent procedures are inapt, impartial procedures can serve as

---

11. Waldron hints at such a view in questioning what he calls "rights-instrumentalism" (although he does so in the context of discussing the value of participation, not of impartiality), see WALDRON, LAW AND DISAGREEMENT, supra note 5, at 252–54, and in his endorsement of the principle of majority rule, see Waldron, Core Case, supra note 3, at 1387–88. Lawrence Solum similarly asserts "that participation has a value that cannot be reduced to accuracy," and his understanding of participation seems necessarily to include a reasonably impartial decisionmaker. See Solum, supra note 10, at 274, 305. David Estlund describes, and critiques, noninstrumentalist understandings of what he calls procedural "fairness" in ESTLUND, supra note 10, at 65–84.

an acceptable substitute. In Case *A*, what is at stake has such small value that the costs of establishing some reasonably competent procedure to decide the dispute—submission to some third party, perhaps, who has the time and exper- tise to assess which bargain-hunter deserves the item more—clearly are higher than the benefits of doing so. A coin-toss is competent *enough* in such a case; at least it is no less likely than random chance to generate the morally best result (assuming there is such a thing in such a case; more on this below). And the very randomness of the coin-toss ensures that the accuracy of the procedure will not dip below fifty percent thanks to some preexisting bias in favor of one of the disputants. A coin-toss is quick, easy, cheap, and accurate enough given how little is at stake. It is not that accuracy is irrelevant in Case *A*—only that the costs of higher-than-random accuracy outweigh the benefits.

The same is true of Case *B*, though in a different way. There a great deal is at stake: People's lives depend on the outcome of the procedure. But the costs of developing a reasonably competent process (one whose competence is greater than random) are prohibitive: The ship will sink in moments, and if the passen- gers take the time necessary to assess each claim to a place in the lifeboat on its merits, everyone will drown. A stochastically competent and entirely impar- tial procedure (drawing straws) is the most accurate that can be called upon in the circumstances. Again, it's not that accuracy does not matter; it's only that better-than-random accuracy is unattainable.

Case *C* is different in that it involves a circumstance to which the concept of accuracy does indeed seem to be a *non sequitur*. It is a stretch to imagine that there will be a "morally right" answer to the question whether to order pepperoni or mushrooms on a pizza; the dispute here seems not at all a matter of rightness or justice and entirely a matter of competing tastes. And so the impartiality of a coin-toss does indeed seem valuable in such a case for reasons having nothing to do with the "accuracy" of the result; impartiality seems important entirely thanks to noninstrumental considerations of fairness. We should note, however, that purely aesthetic disputes are rarely, if ever, the targets of the law, which is our ultimate subject here. In fact it is often thought that the law should stay out of these kinds of disputes—that aesthetic matters are one of those categories, hinted at in Chapter 2, that usually are beyond the jurisdiction of legal authority. So the possibility that impartiality plays a noninstrumental role in resolving purely aesthetic disputes is unlikely to have direct relevance to a DR account of law's authority.

Note, too, that Case *C* may more closely resemble Case *A* than at first it appears. Often there is what seems like a moral backdrop to even the most trivial dispute between spouses, friends, partners, or siblings: Disputants frequently will make moral-sounding arguments on questions like what pizza to order ("But we ordered your favorite last time!" "But you don't really mind pepperoni, while I absolutely despise mushrooms!"). The use of a stochastic device like a coin-toss to resolve these disputes, then, might appear to the parties less like an acknowledgment that the dispute lacks any moral content, and more like a capitulation to the high costs of attempting to sort out the moral issues with any real accuracy.

We need not dwell on these issues; my point here is simply that the presence of certain cases in which impartiality seems important while competence does not should not be taken to prove that impartiality plays a noninstrumental role in legal dispute resolution. This leads to a second, related reason why impartiality might be thought noninstrumental, namely that it might frequently be easier for disputants to agree on impartial procedures than on competent ones. Identifying a reasonably impartial procedure requires only eliminating those procedures with some apparent bias for or against one of the disputants; identifying a reasonably competent procedure requires assessing the respective capacities of various alternatives to recognize the relevant norms and apply them reliably to the facts. This latter task often will seem much tougher than the former one, especially when it must jointly be performed by disputants who disagree about important underlying substantive issues. There is a temptation, then, to think that impartiality is fundamental to dispute resolution in a way that competence is not, and that the fundamental role of impartiality must be related to something other than the goal of generating an accurate result.

But the apparent fundamentality of impartial procedures is simply another function of the fact that establishing highly competent procedures often is very costly. Sometimes, as with Cases A and B (and arguably C) above, the costs of identifying, agreeing upon, and implementing truly competent procedures will be so relatively high that disputants will settle for a procedure that is at least stochastically competent and avoids obvious partiality. Impartiality, indeed, often is easier to identify and agree upon than competence; or perhaps it is more apt to say that partiality often is easier to identify and agree upon than incompetence. So the most salient feature of many real-world procedures will be their avoidance of partiality. (We will see examples of this phenomenon in the next few chapters.) This does not mean, however, that competence does not matter in these circumstances, or that impartiality is best understood as unrelated to the goal of procedural accuracy.

Whether or not impartiality sometimes plays a noninstrumental role, the important point for now is that both impartiality and competence, at reasonable levels (which may vary greatly depending on context), will be necessary components of any agreement among disputants, like Aaron and Betty, to submit their dispute to a reasonably (if not perfectly) accurate procedure, P_I. But will competence and impartiality be sufficient?

5. ACCURACY AND EFFICIENCY

It is worthwhile to make explicit what has been largely implicit in the discussion so far, namely that the value of *efficiency* also will be important to Aaron and Betty in choosing a dispute-resolution procedure. Efficiency is simply the capacity of a procedure to achieve an optimal balance between benefits and costs. On the DR account I am building, the ultimate (or first-order) benefit of a decision-procedure is the resolution of a dispute in a way that is acceptable to both (or all) the disputants and thus avoids the costs of leaving the dispute unresolved. As I've suggested, a means to that end—a second-order benefit of a procedure—is its functioning in a way that both disputants can agree ahead of time is sufficiently accurate; and two means to accuracy (third-order benefits of a procedure) are reasonable competence and reasonable impartiality. An efficient procedure, then, would achieve reasonable competence and reasonable accuracy at the lowest possible cost.

The efficiency of a procedure therefore will be partly derivative of the procedure's other benefits—its competence and impartiality, and hence its accuracy, and ultimately its capacity to peacefully resolve disputes. But it would be a mistake to think of efficiency as entirely derivative. As we have already seen, in some circumstances disputants might be willing to compromise competence in order to avoid high costs. (The same might be true of impartiality.) If Aaron and Betty's dispute is relatively trivial, as in Case A above, they might accept a procedure that is minimally, even stochastically, competent in order to save the resources that would have to be spent on agreeing to or implementing a more-competent procedure. The same might be true if Aaron and Betty's dispute is important but a highly competent procedure is unavailable or prohibitively expensive, as in Case B. The benefits of a procedure are internal—they relate to the objectives of the procedure itself—but the costs may be *external*. Disputants like Aaron and Betty will have to weigh P_I's capacity for competence and impartiality against the costs of those features, and they might be willing to settle on a less-competent or less-impartial (and thus less-accurate) procedure in order to avoid some of those costs.

There might, moreover, be *internal* costs of a procedure that must be taken into account. Betty's rejection of Ted as the arbiter of her dispute with Aaron might be an example of this: Even if Betty agrees that Ted would be a highly competent arbiter, she might reject him on the ground that his competence comes at too high a cost to his impartiality. The reverse might also occur. Suppose Betty proposes Irving, the village idiot, as an arbiter of her dispute with Aaron. Aaron might agree that Irving would be completely impartial but reject him because of his salient incompetence. Indeed, it is possible that the internal benefits of a given procedure—its competence and its impartiality—sometimes will be inversely related to each other, such that a greater degree of one accounts for a lesser degree of the other. Irving's perfect impartiality might be a product of the very dim-wittedness that renders him incompetent.[12]

---

12. The Supreme Court's 2002 decision in *Minnesota Republican Party v. White* provides a real-world twist on this possibility. Relying on the First Amendment, the Court struck down a provision of Minnesota's Code of Judicial Conduct that prohibited a candidate

Both external efficiency (the need to balance a procedure's accuracy with its non-accuracy-related costs) and internal efficiency (the need to balance the two aspects of accuracy—competence and impartiality—with respect to each other) will play a role in Aaron and Betty's process of attempting to agree on P_I, and in any process of designing or settling on dispute-resolution procedures. I will not focus much on external efficiency going forward; the kind and extent of external costs of dispute resolution in its various iterations (adjudication, democratic lawmaking, and constitutional law) are, for the most part, simply beyond my scope here. But the possibility of internal trade-offs between competence and impartiality will play an important role in helping us understand, in chapters 4 through 8, the distinctive roles played by adjudication and democratic law-making, and the sort of hybrid role played by constitutional law, within the American system.

6. THIRD-PARTY ADJUDICATION, PARTICIPATION, AND FAIRNESS

Let us pick up again the saga of Aaron and Betty and their attempt to peacefully resolve their dispute. Where they now stand is as follows. Each has determined that the anticipated costs of leaving the dispute unresolved are high enough to motivate an attempt to resolve that dispute peacefully. Unable to negotiate an acceptable compromise themselves, they've decided to search for some mutually agreeable procedure that might resolve their dispute for them. Of course each would be willing to accept a procedure, P_A, that he or she believes is perfectly accurate, that is, would guarantee the morally correct result; but there is no such perfectly accurate procedure available, at least none that both can agree on. So Aaron and Betty must look for a procedure, P_I, that each believes to be accu-rate enough—likely enough to generate the morally correct result—to merit

---

for state judicial office from "announc[ing] his or her views on disputed legal or political issues." 536 U.S. 765, 770, 788 (2002). Minnesota defended the provision as necessary to ensure judicial impartiality by, among other things, preventing judges from forming predispositions about the legal issues that may arise in cases that come before them. *Id.* at 775. Writing for the majority, Justice Antonin Scalia rejected this argument:

A judge's lack of predisposition regarding the relevant legal issues in a case has never been thought a necessary component of equal justice, and with good reason. For one thing, it is virtually impossible to find a judge who does not have preconceptions about the law. Indeed, even if it were possible to select judges who did not have preconceived views on legal issues, it would hardly be desirable to do so. "Proof that a Justice's mind at the time he joined the Court was a complete tabula rasa in the area of constitutional adjudication would be evidence of lack of qualification, not lack of bias."

Id. at 777–78 (quoting *Laird v. Tatum*, 409 U.S. 824, 835 (1972) (memorandum opinion)).

their *ex ante* commitment. To settle on P_1, Aaron and Betty will have to agree that the procedure is reasonably (if not perfectly) competent (capable of generating the correct result) and reasonably (if not perfectly) impartial (immune to extrinsic factors that favor one side over the other). They will have to weigh the expected accuracy of P_1 against its external costs, and they may have to accept internal trade-offs between the two elements of accuracy (competence and impartiality).

What basic form of procedure might they agree on? Note that some superficially attractive candidates will, in light of the foregoing discussion, quickly be pushed off the table. Resolving their dispute using some stochastic device, like tossing a coin or drawing straws, will have to be ruled out unless they both agree that what is at stake is quite trivial (like the $5 garage-sale item in Case *A*), or that the need to resolve the dispute quickly is quite urgent (as with the sinking ship in Case *B*), or that the dispute really has no "right" or "wrong" answer (as with the pizza order in Case *C*).

Aaron and Betty also will have to rule out another potentially attractive candidate for P_1: majority vote. A majority vote might be a reasonably impartial procedure: While it may be influenced by factors extrinsic to the merits of the dispute (a voter can vote for a given result for any reason she likes, or for no reason at all), those factors would not necessarily favor one side over the other, as each person's vote would have an equal influence on the outcome. A majority vote might be a reasonably competent procedure as well, if one believes a "many minds" argument like the one made by J. S. Mill (among many others) and mentioned in Chapter 2, or if the group of voters in question has some special expertise in the subject. The salient problem in Aaron and Betty's case, however, will be that a majority vote is incapable of generating any outcome at all, because it would involve only two voters, each of whom presumably would vote for the result he or she favors. In this sense, a majority vote among the disputants is (obviously, but in a sense worth mentioning here) a perfectly *in*competent way to resolve a bipartite dispute.

As the discussion to this point has hinted, there is a potential third option for Aaron and Betty that might avoid these problems: They could submit their dispute for resolution by some third party. It seems plausible that Aaron and Betty could agree on a third party whose competence is likely to exceed the level of random chance, and whose preexisting relationships with the parties and their dispute (or lack thereof) suggest an acceptable degree of impartiality. Perfect accuracy, again, is impossible, and we have posited that Aaron and Betty's mutual impulse to resolve their dispute peacefully is fairly strong. So Aaron and Betty might not find it especially difficult to settle on a suitable third-party arbiter, given the distasteful alternatives of resolution by chance (e.g., a coin-toss) or no resolution at all.

Suppose Aaron and Betty agree to submit their dispute to Julia, whom both agree is reasonably well-versed in the customs and mores that should apply to their dispute and has no potentially compromising relationship with either of them or stake in the matter that must be decided. It seems unlikely that the disputants will simply recruit Julia and then leave her to her own devices. For one thing, Julia's impartiality may imply that she is not already intimately familiar with the details of Aaron and Betty's dispute. Someone—most logically Aaron and Betty themselves—may have to inform Julia of the relevant facts. And with so much at stake, Aaron and Betty each will have an incentive to monitor Julia's decisionmaking process rather closely, to ensure that Julia really is reasonably competent and impartial after all.

These considerations will point toward some degree of *participation* by the disputants in the process of resolving their dispute. Aaron and Betty themselves, or people acting on their behalf, seem best suited to acquaint the third-party arbiter, Julia, with the facts they believe relevant to the dispute. This will involve the disputants' presentation of facts (what in modern adjudication we refer to as "evidence") to Julia as part of the process. Of course, the disputants may disagree about the relevant facts—this may in part be what their dispute is about—and so each disputant must have a roughly equal chance to tell his or her side of the story. The terms of participation, that is, must be *fair*. They must not give either disputant an arbitrary advantage, one unrelated to the merits of the dispute. Procedural fairness in this sense is simply an aspect of the impartiality of the procedure.

The process of third-party arbitration of the dispute that Aaron and Julia agree to, therefore—what Aaron and Julia will settle on as P_I—is likely to be reasonably participatory and reasonably fair. Participation can enhance the competence of the procedure; procedural fairness can promote its impartiality. A suitably fair and participatory procedure might be as simple as each party's presenting Julia with an oral narrative of what he or she thinks happened. Or it might expand to include many of the accoutrements of modern litigation: written submissions to the court, the calling and questioning of witnesses, the presentation of documentary and physical evidence, and so on. It might even include arguments to Julia about what the applicable norms are, or should be, and how they apply to the facts. The nature and complexity of the procedure will depend on factors like the intricacy of the dispute itself and the relative formality or informality of relationships in the society in which Aaron and Betty live. In chapters 5 and 6, I will discuss in more detail the elements of participation and procedural fairness in modern American adjudication.

Having agreed to submit their dispute for resolution by P_I—a fair and participatory procedure with Julia as third-party arbiter—Aaron and Betty now face the certainty that one of them, at least, will be substantively unhappy with the resulting decision. From that *ex post* perspective—at the point in time when P_I has produced a decision with which at least one of the disputants substantively disagrees—what might motivate that losing disputant nonetheless to accept the decision?

7. DISPUTE RESOLUTION AND CONSENT

Suppose Julia renders a decision in favor of Betty and against Aaron. Aaron now must decide whether to accept that decision—to treat it as an authoritative resolution of the dispute and abide by its terms. This decision, remember, is distinct from the one Aaron made *ex ante*, when he agreed to submit the dispute to Julia in the first place.

Aaron's reasons *not* to accept Julia's decision will be obvious. They are the same reasons that underwrote his original position in the dispute—his reasons for believing that his preferred location of the fence is the (morally) correct or best location, and that Betty's preferred location of the fence, now adopted by Julia, is a (morally) incorrect or suboptimal location. Aaron's reason for non-acceptance, in other words, is simply that he believes Julia's decision is substantively wrong as a moral matter.

We should note here, in passing, the possibility that Julia's decision in Betty's favor will motivate Aaron to reconsider his initial moral position in the dispute. Aaron agreed to submit the dispute to Julia in the first place because he believed Julia would be a reasonably competent and impartial arbiter. The fact that a reasonably competent and impartial arbiter has now rejected Aaron's substantive position may cause Aaron to rethink that position; and his rethinking may cause him to change his mind. It is possible, in other words, that Aaron will be motivated to accept Julia's decision simply because the source of that decision has caused Aaron to agree with its substance.

Notice the superficial affinity between this possibility and an EG account of legal authority. An EG account supposes that legal subjects will be motivated to obey the law out of recognition that the law is likely to be wiser than they are about what to do. And indeed it is possible that, in any given instance, a person told to do something he otherwise would think wrong will decide to do that thing out of deference to the epistemic authority of the person, institution, or procedure issuing the command. The fact that a process we believe to be suitably accurate—P_I—concludes that something is right might cause us to reverse our initial opinion to the contrary, or at least to question the correctness of our initial opinion sufficiently to defer to P_I.

Notice too, however, that if this occurs, the operable phenomenon need not be one of *authority*, properly understood. It might instead be a phenomenon of influence or persuasion: A person might accept the decision of P_I not because of some content-independent reason having to do with the source of that decision, but because the decision has caused that person to reassess the applicable content-*dependent* reasons. This possibility, while real, lends no credence to the viability of an EG account of legal authority, which depends on the proposition that the relative expertise of legal procedures creates a prevalent and strong content-independent reason for legal subjects to act against (what they believe to be) the balance of content-dependent reasons.

On the other hand, it is possible that the person in question (say, Aaron) might accept the decision of P_I as correct solely because of its source—because he recognizes P_I to be accurate—and without himself reassessing the content-dependent reasons. In that event, Aaron really has deferred to the authority of P_I. This possibility is not ruled out by the fact that EG accounts of legal authority suffer from the Encroachment Flaw. The Encroachment Flaw, rather, describes the possibility (indeed the likelihood) that Aaron's assessment of P_I's authority will be influenced by his assessment of the content-dependent considerations applicable to the situation. If Aaron's assessment of the content-dependent reasons points to one substantive conclusion while the decision of P_I points to another, Aaron might still defer to P_I for the content-independent reason that P_I possesses epistemic authority; it is only that the likelihood of his doing so will be reduced in direct proportion to the force with which the content-dependent reasons seem to undermine P_I's epistemic authority.

I will return to these conceptual mechanics shortly. For now, let us assume that Aaron is not persuaded by Julia's decision to change his mind about the morally best result: He continues to believe that the morally optimal thing to do is to locate the fence somewhere other than where Julia, siding with Betty, has now declared it should go. If he is nonetheless to accept and abide by Julia's decision, then, he will need some strong content-independent reason (or reasons) to do so.

One obvious source of such a reason is the fact that Aaron *consented, ex ante,* to submit the dispute to resolution by P_I. As we saw in Chapter 2, consent might provide a powerful reason, perhaps even a *prima facie* moral duty, to do something that one otherwise might think morally suboptimal, including adhering to the result of a procedure to which one consented. If we assume that Aaron, *ex ante*, freely and knowingly gave his consent that P_I would resolve the dispute, Aaron now, *ex post*, has a strong moral reason to live up to that commitment. And that reason is a content-independent one: Its existence and force have nothing to do with the substance of the decision issued by the procedure to which Aaron consented.

In other words, Aaron is likely to recognize that Julia's disappointing decision now has at least some authority over him by virtue of his *ex ante* consent. Of course, that authority is unlikely to be absolute: There may be reasons (including content-dependent reasons relating to the substance of the decision) for Aaron nonetheless to disobey that decision, and it's even possible that those countervailing reasons will be sufficiently weighty to overcome Aaron's consent-based reason to recognize the decision's authority. But the decision will be able to claim at least some measure of authority by virtue of Aaron's consent, and it is plausible to think the force of that authority will be relatively strong.

Note, too, that the fact of Aaron's *ex ante* consent will not be the only content-independent reason for Aaron, *ex post*, to abide by Julia's decision. Another such reason is that accepting Julia's decision, however substantively wrong

(Aaron thinks) it is, will bring peace between Aaron and Betty. Aaron's reasons for seeking a peaceful resolution of the dispute in the first place thus also will serve as reasons for accepting that resolution once it is offered. Indeed, those reasons may be even stronger *ex post*, because Aaron and Betty will have undergone the presumably time- and resource-consuming process of agreeing on and participating in P_J. Rejecting the resolution offered by P_J now, after Betty has invested resources to achieve it, may effectively create a new dispute with Betty, increasing Aaron's dispute-related costs going forward. Disobeying Julia's decision thus may make Aaron worse off than he was before he agreed to submit to it.

As the losing party, then, Aaron will have at least two potentially strong content-independent reasons to abide by the result of P_J. The first reason is that he willingly consented, *ex ante*, to abide by that decision *ex post*. The second reason is that failing to abide by it would reintroduce, and perhaps worsen, the costs of leaving his dispute with Betty unresolved. The conjunction of these reasons might cause Aaron to acknowledge that the decision has at least some degree of authority over him.

8. CONSENT AND PROCEDURAL ACCURACY

We cannot predict precisely how strong these two content-independent reasons (and the authority they support) will be or, in particular, whether they will be strong enough to outweigh Aaron's existing content-dependent reasons to disobey the decision of P_J. It seems quite plausible, at least, that they will be strong enough to do so, but ultimately that will depend on the particular circumstances of P_J and the dispute it purports to resolve. Let us suppose, though, that in light of these content-independent reasons, Aaron decides to defer to the authority of Julia's decision and abide by it peacefully.

Imagine, then, that Aaron and Betty now find themselves in yet another dispute, this time (let's suppose) over the ownership of some commonly grazed cattle. Betty proposes to Aaron that they again submit their dispute for resolution by P_J, that is, by Julia according to the same participatory and fair process used the previous time. Given the disappointing result generated by P_J the first time, is it conceivable that Aaron would agree to Betty's proposal now?

Note that the fact that P_J generated what was, for Aaron, an incorrect result last time will not necessarily preclude Aaron from agreeing to use that procedure again. Aaron will, first of all, be facing the same kinds of Hobbesian costs of leaving the dispute unresolved that he faced in the first episode; he is likely, then, to be motivated to seek a peaceful resolution of this dispute as well. And the same factors that convinced him to agree to P_J in the previous case may point in that direction now: P_J may still appear reasonably accurate (that is, reasonably competent and reasonably impartial).

It is true that the decision generated by P_1 in the earlier dispute, which Aaron believes to have been incorrect, may now cause Aaron to reassess his earlier conclusion that P_1 is suitably accurate. Accuracy is the tendency to generate correct decisions, and the fact of a decision that is, in Aaron's view, incorrect constitutes some evidence (for Aaron) against a procedure's accuracy. But an incorrect decision need not be *conclusive* evidence of inaccuracy. Remember that Aaron already will have come to grips with the unavailability of a *perfectly* accurate procedure (or at least the impossibility of agreeing with Betty on a perfectly accurate procedure). Aaron's view that P_1 generated an incorrect decision in the prior case only confirms that P_1 is less than perfectly accurate; and Aaron was willing to live with that fact when he agreed to allow P_1 to resolve the earlier dispute. Why shouldn't he be willing to live with that fact again now?

This is not to suggest that P_1's decision in the first case will be irrelevant to Aaron's moral calculus regarding whether to consent to P_1 again. If Aaron believes the earlier decision was so incorrect that no reasonably accurate procedure could have generated it—that it must have been the result of some gross failure of competence or impartiality—then he is unlikely to consent to using P_1 a second time. Similarly, if P_1 has generated many prior decisions that Aaron thinks were wrong, Aaron may conclude that his initial assessment of P_1's accuracy was mistaken. The point is only that the mere incorrectness (in Aaron's view) of a single prior decision by P_1 need not, standing alone, convince Aaron that P_1 is too inaccurate to decide a subsequent dispute.

It also is true—importantly so—that, for reasons quite apart from the substance of the earlier decision, Aaron's experience with P_1 in the earlier case may bear on his evaluation of P_1's accuracy now. Something that occurred during P_1's decision-process might have convinced Aaron that Julia really is not very competent after all, or that she in fact harbors some bias against him or in favor of Betty. On the other hand, Aaron might have become convinced of Julia's competence and impartiality despite her ultimate decision against him. A person's experience with, or observations of, a procedure might well influence his assessment of that procedure's general accuracy in a way that is entirely separate from his evaluation of the substantive decisions the procedure has produced.

Let us suppose that Aaron believes P_1's decision in the prior case, while incorrect, was not so grossly wrong as to vitiate P_1's reasonable impartiality or competence; and let us suppose that Aaron's first-hand experience of the operation of P_1 in that earlier case did not give him any independent reason to question P_1's reasonable accuracy. We can also suppose that no alternative procedure has turned up, in the interim between the previous dispute and the instant one, that both Aaron and Betty can agree is *more* accurate that P_1; P_1, though not perfect, is the best game in town. Under these not-implausible circumstances, it is entirely conceivable that Aaron would agree to submit this new dispute with Betty to resolution by P_1, even though P_1 resolved their prior dispute with what Aaron thinks is an incorrect decision.

Indeed, it's conceivable that Aaron and Betty might make a longer-term commitment with respect to P_I, agreeing to submit as-yet-nonexistent future disputes for resolution by that procedure as well. Suppose that P_I resolves Aaron and Betty's second dispute in favor, this time, of Aaron. Now any doubts Aaron may have had about P_I's accuracy will have been mollified, if not entirely eliminated. And, while the latest decision may engender some new doubts in Betty, she may well adopt the same attitude that Aaron adopted after P_I's earlier ruling against him (an attitude that might be somewhat easier for her to assume than it was for Aaron, given that P_I has gotten it right at least once in Betty's lights). Suppose further that Aaron and Betty, who are neighbors with rather contentious personalities, anticipate that further disputes are likely to arise between them over the years. It seems plausible that they might agree ahead of time to submit any further disputes to resolution by P_I (which still appears to both of them to be the most-accurate procedure available).

Suppose, then, that Aaron and Betty agree that for a period of five years, any disputes arising between them that they cannot resolve informally will be submitted for binding resolution to P_I (that is, to Julia, who will resolve them following a procedure that is participatory and fair). As future disputes arise and are submitted to and resolved by P_I, the loser of each dispute (or losers, plural—remember, again, that any given dispute might be resolved in a way that fully satisfies neither disputant) will have the same set of reasons to abide by P_I's decision that Aaron had in the initial case. Reason number one is consent: The loser of each dispute has consented, *ex ante*, to be bound by P_I's resolution of that dispute. Reason number two (actually likely to be an agglomeration of reasons) is that failing to abide by P_I's decision will reopen and perhaps aggravate a dispute, with potentially costly consequences.

9. DISPUTE RESOLUTION, PROCEDURAL ACCURACY, AND CONSTRUCTIVE CONSENT

The saga of Aaron and Betty so far has revealed both consensualist and Hobbesian strains in the idea of legal authority. Aaron and Betty might be considered bound, at least presumptively, by the results of P_I, both because they have consented to be so bound, and also because failing to obey P_I will reopen costly disputes. The decisions—the protolaw, if you will—generated by P_I seem to possess some authority over Aaron and Betty for these twin reasons. As the discussion of consensualist and Hobbesian accounts of legal authority in Chapter 2 suggested, however, we will run into problems if we try to extrapolate from Aaron and Betty's simple narrative to a more general justification of the authority of law.

The problem with generalizing the consensualist strain in the narrative is that consent-based authority is plausible only in rather microcosmic and, in the modern world, mostly artificial circumstances like those I have posited for Aaron and Betty. Aaron and Betty, the (proto) legal subjects in my simple model, have actually consented to be bound by the (proto) law generated by P_I; but few if any legal subjects in real-world legal systems can be said to have actually consented to be bound by every law, or even most of the laws, that supposedly govern them. It will be rare that a real-world legal subject, faced with the decision whether to obey what she believes to be an incorrect legal command, can count the fact of her actual *ex ante* consent to be bound by that command as a strong reason for obedience.

The problem with generalizing the Hobbesian strain in the account is that a bare Hobbesian justification of authority—that disobedience will reopen and perhaps aggravate a dispute, with costly consequences—proves too much. Unlike consent, this Hobbesian reason might apply to legal subjects in real-world legal systems: In many actual cases, disobedience to legal commands will indeed open or aggravate costly disputes, and widespread disobedience surely would create the risk of Hobbes's brutal "war of every one against every one." Real-world legal subjects, that is, often will have Hobbesian reasons to obey (what they believe to be) incorrect legal commands. The problem, though, is that these reasons will exist regardless of the source of those commands. Consent, as a basis for authority, is connected to the nature of that authority, to the source of authoritative commands: Aaron and Betty consented to P_I *ex ante* because they believed P_I to be a reasonably accurate procedure for resolving disputes. But the bare Hobbesian basis for authority—that disobedience would reopen or aggravate a costly dispute—is entirely disconnected from the nature of that authority. If avoiding a dispute is a reason to obey a command, it is a reason that applies regardless of what procedure generated that command. Aaron and Betty would have had a bare Hobbesian reason to obey P_I even if P_I had been blatantly incompetent and partial—even, that is, if they never would have consented *ex ante* to be bound by P_I. Standing alone as a basis for legal authority, the bare Hobbesian reason thus could justify the authority of any legal procedure—including, not incidentally, the system of absolutist government that Hobbes himself favored.

So (again) we cannot rely on actual consent as a general foundation for legal authority, and we dare not rely on the bare Hobbesian dispute-resolution impulse. And yet the story of Aaron and Betty still has been useful as the prototype of a general account of the authority of law—because it has pointed the way toward a different sort of reason, closely connected to but distinct from both actual consent and the Hobbesian impulse, that legal subjects may have for obeying what they believe to be incorrect laws.

To grasp this reason, imagine that Aaron and Betty mistakenly submit a dispute for resolution by P_I without realizing that their agreed five-year time period has expired. Suppose that after P_I renders a decision in Betty's favor, Aaron remembers that P_I's jurisdiction over him, as it were, is no longer valid. Actual consent therefore does not exist as a reason for Aaron to abide by P_I's decision against him. Will Aaron's moral calculus be meaningfully different from what it would have been a few months earlier, while his actual consent to P_I remained in force? Will he have substantially less reason to abide by P_I's decision now than he would have had then?

If Aaron is honest with himself, he may realize that his situation really is not all that different, morally speaking, from one in which he has actually consented to be bound by P_I. To see why, imagine Aaron again at that point in time after P_I has rendered its initial decision against him, when Aaron had to decide whether to submit a second dispute to P_I. Recall that while P_I's initial decision was (by Aaron's lights) incorrect, that fact need not have destroyed Aaron's belief that P_I was, generally speaking, a suitably accurate procedure. More broadly, Aaron still might have believed that he did the morally right thing by consenting to submit to P_I in the first place—that the costs of leaving his dispute with Betty unresolved, combined with the reasonable accuracy of P_I as a method of resolving that dispute, made his consenting *ex ante* to submit to P_I the morally correct thing to do.

With this point in mind, fast-forward to Aaron's position now—faced with the decision whether to abide by a decision of P_I to which he has *not* actually consented in advance. Suppose that Aaron continues to believe that P_I is a suitably accurate procedure for resolving disputes; suppose, more broadly, that Aaron believes that he acted morally correctly in consenting to be bound by P_I in the first place (though that consent has now formally expired). If Aaron believes this, then he may also believe that he *would* have acted morally correctly to consent, *ex ante*, to be bound by P_I's resolution of this new dispute—even though he did not, thanks to an oversight, actually do so. And if consenting to be bound by P_I would have been the morally correct thing to do *ex ante*, then it might still be the morally correct thing to do *ex post*. Aaron might conclude, in other words, that the morally correct thing for him to do now, in the face of an adverse (and unconsented-to) decision of P_I, is to act as if he *had* actually consented in advance to be bound by P_I.

The device upon which I am relying here should be familiar, in its basic form, from Chapter 2: It is the device of *constructive consent*. The idea is that Aaron should be held to have consented to be bound by P_I, despite his lack of actual consent, by virtue of the fact that he *would* have consented to be bound by P_I had he been given the opportunity to do so. To put this another way, Aaron's reason for abiding by the decision of P_I after the fact is that he would have agreed to do so ahead of time—that consenting to be bound by P_I *ex ante* would have been the morally correct thing for him to do. The accident of his not having actually consented to be bound ahead of time should not release Aaron from the consequences he would now face had he done so.[13]

---

13. The idea I'm advancing here is, I think, identical to what David Estlund has called "normative consent," and his explication of that notion—though I discovered it only after

We should be clear, again, about the normative mechanics of this notion of constructive consent: It really is a heuristic device designed to reveal someone's existing moral duties, not a source of new moral duties. In suggesting that Aaron should now (after P_l's latest decision against him) act as if he had consented to P_l *ex ante*, I am not claiming that Aaron should be treated as if he had actually taken on some new moral duty by consenting to P_l (even though he did not). I am suggesting, rather, that Aaron should be held to the consequences of the moral duty he already possessed. Aaron (I am assuming) had a moral duty to consent, ahead of time, to be bound by P_l's resolution of his latest dispute; it is only that he did not formally consummate this duty thanks to the happenstance of his and Betty's having forgotten that their earlier agreement had expired. The device of constructive consent—of asking whether Aaron would have consented to be bound by P_l ahead of time, had he had the opportunity to do so—simply reveals the existence of a duty to which Aaron already, independently, was subject.

What is that nature of that preexisting duty? Suppose that Aaron and Betty had realized that their five-year agreement had expired, and Betty had asked Aaron whether he would agree, *ex ante*, to submit their latest dispute to P_l. And suppose the morally right thing for Aaron to do in this situation would have been to consent as Betty requested—suppose, in other words, that Aaron would have been subject to a moral duty to consent to submit the dispute to P_l. Aaron's duty to consent would have been more than a duty simply to declare his consent, or to submit to P_l without actually abiding by its result. His duty to consent would have included a duty to make that consent effective—to actually obey the result of P_l once it was rendered. Aaron's existing duty to consent, then, would have included a duty to abide by the resulting decision. If Aaron is bound by that duty now—even absent his actual consent—then he is bound, now, by the duty to submit to the decision rendered by P_l.

It is true that we might think Aaron's duty absent *actual* consent—to be more precise, the complex of moral reasons to obey the decision of P_l that Aaron now faces—is not quite as strong as it would be if his actual consent had been given. Actual consent, on top of constructive consent, might have strengthened the moral argument that Aaron now should obey a decision with which he

beginning to develop the notion on my own—has been crucial in helping me form my arguments in this chapter. Estlund describes normative consent as the phenomenon of being "under [someone's] authority because you would be morally wrong to refuse to consent" to do what that person tells you to do. Normative consent "is hypothetical: you would have consented if you acted morally correctly when offered the chance to consent." Estlund, *supra* note 10, at 9–10. In such cases, Estlund asks, "what happens if we do not consent? Can we escape the authority in that way, by abusing our power to refuse consent?" *Id.* at 117. Estlund's answer, and mine, is no: We can be held, morally, to have consented to something to which we *should* have consented (and thus to which we *would* have been under a duty to consent had the opportunity presented itself).

disagrees in substance. It is not clear, however, that actual consent would add all that much to Aaron's moral calculus. A person's consent to do something he is not already required by morality to do—that is, to take on some new moral duty—might indeed provide a strong reason, perhaps even a duty, for the person to do that thing. But it is not so clear that a person's consent to do something he *is* already required to do creates a new moral duty in this way, or meaningfully enhances the existing one. The golfer Bobby Jones supposedly once remarked that congratulating a competitor for self-reporting a rule violation is "like congratulating a man for not robbing a bank." Committing ahead of time not to rob a bank does not seem to add much to a person's existing duty not to do so.

The important point, in any event, is that Aaron may have a powerful moral reason to abide by the decision of P_I that is distinct from both actual consent and the bare Hobbesian dispute-resolution impulse. That reason, which we might think of as one of constructive consent, is that Aaron was subject to a moral duty (or at least a strong set of moral reasons) to consent ahead of time to be bound by the decision of P_I. That duty included an obligation to obey the decision of P_I once it was rendered; and the duty to obey exists now—once the decision actually has been rendered—just as it would have existed if Aaron had given his actual consent. Aaron must now refrain, as it were, from robbing the bank, even though he did not actually consent ahead of time not to rob it.

This reason of constructive consent is distinct from reasons of actual consent and Hobbesian dispute-resolution; but note that it is connected to both sorts of reason in important ways. It is connected to the idea of actual consent by virtue of the fact that constructive consent does not exist if actual consent would not have been appropriate. Suppose Aaron, after the latest (unconsented-to) decision of P_I in Betty's favor, honestly concludes that he would have been mistaken if he had consented to P_I ahead of time. Perhaps five years of observing P_I in action (including, let us say, many decisions with which Aaron has disagreed) have convinced Aaron that P_I really is not a suitably accurate means of resolving disputes. It is even possible that this latest incorrect (by Aaron's lights) decision of P_I has tipped the balance, for Aaron, toward a conclusion that P_I is not reasonably accurate after all. If Aaron honestly believes now, with the benefit of hindsight, that P_I is not suitably accurate, then he might (honestly) believe that his consenting to P_I ahead of time would have been a moral mistake. And if consenting to P_I ahead of time would have been a mistake, then Aaron cannot be said to have constructively consented to it; he cannot now be bound by the consequences of a (nonexistent) duty to have consented to P_I.

(Of course, Aaron's assessment of the accuracy of P_I, and thus of his moral duties, might be mistaken. And of course there is the substantial risk that Aaron's self-interest, or his strong belief in the substantive correctness of his position in the various disputes decided by P_I, will distort his moral judgment. But such risks are always present when individuals decide whether to obey the law; and we can hardly tell a legal (or protolegal) subject like Aaron not to assess his moral duties incorrectly. The best we can do is to tell people in Aaron's position to do what they believe, in their own best good-faith judgment, is morally best.)

Constructive consent, as a reason to adhere to a decision or other legal command, thus depends entirely on the *ex ante* propriety of actual consent, which itself will be a highly fact-specific, contingent question. One important aspect of that question will be the apparent accuracy of the procedure that has generated the decision or command, and of course the substantive correctness or incorrectness of the decisions that procedure has generated in the past (among other factors) will constitute relevant evidence regarding its accuracy. Another important aspect of the question will be the strength of the need for peaceful dispute resolution itself, coupled with the prospect that a suitably accurate procedure actually will resolve a dispute. (Here is where constructive consent makes contact with the bare Hobbesian dispute-resolution impulse.) Aaron might, in retrospect, honestly believe that he would have been wrong to consent to P_1 because the anticipated costs of an incorrect decision by P_1, coupled with the risks of an incorrect decision (remember that no procedure will be perfectly accurate), would, from an *ex ante* perspective, have outweighed the anticipated benefits of a peaceful resolution of his dispute with Betty. Perhaps the costs of leaving this dispute unresolved would have been relatively low; perhaps the harm from a decision that is (in Aaron's lights) incorrect would have been extraordinarily high. If Aaron honestly believes, *ex post*, that the moral calculus *ex ante* would have weighed against consenting to P_1, then he will have no reason of constructive consent to obey the decision of P_1.

Nor will Aaron have a reason of constructive consent to obey the decision if he honestly believes that Betty would not have consented to P_1 *ex ante*. Suppose Betty had told Aaron, near the end of their five-year agreement to submit their disputes to P_1, that she was dissatisfied with P_1 and did not intend to renew the agreement. If so, Aaron might now believe that Betty, had she been given the opportunity, would not have consented to submit the latest dispute to P_1. Faced with Betty's refusal, it would have done no good for Aaron to agree to submit to P_1—no dispute would have been resolved that way—and thus Aaron would have been under no *ex ante* moral duty to do so. From an *ex post* perspective, Aaron could not then be under a duty to obey the result of a procedure to which he was under no duty to submit in the first place (and to which, remember, he did not actually consent).

In sum, then, Aaron may conclude that he has a *prima facie* duty, or at least a strong moral reason, to adhere to the result of P_1 even absent his actual consent. That reason is not simply that obeying the decision will now avoid a costly dispute, for such a reason would justify obedience to *any* decision, regardless of its source. The reason, rather, is that he should have consented to P_1 in advance and thus is now under an existing duty to obey its results. That duty, however, is contingent on Aaron's continued belief that P_1 is a suitably accurate means for resolving disputes; on his judgment that the costs of leaving the dispute unresolved would have exceeded the costs of submitting to P_1; and on his confidence that his opponent, Betty, would herself have agreed to submit the dispute to P_1.

From the narrative so far, we can begin to see how some of the unsatisfactory accounts of legal authority canvassed in Chapter 2 nonetheless can contribute valuable insights to the DR account I am in the process of building. The idea of actual consent cannot support a full-fledged justification of general legal authority; but it captures a sense in which the DR account might, perhaps must, be socially contingent. On the DR account, legal authority will depend in fact on (legal subjects' good-faith judgments about) the costs of unresolved disputes, the accuracy of procedures for resolving them, and (crucially) the willingness of others in society to submit to those procedures. The idea of consent also helps us imagine how a dispute-resolution procedure would have to look in order to be worthy of consent: It would have to be reasonably accurate, reducing the risk of a bad decision to a level where it is outweighed by the costs of an unresolved dispute. Reasonable accuracy will mean reasonable competence and reasonable impartiality—qualities that themselves can only be assessed by the disputants, further adding to the socially contingent nature of the resulting authority.

If the notion of consent points toward a particular form of dispute resolution and thus of authoritative procedures, the bare Hobbesian dispute-resolution impulse emphasizes the animating reason for legal authority. The costs of unresolved disputes are why disputants need procedures in the first place; imperfections in the procedures must be balanced against those costs. The imperative to peacefully resolve disputes cannot justify obedience to the results of just any procedure at all (including Hobbesian absolutism), but it might justify obedience to the results of procedures that are less than perfectly accurate.

Finally, the concept of constructive consent underscores the morally compulsory nature of legal authority, despite its socially contingent elements. Whether a person should submit to a dispute-resolution procedure—and thus, ultimately, whether a legal subject should obey the law—will depend on, if you will, the particular costs and benefits applicable to her situation: on the costs of leaving the dispute unresolved, on the reasonable accuracy of the available procedure or procedures, on the willingness of her opponent to submit to the same procedure. But in any given circumstance, the calculus of costs and benefits will produce a morally right answer of one kind or another. Either Aaron should, morally speaking, agree to submit his particular dispute with Betty to resolution by P_1 under the applicable circumstances, or he should not (morally speaking) do so. If Aaron is under a moral duty to submit his dispute to P_1, then he cannot avoid the consequences of that fact by failing actually to consent to P_1; he must—or at least he has a strong moral reason to—abide by the decision of P_1 even absent his actual consent.

10. BEYOND THE BIPARTITE DISPUTE

The idea of constructive consent, as I have applied it to the hypothetical series of disputes between Aaron and Betty, holds that where the costs of leaving disputes unresolved are high enough, and where a dispute-resolution procedure (P_I) is accurate enough, disputants have a moral duty to submit their disputes for resolution by P_I and to abide by its results. P_I, that is, might possess authority despite a lack of actual consent to its authority.

It should be obvious by now that if these normative mechanics hold true, P_I might possess authority, not just with respect to participants in a single bipartite dispute, or with respect to repeat players in a series of such disputes, but over a much broader group of disputants and potential disputants. To illustrate this, suppose P_I proves so effective at resolving disputes that other residents of the community in which Aaron and Betty live begin to voluntarily submit their own disputes to P_I. Over time, a custom develops by which disputes are submitted to P_I as a matter of course. Eventually the community—evolving now toward a legal system—unanimously agrees to submit all future disputes that cannot be resolved informally for resolution by P_I.

In this scenario, it is easy to see why members of the community will be bound to submit their disputes to P_I, and to abide by its decisions, going forward: Each of them has actually consented to do so. (For the sake of clarity, we should keep in mind here that even actual consent might not impose an absolute duty of obedience; in any given case, strong reasons to disobey a decision of P_I might outweigh a person's consent. But for present purposes we can speak, in shorthand, of a duty imposed by the act of consent.)

Suppose, however, that a newcomer, Sam, arrives in the community after its members have unanimously agreed to require dispute resolution by P_I. Suppose Sam becomes involved in a dispute with Olive, a longtime member of the community. Sam has never given his actual consent to submit this (or any) dispute to P_I. Is Sam nonetheless under a moral duty to submit his dispute with Olive to resolution by P_I?

The answer might (though it need not) be yes. As we have seen, the existence of a moral duty to submit one's dispute to a suitably accurate process need not depend on actual consent. If the moral costs of leaving the dispute unresolved are great enough, and the expected accuracy of P_I as a way to resolve the dispute is high enough, then Sam will have a moral duty to submit to P_I whether he actually consents to do so or not.

And note—a crucial point—that the costs of refusing to submit to P_I might be higher in this scenario than they would be in a simple bipartite model in which two private parties must agree on a method of dispute resolution, like our original case involving Aaron and Betty. It is likely that Sam, by refusing to submit his dispute to P_I in the face of a community norm requiring it, will create costs greater than those directly related to his dispute with Olive. His dispute with Olive will remain unresolved, resulting in continued uncertainty, lost opportunity costs, and the like. But Sam's refusal also might make his relationship with the community as a whole more costly. Others in the community might determine that they cannot predict how Sam will respond to a dispute, and they might be reluctant to deal with Sam as a result. The sense of security, unity, and well-being within the community that is promoted by the existence of a stable dispute-resolution mechanism thus will have been undermined by Sam's defection from it. Dealings between other members of the community might even be made more tentative for fear that others will follow Sam's example and defect from P_I.

Sam's refusal to submit to P_I, in other words, might threaten a parade of Hobbesian horribles longer than any that would have been triggered by Aaron's refusal, before the establishment of a community norm, to submit his simple bipartite dispute with Betty to P_I. To put the point generally: Defection from a communal dispute-resolution norm is likely to be more costly than defection from dispute resolution in a narrowly bipartite context. Sam, the newcomer who has not given his actual consent to P_I, will have to take account of these increased costs of leaving the dispute unresolved in deciding whether he is under a moral duty to submit to P_I. The likelihood that he has such a duty will be enhanced by the existence of a community norm that would be violated by his refusal.

The same argument would apply to Sam's *ex post* decision whether to abide by the result of P_I. Suppose Sam goes along with P_I under protest, participating in it fully enough that the process with respect to him can be seen as fair; and suppose P_I renders a decision for Olive. We might think that Sam still has not given his actual consent to be bound by P_I, and thus that he still lacks a consent-based moral reason to adhere now to P_I's adverse decision. But the same balance of reasons, more or less, that imposed upon Sam a moral duty to submit to P_I *ex ante* is likely now to impose a moral duty to obey the decision of P_I *ex post*. (I say "more or less" because, as we have already seen, the decision P_I has now rendered against Sam might figure into his calculus regarding the overall accuracy of P_I. If that decision convinces him that P_I is not suitably accurate as a dispute-resolution mechanism, he may conclude he is under no duty to obey its results. On the other hand, refusing to obey P_I's decision once it has been rendered, after Olive (and perhaps others) have incurred the costs of participating in the process, might entail greater harm than declining to submit to P_I in the first place would have.)

The overall point here is this: The existence of a moral duty to submit a dispute for resolution by a suitably accurate procedure, and to abide by the result of that procedure, need not depend on actual consent; and thus such a duty might apply even to members of a community who have not, indeed could not have, given their actual consent to the procedure. Such a duty, of course, will be contingent on a number of relatively case-specific factors. Those factors include:

A. the costs of leaving a given dispute unresolved (including, importantly, not just costs that will be incurred by the disputants themselves, but also costs that will be incurred by third parties and the community as a whole);

B. the expected accuracy of the procedure to which the dispute would be submitted; and

C. the likelihood that other relevant members of the community (including but not necessarily limited to the opposing party in a given dispute) will make a similar moral calculus and perform their own moral duties to submit disputes to the procedure and abide by its results.

11. COORDINATION AND CONSTRUCTIVE CONSENT

I have touched on factor C only lightly so far, so let me elaborate a bit here. As our simple bipartite dispute involving Aaron and Betty shows, no disputant would rationally agree to submit a dispute to P_I if her opponent would not also be bound by the result; the risk that Aaron will be bound by a result he believes is wrong will be worthwhile to Aaron only if he knows Betty will be bound by a result he believes is right. To put this point in normative terms: Aaron cannot have a moral duty, grounded in dispute resolution, to submit to a procedure to which Betty will not submit. The purpose of submitting to a dispute-resolution procedure is to resolve a dispute, and if only one of two disputing parties submits to the procedure it cannot accomplish that purpose.

This point applies from an *ex post* perspective as well, as I suggested earlier in the chapter. Remember that absent actual *ex ante* consent, Aaron's primary moral reason to obey an adverse result of P_I is one of constructive consent: He *should* have consented to P_I *ex ante*, and thus he should now (*ex post*) behave as if he had done so. By the same token, if Aaron would have been under no moral duty *ex ante* to consent to P_I, then he cannot be under a moral duty *ex post* to act as if he had done so. And Aaron would not have been under a moral duty to consent to P_I *ex ante* if Betty would not have consented to P_I *ex ante*. From an *ex post* perspective, then, if Aaron honestly believes that Betty would not have consented to P_I *ex ante*, Aaron will conclude he is under no duty of constructive consent to obey P_I *ex post*.

The point can be extrapolated to a communal context, although the moral calculus implied by doing so becomes somewhat more complex. Consider again the position of Sam, the outsider in a community whose other members have unanimously consented to submit their disputes to P_I. In deciding whether to abide by the adverse decision of P_I in his dispute with Olive, Sam will have to determine whether Olive would have reciprocally agreed to abide by a decision of P_1 in Sam's favor. If Olive would not have consented to do so, then P_1's decision could not have resolved the dispute between Sam and Olive, and Sam himself would have been under no duty *ex ante*—and is now under no duty *ex post*—to submit to or obey P_1.

But note that Sam also will have to assess the attitudes of others in the community besides Olive. As I suggested above, defection from a community's standard dispute-resolution procedure is likely to bring greater costs than defection in the narrower context of a single bipartite dispute: The distrust and uncertainty a defection generates will be broader. In essence, a person who defects from a communal dispute-resolution procedure is leaving unresolved, indeed perhaps creating, a dispute with the community itself, or at least with those in the community likely to deal in the future with that person, in addition to the narrow bipartite dispute the process has attempted to resolve. A moral reason against Sam's defection in the social context, then, will be the avoidance of these broader social costs. But it is unlikely that Sam is under a moral duty to avoid these costs by submitting to P_1 if others in the community would not themselves submit to P_1. Just as Sam cannot be morally required to avoid the specific costs of his dispute with Olive by submitting to P_1 if Olive herself would not do so, he cannot be morally required to avoid the more general costs of his dispute with the community by submitting to P_1 if others in the community themselves would not do so.

Sam's duty to submit to, and obey the result of, P_1 therefore will turn in part on (his assessment of) the extent to which the results of P_1 are generally obeyed within the community. Once we move into the communal context, aspects of a coordination problem within the notion of legal authority thus become apparent. One aspect is the seeming complexity of the empirical judgment that anyone in Sam's position must make regarding the extent of general obedience to the results of P_1. Here we cannot expect fine-grained precision, even in a community as small and relatively simple as the hypothetical one in which I have imagined Sam (and especially under the conditions of a large, diverse modern legal system). The best we can do is observe that the rough degree of general obedience to law within a given community is likely to be readily apparent. In some communities, known instances of disobedience will be relatively rare, and a person in Sam's shoes will have a correspondingly weak reason to defect. In other communities disobedience will be salient and rampant, and a person like Sam will have correspondingly little reason to unilaterally obey when few others in the community are reciprocating. We are getting a bit ahead of ourselves here—catching a glimpse of an actual legal system through a crack in a door that will be opened more widely in the next two chapters. The important idea for present purposes is that Sam will feel himself under a stronger moral duty to obey the result of P_1 to the extent he observes general obedience within the community, and a weaker duty to the extent he observes widespread disobedience.

Another aspect of a coordination problem in Sam's situation will be the question whether the costs of his defection will be so marginal—such a small drop in such a large communal ocean—that the moral reason against his defecting (in the face, remember, of a result Sam believes is substantively incorrect) will be *de minimis*. Even assuming Sam observes widespread obedience within the community to the results of P_I—perhaps especially assuming this—what difference would his one defection make? I will suggest a more extensive response to this problem in Chapter 4, in the context of discussing the authority of legal rules (rather than, as here, ad hoc legal decisions). But we can see the beginnings of such a response by remembering that the avoidance of broad social costs is not the only, or even the strongest, moral reason for Sam to obey P_I. Another, perhaps even stronger, reason is to peacefully resolve Sam's instant dispute with Olive. And Sam's refusal to obey the result of P_I almost certainly would frustrate the resolution of that dispute, with all the attendant costs to Olive and Sam. The social costs that create potentially complex coordination problems, in other words, may be at best makeweights in the more direct moral calculus in which Sam must engage, a calculus whose primary factor may be the immediate and relatively obvious costs of leaving a particular dispute unresolved.

12. THE ENCROACHMENT FLAW REDUX?

Let me now briefly review my steps in assembling a basic model of dispute resolution in this chapter.

1. The potentially high costs of unresolved disputes may lead disputing parties to consider procedures for resolving them peacefully.
2. An acceptable procedure, P_I, would have to be seen by the disputants as reasonably accurate, although it will not be perfectly so. Reasonable accuracy includes reasonable competence and reasonable impartiality.
3. A disputant might have a moral duty to obey the result of P_I *ex post* even if he did not actually consent to it *ex ante*—if he *should* have consented to it *ex ante*, had he been given the opportunity to do so.
4. Whether a disputant should have consented to P_I *ex ante*, and therefore should obey its result *ex post*, will depend on three contingent factors:

   a. the costs of leaving the dispute unresolved (including any enhanced costs of defecting *ex post* from the decision of P_I);
   b. the degree of general accuracy of P_I (the assessment of which might be affected by the most recent decision of P_I but need not be affected decisively by it); and
   c. whether the disputant's opponent committed, or would have committed, to be bound by the result of P_I.

5. In a communal context, additional costs of distrust and uncertainty might flow from a person's refusal to obey the results of P_l, thus strengthening that person's moral reason to obey those results; but these communal costs will depend in part on the extent to which P_l is generally obeyed within the community.

The model sketched above connects the notion of a duty to obey an authoritative command with what I have called the procedural accuracy of the process generating that command—with the tendency of that process to produce correct decisions. In light of this connection, it is only natural to wonder whether the Encroachment Flaw that (as described in Chapter 2) taints EG accounts of legal authority also infects this dispute-resolution model, and thus the DR account of general legal authority I will try to build from it.

The Encroachment Flaw, remember, is the fact that legal subjects assessing the authority of legal commands will, on the EG account, use their substantive disagreement with a command as evidence against its supposed epistemic authority—that is, against its capacity to produce a correct decision in that case. Content-dependent reasoning thus infiltrates the supposedly content-independent concept of legal authority on the EG account. And the model I have described in this chapter might be thought to incorporate the same difficulty. In that model, a person's reasons for obeying a command (absent actual consent) prominently include an assessment that the procedure issuing the command is reasonably accurate; and that assessment might be affected negatively by the fact that the command is (in that person's judgment) substantively incorrect. Doesn't this make the supposedly content-independent authority of the command contingent on the content-dependent question of whether it is substantively correct—thus replicating the Encroachment Flaw?

The answer is: yes, but not fatally so. It is true that on the model of dispute resolution I have sketched here—and thus on the DR account of legal authority it predicates—the content-dependent question of a legal command's substantive correctness will, unavoidably, be relevant to the question of its authority. Even on the DR account (at least the version I am constructing), authority cannot be entirely isolated from the question of substance. I suggested in Chapter 2 that the DR account can avoid the Encroachment Flaw; and indeed it can in a bare Hobbesian form, as I will explain below. But as I also will explain, the Hobbesian version of the account that must be adopted to evade the Flaw will be so unpalatable to modern sensibilities—prioritizing, as it does, the imperative to resolve disputes over literally everything else—that the cure it offers will prove worse than the disease.

My version of the DR account, which turns in part on procedural accuracy, does then reintroduce the Encroachment Flaw. But, crucially, it does so using different conceptual mechanics than the EG account, and in the process it dilutes the Encroachment Flaw to a more-acceptable level of toxicity. Recall that on the EG account, the basis of a legal command's authority is its supposed capacity to instruct legal subjects about the right thing to do in any particular case. A legal subject's disagreement with the substance of a command in her case thus directly undermines the supposed basis of that command's authority in that case.

In contrast, in the version of the DR account that I am building, the basis of a legal command's authority is its supposed capacity to *resolve a dispute* about the right thing to do in a particular case. The capacity of a command to resolve a dispute—and thus its authority on the DR account—does not depend on whether that particular command is substantively correct; that, after all, is precisely what the dispute is about. The capacity of a command to resolve a dispute depends (in part) on whether the procedure that generated that command is, generally speaking, reasonably accurate—whether it is acceptably likely to issue substantively correct commands, given that it will not do so in every case. Disputants have reason *ex ante* to submit their disputes to a process, P_I, and thus to abide *ex post* by the results of P_I, so long as P_I is, in their lights, suitably accurate. In submitting *ex ante* to P_I, each disputant is accepting the risk that the result, in that case, will be incorrect; and so, in obeying the result of P_I *ex post*, a disputant's belief that the result is incorrect cannot, by itself, defeat P_I's authority. Only if that (apparently) incorrect result vitiates the disputant's belief in the general accuracy of P_I will the disputant reject the authority of P_I and its commands.

It is possible, of course, that a single (apparently) incorrect decision of P_I will, by a disputant's lights, be sufficient to disprove the general accuracy of the procedure. Keep in mind, however, that there will be other indicia of general accuracy available to the disputant: perhaps past decisions generated by P_I, and certainly procedural markers of accuracy like meaningful participation and fairness (or the lack thereof). And, importantly, remember that the underlying purpose of the procedure is to resolve an otherwise costly dispute. The higher the likely costs (including the broader communal costs) of leaving the dispute unresolved, the lower will be the standard of accuracy that the disputant can reasonably demand of the procedure.

On an EG account, then, law's authority in a given case depends entirely on its being right in that case; but on (my version of) a DR account, law's authority in a given case depends only in part—and (depending on the circumstances) perhaps in rather small part—on its being right in that case. The encroachment of substance on the question of law's authority therefore is proportionately smaller, and perhaps much smaller, on the DR account than on the EG account. A disputant—ultimately a legal subject—will have to weigh the (apparent) substantive incorrectness of a particular legal command against many other potential indicia of the accuracy of the procedure that generated that command, and also against the costs (including any broad social costs) of disobeying the command. The Encroachment Flaw exists on my version of the DR account, but it is likely to cause only a relatively small crack in the edifice, not (as on the EG account) a potentially fatal weakness in the foundation.

The Encroachment Flaw could be eliminated from the DR account by adopting a bare Hobbesian model of dispute resolution. If we assume, as Hobbes did, that the costs (including the social costs) of unresolved disputes override all else, then we will not need to worry about the acceptability of dispute-resolution procedures; all we will need is what Hobbes prescribed, namely an all-powerful absolutist ruler to impose its resolutions of disputes on the rest of society. The accuracy of the ruler's decisions will be irrelevant. And if accuracy is irrelevant, then the substance of any particular decision is irrelevant as well. All that matters, on the bare Hobbesian account, is that disputes be terminated before they do harm, and that goal can be achieved by substituting raw power for the mutual acceptability that might flow from procedural accuracy and its ingredients, competence and impartiality.

Thus the absolutist Hobbesian version of the DR account can avoid the Encroachment Flaw, because it can divorce legal authority entirely from the substance of legal commands. As I will describe in Chapter 4, however, John Locke exposed a different fatal flaw in the bare Hobbesian account. Locke pointed out that the patent partiality of absolutist rule is, over time, likely to provoke rebellion, accompanied by precisely that nasty, brutish chaos Hobbes sought to avoid. Locke's analysis suggests that in the circumstances of most real-world legal systems, raw power ultimately cannot substitute for accuracy in dispute resolution; it cannot really *resolve* disputes. Certainly Hobbesian absolutism is, to put it mildly, out of fashion today (which is not to say that it lacks practitioners— only that it lacks serious defenders). As I hope the discussion in the remainder of the book will illustrate, dispute-resolution procedures that are acceptable to those who will be bound by them—meaning procedures that are reasonably competent, reasonably impartial, and thus reasonably accurate—are the *sine qua non* of the American system of law and government (and of course of many other systems). Once accuracy becomes a factor in the calculus of legal authority, as I believe it must within our system, the Encroachment Flaw unavoidably follows in some measure. The key point, however, is that the extent of the Flaw is likely to be substantially more modest on (a palatable version of) the DR account than on (any version of) the EG account.

13. BUILDING FROM THE BASIC MODEL

The basic model outlined above illustrates the normative mechanics of the DR account in the context of ad hoc, bipartite dispute resolution. It suggests a plausible source of a disputant's duty to obey the resolution of a particular dispute with which he disagrees in substance. But a modern legal system consists of more, much more, than ad hoc resolutions of discrete bipartite disputes. It also consists, most notably, of *legal rules* and similar general norms designed to govern the resolution of many disputes or to avoid disputes altogether.

The next chapter applies the insights gleaned from the basic model to the phenomenon of legal rules. Chapters 5 and 6 then extend the account to the process of implementing general rules in particular cases—that is, to adjudication— and thus return to the phenomenon of case-by-case dispute resolution.

4. DISPUTES, LEGAL RULES, AND DEMOCRACY

1. MADISON'S INSIGHT

Aristotle's Challenge asks why a government official or other legal subject should think she has a moral duty to obey the law—to accede to its commands even when she disagrees with them in substance. I am building, in response to Aristotle, a Dispute-Resolution (DR) account of legal authority, which traces a duty to obey the law to the law's capacity to avoid or resolve costly disputes. In Chapter 3, I laid the foundation of that account by describing how parties to discrete disputes might have a moral duty to obey the results of a reasonably competent and impartial decision-procedure.

But law in the modern world does not consist solely of *ex post* resolutions of discrete disputes. Modern law includes a prominent place for what we can call, in shorthand, *legal rules*: norms that apply to many different disputes and even, typically, to the conduct of people who are not involved in particular disputes at all. Problems of legal authority thus often present, not the question of whether to accept the disappointing resolution of a discrete dispute offered by some arbiter, but rather the question of whether to act in accordance with some general rule that seems to prescribe an incorrect course of conduct. The hypothetical cases presented in Chapter 1—the Cases of the Sick Child, of the Unjust Statute, and of the Obstructionist Constitution—all posed the problem of legal authority in the context of general legal rules.

If the DR account is to become persuasive as a general account of legal authority, it must explain not only the authority of resolutions of discrete disputes, but also the authority of legal rules. Providing such an explanation is the central goal of this chapter.

A good place to begin is with an insight offered by James Madison in his classic essay *Federalist No. 10*. Madison compared legislation—the process of creating general legal rules—with adjudication—the process of resolving particular disputes:

> [W]hat are many of the most important acts of legislation, but so many judicial determinations, not indeed concerning the rights of single persons, but concerning the rights of large bodies of citizens? And what are the different classes of legislators but advocates and parties to the causes which they determine? Is a law proposed concerning private debts? It is a question to which the creditors are parties on one side and the debtors on the other.

Justice ought to hold the balance between them. Yet the parties are, and must be, themselves the judges . . .[1]

Madison's insight was that lawmaking, too, is a type of dispute resolution, and that legal rules thus can be understood as resolutions of disputes.[2] I begin

---

1. THE FEDERALIST No. 10, at 123, 124–25 (James Madison) (Isaac Kramnick ed., 1987) [hereinafter Madison, FEDERALIST No. 10].

2. In fact, what I've referred to as Madison's insight here owes much to Hobbes and Locke, both of whom similarly recognized that the need for authoritative legislation was inherent in the need for authoritative dispute resolution. Hobbes's Leviathan would have the inherent power, not just (or even primarily) to adjudicate controversies over how laws should apply to particular circumstances, but also to "Judge. . . the means of Peace and Defence" of the commonwealth, to "Judge of what Opinions and Doctrines are averse, and what conducing to Peace," and to "prescrib[e] the Rules, whereby every man may know, what Goods he may enjoy and what Actions he may doe, without being molested by any of his fellow Subjects." THOMAS HOBBES, LEVIATHAN part II, at 232–34 (C. B. Macpherson ed., 1968) (1651). In listing the "rights of sovereigns," Hobbes placed these legislative powers before "the Right of Judicature; that is to say, of hearing and deciding all Controversies, which may arise concerning Law. . . or concerning Fact." Id. part II, at 234. This suggests that for Hobbes, the sovereign's power to judge disputes over the content of general laws took precedence over its power to judge disputes over the application of those laws to particular controversies—certainly a logical progression.

Note that Hobbes chose the somewhat curious label "judge" to describe the sovereign's legislative powers. (James Madison later adopted this metaphor in equating statutes with "judicial determinations." See Madison, FEDERALIST No. 10, supra note 1, at 124.) This reflected Hobbes's view that disagreements in a prelegal state of nature would extend not only to the implications of the laws of nature, but to their content as well. The laws of nature were, for Hobbes, "dictates of Reason," but the human capacity for reason was famously and demonstrably fallible, and so people inevitably would disagree about the content of natural law. HOBBES, supra, part I, at 111, 216. The only way to resolve those disagreements peacefully was to "set up for right Reason, the Reason of some Arbitrator, or Judge"—the sovereign as legislator, who could decide what reason requires and embody those requirements into positive law. Id. part I, at 111.

Locke also recognized that the sovereign's authority to "judge" disputes about the content of standards of conduct came lexically prior to the authority to judge disputes about the application of those standards. "[I]n the state of Nature here are many things wanting," Locke wrote:

First, there wants an establish'd, settled, known Law, received and allowed by common consent to be the Standard of Right and Wrong, and the common measure of all Controversies. . . For though the Law of Nature be plain and intelligible. . . yet Men being biassed by their Interest, as well as ignorant for want of study of it, are not apt to allow of it as a Law binding to them in the application of it to their particular Cases.

JOHN LOCKE, Second Treatise of Government, in TWO TREATISES OF GOVERNMENT 305, § 124, at 396 (Peter Laslett ed., 1960) (1689–1690). Second, of course, was the lack of "a known and indifferent Judge, with Authority to determine all differences according to

this chapter by exploring two interconnected ways in which Madison's insight holds true.

Of course, if legal rules are ways of resolving disputes, then the process of creating legal rules—of legislation—is a type of dispute-resolution procedure; and as such, it must be reasonably accurate (reasonably competent and impartial) in order to claim authority on a DR account of law. The second half of this chapter articulates a case for viewing majoritarian democracy as a reasonably competent and impartial procedure for generating legal rules—that is, a DR justification of democracy. That analysis also sows the seeds of the DR defense of constitutional law I will mount in chapters 7 and 8.

2. LEGISLATION AS DISPUTE RESOLUTION

Madison suggested that legislation—the creation of general legal rules—is itself a kind of dispute resolution, and here I want to explore two interconnected ways in which this might be so.

A. Legal Rules as *Ex Post* Dispute Resolution

First, legal rules can help resolve discrete disputes by specifying, from an *ex post* perspective, the content of the general norms that apply to such disputes.[3]

To illustrate this point, recall from Chapter 3 our hypothetical dispute between Aaron and Betty over the location of the boundary fence between their lots. The dispute might include disagreements between Aaron and Betty about factual issues, such as how long the fence has been there and where the true survey line lies. But Aaron and Betty might also disagree about the general norms that should apply to their dispute. Aaron, for instance, might believe that property owners effectively waive claims against others for trespassing on their property if they fail to protest the alleged trespass in a timely fashion; Betty, for her part, might believe that property rights cannot be waived without an express declaration of intent to do so. If Aaron and Betty dispute the content of some substantive norm of conduct that is relevant to their dispute, then their overall disagreement cannot effectively be resolved without resolving that normative aspect of it as well.

---

established law"—that is, authority to apply general legislative rules to particular disputes. *Id.* § 125, at 396.

Hobbes and Locke thus understood that the function of peaceful dispute resolution must include the authoritative establishment of "settled, known" general rules of conduct, rules according to which particular disputes could be determined.

3. An excellent discussion of the *ex post* dispute-resolution function of legal rules appears in LARRY ALEXANDER & EMILY SHERWIN, THE RULE OF RULES: MORALITY, RULES, & THE DILEMMAS OF LAW (2001), in particular Part I.

Imagine, however, that Aaron and Betty now live in a society that includes legal rules that bind all its members. The existence of legal rules can avoid or mitigate these kinds of *ex post* disputes about the content of applicable norms. If, for example, their society's legislature has promulgated an authoritative statute, S, providing for the implied waiver of certain property rights under carefully defined circumstances, then Aaron and Betty's normative dispute might be made to disappear: All that will be left for them to fight about will be the particular facts of their case and the application of the general statute to those facts. These are potentially significant issues, to be sure, but at least the scope of their dispute will have been narrowed substantially by the existence of S. In essence, the presence of authoritative legislation governing the disputed normative issue will have preempted the purely normative part of their dispute, resolving it ahead of time by means of the legislative process rather than leaving it to be resolved *ex post* by an ad hoc decisionmaker, such as a court.

The first sense in which legislation is a form of dispute resolution, then, is an *ex post*, retrospective one: The existence of authoritative general legal rules can narrow the grounds for disagreement in particular cases, thus facilitating resolution of those specific disputes.

B. Legal Rules as *Ex Ante* Dispute Resolution

But of course legal rules typically do more than provide standards by which to assess the normative consequences of disputants' past behavior. Legal rules also (and often primarily) are prospective, providing standards to which people will attempt to conform their conduct in order to avoid creating disputes in the first place or, at least, to enhance their chances of winning future disputes if they arise.

So, for example, Charles, whose neighbor Deborah is building a garage that Charles believes might encroach on his property, will have good reasons to comply with the provisions of S in order to avoid waiving his own objections to Deborah's garage in a way that might prejudice him if a dispute arises. One such reason is that complying with S might prevent any dispute with Deborah from arising at all: Knowing that Charles has (say) expressly objected to the planned location of Deborah's garage in a way that will preserve his property rights under S, Deborah might decide to build her garage elsewhere and avoid what would be, for her, a losing legal fight. Another reason is that compliance with S will produce a favorable result for Charles should a dispute arise: If Deborah persists in building her garage too close to the property line, Charles's adherence to the requirements of S will mean that he can successfully sue Deborah to remove the garage.

In these ways, Charles's conduct might be shaped, going forward, by the requirements of the legal rule embodied in S. And note that S's effect on Charles's prospective conduct flows, not directly from a sense of being "bound" by S, but indirectly, from Charles's prediction of the consequences of his not following

S should a dispute later arise between him and Deborah. Charles's failure to comply with *S* might encourage Deborah to build her garage too close to the property line, and it might result in a ruling for Deborah if Charles sues her for doing so. In this sense the prospective "binding" character of legislation derives from its (anticipated) retrospective binding effect.

It is important to note that I am describing here ways in which legal rules can help avoid or mitigate disputes—*not* (necessarily) reasons why a legal subject, acting as a good-faith moral reasoner, might obey a legal rule with which he disagrees. Suppose, for example, that Charles thinks the requirements imposed by *S*—that property owners waive their objections to certain encroachments unless they state them expressly, at the proper time and in the proper form—are substantively bad requirements; he thinks, in other words, that *S* is a morally suboptimal rule. Acting as a good-faith moral reasoner, Charles still might have reason to obey *S*, namely that doing so will avoid a costly conflict with Deborah. But Charles also might be motivated to obey *S* out of concern solely for his own self-interest: He does not want Deborah to build her garage close to the property line, and if Deborah does so he wants to win the dispute that will arise when that occurs. This purely self-interested motivation would not embody any recognition of the *authority* of *S* in the sense in which I've been using the concept of authority in this book. (Remember I am assuming that, for purposes of justifying legal authority, legal subjects will act in good faith.) Charles, to the extent he is motivated by self-interest to follow *S*, would be acting as Oliver Wendell Holmes's "bad man," obeying the law not from a recognition of its legitimate authority over him—not from what H.L.A. Hart called an "internal point of view" about the law's moral force—but rather for purely strategic reasons having to do with his own advantage.[4]

My point for the moment, though, is not that *S* has legitimate authority over Charles, but rather that the existence, within a legal system, of legal rules like *S* can mitigate or avoid disputes by prospectively governing people's conduct. Some of that governance might flow from the recognition, by legal subjects such as Charles, of the legitimate authority of rules like *S*; some of it might flow from calculations of strategic self-interest. To the extent legal rules govern by triggering this Holmesian calculus, they are not governing *authoritatively* in the sense in which I mean that concept in this book (although they might well be governing effectively by other measures). I will explore further below the question of the *authority* of legal rules—of why a legal subject who, like Charles,

---

4. Holmes famously opined that law is best understood from the perspective of the "bad man," who concerns himself solely with "the prophecies of what the courts will do." Oliver Wendell Holmes, *The Path of the Law*, 10 Harv. L. Rev. 457, 460–61 (1897). Hart understood Holmes to be ignoring what Hart called the "internal aspect" of law: the sense in which those subject to law feel themselves morally bound to obey it. *See* H.L.A. Hart, The Concept of Law 57 (2d ed. 1994).

disagrees with their substance might nonetheless have good-faith moral reasons to obey them. For now it is enough simply to recognize how legal rules can work to motivate prospective conduct in a way that can avoid disputes.

(i) **Civil vs. Criminal Legislation** There are two complicating factors that I should mention briefly at this point. First, the examples given so far of how S might apply—to help resolve a dispute between Aaron and Betty, or to motivate Charles to act so as to avoid or win a potential dispute with Deborah— involve the role of statutes in what modern lawyers call *civil* cases, that is, disputes between private parties involving their rights and obligations to each other. Charles's conformance to S would be motivated by his desire either to avoid such a civil dispute with Deborah, or to obtain an advantageous resolution of such a dispute should it arise. But much legislation in the real world is *criminal* legislation—legal rules proscribing acts considered harmful to society as a whole and specifying punishment for committing those acts. (A statute, C, making it a misdemeanor to intentionally trespass on another's property, and imposing a fine for doing so, would be an example of a criminal statute.) It might seem as though criminal statutes are "directly" binding in a way that civil statutes are not. A person who violates the terms of a criminal statute, after all, can suffer the consequences regardless of whether any private dispute arises from that conduct.

In fact, however, the prospective binding force of a criminal statute also flows from the binding force it would possess *ex post* in a dispute; it's simply that the nature of the dispute in question is likely to differ from that of a purely civil dispute. Suppose, for instance, that Deborah builds her garage on part of Charles's property and the local sheriff cites Deborah for criminal trespass. Now the dispute in question is between Deborah and the community as a whole, not just between Deborah and Charles. The existence of a criminal statute, C, that authoritatively describes the normative standards applicable to Deborah's conduct can serve the same function that a statute like S can serve in a purely civil dispute: It can remove or mitigate one potential area of disagreement, thus helping to resolve the dispute. And the existence of C as a normative standard that will be applied, retrospectively, in a criminal dispute arising from Deborah's conduct also serves, like the existence of S, to motivate Deborah ahead of time to act consistently with C and thus to avoid the painful consequences of not having done so.

This is not to say that there are no important distinctions between the motivational force, or "bindingness," of criminal statutes and that of civil statutes. When a criminal statute like C proscribes and penalizes certain conduct, it declares that conduct to be antisocial—harmful to the community as a whole— and there might be a special moral stigma attached to such conduct. If so, a person like Deborah is likely to be motivated to avoid that conduct not only by a desire to avoid the consequences of losing a subsequent dispute, but also by a fear of social stigma. And criminal sanctions often (though not always) are more severe than the consequences of an unfavorable civil judgment; imprisonment, for example, is imposed only for criminal (not civil) liability in most modern legal systems. But these facts are ancillary to the main point here, which is simply that the prospectively binding nature of criminal legislation, like that of civil legislation, flows primarily from the desire to avoid a potential dispute and the consequences (official and otherwise) associated with that dispute.

(ii) **Legal Rules and** *Stare Decisis* The second complicating factor is that the prospective binding effect produced by statutes also might be produced by ad hoc acts of dispute resolution, such as adjudications in court. This will be true, however, only if there is some attempt within the system in question to maintain consistency in the resolution of disputes. Common-law systems of adjudication, like those of the United States and Great Britain, typically adhere to *stare decisis*—the principle that like cases should be decided alike, and thus that the decision of one case becomes a "precedent" that guides the decision of subsequent, relevantly similar cases. In such a system, a precedential decision can play the role of a statute in certain ways, serving as a retrospective standard by which to judge the parties' conduct in future similar disputes—and thus as a prospective standard to which parties, seeking to avoid disputes, will conform their conduct. In the next chapter, I will discuss at greater length some of the complexities that arise when the resolutions of specific disputes (such as a court decision) are used as the basis for binding legal rules.

(iii) **The Generality of Legal Rules** With these qualifications, we can see that legal rules typically operate not just retrospectively, to specify (and thus avoid or mitigate disagreements about) what substantive norms will apply in resolving a dispute; but also prospectively, to motivate a person to act in a way that conforms to the rule (and thus avoids a potential dispute or makes it likely that it will be resolved in that person's favor). Notice also that the typical *generality* of legal rules will result in their binding not just individual disputants and potential disputants, but entire classes of disputants and potential disputants. If S requires, say, that a property owner who believes a neighbor's structure has encroached on her land must object in writing within five years of the encroachment or waive any claim, then a potentially large class of property owners within the community will be bound, one way or another—prospectively or retrospectively— by that normative rule. S binds Aaron and Betty in the case of Aaron's fence, Charles and Deborah in the case of Deborah's garage, and probably a great many others—Emily and Fred in the case of Fred's patio, Ginger and Horace in the case of Horace's driveway, Isabel and Jack in the case of Isabel's tool shed, and so on.

(iv) **Legal Rules and Disputes about Prospective Conduct** This property of generality, combined with the prospectively binding quality of legislation, makes legislation a form of dispute resolution in an *ex ante* as well as an *ex post* sense. The contents of legislation typically will matter to a great many people, some of whom will become involved in disputes but many, perhaps most, of whom will try to conform their behavior to the legislation in order to avoid disputes. As Madison put it, acts of legislation are in essence "judicial determinations, not. . . concerning the rights of single persons, but concerning the rights of large bodies of citizens."[5] And of course people inevitably will disagree about the nature and content of the general binding norms that should be embodied in a given piece of legislation. Proponents of efficient land use might argue for a regime of statutory rules allowing the implied waiver of property rights (what American courts call "adverse possession" or "easement by estoppel") under certain conditions; advocates of strong property rights might disagree.

We should remind ourselves here that people need not be materially self-interested in these issues to disagree about them. For example, Kathy, who owns no real property, still might favor a regime of strong property rights on the ground that society is better off that way or that property rights are an important aspect of political morality. Kathy might hold her belief as a matter of ideological principle, as it were, despite the irrelevance of the issue to her own self-interest. (Remember once again our baseline assumption that legal subjects will act as good-faith moral reasoners.) The presence of disagreement about the content of prospective legal rules therefore is likely to be quite widespread, extending well beyond those members of a society who happen to have a material interest in an issue governed by a rule.

This phenomenon—disagreement within a society about the proper substantive content of prospective legal rules—poses the same danger as disagreement about the resolution of particular disputes, but on a larger scale. In a discrete dispute, the worry is that the loser will refuse to accept the proffered resolution and the dispute therefore will not be resolved. Likewise, when the members of a society disagree about the content of prospective legal rules, the risk is that a significant number of them will refuse to accept a rule they find substantively objectionable. Widespread social disobedience of legal rules would frustrate the goal of dispute resolution in two ways.

First, it would allow many otherwise avoidable disputes to occur, in circumstances where some members of society obey rules that others disobey, or where no one obeys a rule and there is nothing to take its place. Suppose Charles considers himself bound by S while Deborah does not. Charles's attribution of authority to S gives him a reason to obey it, but Deborah lacks that reason. Deborah therefore may decide to disobey the rule—by, e.g., building her garage over the property line despite Charles's legally proper objections—and a dispute might then result, one that would have been avoided had Deborah obeyed the rule. Or suppose neither Charles nor Deborah recognizes the authority of S. Unless there is some other relevant legal rule whose authority both recognize, Charles and Deborah will find themselves in a normative no-man's-land, devoid

---

5. Madison, FEDERALIST NO. 10, *supra* note 1, at 124–25.

of any standards that they can anticipate will be applied to their conduct in a dispute. Even if both parties want to avoid a dispute if they can, there is a significant risk they will find themselves in one, merely because one or both of them will have (unknowingly) acted in a way the other finds morally improper.

Second, widespread disobedience of legal rules would frustrate dispute resolution *ex post*, once disputes already have arisen, by allowing (indeed requiring) the disputants to fight about the norms applicable to their conduct. If Charles sues Deborah over the placement of her garage, and if neither recognizes the authority of S, then they will have to adjudicate not only the facts of the case and the application of the relevant legal rule to those facts, but also the content of the relevant legal rule itself. Their dispute will be that much more difficult and expensive to resolve.

And of course widespread disobedience of legal rules might have ramifications beyond the confines of particular disputes, as we got a sense of near the end of Chapter 3. Widespread disobedience means that no one in a society can act with much confidence that her conduct will not precipitate a dispute, or that she will prevail if a dispute arises. Such a society (if that term is appropriate) seems likely to devolve into a Hobbesian nightmare world of conflict and uncertainty, with "no place for Industry;. . . no Culture of the Earth; no Navigation; no commodious Building;. . . no Arts; no Letters," and the like.[6]

3. THE AUTHORITY OF LEGAL RULES

Legislation—the creation of generally binding, prospective legal rules—thus can be seen as a form, perhaps even a necessary component, of dispute resolution. But in order to successfully avoid or resolve disputes about the content of binding norms, a legislative process must solve the same problem that a process of discrete *ex post* adjudication of disputes must solve: It must give those who disagree with its results a strong moral reason nonetheless to obey them. Without such a reason, a legal rule will lack authority in the sense in which I mean that concept in this book. And if such a reason is lacking in a significant number of cases within a system, it will be difficult to see that system as possessing general legal authority.

We have already identified one likely source of a moral reason to obey even a substantively disagreeable legal rule. Obedience to a rule might avoid a costly dispute, by making it clear to the potential disputants what the result would be and thus removing any incentive actually to dispute the question. If Charles follows the procedures laid out in S to object to Deborah's encroaching garage, Deborah is (for that reason) less likely to persist in her encroachment, knowing

---

6. HOBBES, *supra* note 2, part I, at 186.

that to do so would be to precipitate a dispute she cannot win. This fact gives Charles, and for that matter Deborah, what is likely to be a fairly strong moral reason to follow *S*, even if one or both of them disagrees substantively with what *S* requires. That moral reason is the familiar Hobbesian dispute-avoidance impulse—the desire to avoid the moral harm of costly conflict.

But will this reason be sufficient to support a general duty to obey the law—that is, a general account of legal authority—in a typical modern legal system? The potential doubt in this regard takes the following form. Statutes and other legal rules sometimes (perhaps often) seem to apply in circumstances where obeying them would not help a legal subject avoid or resolve a potential dispute. If a legal subject's only moral reason to obey a disagreeable rule is the avoidance of a dispute, and no dispute would be avoided by obeying a rule in a particular case, then the subject can have no duty to obey in that case; the rule lacks authority over that subject. And if such cases are sufficiently numerous, then it becomes problematic (to say the least) to assert that the DR account justifies a general duty to obey the law.

To illustrate this potential difficulty, imagine a criminal statute, *C*, that prohibits trespassing on someone else's land. Suppose a legal subject, Larry, is considering riding his mountain bike on his neighbor Maureen's property without permission—a violation of *C*—and believes he can do so without being detected. If no one will ever know whether Larry has violated *C*, it is hard to see how obeying *C* could contribute to the resolution of any dispute. Larry's riding his bike on Maureen's property without Maureen's knowledge will not instigate some dispute with Maureen. Nor will Larry find himself in a dispute with the local authorities, or with the public at large, if no one ever finds out about his violation of the statute.

Does the absence of any apparent dispute, or of the threat of one, vitiate the moral duty to obey *C* that Larry otherwise might have? If so, then the capacity of a DR account to justify the general authority of legal rules would be in doubt, as it seems plausible that many cases similar to Larry's will arise within a large and complex legal system. Many violations of legal rules within such a system will go unnoticed, neither creating nor aggravating any actual disputes, public or private.

I do not believe the DR account actually is threatened by cases like Larry's, however. There are two reasons for this. The first is that cases like Larry's often will produce disputes after all, despite initial appearances, and thus often will in fact implicate the dispute-resolution justification of legal authority. Most obvious in this connection is the danger that Larry's prediction that he will not be caught violating *C* will turn out to be incorrect. If Larry in fact gets caught riding his bike on Maureen's land, two disputes are likely to materialize—one with Maureen, whose legal rights have been aggrieved, and one with the community as a whole, whose general prescription against trespassing has been violated. Larry's obedience to *C* would have avoided these disputes. And Larry, in deciding whether to violate *C*, should, morally speaking, have taken account not just of the likelihood that he would be caught, but also of the possibility that he might underestimate the likelihood of getting caught. It seems plausible that, in the real world, the circumstances in which a legal subject can be absolutely certain that he or she will not be caught violating a legal rule will be rather rare. If avoiding a dispute is a reason to obey a legal rule, as the DR account holds, then that reason—and the authority of the rule that it supports—remains in effect so long as a dispute is possible.

It is true that by this reasoning, the authority of a legal rule appears to vary in proportion to the risk that some dispute would arise or continue if the rule is violated (and also in proportion to the cost of that potential dispute). The lower the risk or the cost of a resulting dispute, the weaker the rule's authority in the case; the higher the risk or the cost of a dispute, the stronger the rule's authority. Far from being a weakness of the DR account, however, this phenomenon— a roughly direct relationship between the likely cost of a dispute and the force of a law's authority—seems to describe the real-world experience of law fairly accurately. Many (though far from all) circumstances in which disobedience to law seems most justifiable are those in which a costly dispute is unlikely to result. Consider the act of jaywalking on a deserted street, for example; or consider the common practice in the United States of exceeding the posted speed limit by up to ten miles per hour, which typically is tolerated by law enforcement, not because it goes unnoticed, but precisely because it has become so common that a tacit agreement to look the other way has arisen. Conversely, we are likely to insist upon strict enforcement of the law in those cases in which the costs of disobedience seem especially high. Recent high-profile instances of financial fraud—Enron, WorldCom, Bernard Madoff—have prompted harsh reactions from legal officials and public calls for more-stringent legal rules, in large part because of the chaos and devastation they (and similar conduct) frequently leave in their wake.[7]

So the existence of a rough correspondence between the duty to obey the law and the likelihood of dispute-related harm from disobedience need not threaten the descriptive accuracy or normative attractiveness of an account of

---

7. *See* Paul S. Miller, *Congress, Corporate Boards, and Oversight: A Public Law/Private Law Comparison*, 44 U. RICH. L. REV. 771, 789–90 (2010) (explaining the Sarbanes-Oxley Act as a reaction to the "willfully oblivious board [of directors]" in the cases of Enron and Worldcom); Roberta Romano, *Does the Sarbanes-Oxley Act Have a Future?*, 26 YALE J. ON REG. 229, 235 (2009) (describing WorldCom's filing of bankruptcy as "the culmination of a series of spectacular accounting scandals commencing with Enron's collapse"); Diana B. Henriques, *Madoff Is Sentenced to 150 Years for Ponzi Scheme*, N.Y. TIMES, June 29, 2009, http://www.nytimes.com/2009/06/30/business/30madoff.html?_r=1 (noting that Judge Denny Chin sentenced Madoff to a period three times longer than the recommendation of the federal probation office and described Madoff's crimes as "extraordinarily evil").

legal authority—at least not if the large majority of instances of disobedience will produce some harm, as seems likely to be true in modern legal cultures. There will be relatively few cases in the real world in which a legal subject like Larry can be so confident that his disobedience will not cause a dispute that he lacks a powerful dispute-resolution basis for obedience.

There also is a second reason—a less-contingent and thus, I think, a more-powerful one—why cases like Larry's do not threaten the DR account as a justification of general legal authority. Recall that the rule to which Larry arguably is subject, *C*, not only represents a prospective tool to avoid disputes about the consequences of people's behavior or to resolve those disputes if they arise; it also represents the settlement of an *ex ante* dispute about how people should behave going forward. A law against trespassing embodies (part of) a settlement of contested issues within the society regarding the importance of private property, its relationship to individual autonomy, and related questions. By trespassing in violation of *C*, Larry risks frustrating this *ex ante* settlement, even if there is little or no danger that he will instigate some additional, smaller-scale dispute by doing so.

Of what might this *ex ante* settlement consist? I will address that issue at some length in the next chapter; but for now let me suggest two complementary possibilities. First, the legislature that enacted *C* did so by means of a particular statutory text, and if Larry's trespassing violates a prohibition communicated by the statute's text, then it seems reasonable to conclude, at least presumptively, that Larry is violating the settlement embodied in the statute. By trespassing in contravention of the statutory language, Larry would be frustrating the settlement reached by the legislature, even if he is never caught doing so. And remember why Larry might be said to be bound by the *ex ante* settlement represented by *C*: If Larry should have consented to be bound by the legislative process that generated *C*, had he been given the opportunity to do so *ex ante*, then he has reason to act *ex post* as if he had so consented. If that reason exists, it exists quite apart from the desirability of avoiding any future disputes that might arise from Larry's disobedience to *C*.

Second, Larry's act of trespassing might contravene some purpose or justification that is reasonably attributable to *C*. Suppose, for example, that the best understanding of *C*'s justification holds that trespassing on the property of others is a serious moral wrong, even if no physical harm is caused and the property owner is unaware of the trespass. *C* might then be thought to embody a legislative settlement on the issue of whether trespass is morally wrong, and by trespassing on his neighbor's land in violation of *C*, Larry would be frustrating that settlement, even (again) if he is never caught doing so. Larry then would have a reason of constructive consent to obey the settlement *ex post*.

I hope to make both these suggestions about statutory meaning more concrete in the next chapter. For now, the point is that violating a legal rule (whatever that might mean) often will violate an *ex ante* settlement even if it does not generate an *ex post* dispute. Where this is so, legal subjects like Larry will have a moral reason to obey the rule, even if doing so will not avoid or mitigate some prospective dispute. That moral reason is simply that obedience to the rule risks contravening the *ex ante* settlement the rule represents. If Larry has (or would have had, given the opportunity) a moral duty to consent, *ex ante*, to be bound by *C* and other legal rules generated by the legislature, then he might also have a moral duty of constructive consent, *ex post*, to consider himself so bound. Disobeying *C* would violate Larry's moral duty to agree to, and subsequently to honor, the settlement embodied in that rule, even if disobedience would not create or aggravate any additional disputes going forward.

For these reasons, it is unlikely that the possibility of cases like Larry's poses a significant threat to the viability of the DR account as a general justification of the authority of legal rules. Legal subjects typically will have two types of strong moral reason to obey disagreeable rules: the potential to avoid some costly dispute in the future, and the duty to uphold the existing settlement embodied in the rule.

4. ACCEPTABLE LEGISLATION

So legislation—the promulgation of general rules—constitutes dispute resolution on two levels or, more precisely, from two different chronological perspectives. It avoids, and at least partially resolves, many disputes *ex post*, by specifying the standards against which people's behavior will be judged in those disputes. And it resolves disputes *ex ante*, by settling disagreements about how people should behave going forward.

If legislation is a type of dispute resolution, then its legitimacy on the DR account—that is, its capacity to generate legal authority—depends on its capacity actually to resolve, avoid, or mitigate disputes. As we have seen, the concept of authority means that a legal subject who disagrees with the substance of a statute or other legal rule must recognize strong moral reasons—amounting to a *prima facie* moral duty—nonetheless to obey that rule. How might such reasons be generated in the context of general, prospective rules rather than *ex post* decisions of discrete disputes?

As in the context of discrete disputes, those who disagree with the content of legal rules typically will have a bare Hobbesian reason to obey those rules, namely that doing so will avoid or resolve a potentially costly dispute. But, as in the context of discrete disputes, this bare Hobbesian reason seems inapt as a justification of legislative authority; for it could justify the authority of *any* form of legislation, whatever its source.

Consider in this regard John Locke's critique of Thomas Hobbes in his *Second Treatise of Government*. Locke pointed out that Hobbes's absolutist model of law and government ultimately was likely to fail at the overriding task of dispute resolution that supposedly justified it. Hobbes thought absolutist government—"a common Power to keep [the people] in awe"[8]—was necessary to avoid violent private conflict; but Locke noted that a Hobbesian absolute monarch would frequently find himself in conflict with his subjects. Because the monarch, who would hold all the power, would act as a self-judge in such conflicts—inevitably resolving them in his own favor and implementing those resolutions by force—his subjects would be unlikely to accept his decrees; eventually they would revolt, plunging the society into precisely the general chaos that Hobbes sought to avoid.[9]

---

8. HOBBES, *supra* note 2, part I, at 185.

9. Locke pointed out that the "inconveniencies of the State of Nature" so well cata-logued by Hobbes "necessarily follow from every Man's being Judge in his own Case" in that condition—from every individual's possession of the "Power, not only to preserve his Property, that is, his Life, Liberty, and Estate, against the Injuries and Attempts of other Men; but to judge of, and punish the breaches of [the] Law [of nature] in others, as he is perswaded the Offence deserves." LOCKE, *supra* note 2, §§ 87, 90, at 367–69. The problem was that such a power, thanks to the human failings of "Self-love. . . ll Nature, Passion, and Revenge," was of course subject to abuse; individuals in the state of nature inevitably would use their freedom to invade each other's property, putting themselves in a "State of War" with one another. *See id.* §§ 13, 16–20, at 316, 319–22. The establishment of govern-ment and law was the solution to these "inconveniencies," for government and law con-stitute a common authority to which every member of society is subject—"a Judge on Earth, with Authority to determine all the Controversies, and redress the Injuries, that may happen to any Member of the *Commonwealth*." *Id.* § 90, at 369; *see generally id.* §§ 21, 87–90, 95, at 323, 367–69, 374–75.

To this point Locke's justification of legal authority closely resembles Hobbes's: Both locate legitimate legal authority in the function of dispute resolution. But Locke noted that a Hobbesian absolute monarch was *himself* a judge in his own case—and an extremely powerful self-judge at that, one who happened to "command[] a multitude. . . and may do to all his Subjects whatever he pleases, without the least liberty in any one to question or controle those who Execute his Pleasure." *Id.* § 13, at 316–17. Absolutist government, that is, simply replicated the inconveniences of the state of nature on a grander, much more dangerous scale, putting the absolute monarch effectively into a state of war with his subjects. *See id.* §§ 90–94, at 369–74. As such, absolutism was "*inconsistent with Civil Society*"—inconsistent with the very point of establishing legal authority. *Id.* § 90, at 369 (Locke's own emphasis here). A *de facto* state of war between the sovereign and his subjects was inherently unstable, leading inexorably to a "long train of Abuses" by the monarch that would in turn generate rebellion and civil war, which was precisely what the institution of law and government was supposed to avoid. *Id.* § 225, at 463. (Thomas Jefferson later cribbed the phrase "long train of abuses" in the Declaration of Independence from Locke, along with the underlying idea of a right to rebel against an arbitrary sovereign.)

Simply put, Locke recognized that absolutist government typically would fail at the central task of government and law, namely the peaceful resolution or avoidance of conflict. Absolutism is a form of self-judging; and on a Dispute-Resolution account of legal authority, one has little reason to obey the commands of a self-judge, just as on an

As Locke's rejoinder to Hobbes suggests, legal rules, in order to resolve disputes about what ought to be done going forward (and thus to contribute to resolutions of disputes about the consequences of past conduct), must be generated by a process that is acceptable even to the losing parties, just as adjudications of discrete conflicts must be. By mechanisms I outlined in Chapter 3, a person has an additional reason—over and above the bare Hobbesian impulse—to obey a resolution produced by an acceptable process. This is a reason of constructive consent: That person would have had a moral reason to consent to the process *ex ante*, had she had the opportunity to do so, and so now she has reason *ex post* to behave as if she had so consented.

I argued in Chapter 3 that an acceptable dispute-resolution procedure—one capable of giving rise to a strong moral reason, perhaps a duty, to consent *ex ante* and to acknowledge constructive consent *ex post*—must be reasonably accurate under the circumstances, meaning it must be both reasonably competent and reasonably impartial. And the same holds true with respect to an acceptable legislative procedure—that is, a procedure for resolving disputes about the content of generally binding, prospective legal rules. Members of a society who seek in good faith to do what morality requires—to develop and adhere to morally desirable rules—will have reason to submit their disagreements about what those rules should be to a process that is reasonably competent and impartial, for such a process will be likely to generate morally good rules more often than not. And thus members of the society can be said to have constructively consented to abide by the results of such a process, even if they disagree with the substance of those results.

In fact, we can understand Locke's critique of Hobbesian absolutism as in essence an objection to its lack of impartiality. "[I]t is unreasonable for Men to be Judges in their own Cases," Locke wrote, because "Self-love will make Men partial to themselves and their Friends"; self-judging is the ultimate form of partiality. But "Absolute Monarchs are but Men"—susceptible to the inevitable partiality of self-love—and an absolute monarch "has the Liberty to be Judge in his own Case, and may do to all his Subjects whatever he pleases." Absolutism is unacceptable as a dispute-resolution procedure because it is inherently and severely partial.[10]

Epistemic-Guidance account one has little reason to obey commands one strongly believes to be wrong. The "self-love" and "ill nature" of an absolute monarch necessarily corrupt his commands, tilting them toward his own interests and away from those of the political community he is supposed to serve—and ushering in Harrington's "empire of men, and not of laws." *See* JAMES HARRINGTON, THE OCEANA AND OTHER WORKS 144–45 (John Toland ed., 1771) (1656), *available at* http://oll.libertyfund.org/EBooks/Harrington_0050.pdf.

10. *See* LOCKE, *supra* note 2, § 13, at 316–17 (emphasis altered). As usual, Aristotle made essentially the same point much earlier: "[J]ustice exists only between men whose

Like a process for resolving discrete disputes, a process for creating legal rules (viewed from the perspective of a DR account) must be, and must be seen by a significant majority of the society to be, reasonably competent and reasonably impartial. Absolutist government fails on at least the latter ground; but a system of procedures commonly labeled *democracy* will show considerably more promise on both fronts.

5. WHAT IS "DEMOCRACY"?

The term "democracy," like "freedom," "the rule of law," and many other terms common in political discourse, can be and often is used to mean many very different things. This is not just because people typically are confused about what "democracy" is or use the term in bad faith (although both these phenomena no doubt occur with some frequency). It is also the product of two related facts.

First, democracy is a concept that includes many reasonable conceptions which often diverge greatly from or even contradict each other. The American Founders, for instance, sometimes referred to the system of representative government they were creating as "democratic,"[11] while at other times they reserved the term "democracy" for a system of lawmaking by direct popular vote.[12]

Second, even within a single conception of democracy, various democratic values might find themselves in tension with one another. Americans often speak of both free speech and majority rule as core "democratic" values, for example, despite the fact that the two sometimes prove incompatible.

In referring to democracy, democratic government, and related concepts throughout the remainder of this book, I will assume the following working definition: *Democracy* is *a system of government in which ultimate decisionmaking authority resides in the body of competent adult citizens, which typically exercises that authority through regular elections and by simple majority vote.* This working definition incorporates three central features that figure prominently in most

---

mutual relations are governed by law. . . . This is why we do not allow a man to rule, but rational principle, because a man behaves thus in his own interests and becomes a tyrant." ARISTOTLE, *Nicomachean Ethics, in* THE BASIC WORKS OF ARISTOTLE 935, book V, at 1013 (W. D. Ross trans., Richard McKeon ed. 1941).

11. *See, e.g.,* THE FEDERALIST No. 58, at 351 (James Madison) (Isaac Kramnick ed., 1987) (distinguishing generally "democratic" systems of government from generally "oligarchic" ones).

12. Madison, FEDERALIST No. 10, *supra* note 1, at 126 (defining democracy as "a society consisting of a small number of citizens, who assemble and administer the government in person"); THE FEDERALIST No. 14, at 140, 141 (James Madison) (Isaac Kramnick ed., 1987) ("[I]n a democracy the people meet and exercise the government in person; in a republic they assemble and administer it by their representatives and agents.").

mainstream conceptions of democracy, both historical and contemporary. The first is *broad participation* (or, if you prefer, *populism*), meaning that the decision-making body possessing ultimate authority within the relevant political community consists of all competent adult citizens of the community. The second is *regular voting*, meaning that the body of citizens exercises its authority with reasonable frequency and regularity in the form of elections of government officials or other popular votes (e.g., referenda). The third is *majority rule*, or *majoritarianism*, meaning that decisions by the relevant body typically are made by simple majority vote.

My working definition leans toward the general, as I want my discussion of democracy to turn as little as possible on contested particular features of democratic systems. For example, I do not want anything in my arguments to depend on how one resolves relatively fine-grained questions such as unicameral versus bicameral legislatures, presidential versus parliamentary systems, federalist versus unitary structures, and the like. (I will focus to some extent on particularistic features of the American system of government in discussing constitutionalism and judicial review in chapters 7 and 8. But my analysis of democratic government in this and the next two chapters will stick to relative generalities.) Even given the abstractness of my definition, there will be room for debate about the meaning of some of its core terms: about what constitutes "ultimate" decisionmaking authority, who qualifies as a "competent adult citizen," what amounts to a system of "regular" elections, and what type and frequency of departures from majority rule are enough to vitiate its "typicality." Suffice it to say that I mean the definition to be quite capacious indeed and to encompass at least those contemporary systems of government widely recognized as democratic, including those in the United States, Great Britain and most of the Commonwealth countries, Japan, and the nations of Western Europe.

6. DEMOCRACY AS A REASONABLY ACCURATE PROCEDURE

I will argue here that democracy, particularly in comparison with minoritarian forms of government like autocracy and oligarchy—in comparison, that is, with "all those other forms [of government] that have been tried from time to time," as Winston Churchill famously quipped[13]—is a reasonably accurate means of resolving prospective disputes about the content of legal rules. Democracy is relatively impartial, chiefly by virtue of the short-term atomization of decisionmaking typically accomplished by majority rule and the long-term

---

13. "Democracy is the worst form of government, except for all those other forms that have been tried from time to time." Winston Churchill, Speech to the House of Commons (Nov. 11, 1947).

laundering of partiality typically achieved by regular elections. And it is relatively competent, thanks primarily to the diversity and deliberation of its broad populism and the trial-and-error nature of its periodic power shifts.

Of course, even democracy perfectly executed—a fantasy in the real world—will not be perfectly impartial or competent. As I will suggest below, democracy is best understood as a primarily negative ideal—as a means of avoiding the salient indicia of partiality and incompetence inherent in nondemocratic forms of governance. But when democracy functions reasonably well—a significant caveat, as I will discuss at length in Chapter 7—it can claim sufficient systemic accuracy to imbue the legal rules it generates with general authority. Or so I will contend in what follows.

A. Democracy and Impartiality

Democracy's most salient advantage over other types of government is its relative impartiality. The principal engine of that impartiality is majority rule: Important decisions are made by giving each citizen a single equally weighted vote, with the option that receives a majority of the votes (or sometimes, in cases with more than two options, a plurality of the votes) being declared the winner. Majority rule often is credited as an almost miraculously fair system for resolving disagreements. Jeremy Waldron, for example, writes that majority rule, "[b]etter than any other rule,. . . is neutral as between the contested outcomes, treats participants equally, and gives each expressed opinion the greatest weight possible compatible with giving equal weight to all opinions."[14]

We need to be a bit wary of taking such pronouncements at face value, however. Majority rule is "neutral as between the contested outcomes" only in the rather trivial sense that it generates results based not on some inherent preference for one substantive outcome over another, but rather on an inherent preference for whichever outcome passes a certain procedural test, namely earning the most votes. For instance, suppose a small group—say, a jury—votes by majority rule to find a defendant liable to a plaintiff. There is nothing innate in majority rule that prefers a finding of liability to a finding of no liability; the verdict of liability has won, not because majority rule inherently favors the substantive outcome of liability over the substantive outcome of no liability, but simply because the substantive outcome of liability happens, in this instance, to have earned the most votes.

This is a relatively trivial sort of neutrality, though, because it is one that any reasonable decision-procedure will possess. Suppose the rule in the applicable jurisdiction is that verdicts in civil cases must be unanimous. This procedure—a form of minority rule, as it gives disproportionate power to a small number of

---

14. Jeremy Waldron, *The Core of the Case Against Judicial Review*, 115 Yale L.J. 1346, 1388 (2006).

holdouts—also is "neutral as between the contested outcomes" in the sense that it does not incorporate some inherent preference for one verdict over the other. Only a procedure that expressly incorporates a preference for a particular substantive option—"Always find the defendant liable"—lacks neutrality in this sense; but such a rule would hardly be worthy of the label "procedure."

Majority rule *is* neutral as between the *participants* in a procedure: Unlike autocracy and other forms of minority rule, majority rule avoids giving any single participant a greater likelihood of achieving her preferred outcome than any other participant enjoys. Of course, this version of neutrality is simply another way of expressing the point that majority rule "treats participants equally," which itself is a way of stating that majority rule "gives each [individual's participation] the greatest weight possible compatible with giving equal weight to all [individuals' participation]."

The brief for majority rule thus essentially comes down to the point that it does not inherently favor any individual participant in the decision-procedure over any other individual participant. How does this property relate to the concept of impartiality as I elucidated it in Chapter 3?

(i) Impartiality and Majority Rule An impartial procedure, remember, is one in which factors extrinsic to the merits of a dispute have no tendency to favor one side of the dispute over another. This turns out not to be quite the same thing as neutrality in the sense apparently meant by Waldron. Majority rule does not favor any individual voter over any other; but it might allow factors extrinsic to the merits of a dispute to favor one position in that dispute over another.

Suppose, for example, that one member of a jury, Naomi, votes for a verdict of liability based not on her assessment of the merits of the case, but simply because the defendant is a hospital and she has a deep personal aversion to hospitals. And suppose the jury opts for liability by a vote of seven to five. The outcome of the majority-rule procedure (a verdict of liability) has been determined in part by a factor extrinsic to the merits of the dispute (Naomi's personal aversion to hospitals). The procedure thus has been a partial one in the sense in which I mean that concept here: A factor extrinsic to the merits has favored one side over the other.

Majority rule cannot magically eliminate the possibility of such partiality. In fact it surely is commonplace for democratic citizens to vote partially—based on clearly irrelevant factors (a candidate's physical attractiveness), factors of mere self-interest, or other considerations extrinsic to the merits. (Partial voting will occur even among people acting in good faith: A voter might act partially without intending it or even realizing it.)[15] The advantage of majority rule, then,

---

15. Note, however, that we need not indulge an assumption that democratic citizens, acting in their capacity as *voters*, will be good-faith moral reasoners. The baseline premise of good faith I articulated in Chapter 1 applies to people (including democratic citizens)

cannot be its (nonexistent) capacity to eliminate partiality altogether from the process of legislation.

The great advantage of majority rule, rather, is its capacity to limit the scope of partiality in comparison to the minority-rule alternatives. Rather than concentrate all of a group's decisionmaking authority in a single individual or small subset of the group, majority rule atomizes that authority, dividing it into a number of equally weighted individual votes and distributing it evenly across the entire group. As a result, the partiality of any particular member of the group is relatively unlikely to determine the outcome. Naomi the juror's aversion to hospitals cannot, by itself, decide the question of the defendant's liability in her case; her vote will be ineffective unless it is combined with enough other votes for liability to comprise a majority. Each of those other votes might be impartial, or might be partial but in a different way. One or more votes on the opposite side, moreover, might themselves be partial, in effect canceling out Naomi's partial vote. No single juror's partiality alone can resolve the issue.

And as the size of the body deciding by majority rule grows larger, of course, the effect of any single partial vote becomes proportionately smaller. Of the roughly 130 million Americans who voted in the 2008 presidential election, surely many of them voted in a partial manner; but any given partial vote had a negligible influence on the outcome. Probably most partial votes were countered by equally partial votes for another candidate; and every partial vote was a tiny drop in a huge bucket, swamped by a tide of millions of votes, some partial, some impartial, many partial in different ways. In this respect, the broad participation characteristic of democratic government combines with majority rule to reduce the (inevitable) instances of individual partiality to proportional insignificance.

Compare democracy in this regard to an autocratic system, in which the decision of one individual member of the group is conclusive by itself. If the

---

acting as *legal subjects*, that is, as moral agents who must decide whether to obey a law or other legal command directed at them. In voting on what the content of the law should be, however—either directly or (more often) indirectly, through the selection of legislators— citizens are acting, not as *subjects* of the law, but as *authors* of the law. They are deciding, not whether to submit to authority, but how to exercise it. The same is true more obviously of democratic legislators when they cast votes in the legislature. My assumption of good-faith moral reasoning is meant to apply to legal subjects deciding how to act in light of some legal command; as I explained in Chapter 1, the point of the assumption is to support a case for why people in this position *should*, morally speaking, obey the law. We cannot, however, indulge a similar assumption of good faith on the part of those purporting to exercise legal authority (including citizens acting in their capacity as voters). As I will suggest in Chapter 7, the duty of legal subjects to obey the law—that is, the authority of the law—may depend in part on whether those claiming authority are *in fact* acting in good faith. To assume that they are therefore would beg a central question about legal authority.

autocrat acts based on extrinsic factors—bias, self-interest, general irrationality—then those factors inevitably will determine the outcome of the decision. The same holds true in lesser degrees for less-extreme versions of minority rule. An oligarchy, in which a small minority has the power to decide a question, gives disproportionate effect to the partiality of any member of that minority; one partial vote will matter more, perhaps much more, than it would if the same body utilized majority rule.

And there is a related danger of autocracy and oligarchy. It's not just that an individual's partiality matters more in those minoritarian systems; it's also that the relevant individuals are more likely to share in a given type of partiality. This occurs by definition in an autocracy: The autocrat's decision is the only one that matters, and if he is partial in a certain way (say, because of self-interest), then that particular partiality by definition determines the outcome. It may well occur in an oligarchy as well: An oligarchy seems especially susceptible to the danger that all or most of its (relatively small) controlling group will be subject to the same sources of partial decisionmaking. Consider the existence for many years of rule by a white minority in South Africa; it seems likely that many of that minority were united in their bias against their black countrymen or in their self-interested desire to preserve power (or both). A group of oligarchs is disproportionately likely to constitute what James Madison referred to as a "faction"—"a number of citizens. . . united and actuated by some common impulse of passion, or of interest."[16] If a group of oligarchs becomes a faction in this sense, then its partiality is functionally indistinguishable from that of an autocracy: It speaks with a single, partial voice, and the resulting decisions inevitably will be partial ones.

As Madison recognized, the likelihood of a majority faction—a majority united by partiality—is lower than that of a minority faction, simply by the law of numbers. (This property was the basis for Madison's argument for a large republic in *Federalist No. 10*.[17]) In Chapter 7, I will suggest that democratic majorities can indeed become factions, and that when this happens the typical atomizing function of majority rule, and with it its relative impartiality, is lost. The happier point for now, however, is that majority rule forms a more effective hedge against partiality than nonmajoritarian forms of governance. It is this property—not some fantastic capacity to eliminate partiality altogether—that sets majority rule apart from the minoritarian alternatives.

---

16. Madison, FEDERALIST NO. 10, *supra* note 1, at 123.

17. *See id.* at 127–28. The argument is reiterated in *Federalist No. 51*, which probably, but not certainly, was authored by James Madison. *See* THE FEDERALIST No. 51, *supra* note 11, at 321–22 (attributing authorship to James Madison); *see also* DAVID F. EPSTEIN, THE POLITICAL THEORY OF THE FEDERALIST 136 (1984) (attributing authorship of *The Federalist No. 51* to James Madison).

(ii) Impartiality and Regular Elections Even with majority rule in place, it is conceivable that partiality sometimes might play an unacceptably large role in democracy—for example, if a majority acts as a faction on a particular issue. But democracy can temper the effects of partiality in another way: By allowing majorities to be replaced, and policies changed, through regular election cycles, democracy can in effect launder partiality, rendering itself reasonably impartial over the long run.

Consider Madison's still-timely example, in *Federalist No. 10*, of a proposed "law. . . concerning private debts," with respect to which "the creditors are parties on one side and the debtors on the other."[18] Suppose creditors, riding a wave of anger against supposedly irresponsible debtors, carry the day during one election cycle, succeeding in seating a majority of creditor-friendly representatives in the legislature and thus in enacting procreditor bankruptcy and consumer-credit laws. Even if this result is tainted by partiality—even if some crucial percentage, perhaps even a majority, of the electorate was driven by some irrational or self-interested procreditor or antidebtor bias—the resulting damage, under the circumstances of well-functioning democracy, remains reparable. If the consequences of the legislature's procreditor laws come to be widely disfavored, the next election cycle might feature a wave of prodebtor sentiment, resulting in the replacement of enough procreditor legislators to repeal or amend the unpopular laws. On the other hand, if the procreditor laws work well and remain popular, they may be retained at the next election cycle, and the next, despite the tainted circumstances of their origin. In this way well-functioning democracy, by means of regular elections, can work itself pure; just as the scope of a single voter's partiality is limited by majority rule, the impact of a given partial result can be diluted by a sequence of results over time.

There are democratic hazards that can threaten this partiality-cleansing mechanism too. Suppose a majority faction, animated by some dominant self-interest or bias, decides to disrupt the normal cycling of democracy and succeeds in doing so—by, for example, enacting laws that punish opposition to its policies and thus reduce the likelihood that the majority will be replaced in a subsequent election. Such artificial entrenchment of majority power is another of the possible democratic breakdowns that I will canvass in Chapter 7. When it avoids these perils, however, democracy, through regular elections, can cabin the effects of partial outcomes over time, just as it can limit the impact of partial voting on any given outcome.

B. Democracy and Competence

Democracy is committed not just to majority rule, but to majority rule among a broad spectrum of participants. From the perspective of impartiality, a system of

---

18. Madison, FEDERALIST No. 10, *supra* note 1, at 125.

majority rule among a small, privileged segment of society, with many or most of those who will be bound by its decisions left out of the process, is scarcely better than autocracy: Extrinsic factors are likely to have a disproportionate influence on outcomes. Impartiality thus counsels in favor of broadening the relevant decisionmaking body as well as instituting evenhanded decision-procedures within that body.

It seems likely that decisionmaking competence also generally is enhanced by broad participation, although here there are many questions and caveats. Consider three prominent kinds of argument linking broad participation to competence.

(i) Broad Participation and Diversity Generally speaking, the more broadly decisionmaking authority is distributed, the greater the number and variety of viewpoints and interests that will influence the outcome. Democratic theorists often argue that incorporating diversity into decisionmaking in this way tends to improve the quality of the resulting decisions. Here there are three main subsidiary points.

First, broad-based decisionmaking increases the likelihood that some of the decisionmakers will have relevant first-hand experience. This was an important part of John Stuart Mill's case for extending the franchise to the working class in nineteenth-century England:

> [Under the existing system, does] Parliament, or almost any of the members composing it, ever for an instant look at any question with the eyes of a working man? When a subject arises in which the labourers as such have an interest, is it regarded from any point of view but that of the employers of labour? I do not say that the working men's view of these questions is in general nearer to the truth than the other: but it is sometimes quite as near . . . On the question of strikes, for instance, . . . in how different, and how infinitely less superficial a manner the point would have to be argued, if the classes who strike were able to make themselves heard in Parliament.[19]

John Dewey later echoed Mill's sentiment when he defended democracy on the ground that "[t]he man who wears the shoe knows best that it pinches and where it pinches."[20]

Second, broadly participatory government allows decisionmakers to look after their own interests, something they are likely to be highly motivated to

---

19. JOHN STUART MILL, CONSIDERATIONS ON REPRESENTATIVE GOVERNMENT (1861), *reprinted in* JOHN STUART MILL, UTILITARIANISM, ON LIBERTY, AND CONSIDERATIONS ON REPRESENTATIVE GOVERNMENT 187, 225–26 (H. B. Acton ed., 1972).

20. JOHN DEWEY, *The Public and Its Problems, in* 2 JOHN DEWEY: THE LATER WORKS 1925–1953, 235, 364 (Jo Ann Boydston ed., 1984) (1927).

do well.[21] Not only do laborers know what it is like to strike, but they have strong personal and pecuniary interests in protecting the right to strike; if they are allowed to participate in government, the case for a right to strike therefore will be articulated as forcefully and persuasively as possible. Herbert Spencer (ironically, no friend of the right to strike) put it this way:

> Manifestly, on the average of cases, a man will protect his own interests more solicitously than others will protect them for him. Manifestly, where regulations have to be made affecting the interests of several men, they are most likely to be equitably made when all those concerned are present, and have equal shares in the making of them.[22]

Third, broadening participation, all else being equal, increases the chance that talented decisionmakers—the virtuous (in Aristotle's terms) and the enlightened (in James Madison's)—will use their talents to improve the quality of the resulting decisions. Consider Thomas Jefferson's response to John Adams's belief in "a natural aristocracy among mankind":

> [I] agree with you that there is a natural aristocracy among men. The grounds of this are virtue and talents. . . . There is also an artificial aristocracy founded on wealth and birth, without either virtue or talents . . . . The natural aristocracy I consider as the most precious gift of nature for the instruction, the trusts, and government of society. . . . May we not even say that that form of government is the best which provides the most effectually for a pure selection of these natural aristoi into the offices of government? The artificial aristocracy is a mischievous ingredient in government, and provision should be made to prevent its ascendency. . . . I think the best remedy is exactly that provided by all our constitutions, to leave to the citizens the free election and separation of the aristoi from the pseudo-aristoi, of the wheat from the chaff. In general they will elect the real good and wise.[23]

Jefferson's point is not simply the limited (and highly debatable) one that democratic elections are likely to produce good political leaders. His assertion is more general: that democracy, by broadly and evenly distributing political power, removes the arbitrary barriers to governing authority that protect the

---

21. Remember that accounting for the possibility of—even assuming the likelihood of—self-interest as a motivation for democratic citizens as *voters* does not vitiate our standing assumption that individual *subjects* of the law will act as good-faith moral reasoners in deciding whether to obey it. *See supra* note 15.

22. HERBERT SPENCER, *Representative Government—What Is It Good For?*, in THE MAN VERSUS THE STATE 331, 375 (1981) (1892).

23. *Letter from Thomas Jefferson to John Adams* (Oct. 28, 1813), in THE PORTABLE THOMAS JEFFERSON 533, 534–35 (Merrill D. Peterson ed., 1975). For a description of Adams's belief in (and wariness of) a "natural aristocracy," see DAVID McCULLOUGH, JOHN ADAMS 377–78 (2001).

artificial aristocracy. The accidents of wealth and birth do not ensure the possession of virtue or talent, that is, of governing competence. Jefferson suggests that democracy, by making those accidents formally irrelevant to the wielding of political power, enhances the likelihood that governance will be carried out by those truly competent to perform it.

(ii) Broad Participation and Deliberation It may not be simply the diversity of viewpoints and interests that enhances decisionmaking in a democracy, but also the way those viewpoints and interests interact with and react to each other. Madison famously argued to this effect in *Federalist No. 10*:

> The smaller the society, the fewer probably will be the distinct parties and interests composing it; the fewer the distinct parties and interests, the more frequently will a majority be found of the same party; and the smaller the number of individuals composing a majority, and the smaller the compass within which they are placed, the more easily will they concert and execute their plans of oppression. Extend the sphere and you take in a greater variety of parties and interests; you make it less probable that a majority of the whole will have a common motive to invade the rights of other citizens; or if such a common motive exists, it will be more difficult for all who feel it to discover their own strength and to act in unison with each other.[24]

Madison's argument here is in a sense negative: He saw an array of competing interests as a way to prevent any single one of them from dominating, that is, as a hedge against the formation of the kind of resilient majority factions mentioned above. In a broadly participatory form of government, even relatively popular (and thus relatively powerful) interest groups would be forced to negotiate and reason with others, tempering public policy away from extremism and narrow parochialism (Madison's "impulse[s] of passion, or of interest") and toward "the permanent and aggregate interests of the community."[25]

There is a more sanguine way to make a similar point. Consider the views of Cass Sunstein, a contemporary admirer of Madison's "deliberative democratic" views:

> [A] large point of the system [of representative democracy] is to ensure discussion and debate among people who are genuinely different in their perspectives and position, in the interest of creating a process through which reflection will encourage the emergence of general truths. A distinctive feature of American republicanism is extraordinary hospitality toward disagreement and heterogeneity, rather than fear of it. The framers believed that a diversity of opinion would be a creative and productive force. . . .

---

24. Madison, Federalist No. 10, *supra* note 1, at 127.
25. *Id.* at 123.

. . . Public deliberation may reveal the truth or falsity of factual claims about the state of the world or about the likely effects of policy proposals. Through confrontation among people who disagree, errors of fact may be revealed as such.[26]

Sunstein places less emphasis here on the negative, interest-checking function of broad participation and more on its "creative and productive" possibilities, as a means of generating fresh ideas and subjecting them to a sort of trial by deliberative fire. Sunstein's views thus owe much not only to Madison, but also to the well-known defense of free speech mounted by J. S. Mill[27] (and later echoed by Justices Oliver Wendell Holmes and Louis Brandeis, who conceived of democracy as a sort of "marketplace of ideas"[28]).

(iii) Broad Participation and Aggregation Sometimes broad participation is defended based solely on the epistemic power of numbers—the capacity of larger groups of people to reach more-accurate results than smaller groups, all else being equal. In the eighteenth century the Marquis de Condorcet proved mathematically that, if the average member of a group is even slightly more likely than not to correctly answer a yes-or-no question, the probability of a majority of the group's getting the answer right increases as the size of the group increases.[29] Condorcet assumed that *each* member of the posited group would have a better than 50 percent chance of getting the answer right, but more recent work shows that the theorem also holds if we assume an *average* competence within the group of over 50 percent.[30] This suggests that broader participation in decisionmaking is better than narrower participation, all else being equal (and assuming the average member of the relevant group has a better-than-random chance of getting the correct answer).

Modern empirical research backs up Condorcet's "Jury Theorem" and in fact extends it, suggesting that decisionmaking groups consisting of large numbers of people are, on average, more likely to get things right than individuals or small groups, even when those small groups are made up of experts.[31] (Contemporary American and British readers familiar with the popular TV game show "Who Wants to Be a Millionaire?" see this principle acted out on a regular basis,

---

26. Cass R. Sunstein, Democracy and the Problem of Free Speech 241–43 (rev. ed. 1995) [hereinafter Sunstein, Free Speech].

27. *See* John Stuart Mill, *On Liberty, in* Utilitarianism, On Liberty and Considerations on Representative Government, *supra* note 18, at 69, 85.

28. *See, for example,* Holmes's dissents (joined by Brandeis) in *Abrams v. United States,* 150 U.S. 616 (1919), and *Gitlow v. New York,* 168 U.S. 652 (1925), and Brandeis's concurrence (joined by Holmes) in *Whitney v. California,* 274 U.S. 357 (1927).

29. *See* David Estlund, *Making Truth Safe for Democracy, in* The Idea of Democracy 71, 92–94 (David Copp et. al. eds., 1993) [hereinafter Estlund, *Safe for Democracy*].

30. *See id.* at 99 n.42.

31. *See* James Surowiecki, The Wisdom of Crowds (2004).

when a contestant polls the studio audience for the answer to a multiple-choice question. It turns out that a plurality of the audience is correct a whopping 91 percent of the time; by comparison, the "phone-a-friend" option, in which the contestant calls a supposedly knowledgeable acquaintance for the answer, yields a respectable but far lower 65 percent accuracy rate.[32])

(iv) The Limits of Participation The causal connection between broadening participation in decisionmaking and generating good decisions surely has its limits. Some recent research suggests that diversity and deliberation some-times can interact in negative ways, with conflicting viewpoints becoming more rather than less entrenched when they are confronted with their opposites.[33] And aggregating many different opinions might actually reduce decisionmaking competence if most of those opinions are biased or ill-informed—not an unlikely state of affairs in the conditions of modern democratic politics.[34] Even assuming the group whose opinions are being aggregated is reasonably competent and impartial on average, there may be many instances in which a smaller but better-informed group of people—a blue-ribbon panel of experts, say—would tend to generate more-accurate decisions than the larger but less-well-informed public.

In assessing the relationship between democratic participation and decision-making competence for purposes of the DR account, however, we need to consider both the need for general acceptance of a decision-procedure and the possibility of trade-offs between (perceived) competence and (perceived) impartiality. Democratic theorist David Estlund points out that even if there were, out there in the world somewhere, a group of elites—perhaps Plato's Guardians—whose decisions were usually or always more accurate than those generated by a democratic majority, it would be highly unlikely that most members of the society could agree on the group's expertise and thus accept its decisions as binding on that ground.[35] Recall from Chapter 3 that acceptable dispute resolution requires, not procedures that are accurate per se, and certainly not procedures that some subset of the disputants believes to be accurate, but rather procedures that all (or, in the realistic conditions of a modern pluralistic society, the substantial majority) of the disputants can *agree* are reasonably accurate. The larger and more diverse the society, the less likely it seems that a large majority of its

32. See id. at 3–4.

33. See CASS R. SUNSTEIN, INFOTOPIA: HOW MANY MINDS PRODUCE KNOWLEDGE 65–71 (2006) (discussing the problems of group deliberation); Cass R. Sunstein, *Deliberative Trouble? Why Groups Go to Extremes*, 110 YALE L.J. 71, 105–06 (2000).

34. See Estlund, *Safe for Democracy*, supra note 29, at 99 n.42; see generally SUNSTEIN, FREE SPEECH, supra note 26, at 22–23 ("[I]t would not be an overstatement to say that much of the free speech 'market' now consists of scandals, sensationalized anecdotes, and gossip.").

35. See Estlund, *Safe for Democracy*, supra note 29; DAVID M. ESTLUND, DEMOCRATIC AUTHORITY: A PHILOSOPHICAL FRAMEWORK (2008) [hereinafter ESTLUND, DEMOCRATIC AUTHORITY].

members will be able to agree that a small group of Guardians from among them are sufficiently expert to be entrusted with all the society's important decisions. Broad democratic participation, warts and all, might turn out to be a reasonably competent, more-acceptable alternative than elitist oligarchy.

And, again, reasonable competence is not the only necessary ingredient of accuracy; reasonable impartiality matters, too. Even if the vast majority of society somehow could agree on the relative expertise of a cadre of Guardians, their impartiality almost certainly would be the subject of great suspicion. Expertise is one thing, disinterested virtue quite another. The relative impartiality of broadly participatory majority rule, even in the face of potentially more-competent alternatives, might be sufficient to tip the balance in favor of democracy and against oligarchy.

(v) **Competence and Regular Elections** Finally, just as regular democratic election cycles can launder the partiality in any given vote, they also can contribute to the competence of the system as a whole. Regular elections allow for a process of trial and error, by which policies adopted during one election cycle are tested by the pressure of ensuing cycles. All else being equal, good policies—that is, policies thought by successive majorities to be good—are more likely than bad policies to survive the test of repeated elections. Democracy thus creates a reasonable impression of competence compared, say, to a system in which those in power entrench that power by imposing arbitrary barriers to their subsequent removal.

7. DEMOCRACY AS A NEGATIVE IDEAL

To sum up, then: Democracy can claim an accuracy advantage over its competitors along a number of dimensions. Majority rule tends to limit the impact of any particular decisionmaker's partiality. Broadly populist political participation further limits the impact of individual partiality; it also enhances likely competence by providing diversity, encouraging deliberation, and aggregating the judgments of many minds. And the regular opportunities democracy provides to assess and replace leaders and policies promote both long-term impartiality (by laundering the effects of particular partial outcomes) and long-term competence (by allowing for meaningful trial and error).

But democracy, even when it functions well, is far from perfect; and it is important to expand here upon a point I first raised in Chapter 3, namely that competence and impartiality in dispute-resolution generally, and thus in democracy more specifically, probably are best understood as primarily negative ideals. By this I mean that they are important more for what they clearly avoid than for what they arguably accomplish. Systems we think of as democratic are so characterized mostly because they avoid certain salient indicia of incompetence and partiality, not because they can confidently be said to approach ideal levels of competence and impartiality.

A. Democracy as Reactive

As a matter of both intellectual and political history, democratic systems have developed primarily to remediate the obvious flaws of autocracy and oligarchy. Recall that Locke's critique of Hobbesian absolutism focused on its salient faults, not on its failure to live up to some ideal: Locke pointed out that a Hobbesian monarch was a self-judge, an inevitably biased arbiter of his own cause. And Locke's protodemocratic solution—a system in which government ultimately would be responsible to majority rule,[36] and government officials would themselves be subjected to law[37]—was hardly a prescription for entirely impartial, competent government; it was, rather, a sketchy response to the obvious defects of the Hobbesian model.

In political history, key moments in the evolution from more-autocratic to more-democratic models usually have been defined by reactions to the abuses of autocracy or oligarchy. Consider the Magna Carta, by which the English nobles rebelled against what they perceived as King John's abuses of power; the English Declaration of Rights, by which Parliament sought to check the absolutism favored by the deposed king, James II, and in many continental nations of the period; the American Revolution, spurred by complaints about "taxation without representation"; the French Revolution, triggered by the decadence of the Bourbon regime; and, more recently, the reform of the South African constitution after the fall of apartheid. There are of course many other examples.

The relative competence and impartiality of democratic systems thus can be understood largely as a reaction to disastrous experience under less-broadly and less-fairly participatory regimes. It should not be surprising, then, that general agreement on the definition of democracy, and on the substance of the procedures that democracy entails, probably exists in most modern real-world societies at a relatively abstract level. It is noncontroversial to say that democracy requires such things as regular, meaningful elections, one person–one vote, a baseline principle of majority rule, and robust protection for political speech; these are precisely the features that are missing from unacceptable autocratic and oligarchic systems, contemporary and historical. There is less agreement, however, on details like how frequent elections should be, whether and when

---

36. On the idea that majority rule can be implied from the original social compact, see LOCKE, *supra* note 2, §§ 95–99, at 374–77. On the related idea of what has sometimes been called a "right of revolution"—the idea that a majority of society can rise up and depose a sovereign who abuses his power—see *id.*, §§ 199–243, at 446–77.

37. *See id.*, §§ 134–42, at 401–09.

one person–one vote and majority rule may be compromised, what constitutes "political" speech and when it may be impaired, and so on.

For present purposes, the point is that democracy entails certain fundamental indicia of competence and impartiality in the form of fairly participatory procedures—features that serve the purpose of acceptable dispute resolution not because they guarantee accuracy, but because they avoid the salient obstacles to systemic accuracy displayed by autocratic and oligarchic regimes.

B. Democracy as Imperfect

Even with respect to the central democratic procedures and institutions about which there is widespread agreement, real-world democracies are likely to fall somewhat short. Consider the feature of broad participation by the governed in the process of making public policy. An ideally participatory system would allow all of those who will be bound by the laws in a significant way to participate in making those laws, unless there is some strong accuracy-related reason to exclude them. And the participation of the affected parties would be meaningful, that is, capable of actually making a difference in the content of the laws. But no government of a modern nation, and probably no government at all, could be fully participatory according to these measures.

Size is a major obstacle here, for three related reasons. First, the larger the size of a political unit, the less logistically feasible it becomes to allow every affected party to participate in making every important decision. Modern technology might be capable of mitigating this problem (by, for example, allowing every citizen to vote on legislation using the Internet), but that would only exacerbate the second obstacle to full participation: Most members of a society will have so many other things to do (jobs, families, hobbies, etc.) that they will be unable to devote substantial attention to the issues implicated by proposed laws. (The impracticality of adequately informed participation by every citizen is not an obstacle to broad participation so much as a counterweight to it; a good reason for avoiding full participation in the making of every law is that its advantages with respect to systemic accuracy probably would be outweighed by this disadvantage.) The third obstacle posed by the size of a polity is that, in any but the smallest political communities, the participation of a single member, at least in the form of voting, is such a tiny percentage of the sum total of participation that it is virtually guaranteed never to make a difference to the outcome. These facts undermine the meaningfulness, or effectiveness, of participation in real-world systems.

There also are intractable boundary issues regarding participation. A New England town meeting seems extraordinarily participatory, until we realize that the citizens of the next town down the road—who may be affected in a profound sense by the first town's laws regarding, say, zoning or water use—lack a vote, as does the tourist ticketed in the local speed trap. Democratic participation is "full" only with respect to those defined as citizens, and yet typically many noncitizens will be affected, directly or indirectly, by a society's laws. Aliens living within the United States are not allowed to vote in most local, state, or federal elections, and yet they are bound by the legislation that results from those elections. Citizens and subjects of other nations may be deeply affected by American policies on matters like foreign affairs, energy, pollution, trade, and the like, and yet they have no direct electoral influence in the making of those laws.

No actual political community, then, can entirely live up to the ideal of fully participatory government. The best we can ask for is that a system of government be reasonably participatory in light of the practical obstacles to full, and fully meaningful, participation. So we can recognize that political realities currently prevent the elimination of national borders and the consequent drawing of admittedly arbitrary boundaries between the peoples of different states, and we can account for the likelihood that entirely universal suffrage even within a set of arbitrarily drawn borders—extended to young children, for example—may harm decisionmaking accuracy more than it would help. We can focus instead on whether the internal political system within a society has eliminated saliently arbitrary barriers to participation, such as race, gender, property ownership, membership in the dominant tribe, or affiliation with the leading political party.[38] And we can acknowledge the need for indirect forms of participation in many or most contexts—for citizen participation, through voting, in elections to determine who will then represent those citizens in the process of legislation (that is, for representative government)[39]—and ask whether the system of representation is functioning as well as it reasonably can, to allow a majority of citizens to control at least the general direction of policy if not the minute details.

---

38. Whether a given ground for excluding participation is justifiable (like, arguably, the exclusion of young children) or arbitrary (like the exclusion of African Americans and other nonwhites prior to the Fourteenth Amendment in the United States, or of women prior to the Nineteenth Amendment) may, of course, be open to debate. Indeed it was precisely these kinds of debates that were resolved only with the enactments of these Amendments in, respectively, 1870 and 1920. I will argue in Chapter 7 that debates about the grounds of participation, or of exclusion from participation, in democratic politics, in order to be resolved impartially, often must be submitted to an extrademocratic constitutional process rather than left for decision by ordinary democratic politics.

39. Madison believed representative government to be an improvement over direct democracy, as it would

refine and enlarge the public views by passing them through the medium of a chosen body of citizens. . . . Under such a regulation it may well happen that the public voice, pronounced by the representatives of the people, will be more consonant to the public good than if pronounced by the people themselves. . . .

Madison, FEDERALIST No. 10, *supra* note 1, at 126.

Even by standards necessarily watered down by reality, any real-world system, including many we comfortably think of as democratic, inevitably will prove wanting in some respects. Participation through representation, for example, does not in fact always work as well as it could in the United States. But still we can distinguish between political communities in which participation is reasonably broad and reasonably meaningful and political communities in which it clearly fails in one or both respects. In the United States, my focal point here, citizens enjoy nearly universal suffrage (extending to everyone age eighteen or older except imprisoned felons in most states and all convicted felons in a few); most noncitizens may apply for naturalization; legislators and heads of the executive branch are subjected to regular elections and, with rare historical exceptions (none at the highest levels of the federal government), peacefully leave office when removed by the voters; and—an important point, to be taken up in part in the next chapter—low-level officials typically enforce the laws as written by the legislature. As a result, public policy generally seems to change, if often slowly and clumsily, in accordance with medium- to long-term trends in public opinion.

There are of course many examples, current and historical, toward the opposite end of the scale: systems in which most actual lawmaking power (or, just as importantly, the power to enforce the laws) is held by one person on the Hobbesian model, by a single family or small cadre of oligarchs, or by a ruling party; in which the right to vote is severely limited; in which elections are rigged, irregular, or both; in which power is grabbed or held by means of force rather than electoral transition; in which officials on the ground "enforce" something other than the laws as written; or, in many cases, in which some combination of these phenomena is present. The more numerous and widespread are these defects in a particular legal system, the further is that system from attaining even a pragmatically reasonable level of participation, and thus from deserving the label "democracy."

C. Expecting Too Much of Democracy

All of which suggests that we should not expect too much of democracy. Political theorists sometimes argue that, because democracy is not demonstrably superior, in an epistemic sense, to a benevolent autocracy or a Platonic oligarchy, it must be justified in entirely noninstrumentalist terms—that is, without regard to accuracy—or not at all.[40] But this misses the point, which is that democracy avoids the salient indicia of systemic inaccuracy that these rival systems inevitably display. Contemporary Americans can agree that democracy, with its reasonable fairness and participation, is a general improvement over autocracy and

---

40. *See, e.g.*, David Copp, *Could Political Truth Be a Hazard for Democracy?*, in THE IDEA OF DEMOCRACY, *supra* note 29, at 101.

oligarchy, with their historically documented shortcomings, without committing to the implausible and certainly unprovable positions that every conceivable democracy is superior to every conceivable autocracy or oligarchy, or that every democratic decision is more accurate than every autocratic or oligarch one. What is important is the avoidance of obvious markers of inaccuracy, not the achievement of perfect accuracy.

I should note here that this worry about democracy's relative accuracy may be aggravated by the influence of an Epistemic-Guidance (EG) account of legal authority. On an EG account, epistemic expertise is the point of law, and so it matters in every case whether the legislator is likely to have expertise in that case. A benevolent dictator or a bevy of Platonic Guardians often may seem to have the advantage over democracy if this is the standard. But the DR account recognizes that the point of law is not to get it right in every case, but to resolve disagreements over what is right. The avoidance of obvious threats to systemic accuracy in the legislative process—of self-judging, bias, arbitrarily restricted information, and other indicia of incompetence or partiality—may be enough to satisfy the requirement of acceptability and allow these disputes to be resolved. The historically recent success of fundamentally democratic systems suggests that these prophylactic aspects of democracy have in fact been sufficient in most instances.

This is not to suggest that threats to systemic accuracy in democratic systems do not matter. If such threats are salient and endemic enough, a majority's belief in the system's general accuracy may start to decay, and the system may eventually cease to perform its dispute-resolution function with sufficient regularity. (I will suggest in Chapter 7 that constitutional law can be justified as a prophylactic response to this possibility.) And there are many institutional and procedural choices to be made within a generally democratic system that may have an effect on systemic accuracy and social perceptions of it. Much of the remainder of this book is devoted to a discussion of these kinds of choices.

8. DEMOCRACY AS LAW

So here is where we now stand. Legislation, by resolving many normative questions ahead of time, can facilitate dispute resolution (or avoidance) within a society. But legislation is itself a matter of dispute; as Madison saw, legislators, and citizens, are in essence "parties to the causes which they determine" when they legislate, and as such they inevitably disagree among themselves about the desirable content of positive law. These legislative disputes must be resolved in a way that is acceptable to those who disagree with the results—in a way that is reasonably systemically accurate. Democracy can be understood as an approach to legislation that, in its majoritarianism, broad participation, and regular election cycles, eliminates the most salient forms of systemic inaccuracy.

We might think of democracy, then, as a particularly *legal* form of government, a system that borrows the DR justification of legal authority from the *ex post* adjudicative context and applies it to the *ex ante* legislative process. Democratic processes generate law; but in this sense, democracy just *is* law. We can begin now to see why the ideas of democracy and "the rule of law" tend to travel together in contemporary rhetoric, and to understand how Adams could think of democracy as "a government of laws and not of men."

But democratic legislation can only do part of the dispute-resolving work of law. Legal rules are inherently indeterminate; by itself, a legal rule cannot resolve disagreement about how it applies in a particular case. And, for reasons we have already gotten some sense of, such disagreements are frequent in the law. The language with which legal rules are expressed in statutes, regulations, and similar forms inevitably is vague or ambiguous in many contexts. Such cases—and they are more the rule than the exception in any complex legal system—require something besides rules to resolve them; they require a mechanism of interpreting legal rules and applying them to the facts of particular disputes. They require adjudication.

What, on a DR account of law and (now) democracy, should this process of adjudication look like? How should judges, and other participants in adjudication, go about the task of transforming statutes and other general legal rules into resolutions of particular disputes? These are the central questions of the next two chapters.

5. DEMOCRATIC ADJUDICATION

We saw in Chapter 4 that legal rules can facilitate dispute resolution by determining, ahead of time, the norms that will apply to particular disputes. We also saw that the content of legal rules will itself be the subject of dispute—not only because that content influences the decisions of discrete disputes among members of a society, but also, and perhaps primarily, because the content of legal rules sets *policy* for the society: It governs, with purported authority, the actions and interactions of members of that society going forward.

And we saw that democracy is, or can be, a reasonably accurate way to resolve disputes about public policy and thus to generate legal rules. In light of this conclusion, it is tempting to imagine that democratically enacted legislation is, by itself, capable of avoiding or resolving most or all disputes within a society. It turns out, however, that democratic legislation alone cannot liquidate every dispute within a society. There are two reasons for this.

One obvious (and noncontroversial) reason is that people often will have disputes about *facts*—about what has happened, is happening, or (sometimes) will happen—even if they agree about the norms that govern those facts. If a democratically enacted statute tells two neighbors, Aaron and Betty, that property owners (like Aaron) waive objections to others' trespasses (like Betty's encroaching fence) unless they object within a certain period of time, the neighbors still might disagree over whether Aaron actually objected to Betty's fence within the prescribed period, or about whether Betty's fence in fact encroaches on Aaron's property. Some process must be available to acceptably resolve such factual disputes; and it can hardly be the full democratic process that generated the statute in the first place, for that process (except perhaps in very small communities) will be too involved and cumbersome to address every factual dispute that arises from the application of the statute.[1]

No observer of any modern legal system denies the necessity of some process for the *ex post* liquidation of purely factual disputes. Some contemporary legal scholars and judges, however, insist that once disputes over facts are put to

---

1. There have, historically, been relatively small societies in which *ex post* disputes have been resolved by collective processes resembling legislation. The medieval Iceland of the sagas is an example. *See* WILLIAM IAN MILLER, BLOODTAKING AND PEACEMAKING: FEUD, LAW, AND SOCIETY IN SAGA ICELAND 17–21 (1990) (describing annual meetings called the "Thing" and the "Allthing" used to resolve all lawsuits and administrative matters). So are the Germanic tribes that occupied much of Western Europe after the fall of the Roman Empire. *See* THOMAS GLYN WATKIN, AN HISTORICAL INTRODUCTION TO MODERN CIVIL LAW 372–73 (1999).

one side, democratic legal rules are capable of conclusively resolving most or all *normative* disputes to which they apply—disputes over the content of the applicable legal norms, and over the application of those norms to a given set of facts. These *legal formalists* divide into two main camps: *textualists*, who believe that the text of a legal rule by itself can resolve most or all normative disputes within the rule's scope, and *originalists*, who deny that text alone can resolve all normative disputes but think that appeal to the "original intent" or similar mental state of the rule's enactors will do the trick.[2]

Both textualism and originalism fall victim to the second reason why democratic legislation cannot, by itself, liquidate every dispute, namely that rules are, inevitably, *indeterminate* with respect to their applications in particular circumstances. A general rule alone cannot resolve controversies over whether and how it applies in a particular case; and given the nature of both rulemaking and language, such controversies inevitably will arise.

We can understand this phenomenon of legal indeterminacy by adapting a well-known example offered by H.L.A. Hart.[3] Suppose a city ordinance bans "vehicles" from a public park; and suppose that Olive wants to pull her toddler through the park in a children's four-wheeled toy wagon. Assuming that Olive accepts the (democratically enacted) ordinance as authoritative with respect to her actions, does the ordinance prohibit her from bringing the toy wagon into the park?

1. THE INDETERMINACY OF TEXT

The first thing to notice about Olive's case is that the text of the ordinance itself cannot answer the question of whether the ordinance applies to Olive's toy wagon. The pertinent question is whether the toy wagon is a "vehicle" within the meaning of the ordinance, and the word "vehicle" allows for reasonable arguments either way. In some respects the wagon seems like the kind of object we mean when we speak of a "vehicle": It has wheels, it can be directed by a person, it can carry people or objects from one place to another. But in other respects

---

2. Perhaps the leading contemporary textualist is Justice Antonin Scalia. For Scalia's most extensive statement of his own textualist views, see Antonin Scalia, *Common-Law Courts in a Civil-Law System: The Role of United States Federal Courts in Interpreting the Constitution and Laws*, in A MATTER OF INTERPRETATION: FEDERAL COURTS AND THE LAW 3, 47 (Amy Gutmann ed., 1997) [hereinafter Scalia, *Common-Law Courts*]; Antonin Scalia, *Response*, in A MATTER OF INTERPRETATION: FEDERAL COURTS AND THE LAW, *supra*, at 129, 140. Former federal judge Robert Bork articulates and defends his prominent originalist approach in ROBERT H. BORK, THE TEMPTING OF AMERICA: THE POLITICAL SEDUCTION OF THE LAW (1990).

3. *See* H.L.A. Hart, *Positivism and the Separation of Law and Morals*, 71 HARV. L. REV. 593, 607 (1958) [hereinafter Hart, *Positivism*].

the toy wagon does not seem like what we mean by a "vehicle" at all: It has no on-board means of propulsion, it is not typically used for transportation, it requires no license or special training to operate. Neither conclusion—that the toy wagon is a vehicle or that it is not one—is conclusively required, or conclusively prohibited, by the language of the ordinance itself. And of course, as Hart cheekily put it, "[t]he toy [wagon] cannot speak up and say, 'I am a vehicle for the purpose of this legal rule.'"[4]

This is not to say that arguments about whether the toy wagon is a "vehicle" within the meaning of the ordinance are utterly meaningless. Olive might, for instance, go to the local library, thumb through dozens of dictionaries, and determine that, given the many definitions of "vehicle" and examples of "vehicles" she has found, her toy wagon is insufficiently like the typical "vehicle" to fall within the ordinance's purview. There would be nothing nonsensical about Olive's conclusion or her process of reaching it; the point here is not that we cannot reasonably conclude that the toy wagon either is or is not a vehicle.

The point, rather, is twofold. First, any arguments or reasoning regarding whether the toy car is a "vehicle" within the meaning of the statute must be based in part on something other than the text of the ordinance itself—on dictionary definitions of "vehicle," perhaps, or on comparisons of the toy wagon to other objects that we think clearly are or clearly are not vehicles. The text alone cannot resolve the issue for us. And second, as I suggested above, there are likely to be reasonable arguments on either side of the question, i.e., for or against the proposition that the toy wagon is a "vehicle" within the meaning of the ordinance.

Olive's case thus demonstrates that, at least in some (not far-fetched) circumstances, the text of a legal rule cannot by itself liquidate potential disputes about applicable norms. Some mechanism other than the process that created the rule's text will be required to resolve such disputes.[5]

And note that there is no quick fix, at the legislative end, for this problem of indeterminacy. The indeterminacy of the "no vehicles" rule in Olive's case—the fact that the rule itself, as expressed by its language, cannot answer the questions

---

4. *Id.*

5. For simplicity's sake, I am assuming here that the "no vehicles" ordinance is the only legal norm that might plausibly govern Olive's conduct in this case. The shortcomings of textualism become even more apparent in the event this assumption does not hold. Suppose, for example, that the city council has enacted another (authoritative) ordinance allowing the use of "baby carriages" in the park. Does Olive's toy wagon, when used to tote her toddler, qualify as a "baby carriage" permitted by this ordinance, or rather as a "vehicle" prohibited by the "no vehicles" law? Even if the language of each ordinance clearly applies to Olive's wagon—that is, even if Olive's wagon clearly is both a "vehicle" under the first ordinance and a "baby carriage" under the second—the texts of the respective ordinances would not, by themselves, solve the problem of what to do when their two rules conflict.

of whether and how it applies in that case—flows from certain unavoidable realities about the creation and communication of general rules. If a rulemaker wants its rule actually to be understood and followed, it must attempt to communicate the content of that rule by means of language. But, as Aristotle recognized and we saw illustrated in Chapter 1, no rulemaker can anticipate every possible particular meaning of the words it chooses for the rule; the city council that enacted the "no vehicles" ordinance, for example, could not have foreseen every item that might, at some time in the future, arguably fall within the scope of the term "vehicle." If a rulemaker has not anticipated a particular possible question about the meaning of the rule's language—whether a toy wagon is a "vehicle"—then it cannot add more detail to the language (say, prohibiting "vehicles, including toy wagons") to address that particular meaning ahead of time. And even if the rulemaker has anticipated a particular question about the meaning of a rule's language, any attempt to foreclose that question by means of additional language will itself, inevitably, run up against the same problem: Prohibiting "vehicles, including toy wagons" does not answer the question whether, say, a soapbox derby racer is a "toy wagon" within the meaning of the rule. There will always be some potential application of the rule—just around the next corner, as it were—that will not clearly be determined by the rule's text itself, no matter how specific that text gets.

A textualist, however, might respond that Olive's case is anomalous, or at least can be made anomalous by precise legislative drafting. Even if detailed drafting cannot eliminate all indeterminacy with respect to a legal rule, perhaps it can reduce the incidence of indeterminacy to such an insignificant level that the textualist thesis will hold in the vast majority of cases. Legislators may not be able to anticipate every potential meaning of a rule's language, but perhaps they can anticipate most of them. Moreover, it seems plausible that some legal rules can be expressed with a high degree of textual determinacy *without* the drafters' having to anticipate, and include, a long list of exceptions and clarifications. Consider, for example, the rule "Persons under the age of eighteen are not permitted in the park after 10:00 p.m."

In fact there is much truth to these suggestions. The fact that the text of a rule is not self-defining or self-applying does not mean that, in practice, its meaning will always (or even often) be controversial. The "no vehicles" ordinance may not clearly apply to Olive's toy wagon, but it does clearly apply to Paul's fully functional SUV; in H.L.A. Hart's terminology, the SUV is well within the "core of settled meaning" of the word "vehicle."[6] And the 10:00 p.m. curfew for persons under eighteen will apply clearly and noncontroversially in almost every case we might imagine. Textualism thus carries more than a grain of truth: Depending on the rule, its text sometimes, perhaps often—perhaps virtually

---

6. Hart, *Positivism, supra* note 3, at 607.

always—will have significant constraining force, clearly ruling out some results and clearly requiring others.

For our purposes, however, we need to keep in mind two important points. First, even in these noncontroversial, seemingly determinate examples, it is not the text of the rule, strictly speaking, that is creating determinacy by itself; it is rather our understanding, as the audience, of that text's meaning under the circumstances in which we encounter it. It is, in other words, text combined with context; and context is socially contingent. To say that a contemporary audience of English speakers would accept a fully functional SUV as a "vehicle" within the meaning of the ordinance but may disagree about whether a child's toy wagon is a "vehicle" is simply to say that, at this particular time and place, the latter application of the word "vehicle" is reasonably debatable while the former is not.[7] But social contexts can change, and so, therefore, can the meanings of texts.

Social context can alter textual meaning in two senses. First, the applications of a word's or phrase's core meaning might vary with time and place. Consider the question of whether a bicycle is a "vehicle," which might have been answered differently in the late nineteenth century than it would be today.

Second, the core meaning of a word or phrase can itself change over time. Consider the path of the word "awful," which once meant "inspiring of wonder" but now means something quite different.

Because textual meaning is mutable in response to changing social conditions, there is no guarantee that a noncontroversial application of the text of a legal rule (say, counting an SUV as a "vehicle") will not become controversial over time. Inevitably this will occur with respect to at least *some* legal rules in a society; but that society's rulemaker will not be able to anticipate accurately whether, and how, it will happen—whether and how the meanings of the words it uses will change as the social context changes. The rulemaker thus will not be able to foreclose, *ex ante*, the development of controversies over the meanings of certain rules in particular contexts. Instead, the society will have to develop some post-legislative institutions and procedures for resolving those controversies.

The second important point here is related to the first: Democratic legislators may have good reason to sacrifice determinacy for flexibility in their drafting of a rule's text. Adding textual specificity to a rule—by, for instance, attempting

---

7. *See* HENRY M. HART, JR. & ALBERT M. SACKS, THE LEGAL PROCESS: BASIC PROBLEMS IN THE MAKING AND APPLICATION OF LAW 1375 (William N. Eskridge, Jr. & Philip P. Frickey eds., 1994):

> In deciding whether words will bear a particular meaning, a court needs to be linguistically wise and not naïve. It needs to understand, especially, that meaning depends upon context. But language is a social institution. Humpty Dumpty was wrong when he said that you can make words mean whatever you want them to mean.

to catalog every vehicle-like object that should or should not be excluded from the public park—takes time and resources, and at some point a legislature might determine that this cost exceeds the likely benefit in terms of liquidating future disputes. Adding textual specificity also might create its own *ex ante* disputes within the legislature, between, for example, those who want to ban toy wagons and those who do not. The legislature might elect to defer these ancillary disputes in order to more efficiently achieve important goals that are the subject of broad agreement (e.g., banning SUVs and other obvious vehicles from the park), and so it might intentionally draft text that clearly serves these central aims while remaining indeterminate with respect to lesser issues. Or the legislature, recognizing that it cannot anticipate every particular question involving putative vehicles in the park (even if it could agree on those questions), might draft language that clearly covers a group of noncontroversial core cases (SUVs, cars, motorcycles) in the hope that some future decisionmaker, informed by these core cases, will resolve the unforeseen cases in reasonable ways.

In other words, the text of a legal rule might be indeterminate in some cases, not accidentally, but on purpose, that is, by legislative design. In such cases, we might understand what the legislature has done as essentially a delegation of authority to some future decisionmaker to liquidate the rule's meaning in controversial cases. And, given the ubiquity or near-ubiquity of the circumstances to which such delegations respond—limits on legislative time and resources, the risk of legislative disagreement about ancillary details, the impossibility of predicting every application of a rule—there is no reason to think that textual indeterminacy in legal rules is likely to be a rare phenomenon in a modern democratic society.

If textual indeterminacy in legal rules is more than a trivial occurrence within a society, then that society will need procedures to resolve disputes about the meaning and application of legal rules. It turns out that textualists typically take a certain kind of position on the question of how these disputes should be resolved: They contend that reasonable questions about whether the text of a rule covers a given case always should be answered in the negative. I will assess this position in a general fashion later in this chapter; in Chapter 8 I will critique it in the special context of constitutional law. For now, the basic point is this: A democratic society will not be able to rely on the text of its legal rules alone to avoid or resolve disagreements about whether and how those rules apply.

2. THE INDETERMINACY OF LEGISLATIVE INTENT

Some formalists acknowledge that the text of legal rules often is indeterminate, but nonetheless believe determinacy can be salvaged by referring to the specific intent of whoever made the rule. These *originalists* would resolve a case like

Olive's by asking whether the rule's enactor (the city council) intended to include toy wagons as "vehicles" barred from the park by its ordinance. If the rulemaker intended to include toy wagons as "vehicles," then (on this view) Olive's wagon is barred from the park; if the rulemaker intended not to include toy wagons as "vehicles" (or, perhaps, simply did not intend to include them), then Olive's wagon is not barred.

As the previous sentence suggests, there is a significant potential ambiguity in the originalist approach to the meaning of rules. Originalists hold that if the rulemaker affirmatively intended to include a particular case (e.g., the use of a toy wagon) within the scope of its rule (e.g., the "no vehicles" ordinance), then the rule should be understood as including that case. But suppose an affirmative intent to include is absent; e.g., suppose the city council did not intend to include toy wagons within the ordinance's purview. Two possibilities remain. One is that the city council affirmatively intended to *exclude* toy wagons from the reach of the ordinance; the other is that the city council simply formed no intent whatsoever on the matter.

Originalism has a clear prescription for the former possibility: If the rule-maker affirmatively intended to exclude a case from the scope of the rule, the rule should be read as excluding that case. The potential ambiguity lies in how to handle the second possibility. An originalist might insist that the absence of an original legislative intent on the issue means the rule must be understood to exclude the overlooked case. Alternatively, she might accept that an originalist approach, having failed to identify any actual legislative intent, simply does not resolve the issue, leaving it to be resolved by other means.

It turns out that most contemporary originalists hold the former view: that the absence of a legislative intention regarding a case means the case must be excluded from the scope of the rule. In fact this claim is the analogue to the typical textualist position, mentioned above, on the equivalent ambiguity within textualism. Textualists too face the question of what to do when their preferred source of a rule's meaning—its text—proves indeterminate, and typically they too hold that a rule is simply inapplicable in such cases.

As I promised above, I will critique both the textualist and the originalist versions of this position in the next section. In this section, however, I want to press two points about originalism. First, the circumstances in which the meaning of a rule cannot be fully determined by its text but *can* be fully determined by the rulemakers' intent will be exceedingly rare; original intent, even more than text, is endemically indeterminate. Second, some procedure other than the process that created the rule itself will be necessary to resolve disagreements about the existence and content of legislative intent.

To appreciate just how rare a determinate original intent will be, consider precisely what it is that an originalist must look for in a rule. Originalism is virtually always presented as a sort of backup strategy for cases of textual indeterminacy;

originalists typically hold that a rule's text should be followed to the extent it is determinate.[8] The originalist project begins, then, only when the textualist project fails. What the originalist is searching for is a legislative intention that has *not* been clearly and noncontroversially communicated in a rule's text.

The chief problem here is this: Why in the world would a legislature or other rulemaker form an intention regarding an issue—e.g., affirmatively decide to include or to exclude toy wagons from the "no vehicles" ordinance—but *fail* to communicate that intention clearly by means of the rule's text? If the legislature has formed an actual intention on that issue, then (by definition) the issue is not one of those that the legislature has failed to resolve textually because it has failed to anticipate its occurrence. Surely a legislature that intends its rule to cover, or not to cover, a particular case has every incentive to make this clear in the text of the rule. There may well be cases involving clerical mistakes in transcribing the text of the statute (e.g., omitting the word "not"[9]), or what modern lawyers call "scrivener's error." And there may be cases that simply involve sloppy drafting (e.g., omitting the modifier "criminal" from a rule requiring the exclusion of evidence that is overly prejudicial "to the defendant"[10]). In the complex world of modern legislation, these cases might not even be all that rare. But they still seem likely to constitute a tiny minority of the whole—a very small drop in a very large ocean.

If so, originalism, as an approach to identifying actual statutory meaning, is in fact a theory of quite limited scope: It can bring determinacy, if at all, only in a very small percentage of the cases where the text by itself does not do the trick, namely those cases in which the rulemaker formed a definite intention but failed to communicate that intention clearly in the rule's text. And if, as I suggested in the previous section, statutory text frequently will be indeterminate, then originalism does not offer a particularly effective Plan B.

But it turns out that originalism's difficulties are only just beginning. Let us suppose that we find ourselves faced with a textually indeterminate legal rule—the city ordinance prohibiting "vehicles" in the public park, as applied to Olive's toy wagon—and that we are determined to search for some legislative intent on that issue, on the off chance that the legislature formed such an intent but failed to communicate it clearly in the statute's text. Consider the formidable problems we now will face in carrying out this task.

---

8. Justice Scalia, for instance, dismisses a well-known instance of judicial pursuit of original intent with the following verdict: "Well of course I think that the act was within the letter of the statute, and therefore was within the statute: end of case." *See* Scalia, *Common-Law Courts, supra* note 2, at 20 (referring to the Supreme Court's ruling in *Church of the Holy Trinity v. United States*, 143 U.S. 457 (1892)).

9. *See, e.g.,* In re Deuel, 101 N.Y.S. 1037, 1038 (App. Div. 1906) (holding "that the omission of the word 'not' was a mere scrivener's error").

10. *See* Green v. Bock Laundry Mach. Co., 490 U.S. 504 (1989).

First, we will have to determine exactly *whose* intent matters. I have been speaking casually thus far about a single "legislative intent," an "intent of the rulemaker" or "lawmaker," and so on; but in a democracy, the lawmaker typically will be a multimember body, not a single individual. In most cases that body will not have acted unanimously in creating a legal rule; some of its members will have dissented from the majority's decision to adopt the rule. Whose intent, then, should we look for? That of the majority alone? Perhaps only of those members of the body who actually participated in drafting the rule? Or should we also look, somehow, to the intent (whatever that might entail) of some or all of the dissenters?

Second, assuming we somehow can identify the appropriate group whose intent matters, we may have to determine how to resolve *conflicts* between the respective intents of different members of that group. Indeed, the larger and more diverse the relevant group, the more likely it is that some conflict will emerge; legislators who voted against a statute, for example, seem quite likely to have different intentions with respect to the statute's meaning than legislators who voted for it. It seems probable that we will have to prioritize the intentions of some over the intentions of others, but doing so will only beg the question of why we are considering the less-important intentions in the first place—taking us back to the initial question of whose intent matters. Somehow we will have to both identify the relevant group of lawmakers whose intent we care about, and develop a system for prioritizing their intents in cases of conflict that does not contradict our reasons for looking to this group to begin with.

But suppose we manage to solve these problems. We still, third, will have to determine precisely what we mean by *intent*. Any given legislator may experience one or more of a number of distinct mental states regarding an issue, each of which might plausibly be counted as her "intent" with respect to that issue. The variety and complexity of possibilities here turns out to be rather daunting. A given legislator—say, a member of the city council that enacted the "no vehicles" ordinance—might herself believe that a toy wagon really is a "vehicle" and thus is barred by the ordinance. Or she might believe that other legislators think a toy wagon is barred by the ordinance, even though she herself has no opinion on the matter. Or she might believe a toy wagon is barred by the ordinance but also that no other member of the legislature has an opinion on the matter. Or she might believe a toy wagon is *not* barred by the ordinance but *hope* that the ordinance will be understood as barring toy wagons. Or she might attribute this hope to other members of the legislature. And any of these beliefs might be either material or immaterial to the legislator's decision regarding how to vote on the ordinance. Which of these (or a number of other plausible) mental states, alone or in combination, should we be looking for in our search for legislative "intent"?[11]

---

11. *See generally* RONALD DWORKIN, A MATTER OF PRINCIPLE 48–57 (1985) (discussing various types of "intentions" of the Framers that might be thought relevant in constitutional

Fourth, we will have to settle on the proper *methodology* for our search. Where should we look for evidence of original intent, however we define it? Should we confine our search to the relevant legislators' public statements, perhaps on the ground that public statements are most likely to have influenced the legislative process? Or should we look as well to evidence of legislators' private sentiments (in letters or office memoranda, perhaps)? What about legislative committee reports, which might be drafted by staffers rather than the legislators themselves? Should we worry about the incentives our looking at these kinds of materials might create—incentives to be less thorough in actual statutory drafting, perhaps even to "plant" misleading evidence in the legislative history? Are there side constraints (e.g., confidentiality, privacy) that ought to cabin our search somehow?

Finally, we will have to actually *conduct* the search, by whatever methodology we select, for legislative intent however we decide to define it. Given that the intent we're searching for has not been clearly communicated by the rule's text, our search is likely to involve some digging into less-readily available, perhaps even obscure, sources of information (e.g.,—in roughly ascending order of obscurity—records of the work of legislative committees, records of legislators' public statements, legislators' office memoranda, legislators' private notes and correspondence, etc.). The further away in time is the date of our search from the date of the rule's creation, the more difficult the search is likely to become. And we will face the concern of every historian, namely that we may succeed in uncovering only some, but not all, of the relevant information we are looking for, resulting in a skewed picture of the "intent" we are trying to reconstruct.

It should be obvious that, not long after embarking on this search for original intent, we will find ourselves quite far indeed from the formalists' supposed goal of bringing determinacy to legal rules. The originalist version of formalism seeks determinacy in the intent of the rulemaker with respect to a rule's application in a particular case. But the cases in which such determinacy is likely to exist in the absence of a clear textual signal to that effect seem likely to be relatively rare. And the process of identifying the intent in question will itself be rife with the potential for controversy; the search for determinacy is itself indeterminate.

Here again, my point is not that originalism is a fool's errand (although in fact I think it mostly is). My point, rather, is that originalism typically is incapable of liquidating the precise meaning of a legal rule *ex ante*. We cannot use originalism as a way to let the legislator or other rulemaker do all our work for us. We will, rather, require some method of resolving indeterminacy about

---

interpretation); RONALD DWORKIN, FREEDOM'S LAW: THE MORAL READING OF THE CONSTITUTION 267–72 (1996) [hereinafter DWORKIN, FREEDOM'S LAW] (critiquing Robert Bork's position that judges should "be guided by the intention of the framers, and nothing more" when interpreting "the meaning of an abstract constitutional proposition").

a rule's application *ex post*—at the point in time at which people find themselves in a dispute about whether and how an existing legal rule applies to their situation.

3. FORMALISM AS A DEFAULT PRINCIPLE

Despite their characteristic indeterminacy, originalism and textualism might not be fool's errands if these formalist methodologies can provide a sort of default principle in (inevitable) cases of indeterminacy. Perhaps formalism can be understood as a strategy, not for avoiding or resolving indeterminacy in legal rules, but rather for determinately avoiding disputes in the absence of determinate rules.

Formalist theorists often suggest that in cases of rule-indeterminacy—that is, cases in which textualism, originalism, or both (whichever is the theorist's preferred type of formalism) fail to identify a determinate meaning for a legal rule—we (that is, those potentially subject to the rule, and those interpreting and enforcing the rule) simply ought to conclude that the rule does not apply to the case at hand. For example, suppose that formalist interpretive techniques (textualism and originalism) cannot determine whether the "no vehicles in the park" ordinance applies to ban Olive's toy wagon. These "Default Formalists" would hold that, in the absence of a determinate rule *barring* Olive's wagon from the park, Olive's wagon necessarily is *not* barred from the park. On this view, if a legal rule does not *determinately* apply to a particular case, then (for that reason) it does not apply to that case at all.[12]

What might be the attraction of Default Formalism? Here there is both a general answer and an answer that turns on the (probably contingent) facts of contemporary American politics. First (briefly), the contingent answer: Default Formalism almost always results in less government. As such, it often is

---

12. The best overt defense of the Default Formalist view of which I am aware appears in Frank H. Easterbrook, *Statutes' Domains*, 50 U. CHI. L. REV. 533 (1983). Professor (now Judge) Easterbrook argues:

> To delve into the structure, purpose, and legislative history of the original statute is to engage in a sort of creation. It is to fill in blanks. And without some warrant—other than the existence of the blank—for a court to fill it in, the court has no authority to decide in favor of the party invoking the blank-containing statute.

Id. at 539. Typically Default Formalists assume their position without arguing for it, as when they object to the judicial "creation" of constitutional rights in the absence of an explicit textual warrant. *See, e.g.,* BORK, *supra* note 2, at 97–100 (criticizing the Court's decision in *Griswold v. Connecticut* as the "invent[ion] [of] a general right of privacy that the Framers had. . . left out").

attractive to libertarians and political conservatives. I will have a bit more to say about this phenomenon below.

The more general, universal answer is that Default Formalism purports to offer a kind of determinacy, even in the face of inevitable rule-indeterminacy. Where legal rules cannot provide a determinate resolution of a dispute, Default Formalism generates its own determinate answer: Whatever conduct or state of affairs is at issue in the dispute (e.g., Olive's towing her toddler through the park in a toy wagon) may continue to exist unhindered by the law. Default Formalism thus might seem appealing to those who want to avoid or resolve disputes without having to rely, or at least to rely heavily, on some *ex post* mechanism for liquidating legal indeterminacy.

The Dispute-Resolution (DR) account of law suggests that this appeal is superficial and misguided, in a way that is roughly analogous to how bare Hobbesian absolutism is superficial and misguided. Like Hobbesian absolutism, Default Formalism can indeed bring determinacy to potential disputes, thus avoiding the costs associated with those disputes. Where absolutism accomplishes this with the simple rule, "Do whatever the absolute monarch or dictator says," Default Formalism accomplishes it with the nearly-as-simple rule, "Do whatever you want, unless there is a determinate legal rule forbidding you to do it." Provided legal subjects respect the default rule under either system, disputes over how people should behave, or over the consequences of their having behaved in a certain way, will be avoided.

The problem under either system, however, is that the operative default rule ultimately is unlikely to resolve most disputes in an acceptable way. For reasons canvassed in the previous two chapters, the diktats of a Hobbesian monarch are highly susceptible to partiality and incompetence and thus highly likely to be seen as inaccurate. And roughly the same can be said about Default Formalism, which imposes upon actual or potential disputants whatever result happens to be the *status quo*. There is little reason to think the *status quo* typically will be the product of some impartial and competent process; it is just as likely to be the result of one party's superior strength or good fortune or some other arbitrary factor. Default Formalism, like Hobbesian absolutism, thus "resolves" disputes more or less arbitrarily—a state of affairs that, over the long run, is unlikely to be generally acceptable.

This truism is particularly ironic given the libertarian sympathies of many theorists who urge Default Formalism. The DR account suggests that what superficially appears to be a liberty-promoting default rule—"Do whatever you want, unless there is a determinate legal rule forbidding you to do it"—in fact amounts to the imposition of an arbitrary resolution on the order of Hobbes. Default Formalists of a libertarian bent tend to forget that typically it is not just the liberty of the person subject to a rule that is at stake, but also that of those who would be harmed or offended by the absence of the rule. If the "no vehicles" rule does not prohibit Olive from towing her toddler through the park in a toy wagon, Olive's liberty has been preserved—but the liberty of those who want to enjoy the park without having to dodge toy wagons has been compromised. Where the desirability of a particular legal rule is disputed, either outcome—creating and enforcing the rule or not creating and enforcing the rule—will impair someone's liberty. Default Formalism seeks to "resolve" this dispute by arbitrarily privileging the position of those who oppose the rule over the position of those who favor it.

Other Default Formalists emphasize the value of the democratic process, arguing that legal rules should not have authority unless they are the fully pedigreed products of democratic lawmaking.[13] But Default Formalists of this stripe face the paradox of binding people to a thoroughly nondemocratic result in the name of democracy. Terminating disputes by merely enforcing the *status quo* features none of the advantages of participation and fairness that democratic legislation offers, and that those concerned with democratic pedigree purport to value.

Of course—and this is an important caveat—the Hobbesian failure of Default Formalism implies nothing about the wisdom of *democratically enacted rules* that prefer liberty in cases of doubt. Suppose a democratic community considers and adopts, through democratic means, a background rule requiring that no person be punished for committing an act that is not clearly proscribed by some valid applicable law. Now default to the *status quo* no longer is an arbitrary act; it is rather an implementation of a considered, authoritative decision to preserve individual liberty except in cases where the community has specifically chosen to impair it. The failure of Default Formalism tells us nothing about whether such legislated libertarianism is or is not a good idea. And as it happens, legislated libertarianism is fairly commonplace in modern American law; it can be detected, to name just a few instances, in the "rule of lenity" in criminal law, which is a common-law doctrine holding that ambiguous criminal statutes should be construed in favor of the defendant; in the principle of "void for vagueness" in free-speech and due-process jurisprudence, which invalidates prohibitory laws whose terms are overly indeterminate;[14] and arguably in the Ninth and Tenth Amendments to the federal Constitution, which suggest that the federal government cannot impair individual rights (the Ninth) or state prerogatives

---

13. *See, e.g.*, Easterbrook, *supra* note 12; Scalia, *Common-Law Courts, supra* note 2, at 16–18.

14. *See* United States v. Williams, 128 S.Ct. 1830, 1846 (2008) (offering, as examples of statutes held void for vagueness, laws that "tied criminal culpability to whether the defendant's conduct was 'annoying' or 'indecent'") (citations omitted); Kolender v. Lawson, 461 U.S. 352 (1983) (invalidating, as unconstitutionally vague, a statute requiring persons who loiter in the streets to offer "credible and reliable" identification); Colautti v. Franklin, 439 U.S. 379, 380–81 (1979) (invalidating for vagueness a statutory provision criminalizing abortion when a doctor has "sufficient reason to believe that the fetus may be viable").

(the Tenth) without some affirmative constitutional grant of the power to do so.[15] Just as the failure of Default Formalism does not rule out the considered decision to establish a libertarian presumption, however, the potential normative attractiveness of the latter does not somehow salvage the former. It is one thing for a community to decide, through a reasonably accurate process, that those acts which are not clearly prohibited should be allowed; it is another thing to impose that result by default.

4. THE POSSIBILITY OF DEMOCRATIC ADJUDICATION

The DR account therefore illuminates the need for some *ex post* mechanism for resolving (inevitable) disputes about the meaning, in particular cases, of (inevitably) indeterminate democratic laws. Note, however, that this *ex post* mechanism will in a sense be a second-best alternative—necessary only because, and when, democratic legislation fails to generate a perfectly determinate general rule. And this fact—the fallback nature of *ex post* adjudication—begs two additional, important questions under the DR account.

First, given that *ex post* adjudication necessarily will lack many of the attributes of reasonable accuracy possessed by democratic legislation—in particular its broadly participatory nature—can adjudication nonetheless be structured to be reasonably accurate and thus generally acceptable as a means of resolving disputes?

Second, is there a sense in which *ex post* adjudication, despite the failure of formalism, nonetheless can be seen as derivative of democratic legislation—as somehow interpreting and implementing indeterminate general laws (and thus

---

15. Some have argued that the Ninth Amendment embodies a very strong presumption of liberty, which requires government to make at least a threshold showing of necessity before impairing even those aspects of individual liberty that are not expressly protected by other constitutional provisions. *See, e.g.,* RANDY E. BARNETT, RESTORING THE LOST CONSTITUTION: THE PRESUMPTION OF LIBERTY (2004). The Supreme Court has never endorsed such a broad reading of the amendment, however, and in fact only rarely has relied upon it to any extent in reaching a decision.

The Court has given the Tenth Amendment a fairly narrow reading as well, applying it only to prohibit the federal government from "commandeering" the instrumentalities of state government in the service of federal ends. *See* Printz v. United States, 521 U.S. 898, 925–26 (1997) (holding that a federal statute requiring state and local police to conduct background checks on handgun purchasers unconstitutionally compels states to administer a federal regulatory program); New York v. United States, 505 U.S. 144, 176–77 (1992) (holding that a federal statute requiring states either to "take title" to radioactive waste or regulate according to the commands of Congress unconstitutionally commandeers the states' legislative process).

incorporating at least some of the authority of the democratic process) rather than simply authoring its own decisions from scratch?

These questions together go to the larger issue of whether, and how, adjudication can ever truly be *democratic*. I address them in the next two sections of this chapter.

5. PARTICIPATION AND REPRESENTATION IN ADJUDICATION

Seen through the lens of the DR account, any process of interpreting general legal rules and applying them to particular disputes—a process of *adjudication*—must confront something of a paradox, or at least an irony. Democratic legislation cannot, by itself, resolve inevitable questions about its application to particular disputes. This means that the reasonable accuracy, and thus the general acceptability, and thus the authority that flow from the democratic process are potentially compromised where the rubber hits the road—at the point when democratic legislation comes into contact with actual flesh-and-blood controversies.

We have already gotten a sense, in the previous chapter, of the central structural differences between the democratic political process and the paradigmatic system used to adjudicate particular disputes. Democracy, at least in its purest, ideal form—we can continue to put to one side the fact that actual democracies inevitably fall rather short of this ideal—is decentralized and egalitarian; that is, it is highly participatory, with each person who stands to be bound by its results allowed an equal chance (through majority rule) to influence those results. Adjudication, by contrast, appears centralized and elitist—that is, nonparticipatory, with a single decisionmaker (the judge, or sometimes a jury or small group of judges) holding all the power to dictate a result to which it will not even be bound. Indeed, worries about the significance of the seemingly elitist, even paternalistic character of adjudication animate a strong tradition, within the United States, of distrust and criticism of courts as "nondemocratic," a tradition that finds its most insistent expression, as we will see, in attacks on the institution of constitutional judicial review.

But we also have seen hints of the ways in which this stark democracy-versus-adjudication dichotomy is myopic and distorted. Adjudication's concentration of authority in the hands of a neutral arbiter promotes impartiality by avoiding self-judging, even as it compromises the competence and impartiality that flow from broad participation. Accurate dispute-resolution potentially involves trade-offs; greater impartiality might sometimes be worth the price of lesser competence, or vice versa, and there may be more than one way to foster either accuracy-promoting value. I suggested in Chapter 4 that democracy is not perfectly impartial; in Chapter 7, I will catalog the ways in which its impartiality and competence sometimes fail. Still, the overall balance struck by democracy seems accurate enough, especially in comparison to the alternatives. Similarly, I want to suggest in this chapter that a particular mode of adjudication—one characterized by what is often called the "adversary system" of procedure and relying largely on the "common-law method" of decisionmaking—embodies a similarly acceptable balance among the values of impartiality and competence, albeit in a distinctive way.

A. Adversary Adjudication[16]

In the United States, as well as in Great Britain and in other countries whose legal systems have been heavily influenced by the British, adjudication typically follows an "adversary" model: Primary responsibility for initiating court cases, framing the factual and legal issues, investigating and establishing the existence of relevant facts, researching and articulating the legal arguments, and shaping the remedy lies with the disputing litigants, not with the judge. This so-called "adversary system" can be contrasted with the kinds of "inquisitorial" systems employed in Western Europe (influenced by Roman law, canon law, and the Napoleonic codes), in the orbit of the former Soviet empire (shaped by these influences, by the centralizing tendencies of communism, and in some areas by Islamic law), and in much of Asia (influenced by ancient Chinese models, by European colonization, and by modern communism).[17] In inquisitorial systems, judges or other legal officials, neutral as between the litigants, take the lead in framing the issues, investigating the facts, developing the legal arguments, and so on.

The labels "adversary system" and "inquisitorial system" of course describe archetypes; most actual systems combine elements of both while leaning in one direction or the other, and in fact it may be that the systems closest to the opposite ends of the spectrum have, in recent years, reverted somewhat closer to the mean.[18] But still there are substantial, and for our purposes important,

---

16. Two excellent and influential general accounts of adversary adjudication, upon both of which I have relied heavily, are Lon L. Fuller, *The Forms and Limits of Adjudication*, 92 HARV. L. REV. 353 (1978), and MIRJAN R. DAMAŠKA, THE FACES OF JUSTICE AND STATE AUTHORITY (1986). Damaška's book provides not only an excellent summary of the typical features of adversary adjudication, but also a thoughtful comparison, with attention to political theory, between those features and the typical features of the inquisitorial model.

17. *See generally* DAMAŠKA, *supra* note 16; *see also* HERBERT JACOB ET AL., COURTS, LAW, AND POLITICS IN COMPARATIVE PERSPECTIVE (1996).

18. In the United States, at least, a movement toward mandatory disclosure of important evidence and other information, and the interrelated growth of broad-based public interest litigation and what is often called "managerial judging," have pushed adjudication away from an extreme adversary model. On the relationship between mandatory disclosure rules and the adversary system, see Rogelio A. Lasso, *Gladiators Be Gone: The New Disclosure Rules Compel a Reexamination of the Adversary Process*, 36 B.C. L. REV.

distinctions between systems (like that in America) that lie toward the adversary end of the scale and systems (like that, say, in France) that lie toward the inquisitorial end. Adversary systems, as compared to their inquisitorial counterparts, are relatively participatory: Those who will be bound by a decision play leading and often decisive roles in determining the content of that decision.

The United States has, arguably, the most adversary system of justice in the world. Consider the following typical features of adjudication in American courts. (Here I will focus on the process of civil litigation—lawsuits between private parties (or, sometimes, government acting in its private capacity)—although most of the same general principles also apply to criminal prosecutions.)

- The litigants,[19] not a judge, choose whether and when to initiate adjudication. In order for a court to decide an issue, that issue must be material to an actual dispute among two or more persons who have something tangible riding on the outcome, and at least one of those persons must seek the court's resolution of the dispute.[20]
- The litigants, not the judge, determine what legal issues (issues involving the content or application of general legal rules) and what factual issues are presented by a court case and thus must be decided by the court.[21]

---

479 (1995). On the growth of public-interest litigation and its challenge to the traditional adversary model, see Abram Chayes, *The Role of the Judge in Public Law Litigation*, 89 HARV. L. REV. 1281 (1976), and Owen M. Fiss, *Foreword: The Forms of Justice*, 93 HARV. L. REV. 1 (1979). On managerial judging, see Judith Resnik, *Managerial Judges*, 96 HARV. L. REV. 374 (1982).

19. Most litigants in American courts retain attorneys to represent their interests by performing most litigation-related tasks. Attorneys have fiduciary duties to their clients, requiring them to represent their clients' interests in good faith. *See* MODEL RULES OF PROF'L CONDUCT R. 1.1–1.18 (2007). An attorney's duty to her client may be limited, however, by duties to the court and to the public, such as the duties not to assist in the perpetration of a crime or in the conduct of frivolous litigation. *See id.* at R. 1.2(d), 3.1; FED. R. CIV. P. 11. In referring to the "litigants" in this chapter, I mean to include attorneys acting on behalf of litigants (except where I distinguish in the text between attorneys and litigants).

20. For discussions of standing, see *Lujan v. Defenders of Wildlife*, 504 U.S. 555, 560–63 (1992); *Allen v. Wright*, 468 U.S. 737, 750–52 (1984); and *City of Los Angeles v. Lyons*, 461 U.S. 95, 101–07 (1983).

21. This is done initially by means of "pleadings," documents in which the party initiating the lawsuit (the plaintiff) states her "claims," or legal grounds for relief, and the party defending the lawsuit (the defendant) responds with "defenses," or reasons why the relief sought by the plaintiff should be denied. Legal and factual issues can further be expanded or narrowed by amendments to the pleadings and by "motions," or requests that the court take some action during the pendency of the lawsuit.

- The litigants, not the judge, investigate the relevant facts and assemble them in forms suitable for proof.[22]
- The litigants, without the approval of the judge, may choose to terminate the lawsuit and settle their dispute by other means (or, for that matter, to leave the dispute unsettled).[23]
- The litigants have a substantial role in deciding who ultimately will determine the facts relevant to their case—whether it will be a judge or a jury in some cases, and, in most jury cases, who will sit on the jury.[24]
- Each litigant herself chooses what factual evidence to present to the trier of fact (judge or jury) and actually presents it, often in the form of live oral examination or cross-examination of witnesses under oath.[25] Where expert testimony is required, the experts typically are retained, and compensated,

---

22. The formal aspects of this process are called "discovery." Typically they consist of written questions asked of other litigants, or "interrogatories"; requests from other litigants and nonlitigant third parties for relevant documents and other tangible evidence; and interviews conducted of parties and witnesses under oath, or "depositions."

23. In fact, procedural rules and statutes increasingly encourage out-of-court settlement, and far more cases settle than go to trial in American courts. *See* FED. R. CIV. P. 16 (stating that one purpose of a pretrial conference is to facilitate settlement); 9 U.S.C.A. § 2 (West 2010) (providing that an arbitration agreement in a written contract is "valid, irrevocable, and enforceable, save upon such grounds as exist at law or in equity for the revocation of any contract"); 28 U.S.C.A. § 651(b) (West 2010) (requiring all federal courts to authorize the use of alternative dispute resolution in all civil actions through adoption of a local rule). *See also* U.S. DISTRICT COURTS, CIVIL CASES TERMINATED BY NATURE OF SUIT AND ACTION TAKEN TBL. C-4 (2008), http://www.uscourts.gov/judbus2008/appendices/C04Sep08.pdf (revealing that only 2 percent of all cases sampled reached trial); Mia Cahill & Marc Galanter, *"Most Cases Settle": Judicial Promotion and Regulation of Settlement*, 46 STAN. L. REV. 1339 (1994) (explaining that "settlement is the most frequent disposition of civil cases in the United States").

There are exceptions to the general principle that the litigants can settle cases without court approval, including most prominently class action lawsuits, in which one or a few active litigants represent the interests of many absent parties; settlements of such cases require judicial approval in order to protect those absentee interests. *See, e.g.,* FED. R. CIV. P. 23(e).

24. The Seventh Amendment to the U.S. Constitution guarantees the right of trial by jury in some civil cases, but that right may be waived by the parties. *See* U.S. CONST. amend. VII. Where a jury will hear the case, the litigants typically have the right to participate in the process of choosing the jurors, known as *voir dire*, by asking questions of potential jurors (either directly or by submitting questions to the judge), by objecting "for cause" to jurors who may be unqualified for various reasons, and by "striking" a certain number of jurors who are qualified but unsatisfactory to one of the litigants.

25. The litigants' ability to present evidence is substantially constrained by evidentiary rules and similar limitations. For my attempt to justify these phenomena in light of free-speech norms, see Christopher J. Peters, *Adjudicative Speech and the First Amendment*, 51 UCLA L. REV. 705 (2004).

by the parties themselves. The litigants also have a role in deciding what instructions the judge will give the jury before it deliberates.

- The litigants, not a judge, determine whether the result in the trial court will be reviewed on appeal. No appeals court will review an issue—no matter how publicly important that issue may be—unless a party aggrieved by the result in the trial court seeks such a review.

- As with the merits of the claims and defenses, facts and legal arguments relevant to remedies—to the nature and extent of the relief a court can award to an aggrieved party—are identified, investigated, and presented by the litigants, not unilaterally by a judge.

- Norms of legal practice, and in some cases formal rules,[26] require judges to issue written opinions explaining how their major rulings are justified by the facts and the law.

While a typical inquisitorial system resembles the American system in some respects, it differs markedly in others.[27] Judges in such systems independently review the pleadings to ensure their formal sufficiency. Evidence is gathered by a judicial officer rather than the litigants themselves and typically is reduced to written form before it is presented to the trier of fact (which is always a judge or panel of judges). Expert witnesses are appointed and questioned by the court and generally are not subject to examination by the litigants. Litigants in inquisitorial systems play vital roles, to be sure, but judges in such systems do much of the work that litigants do in adversary adjudication.

Mirjan Damaška has argued persuasively that the model of adjudication a society employs typically reflects its broader political commitments.[28] If this is so, it is no accident that broadly democratic systems of legislation tend, as in the United States and Britain, to go hand-in-hand with litigant-driven processes of adjudication. The perception of legitimacy that flows from the presence of an opportunity for those who will be bound to participate in lawmaking naturally suggests a method of interpreting and applying laws in particular cases that is itself participatory. More generally, the DR account of legal authority—which, as we have seen, leads to electoral and legislative processes that incorporate fair participation—also leads to an adjudicative process that is fairly participatory. The Epistemic-Guidance (EG) account, which is concerned that law produce good answers to particular questions, fits better with systems of both

---

26. See, for example, Federal Rule of Civil Procedure 52, which requires judges who serve as triers of fact to write opinions justifying their decisions on both factual and legal grounds. FED. R. CIV. P. 52.

27. For summaries of typical inquisitorial procedures in civil trials, see WATKIN, *supra* note 1, at 389–95; MARTIN SHAPIRO, COURTS: A COMPARATIVE AND POLITICAL ANALYSIS 148–50 (1981).

28. *See* DAMAŠKA, *supra* note 16.

legislation and adjudication that confer disproportionate authority on small groups of experts.

B. Common-Law Representation[29]

The adversary system affords those who will be most directly bound by court decisions, the litigants themselves, the opportunity to participate directly and meaningfully in making those decisions. But often people other than litigants are "bound" in a very real sense—affected, perhaps deeply and irrevocably—by court decisions. This can happen in a number of ways.

  a. Nonlitigants might be bound, not by a court order directed at them, but by the indirect effects of a court order. Suppose, for example, that a jury renders a large damages award in a slip-and-fall lawsuit against an underinsured convenience store. The store's owner is directly bound by the judgment and thus required to pay the damages awarded to the plaintiff. But if paying the judgment bankrupts the store's owner, putting his employees out of work and destroying his family's savings, then these nonlitigants have been meaningfully "bound" by the judgment as well.

  b. Nonlitigants might be bound because they share something in common with one of the litigants that causes them to fear becoming litigants themselves. Suppose a jury renders a large damages award in a lawsuit brought by a fast-food customer burned by hot coffee she had purchased. Fearing similar lawsuits, other restaurant chains may begin serving coffee at reduced temperatures and placing warning labels on their coffee cups.

  c. Nonlitigants might be bound by virtue of actually becoming litigants in future similar lawsuits. Suppose a rival fast-food chain fails to change its coffee service policies as a result of the verdict in example *b* and is itself sued by a customer burned by hot coffee. While this second fast-food chain will not be directly bound by the result of the first lawsuit, a principle called *stare decisis* might nonetheless operate to bind it to that result in a less direct way. In common-law jurisdictions like Britain and the United States, *stare decisis* requires courts to respect, and often to follow, principles of law laid down by earlier court decisions (known as "precedents"). If the judgment in example *b* rested in part on a new

---

29. The account offered here of interest representation through the common-law method owes much to the insights in the following works: on the idea of representation itself, HANNA FENICHEL PITKIN, THE CONCEPT OF REPRESENTATION (1967); on *stare decisis* as an engine of interest representation, R. L. Brilmayer, *Judicial Review, Justiciability and the Limits of the Common Law Method*, 57 B.U. L. REV. 807 (1977); Lea Brilmayer, *The Jurisprudence of Article III: Perspectives on the "Case or Controversy" Requirement*, 93 HARV. L. REV. 297 (1979); and Steven L. Winter, *The Metaphor of Standing and the Problem of Self-Governance*, 40 STAN. L. REV. 1371 (1988).

principle of law established by the court—say, that restaurants have a legal duty to warn consumers even about seemingly obvious hazards like hot coffee—then the court in a subsequent case, through *stare decisis*, may decide to follow the same principle, without giving the second defendant a chance to reargue the matter. Indeed, the subsequent court *must* follow this principle if the previous court was a higher-ranking court in the same jurisdiction.

Note that *stare decisis*, or the doctrine of precedent, drives the binding effect in example *b* as well as example *c*. Other restaurant chains fear being sued in large part because they worry that any court they would face would apply the same legal principles as the court in the original coffee-spill case, thus making a similar result more likely. (These other chains might fear being sued even without *stare decisis*; litigation can be expensive even for the winner. But the existence of *stare decisis* increases the potential costs of being sued. It also increases the *risk* of being sued, by creating an incentive for subsequent plaintiffs, and their lawyers, to file similar lawsuits.)

Note also that *stare decisis* turns courts into rule*makers* as well as rule-*appliers*. If a court, in resolving a legal issue in a certain way, sets a precedent that other courts must follow with respect to the same or similar issues, then the court has in effect created a rule that binds, not only subsequent courts, but also the litigants before those courts (as in example *c*) and those who fear becoming litigants (example *b*). The same functions of *ex ante* dispute avoidance and *ex post* dispute resolution that are served by democratically enacted legislation also can be served by judicial precedents. Where a judicial precedent is itself an application of a legislative rule, *stare decisis* thus can reduce the indeterminacy of legislative rules over time, by in effect amending those rules piecemeal, adding more detail as new issues arise.

Indeed, for much of the history of Anglo-American jurisprudence, it was the system of judicial precedent, not democratic legislation, that served to generate the majority of legal rules. Only in the nineteenth century did statutory law begin to rival judge-made law as a source of legal norms, and only in the twentieth century did statutory law achieve its present state of dominance (although even now much law is judge-made).[30] This accounts for the fact that we now typically refer to the British and American judicial systems and their derivatives as "common law" systems: The "common law" was judge-made law, derived, it was thought, from the customs and traditions of the community rather than from any positive legislative act.[31] In contrast, "civil law" systems like those in

---

30. *See* WILLIAM D. POPKIN, STATUTES IN COURT 30–35, 59–63, 112–19 (1999).

31. Under the influence of English legal theorists like William Blackstone, English and American jurists continued well into the twentieth century to deny that they created law in any meaningful sense when they decided common-law cases. Common-law decisions

Continental Europe, following a tradition going back through the Napoleonic codes and canon law to the law of the Roman Empire, mostly reject the doctrine of judicial precedent, an approach that places the primary burden of rulemaking on detailed legislative codes.[32]

But if a system of judicial precedent is a system of legal rulemaking—either a community's dominant system or, as in modern common-law countries, a system that mostly supplements statutory law—the rules it generates seem to lack the participatory pedigree of democratic legislation. Here the apparent problem is not simply, or even primarily, the perceived "participation gap" in adjudication (which in any case, as we have seen, is not as large in an adversary system as it may at first seem). The apparent problem is that the subsequent litigants who are bound by judicially created rules, and the nonlitigants who adjust their behavior in order to avoid becoming litigants, have not participated at all in the making of those rules, not even to the same extent as the litigants who were parties to the precedent-setting case.

Whatever the participatory pedigree of adjudication with respect to the directly bound litigants, then, its legitimacy with respect to those indirectly bound through *stare decisis* seems problematic. On closer inspection, though, this apparent problem withers away almost to nothing. Consider first the fact that democratic legislation, the paradigm of participatory rulemaking, itself binds a great many people who have not directly participated in making it. Like judicial precedents, statutes reach forward into time, constraining the behavior and affecting the disputes of many who were not there, so to speak, when the law was created. The federal Sherman Antitrust Act, for example, was signed into law by President Benjamin Harrison in 1890 and remains in force today with only minor amendments.[33] Very few judicial precedents remain binding, essentially unaltered, for more than a century. Probably no Americans alive today were alive when the Sherman Act was adopted; any who are were far too young to vote in 1890. And yet the Act binds us now just as it bound our predecessors five generations ago.

---

were "at most, only evidence of what the laws are"—of what custom required—"and are not, of themselves, laws." Swift v. Tyson, 41 U.S. 1, 18 (1842). The American Legal Realists ridiculed this canard (among others) in the early twentieth century; Oliver Wendell Holmes, for example, mocked the idea of the common law as "a brooding omnipresence in the sky," a "transcendental body of law outside of any particular [jurisdiction]." Black & White Taxicab & Transfer Co. v. Brown & Yellow Taxicab & Transfer Co., 267 U.S. 518, 533 (1928) (Holmes, J., dissenting); Southern Pac. Co. v. Jensen, 244 U.S. 205, 222 (1917) (Holmes, J., dissenting). Ultimately, in one of the most significant judicial opinions of the twentieth century, the Supreme Court rejected the Blackstonian view. See Erie R. Co. v. Tompkins, 304 U.S. 64, 79 (1938).

32. See generally SHAPIRO, supra note 27, at 126–56.
33. See 15 U.S.C.A. §§ 1–7 (West 2010).

We tend not to fret about the intergenerational binding effect of statutes because we know that we in the present generation can, if it becomes important enough to us, repeal or amend old statutes using the same democratic process that created them.[34] But the same holds for judicial precedents under the common-law method. Precedent is not absolutely and forever binding; it can be overruled by subsequent courts if a strong enough case for overruling is presented.[35] (In fact the history of the Sherman Act provides an example of this process. The Act's open-ended language—prohibiting "contract[s], combination[s]. . . or conspirac[ies]. . . in restraint of trade"—has required detailed judicial interpretation, and the substance of that interpretation has evolved considerably over the hundred-year history of the Act.) And remember that a court's decision whether to overrule a precedent will itself be made by an adversary process featuring the meaningful participation of the litigants who stand to be bound by that precedent. The analogy to the repeal or amendment of legislation thus turns out to be rather strong.

In fact, there is an argument to be made that the legitimacy of judicial precedent, along the dynamic of intergenerational binding effect, compares not just credibly but favorably to that of democratic legislation. Under the common-law method, overruling is not the only way to avoid being bound by precedent; it is not even the most frequent way, not by a long shot. The most common way to avoid being bound by precedent is to do what lawyers call *distinguishing* the precedential case. *Stare decisis* requires that cases not be decided inconsistently with each other—that like cases be decided alike. This means that a common law "rule"—the binding effect of a precedent, which lawyers call a "holding"—applies only to future cases that are similar to the precedential case

---

34. For the opposite reason we *do* tend to fret about the intergenerational binding effect of constitutional provisions: They cannot so easily be amended or repealed. I discuss this problem at length in chapters 7 and 8.

35. To be precise, a court can choose to overrule a precedent laid down by the same court, or by a court lower in the judicial hierarchy within that jurisdiction. So, for example, the U.S. Supreme Court can overrule its own decisions and can "overrule"—the technical term here is "reverse"—decisions of lower federal courts, such as the Circuit Courts of Appeals. One of the federal Courts of Appeals, however, cannot overrule a precedent of the Supreme Court. Nor can it overrule a precedent of another Court of Appeals, as each Court of Appeals is supreme with its own jurisdiction (or "Circuit"), subject only to reversal by the Supreme Court. But a Court of Appeals can decline to follow a decision rendered by a Court of Appeals in another Circuit. The fact that federal Courts of Appeals typically decide cases in panels of three judges rather than *en banc*, or as a full court, complicates matters further: A three-judge panel within a Circuit cannot overrule or decline to follow a decision of another panel within that Circuit, while the entire Court sitting *en banc* may do so. These details, of course, are at best ancillary to my argument in the text.

in material respects.[36] A court's holding that a restaurant can be held liable for burns caused by spilled coffee, in a case where the restaurant did *not* warn customers about the danger of burns, does not require the same result in a subsequent case in which the restaurant *did* issue a warning. The restaurant's lawyer in the subsequent case would (if she is a good lawyer) point out this material factual difference to that court—thus "distinguishing" the precedential case—and would argue that the factual difference justifies, or perhaps even requires, a different result in that case.

Skilled lawyers and judges in the common-law tradition are very good at making these kinds of arguments of distinction; that is one of the basic skills of Anglo-American lawyering, one that consumes a substantial chunk of the process of legal education. (The complementary legal skill is known as "analogizing," by which lawyers argue that factually different precedential cases nonetheless are similar enough in important ways to require a similar result. When American law professors tell their first-year students that they will learn to "think like lawyers," the ability to analogize and distinguish cases is a large part of what they mean.) And the frequency with which precedents may be distinguished— or, to put it another way, the typical narrowness of judge-created legal rules— means that the force of a precedent often is easier to escape than the force of a statutory rule, which will tend to be broader. Statutes usually bind more broadly than precedents, and so their intergenerational impact—or for that matter their contemporaneous impact—tends to be greater than that of precedents. The breadth of a given precedent, moreover, will (again) be determined by the participation of the litigants through the adversary process.

There is, however, another potentially troubling dynamic of comparison between judicial precedent and democratic legislation. Both bind not only intergenerationally but also contemporaneously, and in this respect legislation seems to have a clear legitimacy advantage. If a state legislature enacts a statute requiring warning labels on restaurant coffee cups, restaurant owners, customers, and other affected parties in the state will have had the opportunity to participate in the legislative process, first by voting for members of the legislature, then by sending letters and e-mails, writing op-eds, demonstrating in the streets, and so on. (We can put aside the unlikelihood that a coffee-cup warning-label

---

36. Again, to be precise (or at least as precise as possible), a "holding" consists of whatever is necessary to justify the particular decision reached by a court. Everything else the court writes or says in connection with its decision is referred to as "dicta" and is not part of the binding rule created by the decision. So, if a court holds that a restaurant can be liable for burns caused by spilled coffee, and if it would have reached a different result if the restaurant had warned the injured customer about the danger of burns, then the lack of a warning is part of the court's holding, and thus part of the binding rule created by the precedent. If this seems mysterious to you, then you haven't attended law school; if it seems inane to you, then you probably shouldn't attend law school.

statute would in fact inspire such passion.) But if a state court (even the state's highest court) issues a ruling with essentially the same effect, only the litigants and the judge (or the judges, plural, of the trial and appellate courts) will have participated in the decision,[37] and none of them has the same accountability to the electorate that members of the legislature have. The litigants have not been elected at all; and while the judges may have been elected (as is the case in most of the American states), professional norms require them to decide legal issues according to their best judgment about the requirements of the law, not in response to popular sentiments or electoral pressures. The adjudicative process, too, typically is less public and transparent than the legislative process, reducing the opportunities for public comment and debate about the proceedings—comment and debate that, given the aforementioned professional norms, is not supposed to influence judicial decisions anyway.[38]

But even in this respect common-law adjudication is not as dissimilar to democratic legislation as at first it appears. We comfortably think of representative democracy as reasonably participatory in large part because of the confidence the electoral process gives us—confidence that our representatives in the legislature will take our best interests (at least those of a majority of us) into account in making legislation. That confidence flows from the incentives created by the electoral process itself: Legislatures who do not do a good job of looking after their constituents' interests can be removed from their jobs at the next election.

The key to the legitimacy of representation in a democracy, then, is the likelihood that representatives will take seriously the interests of their constituents. And, as it turns out, basically the same can be said of common-law adjudication. The litigants to a precedent-setting court case—a case in which a court lays down a new rule of law—are, virtually by definition, likely to be *interest representatives* of similarly situated subsequent litigants (and parties who want to avoid becoming litigants). According to the common-law method, the legal rule these precedent-setting litigants help create will bind future litigants only to the extent the facts of their dispute are materially similar to the facts of the precedential case. This is, again, where the processes of distinguishing and analogizing precedents come in: Lawyers in a subsequent case can argue that the facts of that case are sufficiently distinct from those of the precedential case to fall

---

37. Members of a jury might have participated in the decision of the case, too—but not in the creation of the legal precedent that now will bind future similar litigants. Legal issues are decided by judges, not by juries.

38. To be precise once more: An Anglo-American judge, consistent with professional norms, could be influenced by the *substance* of public commentary and similar phenomena; she might allow such commentary to affect her good-faith judgment about what the law really requires in her case. But she probably could not be influenced by the mere *fact* of public commentary to decide the case, for instance, in the way she believes will get her the most votes at the next judicial election.

outside the scope of its rule, or that they are sufficiently analogous to fall within the rule's purview.

Imagine, for instance, that some time after the precedent-setting coffee-spill case is decided, a different customer sues a different restaurant for injuries she incurred when she spilled her coffee. As in the original case, the coffee cup provided by the restaurant did not feature a label warning that the coffee inside was hot. Unlike in the original case, however, the restaurant employee orally warned the customer to "be careful, that coffee is very hot." In the subsequent case, lawyers for the customer (the plaintiff) will argue that the rule laid down by the original case applies—that the absence of a printed warning on the coffee cup by itself can support liability, perhaps because merely oral warnings might not always be heard by customers. For their part, lawyers for the restaurant (the defendant) will argue that the precedential rule does not apply—that the lack of a printed warning does not support liability where an oral warning has been provided. But the defendant's lawyers will be precluded, by the principle of *stare decisis*, from rearguing the core question decided in the precedential case, namely whether hot coffee spilled without some sort of warning of its temperature—whatever form that warning must take—can impose liability on the restaurant that served the coffee.

We can see two related phenomena at work in this simple example, both relevant to the legitimacy of binding subsequent litigants to a precedential legal rule. The first phenomenon is one of interest representation through similarity of circumstance. The defendant in the subsequent case cannot reargue the question of whether some kind of warning is required to avoid liability; that question was decided in the precedential case. Clearly the subsequent defendant is bound by this rule. But note that, with respect to that rule, the subsequent defendant and the original defendant share the same set of incentives. The original defendant had every motive to argue against a legal rule imposing liability for spilled coffee without adequate warning; it knew that such a rule would result in an expensive judgment against it. Its interest was in doing whatever it could to prevent the creation of the rule; as such, its interest coincides with the interest of the subsequent defendant, who also would like to avoid the rule. In binding the subsequent defendant to the results of the original defendant's efforts, then, the common law treats the original defendant as an interest representative of the subsequent one—a party authorized, in essence, to act on someone else's behalf by virtue of the fact that their interests coincide.

This idea of interest representation is infused throughout modern Anglo-American law. The device of the class action lawsuit, by which one or a small group of parties formally represents a large number of absent parties in litigation, depends on interest representation for its legitimacy.[39] So do the principles

---

39. Three of the four prerequisites for the maintenance of a class action in U.S. federal court relate to interest representation. There must be "questions of law or fact common to

of issue and claim preclusion (often referred to by the older labels "collateral estoppel" and "res judicata," respectively), which hold that those in "privity" with litigants—that is, those whose interests strongly coincide with the litigants'— can be directly bound by the results of lawsuits. Procedural rules typically allow joinder (that is, addition) of third parties to lawsuits where their interests are likely to be affected but will not adequately be represented by the existing litigants.[40]

Perhaps more to the point, the idea of interest representation also holds a prominent place in the theory and practice of representative democracy. Edmund Burke argued that interest representation was in fact more reliable than the incentives created by the electoral system. Where a representative shared his constituents' interests, Burke believed, he could exercise his best judgment about how to act when presented with facts his constituents did not possess, in essence acting as his constituents would have acted had they been privy to the same information and enjoyed the luxury of sufficient time to consider and debate the matter.[41] Many of the American Founders, contemporaries of Burke, also believed that interest representation played a crucial role in government. They rejected a proposal to constitutionalize a right of constituents to "instruct" their representatives how to vote, concluding along Burkean lines that such a right would make truly deliberative government impossible.[42] And they believed that the members of the popularly elected branch of the legislature, the House of Representatives, would share "a communion of interests and sympathy of sentiments" with their constituents that would supplement (and be reinforced by) "the restraint of frequent elections" as safeguards of good government.[43] The combination of these positions—a belief in the likelihood of interest congruity between elected representatives and their constituents, and a Burkean conviction that representatives should freely deliberate and exercise their own

---

the class"; "the claims or defenses of the representative parties" must be "typical" of those of the class; and the representative parties must "fairly and adequately protect the interests of the class." FED. R. CIV. P. 23(a). (The fourth prerequisite, listed first in the Rule, is that the class be "so numerous that joinder of all members is impracticable. *Id.*)

40. *See, e.g.,* FED. R. CIV. P. 19, 20 (addressing required and permissive joinder of parties).

41. *See Letter from Edmund Burke to Sir Hercules Langrishe, M.P.* (Jan. 3, 1792), *excerpted in* BURKE'S POLITICS 477, 494 (Ross J. S. Hoffman & Paul Levack eds., 1959); Edmund Burke, *Speech to the Electors of Bristol* (Oct. 13, 1774), *excerpted in* BURKE'S POLITICS, *supra,* at 114, 115.

42. As Roger Sherman commented in the first Congress against a "right to instruct":

I think, when the people have chosen a representative, it is his duty to meet others from the different parts of the Union, and consult, and agree with them to such acts as are for the general benefit of the whole community. If they were to be guided by instructions, there would be no use in deliberation.

1 ANNALS OF CONG. 735 (Joseph Gales ed., 1834).

43. *See* THE FEDERALIST NO. 57, at 339 (James Madison) (Issac Kramnick ed., 1987).

judgments regarding public policy—explains in large part James Madison's famous confidence that "the public voice, pronounced by the representatives of the people, will be more consonant to the public good than if pronounced by the people themselves."[44]

Practically speaking, it is difficult to deny the role that similarity of interest, or at least the perception of it, plays in contemporary American politics. Markers of a political candidate's identity—gender, race, class, the perception that he is "out of touch" and "elitist" or that she is "a suburban hockey mom" or "someone you could have a beer with"—feature prominently in each election cycle. Rightly or wrongly, voters often find comfort in the belief that a candidate is "like them" in important respects, and thus likely to share their interests and their values— and discomfort in the opposite belief.

The interest representation that is inherent in the common-law method thus brings Anglo-American adjudication into contact with a core principle of representative political legitimacy. Subsequent litigants are bound by precedential rules they did not directly participate in making; but they are bound only to the extent that the litigants who did participate in making those rules shared their relevant interests. Note, by the way, that this latter feature of *stare decisis*— the binding only of others with similar interests—is *not* shared even by representative democracy. And here we should notice a second feature of common-law reasoning that representative democracy lacks, one also exemplified in the spilled-coffee example: Subsequent litigants have the opportunity to, in effect, choose the legal rules that will bind them. The plaintiff in the second coffee-spill case argues that the precedential rule covers her case; the defendant argues that it does not. This dispute itself will be resolved by the participatory process of adversary adjudication, with each side presenting proofs and arguments to support its case.

C. Adjudication and Indeterminacy Redux

This brings us back to the relationship among democratic legislation, legal indeterminacy, and adjudication. The apparent problem here, remember—the problem to which legal formalism presents itself, misleadingly, as a solution—is that democratically enacted general laws, legitimately authoritative though they may be, cannot do all the dispute-resolving work that must be done in any sort of complex society. Democratic laws sometimes, perhaps often, will be indeterminate—incapable of noncontroversially specifying whether and how they apply in a given case. And the full-dress democratic process, cumbersome as it is, can hardly liquidate these inevitable indeterminacies on an *ex post* basis.

---

44. FEDERALIST No. 10, at 122, 126 (James Madison) (Isaac Kramnick ed., 1987).

Democratic legislation therefore seems to fall substantially short, in practice, of its goal of acceptable dispute resolution.

I've argued here, however, that adversary common-law adjudication can step in where democratic legislation leaves off. Adversary common-law adjudication is in effect a sort of democratic process: a reasonably fair, reasonably participatory method of interpreting and applying general democratic laws *ex post* to particular controversies. The adversary system allows those directly bound by a court decision to participate meaningfully in constructing, and constraining, the decision of an impartial arbiter. The common-law method allows those indirectly bound through *stare decisis* to participate by proxy, through interest representation by the precedent-setting litigants.

But an interesting (and ultimately important) question remains: In what sense, if at all, is this participatory, representative process of adjudication—a process that might be seen as incorporating meaningful indicia of competence, impartiality, and thus reasonable accuracy—in some way *derivative* of the full democratic process whose indeterminate laws it must apply to particular disputes? In deciding how to apply indeterminate legal rules, do courts simply fill in gaps in the law, creating (more or less from scratch) their own legal rules whenever a democratically enacted statute fails to resolve the matter? Or might it be possible for courts somehow to apply, or implement, or *interpret* even a general law that does not determinately resolve the issue presented in a case? And if it is possible, might democratic courts in fact have something like a duty to do so?

6. TEXT, JUSTIFICATION, AND DERIVATIVE DEMOCRATIC AUTHORITY

Even once we recognize that adversary common-law adjudication carries a significant amount of "democratic" legitimacy—that its fairly participatory processes bring reasonable accuracy to the resolution of particular disputes—we might still wonder whether adjudication can, and ought to be, tethered in some substantive way to the full democratic process.

Consider in this respect the formalist goal of eliminating indeterminacy in the application of general democratic laws. Formalists often profess a worry about "judicial discretion" as a motive for their approach—a concern that if adjudication cannot be reduced to relatively mechanical implementation of reasonably determinate rules, "nondemocratic" judges will simply impose their (nonauthoritative) will on litigants (and, on big "public law" questions, on society more broadly).[45] I argued earlier in this chapter that the formalist approach

---

45. *See generally* Scalia, *Common-Law Courts, supra* note 2, at 44–47; Bork, *supra* note 2, at 176, 240, 265.

fails to eliminate or substantially reduce indeterminacy in general rules; and the analysis in the previous section suggests that, in any event, the formalist fear of unfettered judicial discretion is substantially overblown.

But there remains a core of normative validity in the formalist project. The possibility of reasonably accurate, and thus reasonably authoritative, adjudication does not vitiate the formalists' concern with democratic pedigree. Democratic legislation bears the imprimatur of the community as a whole in a way that even optimally fair, optimally participatory adjudication cannot. The authority of a court decision that in some meaningful sense *applies* democratic legislation therefore might be greater than the authority of a court decision that merely fills in the gaps where legislation leaves off.

A. Primary and Derivative Authority

Suppose, for example, that a court decides a case in a way that clearly applies an existing democratic statute. Imagine that Paul is prosecuted for driving his SUV through the city park in violation of the "no vehicles" ordinance hypothesized earlier in this chapter. Suppose that everyone agrees that Paul's SUV is a "vehicle" and thus is banned by the ordinance from the park; the question is simply the factual one of whether it was Paul's SUV that was spotted in the park (as the prosecution claims) or rather someone else's similar vehicle (as Paul claims). If the court, following a fair and participatory procedure, finds against Paul on this factual issue and orders him to pay a fine for violating the ordinance, we might see this decision as authoritative with respect to Paul partly by virtue of the fairly participatory, and thus reasonable accurate, adjudicative procedure that generated it. We can think of this as the *primary* authority of the decision, that is, the authority that flows from the nature (as reasonably accurate) of the procedure (of adversary common-law adjudication) that produced the decision.

But we might also think there is an additional reason to ascribe authority to the court's decision (or perhaps an additional source of the decision's authority). That decision is, plainly, an application of a general rule (the "no vehicles" ordinance) that itself possesses a certain primary authority, by virtue of its origin in the process of democratic legislation. The factual aspect of the court's decision—that it was in fact Paul's SUV that drove through the park—has authority as the product of the fair and participatory process of litigation that produced it. But the *legal* aspect of the decision—that Paul's act of driving his SUV in the park violated the law—has authority as the product of the fair and participatory process of democratic legislation that produced *it*. The primary authority of the court's decision (stemming from the court's own procedures) thus is complemented by authority that is derived from the primary authority of the "no vehicles" ordinance (stemming from the process of majoritarian democracy). We can think of this latter type of authority as the *derivative* authority of the court decision, as it flows not from anything about the court's procedures themselves, but rather from the fact that the court's decision is in part an application of the authoritative democratic statute enacted by the city council.

Compare this scenario with one involving a court decision that lacks this second, derivative type of authority. Suppose Olive is prosecuted under the "no vehicles" ordinance for pulling her toy wagon through the park. Imagine that the court, like the court in Paul's case, follows a fair and participatory procedure in resolving a number of factual issues against Olive (e.g., issues relating to the size of the wagon, how long Olive had it in the park, and so on). But imagine that, unlike in Paul's case, the court cannot identify a determinate meaning of the "no vehicles" ordinance as applied to Olive's wagon: The court concludes, rather, that the ordinance simply does not determine whether Olive's wagon is (or is not) banned from the park. Suppose, however, that the judge is not a Default Formalist: She believes it is better to resolve that question using the process of adjudication than to leave it to be resolved arbitrarily by simply ratifying the *status quo*. And so the court—using the same fairly participatory process that it followed in resolving the factual issues—resolves the legal issue by holding that Olive's wagon is in fact banned from the park.

We can understand the court's decision in Olive's case as having primary legitimacy for the same reasons as in Paul's case: The decision in each case has been generated by a fairly participatory (and thus reasonably accurate) process. But notice that the decision in Olive's case lacks the additional derivative legitimacy that was present in Paul's. Because the court has approached its decision as an act of lawmaking *ab initio*, rather than as the application of an existing democratically enacted rule, that decision lacks the imprimatur of the full democratic process. Whatever authority it possesses depends entirely on the nature of the adjudicative process itself.

Notice also that the dispute-resolution task for the court in Olive's case is more daunting than the court's task in Paul's case, in the following sense: The court in Olive's case must resolve a dispute not just about the facts, but about the content of the law as well. The costs of resolving Olive's dispute, all else being equal, thus are likely to be correspondingly higher. This is simply a function of the fact that general legal rules have, in Olive's case, failed at their task of resolving, *ex ante*, disputes about what legal norms apply, *ex post*, to Olive's conduct.

We can charitably understand formalism, our old acquaintance, as an attempt not just to bring more determinacy to *ex post* disputes—thus reducing their costs—but also to bolster the primary authority of adjudication with the derivative authority found in the application of a democratically enacted general rule. This latter goal certainly is understandable if we forget (as most formalists seem to do) that adjudication can itself possess significant primary authority. But even if we recognize adjudication's potential for primary authority, we may prefer to combine that authority with authority derived from the full democratic process, all else being equal. The full democratic process, after all, has significant participation-related advantages over adjudication: It can bring a much greater diversity of viewpoints and interests to bear on decisionmaking. We might then think that democratic lawmaking, generally speaking, is likely to have a greater degree of competence than adversary adjudication. This does not mean that adjudicative decisions lack a sufficient level of reasonable competence; it is only to suggest that a comparison is likely to favor majoritarian democracy, and that the authority of a court decision therefore is likely to be stronger (all else being equal) to the extent it is augmented by the authority of democratic politics.

Likewise, although a comparative strength of adversary adjudication is (or at least can be) its impartiality, that strength becomes attenuated as a judicial decision is imposed upon those who have not directly participated in making it. If we assume that the procedure followed by the court in Olive's case was optimally fair and participatory, Olive herself has a strong reason to recognize the ruling's authority over her. But even in a well-functioning system of common-law adjudication, the next person prosecuted for pulling a toy wagon through the park, finding herself bound by the rule devised by the court in Olive's case, might not have quite so strong a reason for obedience. The subsequently bound litigant, after all, did not actually participate in the process of crafting that rule. And although there may be good reason to think that her interests were well represented in that process—and thus sufficient reason to hold that the rule is authoritative with respect to her—surely that reason is enhanced if the rule is the product, not simply of the efforts of Olive, the prosecutor, and the judge in the earlier court case, but of the full-dress democratic process in which the subsequent litigant has (or could have) directly participated.

The point here is that a court decision that is both primarily and derivatively authoritative is, all else being equal, preferable (on a DR account) to a court decision that has primary authority alone. And of course the formalist point about determinacy remains: To the extent existing legal rules can be applied to a dispute, the need to generate new rules *ex post*, and the costs of disputing their content, can be avoided. We therefore can see the formalist project in a more flattering light: Formalism has the noble goals of increasing the determinacy of general legal rules, thus reducing the costs of *ex post* disputes, and of bringing the authority of the democratic process to the practice of adjudication. The analysis so far suggests that even courts with considerable authority of their own ought to pursue that goal—assuming it is possible to do so.

The problem, of course, now becomes whether it is possible to do so. The formalist strategy fails, as we have seen; adjudication cannot function merely as a mechanical process of applying determinate general rules to particular facts. Is there an alternative strategy? Can we conceive of a way for courts to *apply* indeterminate general rules in specific cases, rather than simply legislate from scratch within the gaps those rules leave open?

B. Legal Positivism as a Theory about Rules

Legal positivism—or a certain version of that approach, anyway—suggests that the answer is no. H.L.A. Hart theorized that law just consists of rules: primary rules that directly govern people's day-to-day activity, and secondary rules that determine whether and how the primary rules can be created, extinguished, or changed.[46] If that is so, then a decision that does not directly apply a primary or secondary legal rule is not a *legal* decision; it is not law. Of course, some secondary legal rule might give a decisionmaker (say, a judge) the authority to create *new* law in situations were no primary legal rule determines the outcome; but doing so would be an act of legislation, not one of interpretation. The authority of the resulting decision, if any, would flow from something about the process used to create the new law (and perhaps, in part, from something about the process used to create the secondary rule that authorized the creation of new law), not from anything about the process of creating the primary rule or rules that, it turns out, do not determine the outcome.

On this understanding of Hartian positivism, the line between applying or interpreting law on the one hand and creating it on the other falls where the determinacy of primary legal rules runs out. If no primary legal rule applies in a clear and noncontroversial way to a particular case, then (on this view) there simply is no existing law that governs the case, and the judge or other decisionmaker must either throw up her hands (the Default Formalist solution) or resolve the case by making new law.[47] The latter choice might carry substantial direct authority, if the adjudicative process by which the law is created is reasonably competent and impartial; but it would not carry any derivative authority flowing from the application of an authoritative general rule. And if primary legal rules are considered authoritative because they are produced by a fair and broadly participatory democratic process, adjudicative decisions within the indeterminate gaps in those rules cannot channel any of the advantages of that process, and thus cannot rest in part upon any of that process' authority.

If legal rules frequently are indeterminate, as I suggested above,[48] then this rule-bound version of positivism implies that adjudicative decisions often lack derivative authority. This might seem intuitively problematic: What is the point

---

46. *See* H.L.A. Hart, The Concept of Law (2d ed. 1994) (particularly Chapter 5).

47. *See, e.g.,* Joseph Raz, The Authority of Law 53–77, 180–209 (1979). Raz argues that "[w]here the facts which are legal reasons"—e.g., the meaning of a statute, the intent of the legislature—"are indeterminate, through vagueness, open texture, or some other factors, certain legal statements are neither true nor false." Such "gaps" in the law are "inevitable" on a positivist account of law, Raz contends, *id.* at 72–74; they create "unregulated disputes" that can only be resolved by "judicial law-making." *Id.* at 193–97.

48. For a critique of Hartian positivism based on the idea that legal rules often incorporate "essentially contested concepts"—that is, that they often are indeterminate—see Ofer Raban, Modern Legal Theory and Judicial Impartiality 11–16 (2003).

of an elaborate democratic process for generating legal rules if those rules, in a great many cases, will make no difference to the outcome? From the perspective of the DR account of law, this intuition can be expressed as the worry that whatever authority is conferred by the democratic process turns out to be missing from a large number of judicial decisions. Adjudication may be narrowly democratic—reasonably fair and participatory with respect to the bound parties; but (the rule-bound view suggests) it is broadly nondemocratic—entirely lacking that pedigree that the full-blown process of majoritarian democratic politics can confer.

C. Linguistic Intention and Justification

Fortunately, rule-bound positivism rests on an erroneous view about the application of rules. On that view, a general rule cannot be applied to a particular dispute unless its meaning with respect to that dispute is clear and noncontroversial. To put this another way, rule-bound positivism holds that in cases in which no legal rule applies clearly and noncontroversially, a court or other decisionmaker must either refuse to decide the case (the solution of Default Formalism) or fashion a resolution entirely from scratch. But this view misses the ways in which even indeterminate rules might contribute to the outcome of a case.

(i) **Linguistic Intention** First, as we have already got some sense of, the language of a rule can limit the permissible outcomes even when it does not conclusively determine the outcome. Within any social context, linguistic terms will have a limited range of permissible meanings; there will be some (typically many) meanings that are not defensible as reasonable interpretations of the language. In the contemporary United States, for example, it would not be permissible for a judge to interpret the "no vehicles" ordinance as not applying to a fully functional SUV, or as applying to a picnic basket. These would be patently unreasonable interpretations of the meaning of the language; an SUV is too well-situated within the "core of settled meaning" of the word "vehicle," while a picnic basket is too far outside that core.[49] Again, the constraint here is a function of more than just the rule's text; it also is a function of the social context in which the language exists. But it is constraint imposed by the rule nonetheless; and by honoring that constraint, a court gives some degree of normative effect to the rule in its decision of the case.

Notice, too, that this constraint is not a product of the psychological "intent" or other mental state of the legislature or some members of it; or rather (to be more precise) it is not a product of the legislators' "intent" regarding any particular application of the general rule. Ronald Dworkin draws a helpful distinction between the "legal" and the "linguistic" intentions of the legislature: Its linguistic

---

49. Hart, *Positivism, supra* note 3, at 607.

intentions are what it intends to say through the medium of a statute, and its legal intentions are the particular consequences it intends should flow from that statement.[50] A judge interpreting the "no vehicles" ordinance is constrained by the city council's linguistic intention to prohibit "vehicles" rather than, say, "nuisances" or "hazardous objects." But this does not mean that (as an originalist would claim) the judge is constrained by whatever the city council, or some subset of it, thought or would have thought about the specific question of whether toy wagons should be allowed in the park—that is, by what Dworkin calls their legal intentions.

If a judge interpreting a statute is constrained, not by its language itself or by the legal intentions of its creators, but by the permissible range of meaning of the statute's language as determined by the social context, then of course (as we have also seen) it will be possible for the meaning of a statute to change over time. The "no vehicles" ordinance might prohibit a bicycle now even if it did not prohibit one fifty years ago when the ordinance was enacted; and—a slightly different phenomenon—it might prohibit SUVs now even though SUVs did not exist fifty years ago.

By the same token, the concept of linguistic intention imposes limits on how much the meaning of a rule can morph. Constitutional theorist Christopher Eisgruber offers the example of a grandfather who, on his deathbed, convinces his grandson to promise that he will "eat only healthy foods."[51] The precise content of this general rule might change over time, along with changing medical understandings of which foods qualify as healthy—from beef and whole milk to sushi and red wine (and perhaps someday, as in the Woody Allen movie *Sleeper*, to cream pies and hot fudge).[52] But if the word "healthy" comes to represent some entirely different concept—say, "trendy" or "delicious"—the grandson would hardly think he is keeping his promise by eating whatever happens to be trendy or delicious. Doing so would contravene his grandfather's (otherwise capacious) linguistic intent in using the word "healthy," and that would be to disobey the grandson's authoritative promise to "eat only healthy foods."

---

50. *See* DWORKIN, FREEDOM'S LAW, *supra* note 11, at 15–38. For a helpful description and application of Dworkin's distinction, see CHRISTOPHER L. EISGRUBER, CONSTITUTIONAL SELF-GOVERNMENT 28–32 (2001).

51. *See* EISGRUBER, *supra* note 50.

52. *Dr. Melik*: This morning for breakfast he requested something called "wheat germ, organic honey and tiger's milk."

Dr. Aragon [chuckling]: Oh, yes. Those are the charmed substances that some years ago were thought to contain life-preserving properties.

Dr. Melik: You mean there was no deep fat? No steak or cream pies or. . . hot fudge?

Dr. Aragon: Those were thought to be unhealthy. . . precisely the opposite of what we now know to be true.

Dr. Melik: Incredible.

In the grandfather-on-his-deathbed hypothetical, it might be reasonable to ask why the grandson should feel himself bound by the grandfather's linguistic intentions rather than his legal intentions. In many cases, after all, it might not be too difficult to glean what the grandfather's legal intentions were or might have been; Grandpa surely would have wanted his grandson to eat lots of red meat and would have been deeply suspicious of sushi. And we might not think there was anything particularly special about the exact formulation of words Grandpa happened to use (with his dying breath!) to extract the promise from his grandson. When the rule in question has been generated by a democratic legislature, however, its language takes on a particular importance. As Henry M. Hart, Jr. and Albert Sacks wrote in their influential teaching materials *The Legal Process*, "[t]he words of a statute are what the legislature has enacted as law, and all that it has the power to enact. Unenacted intentions or wishes cannot be given effect as law."[53] The result of the democratic process has been the adoption of a rule as expressed in a particular body of text; it is the rule *expressed that way* that carries whatever authority the democratic process can confer. Respect for the legislature's authority thus requires giving effect to the particular language it has adopted; it requires implementing its linguistic intent.

The language of a legal rule, then, stakes the outer boundaries of a court's discretion even in a case where the language does not specify the outcome. In this respect, even indeterminate rules can be *applied*: An interpreter applies them by staying within the boundaries imposed by their language.

(ii) Justification There is another sense in which a linguistically indeterminate rule might be applied by a judge or other interpreter. A judge might think that some nonlinguistic aspect of a rule—an aspect I will refer to as the rule's *justification*—is capable of providing interpretive guidance within the outer boundaries set by the rule's language.

By the "justification" of a statute or other rule, I mean the most normatively attractive explanation of why the rulemaker created the rule and used certain language to express it.[54] We can get a sense of what a justification is, and how a judge or other interpreter might identify and apply it, by imagining again that a

---

53. HART & SACKS, *supra* note 7, at 1375. On Hart & Sacks's account of the importance of statutory text, and its similarity to Ronald Dworkin's account, see Vincent A. Wellman, *Dworkin and the Legal Process Tradition: The Legacy of Hart and Sacks*, 29 ARIZ. L. REV. 413, 461–67 (1987).

54. Compare a number of similar descriptions of the inquiry into statutory "purpose": Purpose should be inferred by asking "[w]hy. . . reasonable men, confronted with the law as it was, [would] have enacted this new law to replace it[.]" HART & SACKS, *supra* note 7, at 1378. "A statute's purpose consists of the set of reasons for making those words a fixed part of the body of the law." Wellman, *supra* note 53, at 463 (describing Hart and Sacks's understanding of statutory purpose). "Legislative intention"—the author's label for what Hart and Sacks call "statutory purpose" and I call "statutory justification"—is a hypothesis

judge must decide whether Olive's act of towing her toddler through the public park in a toy wagon violated the "no vehicles in the park" ordinance.

Suppose the judge has concluded that an interpretation of the ordinance as banning Olive's wagon is consistent with, but not required by, the linguistic intention behind the ordinance; that is, she has decided that the word "vehicle" can reasonably be read as either describing or not describing toy wagons. This conclusion is not much help to the judge, for it leaves her free to resolve the ultimate issue either way. But that does not mean the ordinance itself has exhausted its usefulness in the case.

Suppose that although the judge is unsure whether Olive's wagon is a "vehicle," she can readily conjure objects that clearly qualify as "vehicles" and thus fall within the linguistic intention behind the ordinance. An SUV clearly is a vehicle; a truck clearly is a vehicle, as is a car, a bus, or a motorcycle—all of them are well within H.L.A. Hart's "core of settled meaning" of the term.[55] In fact, the judge probably imagined a similar lineup of obvious "vehicles" in trying to answer the linguistic-intention question, that is, to determine whether a toy wagon must, or may, qualify as a vehicle.

Now, however, the judge might have a different purpose in thinking about cases in which the ordinance clearly applies: She might use such cases (we can call them *positive paradigms*) as clues to a justification for the ordinance.[56] Her inquiry would be, not what the typical properties of a "vehicle" are and whether Olive's wagon shares them—that was the inquiry at the linguistic-intention stage—but rather *what it is about these quintessential vehicles that might explain the legislature's decision to ban them from the park*. If there is some property or collection of properties that obvious vehicles possess and that justifies their exclusion from a public park, then the judge might be able to resolve Olive's case by asking whether Olive's wagon also possess that property or collection of properties (and thus also should be excluded from the park).

Suppose the judge notices a number of properties that these quintessential vehicles have in common: they are loud; they produce noxious fumes; they pose a danger to pedestrians in the park; they are made largely of metal; they carry one or more people from place to place; they must be driven or piloted by someone; they are relatively expensive. Some of these properties (the first three) might reasonably justify a statute banning vehicles *qua* vehicles from the public park. Parks are places people go, often with children, to play and relax; excessive noise, noxious fumes, and large speeding objects frequently will interfere with that function. On the other hand, it is difficult to construct a reasonable

---

about the reason for which a certain category [of persons, things, or activities] is treated [by a statute] in a certain way." RABAN, *supra* note 48, at 97.

55. *See* Hart, *Positivism, supra* note 3, at 607.

56. *Cf.* HART & SACKS, *supra* note 7, at 1378 ("Why would reasonable mean, confronted with the law as it was, have enacted this new law to replace it? The most reliable guides to an answer will be found in the instances of unquestioned application of the statute.").

argument why other properties (the last four) would justify excluding vehicles from the park: Nothing in particular about objects that are made of metal, or that carry people from place to place, or that require a driver, or that cost a lot of money is likely to interfere with the function of a public park. So the judge might hypothesize, based on these positive paradigms, that the "no vehicles" ordinance is justified as a means of preventing excessive noise, noxious fumes, and danger to pedestrians in the park.

The judge might also notice that some objects that clearly are *not* vehicles— that is, cases that are *negative* paradigms—also possess one or more of these properties. Fireworks, for instance, produce lots of noise, noxious smoke, and danger to bystanders; and yet they clearly are not banned by the ordinance. Does this suggest that the judge's hypothesized justification of the ordinance—the prevention of noise, fumes, and danger—must be rejected? Probably not; the fact that the legislature has regulated less than the entire universe of activities that cause a certain harm (vehicles but not fireworks in the public park) does not necessarily rule out avoidance of that harm as the justification of the legislation it has enacted. Legislatures have limited time and resources, and often they will try to solve only the most salient manifestations of a problem. Frequently, too, the reason for regulating one type of activity will, if applied to similar types of activity, be outweighed by countervailing reasons against regulation. (Perhaps banning fireworks from the park would ruin the city's annual Fourth of July celebration.) So the judge will have to be cautious about paying too much attention to negative paradigms. But if the judge identifies a great many negative paradigms that happen to possess some or all the properties she thinks justify the statute at hand—that is, lots of things that clearly are not banned from the park but still are loud, smelly, and dangerous—she may be forced to rethink her hypothetical justification of the ordinance.

This point suggests another consideration the judge is likely to make in seeking the justification of the ordinance: She is likely to consider the body of law apart from the ordinance in question, and to ask what understanding of the ordinance's impact on that body of law makes the most sense. Suppose, for example, that the park independently is subject to a noise ordinance that prohibits sounds in excess of a certain decibel level. This would militate against an interpretation of the ordinance as justified in part by concerns about excessive noise; such an interpretation would render the ordinance partially redundant. (There may of course be countervailing considerations here; perhaps a bright-line ban on vehicles is easier to enforce than a decibel limit.) Suppose, on the other hand, that the city sponsors noisy powerboat races every week on the lake in the park; this too would militate against the "no excessive noise" justification of the ordinance, not because it would render the ordinance redundant, but rather because it would render the ordinance useless.

A focus on the state of the law absent the ordinance also suggests a complementary inquiry into the particular problems or events that led the legislature to enact the ordinance. Perhaps the city council adopted the law in the wake of a tragic vehicle-strikes-pedestrian accident in the park; that would suggest that the ordinance is justified at least in part by the goal of preventing such accidents. Note that the judge's attention to the events or states of affairs that precipitated legislative action—to "the mischief that needed remedying," in the words of Hart and Sacks[57]—is distinct from obeisance to the legal intentions of the legislature (or some members of it), that is, to legislators' actual psychological hopes or expectations that the statute generate a particular result. Enactment history "should be examined for the light it throws on *general purpose*," as Hart and Sacks put it (or on the statute's "justification" in my terminology); "[e]vidence of specific intent with respect to particular applications is competent only to the extent that the particular applications illuminate the general purpose and are consistent with other evidence of it."[58]

The judge, then, might attempt to formulate a justification of the ordinance by reference to positive and (to a lesser extent) negative paradigms, to the state of the law absent the ordinance, and to the particular problems that motivated the legislature to enact the ordinance. What the judge is looking for, as I suggested in the previous paragraph, is not some actual mental state of the legislator or legislators; the search is not for legal intent or some other originalist entity.[59] (Avoiding confusion on this point is my motive for using the terminology of statutory "justification" rather than statutory "purpose.") The search, rather, is for a normatively persuasive explanation of what the legislature *did* in enacting the statute. In this respect statutory justification is not subjective (contingent on the psychology of the subject—the legislature—whose action is in question) but rather objective (resulting from the assessment of that action according to some external standard).

By the same token, the search for statutory justification unavoidably has a normative component; the external standard to which a statute is assessed in the pursuit of its justification is a normative one. The judge rejects expensiveness and metallic construction as justifications for banning vehicles from the park on purely normative grounds: Such justifications would be normatively unreasonable.[60] Different judges may reach different conclusions regarding

---

57. *Id.* at 1379.

58. *Id.* (emphasis in original).

59. *Cf.* RABAN, *supra* note 48, at 96 ("Discovering legislative intention is not an exercise in individual psychology: legislative intention is not a fact about what this or that legislator has thought. Rather, it is a hypothesis about the reason for which a certain category is treated in a certain way. . . .").

60. In the language of contemporary American constitutional analysis, a statute banning expensive objects from the public park probably would lack a "rational basis" and thus would fail muster under the Due Process and Equal Protection Clauses. *See* ERWIN CHEMERINSKY, CONSTITUTIONAL LAW PRINCIPLES AND POLICIES 540, 672 (3rd ed. 2006) (describing rational-basis review).

which potential justifications are normatively reasonable, or more normatively reasonable than others. In this sense, the search for justification *is* subjective: It depends on the particular moral judgments of the interpreter charged with identifying the justification.

Still, it is fair to say that the search for justification is a way of applying the underlying statute rather than simply engaging in unfettered, all-things-considered moral reasoning. Suppose our judge, having gone through roughly the process outlined above, determines that the "no vehicles" ordinance is justi-fied by the goal of avoiding harm to pedestrians and other users of the park; and suppose she decides that because Olive's toy wagon presents no real threat of harm to pedestrians or others, it should not be banned from the park as a "vehicle" under the ordinance. The judge can reach this decision even if she believes, as a matter of her own personal moral judgment, that toy wagons are ugly and annoying and should be banned from the park. Her decision not to punish Olive (and thus to allow toy wagons in the park) thus is, or can be, the product of something other than an act of unfettered, all-things-considered moral reasoning. It can be constrained in some way by her idea of statutory jus-tification and her process of identifying and applying it.

The search for statutory justification, in other words, can be understood as a method of *applying* a statute in the face of indeterminacy. When we combine the idea of statutory justification with the idea of linguistic intention, we get a picture of statutory interpretation that really *is* interpretive:[61] It entails, not an all-or-nothing choice between the mechanical application of determinate legal rules (the formalist strategy) on the one hand and *ab initio* judicial lawmaking (the rule-bound positivist alternative) on the other, but rather a process by which normative judgments are guided and constrained by descriptive facts about the language, legal backdrop, and enactment history of a statute.

---

61. The process of applying an indeterminate statute is "interpretive" both in one sense in which that concept typically is used in everyday language—to describe a nonmechan-ical act of making an indeterminate general norm relevant to a particular problem—and in the more technical sense in which Ronald Dworkin has used the term. Dworkin argues (roughly speaking) that judges decide cases by developing a normatively attractive account of the body of relevant legal materials (statutes, court decisions, constitutional provisions, etc.)—one that fits those materials reasonably well and also is morally appealing—and then deciding individual cases in a way that is consistent with that account. He calls this process "interpretation," and it bears an obvious resemblance to the (much narrower) description of the pursuit of statutory justification I offer in the text (or rather my descrip-tion owes an obvious debt to Dworkin's account). More generally, Dworkin believes that law, as a social practice, must be understood interpretively—by devising a normatively attractive account of the practice, that is, an account that fits the descriptive aspects of the practice and also is morally appealing. *See* RONALD DWORKIN, LAW'S EMPIRE (1986) [hereinafter DWORKIN, LAW'S EMPIRE].

To the question, then, of whether adjudication can possess derivative democratic authority absent a determinate and applicable statute, the answer is a qualified "yes." Courts can meaningfully apply even indeterminate legal rules; in doing so, they can channel some of the democratic authority that generated those rules, while also enhancing *ex ante* determinacy as compared to a completely unfettered judicial process. At the same time, courts add considerable *ex post* value to the rule-applying process: They supply the inevitable normative component of interpretation, and of course they resolve disputes about the facts to which general rules, so interpreted, will apply. Thus it remains important for courts to cultivate the primary authority that can flow from a fair and participatory adjudicative process.

D. A Note on the Common Law

Much (and, historically, most) decisionmaking by English and American courts involves not statutory interpretation but the *common law*—a body of judicially created and developed doctrines. While the dominance of the common law has been eclipsed over the past century or so by the proliferation of statutory regulation,[62] many areas of the law—tort, contract, and property law chief among them—still consist largely of common-law doctrines. Common-law decisionmaking differs from statutory interpretation in a number of ways relevant to this book, and I want briefly to canvass them here.

First, the *authority* of common-law decisionmaking differs from that of statutory interpretation. As we have seen, statutory interpretation draws on both the primary authority of a court's own procedures and authority derived from the democratic procedures that generated the statute in question. But common law is court-made law, not legislature-made law; a court interpreting a common-law doctrine is applying the work of other courts, not of a democratic legislature. Precedential common-law decisions lack the full measure of authority that can be conferred by the democratic process, and so subsequent judicial interpretations of those decisions lack the derivative authority present in an act of statutory interpretation.

This distinction, however, should not be overstated. Given the contemporary dominance of statutory law, the persistence of the common law in some subject areas can fairly be characterized as a function—at least partially a function—of legislative choice. In some American jurisdictions (e.g., California), the legislature has gradually codified common-law doctrines in statutes, thus displacing common-law decisionmaking in areas like tort and contract law with what is technically statutory interpretation. But in most American states, these historically common-law subjects still are regulated primarily by the common law.

---

62. On this point, see POPKIN, *supra* note 30; CASS R. SUNSTEIN, AFTER THE RIGHTS REVOLUTION: RECONCEIVING THE REGULATORY STATE 1–46 (1990).

The absence of wholesale legislative displacement of the common law in these jurisdictions probably can be attributed, if not to some conscious decision to defer to the common law, then at least to a general legislative satisfaction with the substance of, and process of developing, that law. Legislative sufferance of the common law implies tacit, if not explicit, approval; and thus we might think of contemporary common-law decisionmaking as incorporating a sort of delegated legislative authority. Common-law doctrines have not themselves been generated by the democratic process, but they bear the implicit imprimatur of that process—and therefore carry a diluted strain of the full democratic authority borne by statutes.

Apart from the implicit endorsement of the legislature, the authority of the common law flows from two sources. First is the authority of the process of adversary common-law adjudication itself, which we have explored at some length already. Second is the tremendous benefit of consistency in the decision of cases. There is a vigorous and ongoing debate—beyond my scope here—over why consistency in the common law (and in other contexts) is valuable (although virtually everyone agrees that it *is* valuable).[63] Seen through the lens of the DR account, consistency in judicial decisionmaking—"deciding like cases alike"—brings a measure of determinacy to the law, thus allowing people to avoid disputes or to resolve them more quickly and inexpensively when they arise. On this view (which is a version of a widespread instrumental understanding of the value of legal consistency), a precedential common-law decision has authority (over litigants and judges in subsequent cases, and thus over those who may become or hope to avoid becoming litigants) because following it will preserve determinacy in the law.

The distinctive nature of the authority of the common law implies, second, a *methodology* of common-law decisionmaking that resembles in some ways and differs in others from that of statutory interpretation. The resemblances follow from the relevance of justification to both methodologies. A court interpreting a statute seeks the statute's justification as a way of "applying" the statute, or extending its normative authority, to cases not clearly resolved by the statutory language itself. A court interpreting a common-law precedent seeks the

---

63. At the heart of the debate is whether consistency—"deciding like cases alike"—has inherent or only instrumental value. For my own description of and positions on that question, see Christopher J. Peters, *Foolish Consistency: On Equality, Integrity, and Justice in Stare Decisis*, 105 YALE L.J. 2031 (1996), contending that consistency in judicial decisionmaking has only instrumental value; Christopher J. Peters, *Equality Revisited*, 110 HARV. L. REV. 1210 (1997), taking the same position on consistency more generally. For contrary positions, see DWORKIN, LAW'S EMPIRE, *supra* note 61, attributing the value of consistency in judicial decisionmaking to a non-instrumental norm called "integrity"; Kent Greenawalt, *Response: "Prescriptive Equality": Two Steps Forward*, 110 HARV. L. REV. 1265 (1997), defending consistency, or "prescriptive equality," as possessing noninstrumental value in many ethical contexts.

precedent's justification as a way to determine the relevant metric of commonality and difference with which to assess consistency. In either context, a justification serves as an abstract norm—in essence, a very general rule—that can be extracted from an existing decision and applied to a new case, thus bridging the earlier and the later decision.

Suppose, for example, that a court in Case A decides as a matter of common law that a fast-food restaurant can be held liable in tort for injuries suffered by a customer who burned herself on hot coffee served in a cup without a warning label. Now a court in Case B is faced with a case involving a burned customer who was orally warned that the coffee was hot. The court in Case B wants to reach a decision that is consistent with the decision in Case A. How is the Case B court to determine which result would be "consistent" with the result in Case A?

The Case B court might accomplish this by identifying the justification of the Case A result—the most normatively attractive explanation of why the Case A court reached its decision and used certain language to express it—and then applying that justification to Case B. Suppose the Case B court reads the opinion in Case A and determines that the decision is justified by a principle of least-cost avoidance: The restaurant was held liable because restaurants are more likely to know whether the coffee they serve is dangerously hot and thus better able than customers to avoid accidents by warning customers about them. Now the court has identified a general rule that might also be applied in Case B. To decide Case B according to that rule is to decide Case B consistently with Case A.

The chief similarity between common-law decisionmaking and statutory interpretation, then, is that in both contexts a court will attempt to decide a case according to a general rule extracted from an earlier decision (a court case in the former context, a statute in the latter). But here the similarities give way to differences between the two modes. One difference is that the justification of a common-law precedent manifests itself in distinctive ways. Statutes sometimes include statements of purpose, but typically legislatures leave the divination of statutory justification to subsequent interpreters, relying on the capacity of statutory language to avoid most potential disputes. Common-law courts, by contrast, see their primary task as resolving particular disputes and explaining their resolutions of them by means of written opinions. A court interpreting a common-law decision, then, will not have a canonical statement of a general rule to work with. Instead it will have a particular result (defendant is liable) on a certain set of facts (hot coffee served by a restaurant to a customer without a warning) accompanied by a relatively detailed explanation of why that result follows from those facts. This written explanation typically performs much of the subsequent court's work for it; it articulates, albeit not always clearly and unambiguously, what the precedential court sees as the justification of its decision. The court in Case B can rely heavily on the court's own statement in Case A of its justification for the result in that case.

But the subsequent court *need not* rely on the precedential court's own justification of its results; and herein lies another difference between common-law decisionmaking and statutory interpretation. Once it has identified the justification of a statute, the superior authority of the legislature—its greater democratic pedigree—militates powerfully against the court's disregarding that statutory justification. Doing so, after all, would be in a real sense to deny the legislature's authority. With an exception of sorts that I discuss below, however, a precedential court has no greater democratic authority than a subsequent court. The reason to follow precedent in the common law is one of consistency and thus of determinacy, not of superior authority. It might be that the demands of consistency should be overridden by case-specific factors with more frequency than the demands of democratic authority should be; and this fact might explain the recognized authority of common-law courts to overrule their own precedents or to ignore the precedents of courts in other jurisdictions. The court deciding the coffee-burn lawsuit in Case B might not (and, in the Anglo-American common-law tradition, probably would not) consider itself as tightly bound by the decision in Case A as it would if that decision took the form of a democratically enacted statute.[64]

It might also be the case that the goal of consistency often should be compromised, if not overridden altogether, in the name of getting a particular case right or sending the law in a new direction. This might explain the celebrated capacity of common-law courts to invent, retroactively, new justifications for precedential decisions, thus allowing subsequent cases to be decided in ways that are technically consistent with precedent but philosophically divergent from it.[65] The judge in Case B, for example, might interpret Case A as justified, not by a principle of least-cost avoidance, but on the ground that hot coffee is an inherently dangerous product and thus the seller is strictly liable for any harm it causes. On the strength (if that's the right word) of this reinterpretation, the judge in Case B might hold the defendant liable despite its oral warning. The result of Case B then would maintain formal consistency with the result of Case A, although its fealty to the goal of determinacy would be rather minimal. The plausibility of such a reinterpretation will depend on how far it departs from the Case A court's own explanation of its decision (and from subsequent

---

64. This truism about the common law—that it is not *as* binding as statutory law—is reflected in the well-known proposal of Judge (then Professor) Guido Calabresi that statutes be treated as common-law precedents are treated; that is, as presumptively but not absolutely binding. *See* GUIDO CALABRESI, A COMMON LAW FOR THE AGE OF STATUTES 85–86 (1982).

65. A famous example is *MacPherson v. Buick Motor Co.*, 111 N.E. 1050 (N.Y. 1916), in which the New York Court of Appeals, in an opinion by Benjamin Cardozo, reinterpreted precedent to hold that plaintiffs injured by defective products need not be in contractual privity with manufacturers in order to sue them in tort.

courts' interpretations of that decision; more on this below); in this respect the constraints on reinterpretation of common-law precedents resemble the constraints on statutory interpretation imposed by linguistic intentions and the plausible meanings of language.

Another distinction between statutory and common-law interpretation is that the rule being interpreted in the latter context typically emerges, not from a single canonical statement, but from a series of prior court decisions and the written explanations offered for them. The court in Case B may in fact be faced with decisions of courts in Cases A_1, A_2, and A_3, each of them dealing with liability in a slightly different factual setting. The Case B court then will have to piece these multiple precedents together into a sort of compound rule, subject to the need for a justification and the possibility of reinterpretation described above.[66] Even this distinction should not be taken too far, however; for judicial interpretations of statutes may over time produce a similar phenomenon, with subsequent courts having to interpret, not only the rule stated in the statute's language itself, but also subsequent supplementations of that rule through ad hoc judicial decisions interpreting and applying the statute.

Finally, I should note that the operation of precedent takes on a different flavor when the courts in question have a hierarchic relationship to each other— that is, when precedent operates *vertically* rather than *horizontally*. So far I have described the common-law practice of one court's attempting to achieve consistency with the decisions of other coequal courts (or perhaps with its own prior decisions). For example, the U.S. federal court system is divided into multiple "circuits," each of which (with some exceptions not relevant here) hears cases from within a particular geographic region and is further divided into "districts" where the cases originate. A trial court in one district is not formally bound by precedents decided by trial courts in other districts or in other circuits; an appellate court within one circuit is not formally bound by precedents decided by appellate courts in other circuits. Nonetheless these coequal courts typically attempt, at least presumptively, to achieve consistency with the decisions of their sister courts. Likewise, a single court of appeals presumptively attempts to achieve consistency with its own precedents. These manifestations of *stare decisis* can be visualized as *horizontal* in their operation.

Stare decisis also operates *vertically*, however: A lower court within a single system (e.g., a federal circuit) is bound by the precedents of superior courts within that system. So a federal district court is bound by the decisions of the federal courts of appeals within that circuit, and every federal court is bound by

---

66. "Nothing in this [common-law] picture is. . . inconsistent with the idea of a rule, for often rules, of which the rules of language and etiquette are common examples, emerge without there being an original canonical rule-formulation." FREDERICK SCHAUER, PLAYING BY THE RULES: A PHILOSOPHICAL EXAMINATION OF RULE-BASED DECISIONMAKING IN LAW AND IN LIFE 175 (1991).

the decisions of the highest court in the system, namely the U.S. Supreme Court. When precedent operates vertically in this way, its binding authority is, or is supposed to be, absolute rather than merely presumptive. (This is simply a function of the hierarchic nature of court systems.) As such, the attitude of a lower court within the system to a precedent rendered by a higher court resembles the attitude of a court toward the legislature whose statute it is interpreting. Like the legislature (although for different reasons), the higher court bears some measure of authority that the lower court lacks. Thus lower courts have much less freedom to play fast and loose with vertical precedents—to creatively reinterpret or overrule them—than courts have with respect to horizontal precedent.

This sketch of common-law decisionmaking is perhaps too bare-bones to do justice to the topic.[67] But it should suffice for our purposes, which are to consider how court decisions (including common-law decisions) might possess authority on the DR account. The central points here are these: Common-law decisionmaking depends chiefly on the primary legitimacy of the adjudicative process itself, not on legitimacy derived from the legislative process; but at the same time the value of determinacy, and the democratic legitimacy that echoes (however faintly) from the legislature's tacit endorsement of the common law, push in the direction of judicial fealty to prior decisions.

7. COURTS, LITIGANTS, AND THE LAW

We now have a picture of authoritative adjudication on the DR account. Adjudication can claim primary authority with respect to litigants because, and to the extent that, it is fairly and meaningfully participatory and representative. The fair participation of the so-called adversary system, and the interest representation of the common-law method, make adjudication *democratic* in a sense: It embodies the same values of fairness and participation (albeit in different forms and a different balance) that democratic politics brings to the creation of legal rules.

Adjudication also can claim, derivatively, the authority that flows from the democratic process itself. Courts can credibly apply even indeterminate legal rules; when they do, they channel and extend the democratic settlements embodied in statutes. Adjudication thus can be doubly democratic—as a partner with the legislature in the elaboration of democratic statutes, and as a participatory and representative way to resolve particular disputes.

---

67. For some influential accounts of common-law reasoning, see BENJAMIN N. CARDOZO, THE NATURE OF THE JUDICIAL PROCESS (1921); EDWARD H. LEVI, AN INTRODUCTION TO LEGAL REASONING (1949); K. N. LLEWELLYN, THE BRAMBLE BUSH (1930); SCHAUER, *supra* note 66, at 167–206; CASS R. SUNSTEIN, LEGAL REASONING AND POLITICAL CONFLICT 62–100 (1996).

This democratic paradigm of adjudication, however, comes under stress when any of its premises—participation, representation, law-application—is tested, or when the premises pull in different directions. And as it happens, these phenomena manifest themselves, in various forms, with some frequency in modern litigation. Judges, like anyone else subject to the law, sometimes feel that applying a governing rule will do more harm than good. Sometimes, on the other hand, judges feel that their duty to apply the law—or to preserve fairness among the litigants—militates against litigant autonomy. Sometimes the traditional adversary model of adjudication seems inadequate to resolve the kinds of far-reaching, multifaceted disputes that arise in modern democracies. And sometimes the goal of bringing determinacy to democratic rules threatens the representative legitimacy of the common-law method.

In the next chapter, I explore several contexts in which these kinds of tensions arise from the fact that a court owes duties to both the litigants and the law. The DR account of law, I suggest, offers some productive ways to think about such problems.

6. THE FORMS AND LIMITS OF DEMOCRATIC ADJUDICATION[1]

I suggested in Chapter 5 that the Dispute-Resolution (DR) account of law can lead to a model of authoritative adjudication within a democratic community. In this chapter, I apply that model to four sets of persistent questions in the contemporary theory of adjudication. Each of them involves, in its own way, the fraught tripartite relationship among the judge, the litigants, and the democratic institutions whose general rules a court must apply.

As we have seen, the primary role of adjudication in a democracy (on the DR account) is to resolve disputes about the application of democratically enacted general laws. This way of looking at the judicial role suggests two distinguishable—and potentially clashing—aspects of that role.

The first aspect is the courts' function as part of a larger system of democratic legislation. Adjudication brings *ex post* determinacy to statutes and other democratic norms that are, inevitably, indeterminate *ex ante*. A focus on this "public" component of democratic adjudication suggests a corresponding responsibility on the part of courts: Courts should attempt to faithfully apply general laws in particular circumstances.

The second aspect is the courts' function as resolvers of discrete disputes. Adjudication resolves disagreements about how general rules apply in specific cases. A focus on this "private" component of democratic adjudication suggests a judicial responsibility to decide using procedures that can be accepted by the litigants (and others) who will be bound by a court's decisions. This in turn entails, as we have seen, a process that is reasonably fair and reasonably participatory.

Some persistent normative issues in modern American adjudication reflect the interplay, and often the tension, between these public and private aspects of the judicial role. Other issues reflect friction between the two components of the private role: fairness among the litigating parties and meaningful participation by those litigants. In this chapter, I explore what the DR account might tell us about the importance of, and proper balance among, these elements of judicial authority in our thinking about those persistent questions.

---

1. My title derives from Lon L. Fuller's famous essay *The Forms and Limits of Adjudication*, 92 HARV. L. REV. 353 (1978). My conclusions here differ substantially from Fuller's, particularly with respect to public-law litigation (*see infra*), although I acknowledge below that the concerns Fuller expressed in his essay—concerns, in essence, about judicial competence—might counterbalance my prescription of broader participation in public-law cases.

1. JUDICIAL PRAGMATISM

Perhaps the most fundamental set of issues in contemporary adjudicative theory has to do with the proper grounds of judicial decisions. While there are many variations of the debate, the basic issue is this: To what extent must judges restrict themselves to good-faith interpretations of existing legal norms, and to what extent may they, on the other hand, base their decisions on nonlegal normative considerations?

The various positions on this question are many and nuanced, but allow me to illustrate the basic issue using two somewhat caricatured poles in the debate. One is a position I will refer to as *judicial pragmatism*. A judicial pragmatist believes judges should strive to reach the morally best results, all things considered. Because the "best result" a judge is trying to obtain is defined by morality, not just by law, a pragmatist judge is not confined to the interpretation of legal norms. Of course, legal sources—constitutional provisions, statutes, regulations, and prior court decisions—might inform a pragmatist judge's calculus of what the best result is; and of course a judge might conclude that the way to achieve the best result is to apply, or perhaps to be seen as applying, only legal norms. But a pragmatist judge is not truly constrained by legal norms; she has no standing moral duty to interpret legal norms and only legal norms in reaching her decision.[2]

At or near the opposite pole is *judicial interpretivism*.[3] A judicial interpretivist believes judges should attempt in good faith to implement existing legal norms, and *only* to implement existing legal norms, in reaching their decisions. An interpretivist judge does not necessarily eschew moral analysis altogether; she may conclude that the applicable legal norms allow or require her to engage in moral reasoning,[4] and she may believe, more generally, that the process of

---

2. My description of judicial pragmatism here is a highly streamlined version of the "legal pragmatism" endorsed by Richard Posner, who, in addition to being a legal theorist, also is a federal appellate judge. *See* RICHARD A. POSNER, LAW, PRAGMATISM, AND DEMOCRACY 24–26, 57–60 (2003).

3. In fact Default Formalism, a version of interpretivism discussed in Chapter 5, probably occupies the opposite pole from judicial pragmatism. Default Formalism counsels judges to seek determinate answers to particular disputes in legal rules and, where those answers do not appear, to hold that the rule does not apply, thus ratifying the status quo. The pragmatist resolves a dispute without feeling bound by existing rules; the Default Formalist either feels completely bound by existing rules or refuses to resolve the dispute at all. Of the two evils, judicial pragmatism probably is the lesser on the DR account, as at least it is reasonably likely to generate a nonarbitrary resolution of a dispute in most cases.

4. She may, for instance, be an "inclusive" or "soft" legal positivist, who believes that although what qualifies as law is determined by social facts, those social facts sometimes make morality relevant to a judge's decisions. For a sympathetic description of inclusive

interpreting an existing legal rule or other norm inherently involves some moral analysis.[5] But she thinks that her decisionmaking authority is both conferred by and constrained by legal norms (as opposed to nonlegal ones).

We can illustrate the disagreement between judicial pragmatism and judicial interpretivism by recalling the Case of the Unjust Statute from Chapter 1. In that case, the judge must decide an issue that is governed by a statute which, if applied faithfully, would require a result the judge believes is morally suboptimal. If the judge in the Case of the Unjust Statute is a thoroughgoing pragmatist, she will reject application of the statute and reach the result she believes is morally best (although she might, for appearances' sake, disingenuously explain her decision as a faithful application of the statute). If the judge is an interpretivist, on the other hand, she will apply the statute in good faith and reach the morally suboptimal result.

As this allusion back to Chapter 1 suggests, judicial pragmatism is a version of Aristotle's position about the authority, or lack of authority, of law. The judicial pragmatist denies that a judge must recognize the authority of democratically enacted legal rules or other norms; she holds that a judge should decide consistently with legal norms only insofar as doing so leads to the morally best result, all things considered. A critique of judicial pragmatism therefore must incorporate a response to Aristotle's Challenge: It must explain why democratic law is worthy, at least presumptively, of a judge's allegiance (that is, it must offer an account of democratic legal *authority* in adjudication). It also must describe how, given pervasive legal indeterminacy, it is *possible* for a judge to apply the law (an account of the interpretation of democratically enacted rules).

My arguments to this point have, I hope, offered plausible accounts on both fronts. The analysis in Chapter 4 suggests that democratic legislation is, or at least can be, authoritative on a DR account of legal authority. That authority flows from the broad participation and basic fairness of the democratic process. A single judge, or a small panel of judges, cannot compete with democratic politics on the score of participation and fairness. A judge or panel's decision might (indeed should) reflect the meaningful participation of the litigating parties; but those parties are likely to be a small slice of the community and thus poor representatives of the community as a whole. And although judicial procedures might (indeed should) be fair as among the directly participating litigants, that

---

legal positivism, see Kenneth Einar Himma, *Inclusive Legal Positivism, in* THE OXFORD HANDBOOK OF JURISPRUDENCE & PHILOSOPHY OF LAW 125 (Jules Coleman & Scott Shapiro eds., 2002). Himma lists as "prominent inclusive positivists" H.L.A. Hart, Jules Coleman, W. J. Waluchow, and Matthew Kramer. *Id.* at 125.

5. This describes the interpretivist position of Ronald Dworkin, who believes the process of judicial interpretation of the law requires judges to see the law in its morally "best light." *See* RONALD DWORKIN, LAW'S EMPIRE 49–55 (1986).

fairness cannot extend to parties who will be affected by the court's decision but have not participated, or been meaningfully represented, in the process.

In other words, while a court decision might possess primary authority with respect to those participating or represented in the process of making it, it lacks the derivative authority of full-fledged democratic legislation—unless that decision is an application, in some sense, of a democratically enacted statute. A purely pragmatic decision—one based directly on nonlegal norms rather than an interpretation and application of a legal rule—lacks the derivative authority flowing from the full democratic process. And, as I argued in the previous chapter, it is conceptually possible for judges to interpret and apply even indeterminate general rules; in doing so, the judge supplements the primary authority of the adjudicative process with the derivative authority of the democratic process that generated the rule.

An argument against judicial pragmatism, then, is that judicial decisions that interpret and apply, in good faith, democratic legal rules are, for that reason, more authoritative than judicial decisions that do not. But why should it matter, in any given case, whether a judge's decision carries derivative as well as primary authority? Mightn't it be sufficient that the decision has primary authority by virtue of the fair participation or representation of those who will be bound by it? So long as this primary authority is present, mightn't (mustn't) a judge be willing to disregard a statute or other legal rule if, as in the Case of the Unjust Statute, she believes applying the rule would produce a morally suboptimal result?

The analysis so far suggests two reasons why derivative authority matters. The first has to do with the dispute-resolving authority of the legislative process itself. As we have seen, a statute is an act of dispute resolution: It resolves a dispute about *policy*, about how the members of the community should behave going forward; and it also resolves a dispute *about* dispute resolution, that is, about how future disputes should be resolved. By enacting a statute banning vehicles from the public park, the legislature is resolving (or foreclosing) a policy dispute about whether vehicles should be allowed in the public park. It also is resolving (or foreclosing) a dispute about what should happen if someone brings a vehicle into the public park.

In refusing to apply a statute, then, a pragmatist judge would be frustrating the settlement of a dispute (actual or potential) that is embodied in the statute. She would be failing to resolve the dispute before her (Olive's wagon or Paul's SUV in the park) as authoritatively commanded by the legislature. And she would be undermining the legislature's determination of public policy (no vehicles in the park) by sending a message, subtly or overtly, that those who bring vehicles into the park may, in appropriate circumstances, be forgiven by a court for doing so.

Derivative authority, in other words, is not just a matter of the litigants' reasons to obey the court's decision; it also is a matter of the court's reasons, and the reasons of others in society who might become litigants or who want to avoid becoming litigants, to obey the legislature's decision. By failing to apply a democratically authoritative statute, a pragmatist judge is directly disregarding the legislature's authority and is encouraging others to do so. This might not be a conclusive argument against pragmatism, but surely it is a valid one.

Of course, the second reason why derivative authority matters is precisely that it enhances the litigants' reasons for obeying the court's decision itself. As I suggested in Chapter 5, a court decision bearing both primary and derivative authority simply has *greater* authority than a court decision without the latter. A litigant has greater reason to respect a court decision that faithfully implements a democratically enacted statute than to respect a court decision that ignores or subverts a statute. This is so for the same reason that a democratic statute is deserving of greater respect—is possessed of greater authority—than the decree of a Hobbesian monarch. As a means of acceptably resolving or avoiding disputes about what should be done, the democratic process, with its indicia of reasonable competence and impartiality, simply is more likely to be successful than even the most earnest moral judgments of a single individual (a judge, an absolutist ruler, a Platonic Guardian).

The core DR argument against judicial pragmatism, then, is that it undermines the authority of both the democratic process and the process of democratic adjudication. Of course, this can never be a wholly decisive argument against pragmatic judging, even if one accepts the basic validity of the DR account. This is true for the same reason that the DR account cannot, more generally, decisively rule out disobedience to the law. Sometimes the morally right thing for a judge to do will be to ignore or subvert an applicable statute in order to reach a certain result. Legal interpretivism, like legal authority generally, is at best a strong operative presumption in favor of obedience. That is the best response the DR account can offer to judicial pragmatism; but no other account of legal authority of which I'm aware can do any better.

Before leaving the subject, I want to sketch one additional objection to judicial pragmatism from the perspective of the DR account. Pragmatism might threaten not just the derivative authority of a court decision, but its primary authority as well.[6]

On the DR account, the primary authority of a judicial decision depends on the extent to which it is a product of the fair and meaningful participation of the litigants. The meaningful participation of the litigants, in the form of presenting proofs and arguments, depends on the existence of a set of known rules according to which participation will occur. These include not just "procedural" rules like those found in codes of civil procedure and evidence—how to file a

---

6. I present a more detailed and comprehensive version of the following argument (which departs from what follows in certain particulars) in Christopher J. Peters, *Participation, Representation, and Principled Adjudication*, 8 LEGAL THEORY 185 (2002).

claim, how to present proof at trial, how to submit legal arguments, and so on—
but also "substantive" rules of law upon which the litigants' proofs and arguments can be based.

Imagine, for instance, that Olive (through her lawyer) must attempt to persuade a court that she should not be convicted and fined for violating the
"no vehicles in the park" ordinance. Olive might want to make legal arguments—
for instance, that the word "vehicles" in the ordinance does not apply to her toy
wagon. She also might want to present factual proofs—perhaps testimony that
she was pulling her wagon outside the park's boundaries when she was cited.

Note, however, that Olive's ability to make legal arguments and present
factual proofs depends on the existence of a legal rule or rules—the "no vehicles"
ordinance in Olive's case, perhaps common-law precedents in another case—
that she knows the court will attempt in good faith to apply. Suppose the judge
announces that she is going to ignore the "no vehicles" statute and simply reach
whatever decision she thinks is morally best, all things considered. How is
Olive going to make "legal" (that is, normative) arguments in light of this
announcement? Which rules or principles of all-things-considered morality or
justice will she invoke in arguing that those rules or principles do not prohibit
her conduct? Only by happenstance will she manage to hit on precisely those
moral norms, and interpret them in precisely those ways, that are amenable to
the judge's own sense of morality. By the same token, which factual "proofs" is
Olive going to offer to demonstrate that her conduct did not in fact violate the
(unidentified) moral norms the judge finds amenable? How is Olive to know
which facts matter, and how they matter, when she is not even clear on the
norms that will apply to those facts?

Legal rules, remember, can mitigate the costs of dispute resolution by
avoiding arguments about what norms should apply to disputes. But a wholly
pragmatic judicial process is a process without governing legal norms; it thus is
a free-for-all in which the litigants must attempt to argue every issue from something like first principles. The chances that any litigant's participation—her
influence on the actual result—will be significant in such a maelstrom seem
minimal. Truly pragmatic judicial decisionmaking threatens to become nonparticipatory decisionmaking—decisionmaking, more or less, by judicial fiat. Its
results therefore might not be worthy even of the primary authority that (good-
faith) adversary common-law adjudication possesses.

Of course, a pragmatic judge seeking to rein in the maelstrom might
pretend that she is deciding the case by applying statutes or other existing legal
rules—thus giving the litigants an ostensible foundation for their proofs and
arguments—while in fact she decides the case in all-things-considered pragmatic fashion.[7] But this would hardly solve the problem of primary authority;

---

7. On the propriety of judicial dishonesty of this type and others, see Scott Altman,
Beyond Candor, 89 MICH. L. REV. 296, 310–12 (1990).

if anything, it would exacerbate that problem. Judicial pretense of this sort would render the litigants' "participation" wholly illusory; they would be playing one game while the judge is refereeing another. The resulting decision would lack authority despite appearing to possess it. And while the deception might work in a particular case—the losing litigant might walk away disappointed but comforted by the (apparent) fairness and participatoriness of the process—it seems unlikely to work over the long run. Systemic pragmatism—pragmatism routinely practiced by a large number of judges within a system—seems likely to produce many cases in which the result is ill-fitted to the proofs and arguments offered by the litigants. Over time, litigants will lose trust in the system, which then will cease to be effective as a means of resolving society's disputes.

Or not; perhaps a cadre of pragmatist judges could go on fooling the public forever. (Modern judicial systems, after all, are labyrinthine and opaque from the perspective of most laypeople; and, as most American lawyers readily acknowledge, a certain amount of pretense—e.g., false professions of strict formalism—is common in judicial opinions and other discourse by and about judges.)[8] If so, then the success of judicial pragmatism must rest upon falsehood, which is something the DR account provides no particular reason either to endorse or to condemn. But the DR account does strongly undermine a case for judicial pragmatism that is built on anything other than systemic dishonesty.

2. MANAGERIAL JUDGING

In the past half-century or so, the traditional judge-litigant balance of power—or, perhaps, of responsibility—in American adjudication has shifted somewhat in the direction of the judge. Some aspects of this shift can be attributed to the contemporaneous trend toward litigation with broad public significance; I explore that phenomenon in the next section. Here I want to focus on the enhancement of the judicial role even in garden-variety litigation involving relatively narrow private disputes.

As procedural theorist Judith Resnik suggests in her germinal work on the subject,[9] managerial judging in private litigation has been spurred by the advent and increasing importance of discovery—the formalized process of

---

8. For example, Chief Justice John Roberts memorably stated at his confirmation hearing that "Judges are like umpires. Umpires don't make the rules, they apply them." *Confirmation Hearing on the Nomination of John G. Roberts, Jr. to Be Chief Justice of the United States: Hearing Before the S. Comm. on the Judiciary*, 109th Cong. 55 (2005) (statement of John G. Roberts, Jr., Nominee to be Chief Justice of the United States).

9. Resnik's account of the modern shift toward managerial judging remains definitive, though it is now more than twenty-five years old. *See* Judith Resnik, *Managerial Judges*, 96 Harv. L. Rev. 374 (1982). Resnik describes the advent of managerial judging in federal civil cases generally, including public-law litigation and garden-variety private litigation;

exchanging and gathering information within the context of a lawsuit. In the U.S. federal court system, discovery was primarily an innovation of the Federal Rules of Civil Procedure, which were first promulgated in 1938 and since have been copied in varying degrees by most state-court systems. Because discovery tugs in the opposition direction from the traditional *adversarial* thrust of the adversary system—as Resnik puts it, "a discovery system ('give your opponent all information relevant to the litigation') was grafted onto American adversarial norms ('protect your client zealously' and therefore 'withhold what you can')"[10]—it generates considerable ancillary conflict within litigation, making judicial oversight necessary. It also results in the production of much relevant information relatively early in a lawsuit, which facilitates early judicial assessment of the merits. And it typically increases the expense and duration of lawsuits, raising their stakes and creating another incentive for judges to intercede and litigants to seek intercession.

Other factors also have contributed to a growth in managerial judging even in run-of-the-mill private lawsuits. In addition to facilitating discovery, the Federal Rules allow (and even encourage) the joinder of multiple parties, claims, and defenses in a single proceeding, often producing unwieldy disputes that must be carefully orchestrated by the judge. Social changes, and changes in the substantive law reflecting them, have led in turn to procedural complexities and judicial responses. Class action lawsuits, for example, evolved as a way to process disputes over shared or widespread injuries; judges took on the task of protecting the interests of absent class members.[11] Consolidation of cases and other "complex litigation" techniques—all of them requiring substantial judicial management—emerged as responses to the problem of interrelated cases arising in multiple jurisdictions.

For my purposes here, it will be useful to focus on three typical aspects of contemporary managerial judging. The first is active judicial encouragement of settlement or other means of "alternative dispute resolution" between the parties (as opposed to judicial disposition of a lawsuit on its merits). The second is judicial oversight and refereeing of the discovery process. The third is judicial willingness to dispose of all or part of a case on the merits without a trial.

A. Encouraging Settlement

Modern American judges, abetted by statutes and procedural rules, typically encourage litigants to settle cases without trial or to resolve their disputes by

---

the work of Owen Fiss and Abram Chayes, respectively, addresses it in the context of public-law litigation, the subject of my next section.

10. *Id.* at 379.

11. See, for example, the provisions of Federal Rule of Civil Procedure 23, which rely heavily on judicial discretion in certifying and defining classes, requiring notice to absent class members, and evaluating proposed settlements for fairness. FED. R. CIV. P. 23.

less-formal "alternative" means.[12] The incentives to do so are obvious: Trials, and the pretrial process that precedes them, are expensive and time-consuming for both the parties and the court. Just as obviously, an agreed settlement serves the goal of peaceful dispute resolution, all else being equal. Parties who settle their differences voluntarily seem at least as likely to respect that settlement as parties who have a settlement thrust upon them in the form of a court judgment.

The potential worry, from the perspective of a DR account, is that all else will not always be equal. For one thing, a settlement, or an agreement to submit to alternative dispute resolution (ADR), might not truly be voluntary.[13] There are of course the usual worries about inequality of bargaining power; one reason for a litigant to seek public adjudication in the first place might be his perception that he cannot privately negotiate a fair settlement. If, having filed (or waited for the other party to file) a lawsuit, this litigant finds himself pressured by the court to do precisely what he was not willing to do without the lawsuit, he is likely to feel that the attempt at adjudication has been a waste of time. Over the long run, a general perception that judges are pressuring litigants to accept unfair settlements would be likely to undermine the institution's authority.

The issue, however, is nuanced, and much depends on how we understand the concept of a judge's "pressuring" litigants to settle. In American courts, judges cannot refuse to adjudicate a lawsuit if the parties refuse to settle; a judge cannot present settlement (or ADR) as the only option. "Pressure," if it exists, takes more subtle forms. The judge's central tool of persuasion is the threat that a litigant who is unwilling to settle will incur her displeasure, which might be manifested in the judge's rulings during the course of the lawsuit. If this threat is felt evenhandedly—if both (or all) litigants equally fear the judge's wrath—then its *in terrorem* effect will be minimal: The litigants might have to put up with a grumpy judge, but neither of them will suffer vis-à-vis the other for his or her failure to settle.

The real worry is that a judge will exert (or be seen as exerting) disproportionate pressure on one or some of the litigants to settle. If this occurs

---

12. Federal Rule of Civil Procedure 16, for instance, permits a court to hold a pretrial conference for the purpose, *inter alia*, of "facilitating settlement." FED. R. CIV. P. 16. Rule 68 supplements the carrot of voluntary settlement with a stick: A litigant who rejects a settlement offer made pursuant to the Rule and then receives a final judgment that is "not more favorable" than the offer must pay the other litigants' litigation costs. FED. R. CIV. P. 68. The federal Alternative Dispute Resolution Act of 1998 requires federal district courts to implement alternative dispute resolution (ADR) programs. *See* 28 U.S.C.A. §§ 651–658 (West 2010). And the Federal Arbitration Act gives federal courts jurisdiction to enforce agreements to arbitrate disputes arising from interstate commerce. *See* 9 U.S.C.A. §§ 2–6 (West 2010).

13. On this point, see Owen M. Fiss, *Against Settlement*, 93 YALE L.J. 1073, 1076–78 (1984).

arbitrarily—because the judge does not like one of the litigants, or thinks that litigant has weaker bargaining power—it is an obvious failure of fairness in the procedure. If, on the other hand, it occurs because, on the judge's assessment, the pressured litigant has a weaker case on the merits, the (potential) problem is a failure of meaningful participation. I've argued that much of the authority of adjudication stems from its adversary nature—adversary in the sense that both (or all) litigants have a full and fair opportunity to present their proofs and arguments to the judge. A judicial evaluation of the merits before this has the chance to happen—before all the facts are in and all the arguments have been made—risks short-circuiting the process. Litigants who feel pressured to settle before they've had a real opportunity to make their case are likely to be dissatisfied with the result; if this happens frequently enough, the systemic authority of adjudication might be threatened.

The concern about prematurely coerced settlements, however, is hardly a decisive argument against judicial involvement in the settlement process. Considerations of external efficiency—of the costs associated with full participation and fairness—must play a role in adjudication; in some cases, one litigant's side will be so weak that a full adjudication would be a waste of time. Judges (facilitated by early discovery[14]) might be in a relatively good position to identify these cases at an early stage, and to encourage an appropriate and efficient settlement. Encouraging a party to settle when that party otherwise will lose—after the expenditure of significant resources—seems an appropriate prioritization of efficiency over (meaningless, indeed wasteful) participation.

Then there is the possibility that judicial involvement in settlement negotiations might actually promote fairness. Wholly private negotiations will be heavily affected by any imbalance in bargaining power, but a judge might be able to temper that imbalance by providing a neutral assessment of the relative merits of the litigants' positions. A litigant cowed by her opponent's superior resources might be reassured when a dispassionate judge takes her case seriously. And a judge might actively discourage heavy-handed negotiating tactics. She might even level the resources playing field somewhat by enforcing equity in the litigation process—e.g., by preventing the wealthier litigant from using burdensome discovery to wear down the poorer litigant (more on this possibility below). The result could be a judicially facilitated settlement that is more fair, and thus more acceptable to the parties and generally, than a wholly private settlement would have been.

From the perspective of the primary authority of adjudication, then, the most we can say is that judicial involvement with settlement is a question of balance. A truly coerced settlement presents an authority gap that is unlikely to be filled

---

14. In the federal court system, litigants in most cases must exchange basic information about the case—relevant witnesses and documents—shortly after the lawsuit is filed. *See* FED. R. CIV. P. 26(a).

by gains in efficiency: Pressuring one party to accept a settlement she thinks inadequate exacts a huge cost in terms of participation (and, if the pressure is arbitrary, in terms of fairness). But evenhanded judicial facilitation, even encouragement, of settlement can promote both efficiency and fairness. By providing a forum for discussing settlement in the midst of a lawsuit, after the pleadings and discovery have revealed the relative strengths and weaknesses of the litigants' respective cases, a court might be encouraging a result that both parties find substantively acceptable. And by preventing the wealthier party from abusing its advantage in resources, a court can facilitate a settlement process that is more fair than what would have occurred privately.

As we have seen, however, primary authority is not the only concern in adjudication. Courts apply general rules produced by the democratic process, and to the extent a court fails to apply or inaccurately applies a statute or other democratically generated rule, its result lacks the democratic authority that can be derived from the rule. Settlement and ADR might threaten this derivative authority in three respects.

First, settlement or ADR might undermine the policy goals of a particular statute. Consider federal laws prohibiting employment discrimination based upon race, gender, religion, and various other characteristics. One justification of these laws might be to compensate for typical inequalities in bargaining power between employers and employees, particularly when the latter are members of historically disadvantaged groups. If employees' claims under these statutes are resolved by means of settlement, or pursuant to an agreement to submit to ADR, the "resolution" might merely recapitulate the bargaining-power problem the statutes are designed in part to address. As I suggested above, settlement with judicial involvement might mitigate this worry; but consider the possibility (the likelihood) that the antidiscrimination laws also have the purpose of deterring discriminatory conduct. In the employment context, settlements and the results of ADR typically are nonpublic; often they are subject to strict confidentiality agreements. They also tend to provide remedies that are less expensive to employers than a jury award would be. Settling rather than fully litigating employment discrimination claims thus might frustrate the statutory goal of deterring future misconduct. A given settlement might fail even to remedy the particular misconduct at issue; a gender-discrimination plaintiff, for example, might accept a cash payment rather than insist that her employer discontinue its discriminatory policies. If a court facilitates settlement or ADR in such circumstances, it contravenes the authoritative justifications embodied in the applicable statutes.[15]

---

15. Courts have struggled with the question whether arbitration agreements, signed by employees as a condition of employment, are enforceable with respect to antidiscrimination and related employment claims. *Compare, e.g.,* Carter v. Countrywide Credit Indus., Inc., 362 F.3d 294 (5th Cir. 2004) (enforcing an employer-employee agreement to arbitrate

Second and more generally, settling or agreeing to arbitrate statutory disputes (or, to foreshadow the subject of the next two chapters, constitutional ones) threatens to compromise the democratic process by depriving its participants of important information about the efficacy of, and need for, public policy. Suppose a large percentage of employment discrimination claims are resolved by confidential settlements or arbitration awards rather than public litigation. As a result, legislators, regulators, and the public will have been denied data about the real extent of employment discrimination; the adjudicated claims will constitute only a fraction of the total number of discrimination disputes. The ability of the democratic process to respond to social problems might be dulled as a consequence. To the extent these claims are at least brought to a court and then settled afterward, the problem is mitigated but not eliminated; meritorious claims (and for that matter nonmeritorious ones) are likely to attract greater public and political attention if they are resolved by a jury verdict or some other public judgment.

Third, settlements and ADR reduce the number of adjudications on the merits, and thus retard the process of bringing determinacy to statutes and other general legal rules. As we have seen, judicial interpretations of statutes (or of common-law precedents) can reduce indeterminacy by resolving, on a case-by-case basis, particular questions about a statute's or precedent's meaning; by the principle of *stare decisis*, judicial interpretations allow courts, litigants, and would-be litigants in future cases to anticipate how a rule will be applied and thus avoid the costs of fighting over its application. Fewer adjudications mean less determinacy in this respect, and thus greater dispute-resolution costs *ex post*.

The DR account thus lends guarded support to the skepticism about settlement and ADR famously expressed by Owen Fiss in his classic essay *Against Settlement*.[16] Fiss' concerns have not prevented the movement toward greater use of settlement and ADR—and greater judicial encouragement of those devices—from gaining momentum in the quarter-century since his essay first appeared. There are a number of probable reasons for this shift, some laudable and others troubling. As I suggested above, settlement and ADR can be more efficient than full-blown litigation, if they can operate as accurately at less cost. They also might enhance fairness—especially under judicial supervision—to the extent they circumvent the advantage of wealth in the litigation process; this prospect

---

Fair Labor Standards Act claims), *with* Ferguson v. Countrywide Credit Indus., Inc., 298 F.3d 778 (9th Cir. 2002) (declining to enforce as unconscionable a virtually identical agreement to arbitrate federal gender discrimination claims). Except in the special context of class actions, however—where the court is obligated to consider the interests of absent parties, see FED. R. CIV. P. 23(e)—courts have not declined to approve or enforce agreements to settle such claims after litigation has begun, absent some departure from the requirements of ordinary contract law.

16. *See* Fiss, *supra* note 12.

probably explains the attraction of ADR to many political liberals. On the other hand, in many contexts they can perpetuate or even aggregate existing imbalances in bargaining power (as the employment discrimination example suggests), thus appealing to relatively well-funded, well-organized interests such as large employers and corporate providers of consumer products and services.

To the extent the shift toward settlement and ADR is responsive to shortcomings in the adjudicative process—inefficiencies and power imbalances—the ideal solution is of course to mitigate or remedy those shortcomings. Here there are many issues well beyond my scope in this book, including worries that efforts to enhance the fairness and participatory nature of adjudication (such as increased discovery) have made the process more expensive and thus less attractive. To the extent the shift represents an effort by powerful interests to avoid adjudication precisely because it is participatory and fair, it should of course be resisted. The DR account suggests, at least, that policymakers and judges pay close attention to the distinctions between the laudable and the corrosive reasons for encouraging ADR or settlement.

B. Overseeing Discovery

Discovery seems at first glance to run counter to the idea of an "adversary" system, as it requires each side to share relevant information with the other, thus mitigating or eliminating any existing advantage of a litigant with better independent access to information. (Modern federal procedure even requires parties to share much information without being asked, further compromising the "adversary" nature of the process.) From the perspective of the DR account, however, there is no inherent reason to be suspicious of discovery; quite the contrary. Recall that the adversary system is valuable as a way of promoting decision-making competence (by giving the affected parties a role in the process) and impartiality (by reducing the potential for arbitrary decision by the judge). Discovery in fact can further both goals. By increasing the availability of relevant information, it can enhance the competence of the procedure. And by requiring parties with greater access to information to share it with their opponents, discovery can mitigate the arbitrary advantage of one disputant over another, which of course is part of the impetus for creating dispute-resolution mechanisms in the first place.

Only if we consider participation to have noninstrumental value—to be a good in and of itself—might we be concerned that discovery somehow corrupts the authority of adjudication. If the point of the adversary system is simply to allow litigants as much control as possible over the process, then discovery is problematic; for it reduces the extent to which the result of adjudication will depend on the particular choices the litigants themselves (through their lawyers) make. I suggested in Chapter 3 that participation is best understood as an instrumental good—a way of promoting competence and impartiality—rather than an inherent one. If I'm right about this, then discovery is not problematic for adjudicative authority. (In fact, the development and rapid expansion of discovery in American adjudication during the past century might constitute some evidence that participation, at least within the American system, is best understood in instrumental terms.)

For discovery to contribute to judicial authority rather than detracting from it, it must operate equitably in fact, not just in theory. Substantial judicial supervision typically is necessary to make that happen. Because discovery is expensive, parties with greater resources can (and have an incentive to) overuse it as a way to drain their opponents' funds. Judicial oversight can temper this problem; it also can ensure that discovery actually serves its function of bringing relevant information to light. And indeed American procedural rules typically afford judges extensive discretion to monitor discovery and rein in abuses,[17] an invitation most judges reluctantly accept.

Concerns for derivative authority also generally support broad discovery under judicial oversight. We can again use federal employment discrimination statutes as an example: A policy against discrimination could hardly achieve its regulatory or remedial goals if courts could not gain access to relevant facts about whether discrimination occurred, what harm it caused, and so on. Broad discovery therefore facilitates the implementation of democratically enacted public policy; it promotes the derivative as well as the primary legitimacy of judicial decisionmaking.

C. Assessing the Merits before Trial

Arguably the most significant procedural development in American civil adjudication during the past century has been the trend toward earlier judicial assessment of the merits of a dispute. Discovery has facilitated this trend; judges now have access to relevant facts about a lawsuit well before the presentation of evidence at trial. And because trials tend to be even more expensive than discovery, and judges tend to have crowded dockets, there are strong incentives to dispose of cases, or parts of them, before a trial begins. Settlement and ADR are two ways to do this, but there are other ways involving direct judicial evaluation of the substance of a dispute. The most prevalent is what the federal courts call summary judgment, by which a judge, after ample time for discovery, dismisses claims and defenses that appear unsupported by the evidence produced. Courts over the years have become ever more aggressive in employing summary judgment.[18] Recently, federal courts have begun dismissing many cases earlier

---

17. *See, e.g.,* FED. R. CIV. P. 26(b)(1) (limiting expensive and burdensome discovery); 26(c) (providing for court orders limiting discovery); 26(g) (requiring litigants and attorneys to certify that discovery is legally justified and not abusive); 37 (affording courts broad discretion to order discovery and sanction litigants for discovery abuses).

18. In this regard, compare the Supreme Court's 1970 decision in *Adickes v. S.H. Kress & Co.*, 398 U.S. 144 (1970), which denied summary judgment where the defendant did not

still, at the pleading stage, where the plaintiff has (in the court's judgment) failed to plead facts that make her claim "plausible."[19]

There are obvious worries about early judicial assessment along the lines of those suggested above in discussing settlement. Premature assessment can deny litigants the opportunity to participate meaningfully by fully presenting their proofs and arguments. In some cases—for example, where a party cannot plead a sufficiently "plausible" claim because crucial facts are solely within the possession of her opponent (and, in a Catch-22, immune from discovery unless the plaintiff can plead a sufficient claim)—early assessment arbitrarily ratifies the status quo; the Hobbesian echoes of dispute "resolution" by superior force are quite troubling in these contexts. And to the extent early assessment disposes of meritorious claims or defenses—a greater risk the earlier the assessment occurs—it frustrates the policy goals embodied in the general legal rules those claims or defenses seek to vindicate.

Indeed, the costs of early judicial assessment are in some respects greater than those of settlement. Settlement at least requires some negotiation and agreement by both (or all) parties; it involves some *quid pro quo*. But an early dismissal of a claim brings no benefit to the claimant, and thus no substantive reason for satisfaction with the result.

On the other side of the equation, of course, are the costs saved when non-meritorious claims or defenses are disposed of early in a case. The DR account, however, should (if nothing else) remind us that whether a claim is "meritorious" is precisely what the disputants disagree about; managing that disagreement in an acceptable way is the reason for having courts. A plaintiff whose claim is dismissed on the pleadings because it is not "plausible" will hardly be consoled by the court's determination that the claim lacks merit. A system that regularly rejects claims without affording claimants a reasonable chance to prove them is, over the long haul, a system that risks a crisis in its authority.

My sense is that the line between justifiable and illegitimate pretrial judicial assessment of a case's merits typically falls at the point where a litigant has had a reasonable opportunity to uncover and produce evidence in support of her claims; it falls, in other words, at the close of discovery. Where a claimant, despite

---

"foreclose the possibility" that the plaintiff could prove his claims, to its decision sixteen years later in *Celotex Corp. v. Catrett*, 477 U.S. 317 (1986), which allowed summary judgment where the plaintiff "failed to produce evidence" supporting her claims.

19. This as yet ill-defined "plausibility" standard emerges from the Supreme Court's recent decisions in *Bell Atlantic Corp. v. Twombly*, 550 U.S. 544 (2007), and *Ashcroft v. Iqbal*, 129 S. Ct. 1937 (2009). It seems decidedly at odds with the longstanding principle of *Conley v. Gibson*, 355 U.S. 41, 45–46 (1957), that a claim should not be dismissed on the pleadings "unless it appears beyond doubt that the plaintiff can prove no set of facts. . . which would entitle him to relief." The Court in *Twombly* purported not to overrule *Conley*, but it downplayed this language as "an incomplete, negative gloss on an accepted pleading standard" that "is best forgotten." 550 U.S. at 547.

the benefit of liberal discovery provisions, is unable to make a credible case, her participation has been meaningful but unavailing, and there is little point in incurring the additional costs of a trial. But where a claimant has had no reasonable opportunity to make her case—as when she must plead a claim without access to information solely in the possession of her opponent—it is difficult to characterize a dismissal as a true "resolution" of the dispute.

3. PUBLIC-LAW LITIGATION (AND JUDICIAL INDEPENDENCE)

The twentieth century saw, not just a trend toward managerial judging in American adjudication, but the related emergence of litigation as a means to achieve broad public-policy goals.[20] The watershed event in this public-law litigation revolution was the Supreme Court's 1954 ruling in *Brown v. Board of Education* that legally enforced racial segregation in public schools was unconstitutional.[21] *Brown* spurred decades of cases in which courts worked out its implications and enforced them using "structural injunctions"—complex court orders requiring ongoing judicial supervision of public school systems.[22] The example of school desegregation inspired structural-reform litigation in other contexts, such as prisons and public mental-health facilities.[23] More broadly, it ushered in an era (continuing to this day) in which ideological plaintiffs of all political stripes routinely use statutory or constitutional claims brought in civil lawsuits as a way to force changes in public policy and the operation of government institutions.

---

20. Now-classic descriptions of this trend can be found in Abram Chayes, *The Role of the Judge in Public Law Litigation*, 89 Harv. L. Rev. 1281 (1976), and Owen M. Fiss, *Foreword: The Forms of Justice*, 93 Harv. L. Rev. 1 (1979) [hereinafter Fiss, *Forms of Justice*].

21. Brown v. Bd. of Educ., 347 U.S. 483, 493 (1954).

22. *See* Richard Kluger, Simple Justice 716–47 (1976) (detailing the struggle to achieve school desegregation after the Supreme Court decided *Brown*); *see also* Johanna Miller Lewis, *Implementing* Brown *in Arkansas, in* With All Deliberate Speed: Implementing Brown v. Board of Education 1, 5–19 (Brian J. Daugherity & Charles C. Bolton eds., 2008); Charles Ogletree, *All Too Deliberate, in* The Unfinished Agenda of Brown v. Board of Education 45, 45–60 (James Anderson & Dara N. Byrne eds., 2004).

23. *See e.g.*, Bell v. Wolfish, 441 U.S. 520 (1979) (pretrial detainees alleged that the conditions of confinement and practices of a short-term custody facility were unconstitutional); Hutto v. Finney, 437 U.S. 678 (1978) (state prisoners alleged that the conditions in prison isolation cells were unconstitutional); Welsch v. Likins, 373 F.Supp. 487 (D. Minn. 1974) (mental patients alleged the treatment and conditions in state mental hospitals violated the Civil Rights Act).

Public-interest litigation puts pressure on the participatory, representative model of adjudication I outlined in Chapter 5. This is because its typical impact is considerably broader than the binding of a small number of actual litigants and a somewhat larger (but still relatively small) group of similarly situated future litigants and would-be litigants. When a court strikes down a statute or policy as illegal, everyone who benefited from or ideologically supported the status quo is adversely affected by the decision. The classic bipartite structure of an adversary lawsuit, however—with a single plaintiff on one side and a single defendant on the other—usually cannot allow for either the participation by or the interest representation of all of these affected parties.

Consider an example that I will explore more fully in Chapter 8: the two law-suits brought in 2003 to challenge the University of Michigan's use of race-based affirmative action in admitting students to its undergraduate and law school programs.[24] In each case, the plaintiff was a white applicant denied admission and the defendant was the university. When the cases reached the U.S. Supreme Court, however, the decisions stood to affect a much wider spectrum of people and institutions: public universities (and perhaps other public institutions) in other states; minority students seeking admission to those universities; white students seeking admission; current students; faculty members; administrators; employers; anyone with a material or ideological interest in higher education, public education, or race relations in America. It is perhaps not too great an exaggeration to say that almost every American had *some* stake in the outcome of the litigation. And yet surely the original parties to the lawsuits—two young white plaintiffs and a single (albeit large) state university—could not adequately represent all, or indeed more than a few, of these diverse interests.

The challenge posed by public-law cases like the Michigan affirmative-action lawsuits is a challenge to the primary authority of a judicial decision. How could the Supreme Court's rulings in those cases have authority over the many affected parties who neither had an opportunity actually to participate in the litigation nor had their interests adequately represented by an actual participant?

The short answer is: They could not, at least not on the DR model of adjudication sketched in Chapter 5. But this concern does not doom public-law litigation on the DR account; it only necessitates adjustments to the traditional adversary common-law paradigm, adjustments that American courts in fact make to deal with such cases. The primary adjustment is a radical expansion of participation in public-law cases. The Federal Rules of Civil Procedure, and (increasingly) state rules based on them, allow for liberal joinder of parties who have an interest in a case or whose own claims or defenses share common issues with those being litigated. Federal Rule 24, for example, gives nonlitigants a right to

---

24. *See* Grutter v. Bollinger, 539 U.S. 306 (2003) (challenging the law school's admissions program); Gratz v. Bollinger, 539 U.S. 244 (2003) (challenging the university's undergraduate admissions program).

intervene—to become parties to a lawsuit—when their interests might be impaired by the lawsuit's outcome and are not adequately represented by existing parties. Rule 19 requires courts to join such parties if they are within the court's jurisdiction and unwilling to intervene voluntarily. These provisions operate to fill gaps in the traditional common-law process of interest representation that are created where, as in most public-law cases, the original litigants cannot be relied upon to protect the interests of all those who will be indirectly bound by the decision.[25] In the Michigan cases, the two trial courts allowed a total of fifty-eight different parties to intervene on the university's side, thus expanding each suit from a bipolar dispute to something approaching a town-hall meeting.[26]

The Federal Rules also allow courts to expand lawsuits in a different way: by certifying litigants as representatives of larger classes whose members will be bound by the result.[27] In some circumstances, class members must be notified of the lawsuit and may directly participate in the litigation.[28] With respect to

---

25. Rule 24 also allows intervention at the court's discretion by nonlitigants whose claims or defenses raise questions in common with those of the existing litigants. *See* Fed. R. Civ. P. 24(b).

26. In *Grutter*,

> 41 individuals and three pro-affirmative action student groups. . . intervene[d] in the case as defendants. The individual intervenors include[d] 21 undergraduate students of various races who. . . attend[ed] the University of Michigan, Wayne State University, the University of California at Berkeley, or Diablo Valley Community College in Pleasant Hill, California, all of whom plan[ned] to apply to the law school for admission; five black students who. . . attend[ed] Cass Technical High School or Northwestern High School in Detroit and who plan[ned] to apply to the law school for admission; twelve students of various races who. . . attend[ed] the law school; a paralegal and a Latino graduate student at the University of Texas at Austin who intend[ed] to apply to the law school for admission; and a black graduate student at the University of Michigan who [was] a member of the Defend Affirmative Action Party.

137 F. Supp. 2d 821, 824–25 (E.D. Mich. 2001). The pro-affirmative action groups were "United for Equality and Affirmative Action (UEAA), the Coalition to Defend Affirmative Action By Any Means Necessary (BAMN), and Law Students for Affirmative Action (LSAA)." *Id.* at 824 n.4.

In *Gratz*, the intervenors were

> seventeen African American and Latino students who ha[d] applied for, or intend[ed] to apply for, admission to the University, joined by the Citizens for Affirmative Action's Preservation, a nonprofit organization whose stated mission is to preserve opportunities in higher education for African American and Latino students in Michigan.

122 F. Supp. 2d 811, 815 (E.D. Mich. 2000).

27. *See* Fed. R. Civ. P. 23.

28. Rule 23 requires notice and an opportunity to participate in some types of class action; it permits but does not require such notice in other types. *See* Fed. R. Civ. P. 23(c)(2), (d)(1)(B). The Rule also grants the court substantial discretion to allow or require

nonparticipating class members, the class representatives and their attorneys must fairly and adequately represent those members' interests, and the court must oversee the litigation with their interests in mind.[29] The Rules therefore make interest representation a matter of formal obligation in class actions. In the Michigan lawsuits, the trial court in each case certified the plaintiff as the representative of a large class of actual and potential nonminority applicants.[30]

Court rules also typically provide for meaningful participation by interested nonlitigants who cannot qualify (or are otherwise unwilling) to formally intervene. For example, after the Supreme Court agreed to hear the Michigan cases, it allowed the filing of no less than *ninety-one* different *amicus curiae* ("friend of the court") briefs supporting one side or the other (or, in a few instances, supporting neither party); many of these briefs, moreover, were filed on behalf of multiple *amici*. Several of these *amicus* briefs were relied upon for important points in the Court's opinions.[31]

---

participation in order to protect the interests of class members, and it requires notice and an opportunity to object to settlements. *See* FED. R. CIV. P. 23(d), (e).

29. The duties of class representatives and their attorneys to absent class members are specified by Rules 23(a)(4) and 23(g)(4), respectively. Rule 23 implicitly requires judges to protect absent class members through the enforcement of these provisions and by ordering notice, structuring the litigation, and defining the relevant classes; it explicitly requires a judge to consider absent members' interests in approving a settlement. *See* FED. R. CIV. P. 23(e).

30. The *Grutter* class was defined as

all persons who (A) applied for and were not granted admission to the University of Michigan Law School for the academic years since (and including) 1995 until the time that judgment is entered [in the lawsuit]; and (B) were members of those racial or ethnic groups, including Caucasian, that Defendants treated less favorably in considering their applications for admission to the Law School.

137 F. Supp. 2d at 824. The *Gratz* class was defined as

[t]hose individuals who applied for and were not granted admission to the College of Literature, Science & the Arts of the University of Michigan for all academic years from 1995 forward and who are members of those racial or ethnic groups, including Caucasian, that defendants treated less favorably on the basis of race in considering their application for admission.

122 F. Supp. 2d at 814 n.2.

31. In her opinion for the *Grutter* majority, for example, Justice Sandra Day O'Connor cited *amicus* briefs filed by, respectively, a group of law school deans and a coalition of colleges for the point that a great many schools have relied on the permissibility of affirmative action to achieve diversity. *See* Grutter v. Bollinger, 539 U.S. 306, 323 (2003). Later, Justice O'Connor rested her holding that racial diversity is a compelling interest in part on assertions by corporate and military *amici* of diversity's importance in global business and in military training. *See id.* at 330–31. Citations to the *amicus* briefs filed by the United States are rife in the Court's opinions in both cases.

As these examples suggest, one response of American courts to the growth of public-law litigation has been to allow (or, often, require) broader participation as cases depart further from the traditional bipartite model. There is plenty of room for a debate (one beyond my scope here) about whether courts—thanks to constraints on the way they gather information and how that information typically is presented to them—become relatively incompetent to decide these "polycentric" disputes as the disputes become more multifaceted and complex.[32] For present purposes, the main point is that adjudication of important public-law issues seems capable of possessing significant primary authority so long as courts provide for suitably broad participation.

We can supplement this point with a more affirmative one: The authority of the democratic process seems to imply some role for public-law litigation. Public-law litigation addresses (alleged) failures by government actors to obey democratically enacted statutes or constitutional provisions. I will discuss the authority of constitutional provisions, and of judicial interpretations of those provisions, at some length in the next two chapters. For now, consider a circumstance in which some government official or agency disobeys a statute. In any given instance, a single government official or agency, because of relative expertise or an appreciation of on-the-ground facts, might be more likely to get things right than the statute to which it ostensibly is subject. But the DR account reminds us that people will disagree about what it means to get things right—a fact the existence of public-law litigation makes quite plain—and so the question in any such case is not whether to do the right thing, but how to resolve a disagreement about what the right thing is. I argued in Chapter 4 that the democratic legislative process is a reasonably accurate means of performing that task. For a government official or agency to reject the decision generated by that process would be to upset that settlement; it would be to take Aristotle's part over John Adams in the debate over the possibility of a rule of law.

The DR account thus requires that statutes be treated as authoritative—that they be enforced, at least presumptively, including against government actors themselves. This is the essence of Adams's "government of laws and not of men." Public-law litigation is a means of accomplishing this; it is a mechanism by which ordinary citizens can require powerful officials to meet their legal obligations. Without that opportunity, a nominally democratic government could become a functionally Hobbesian one.

Note, by the way, that this brief for public-law litigation is in fact an argument for judicial independence more broadly. Courts that are controlled by other institutions of government will hardly be in a position to enforce those institutions'

---

32. On the skeptical side of the debate is Fuller, *supra* note 1; on the sanguine side are Chayes, *supra* note 19, and Fiss, *supra* note 12. For my own attempt to justify certain restraints on the gathering and presentation of facts in court, see Christopher J. Peters, *Adjudicative Speech and the First Amendment*, 51 UCLA L. Rev. 705 (2004).

obligation to obey the law. It is of course no accident that in many superficially "democratic" societies—the countries of the old Soviet bloc come to mind—the lack of real judicial independence saw to it that supposed legal limitations on the power of government actors were never enforced. It may be that periodic American proposals to rein in an "activist" judiciary—by, for example, removing the courts' jurisdiction over certain controversial topics—in fact threaten the efficacy of the very democratic process that judges often are accused of circumventing.[33] (There are, however, countervailing factors with respect to "jurisdiction-stripping" proposals, some of which I discuss in more detail in Chapter 8.)

In sum, then: The DR account suggests that public-law litigation is to some extent necessary in a democratic society, and that concerns for judicial legitimacy can be addressed by appropriately broadening participation in the litigative process.

4. JUDICIAL MINIMALISM

The fact that courts can authoritatively decide broad public-law issues tells us little about their appropriate methodology in doing so. One prominent debate about public-law methodology involves the proper scope of judicial decisions: Should courts behave somewhat like mini-legislatures, attempting to generate their own general rules to supplement the general rules embodied in the statutes, regulations, and constitutional provisions they are interpreting? Or should courts (despite the relative expansiveness of their proceedings) proceed in a more ad hoc, common-law fashion, attempting to tether their decisions closely to the particular facts of a decided case?

While at least one sitting Supreme Court Justice (Antonin Scalia) favors the former approach,[34] the Court as a whole has recently favored the latter in its public-law decisions.[35] Several prominent public-law theorists, moreover, have

---

33. *See* Janet Cooper Alexander, *Jurisdiction-Stripping in a Time of Terror*, 95 CAL. L. REV. 1193, 1193–94 (2007) (noting that "jurisdiction-stripping bills have been introduced" in Congress, but few have been enacted); see also The Marriage Protection Act of 2005, H.R. 1100, 109th Cong. (2005) (attempting to amend title 28 of the United States Code to "limit Federal court jurisdiction over questions under the Defense of Marriage Act"). For an in-depth analysis of the concept of "judicial activism," see Craig Green, *An Intellectual History of Judicial Activism*, 58 EMORY L.J. 1195 (2009).

34. *See, e.g.*, Antonin Scalia, *The Rule of Law as a Law of Rules*, 56 U. CHI. L. REV. 1175, 1178–79 (1989).

35. For a description of this trend, see CASS R. SUNSTEIN, ONE CASE AT A TIME: JUDICIAL MINIMALISM ON THE SUPREME COURT (1999) [hereinafter SUNSTEIN, ONE CASE AT A TIME]. Sunstein's book assesses the work of the Court under Chief Justice William Rehnquist (and featuring Sandra Day O'Connor as its typical swing vote); early indications suggested that its successor Court, under Chief Justice John Roberts and featuring

offered extensive and nuanced normative defenses of what one of them, Cass Sunstein, calls "judicial minimalism."[36] Sunstein urges courts to be cautious about rendering broad, rule-like decisions in public-law cases; doing so risks short-circuiting the democratic process (which sometimes is better-equipped to resolve the relevant issues) and amplifies the danger of judicial error. Minimalist public-law decisions—decisions that are "narrow" (limited closely to their facts), "shallow" (based on analogical reasoning rather than deep theory), or both—in fact can serve democratic values, Sunstein argues, by signaling statutory or constitutional problems while giving the political branches the opportunity to devise their own solutions.[37]

As Sunstein acknowledges, judicial minimalism is not a one-size-fits-all prescription (that itself would be nonminimalist); in some contexts (e.g., where there is a great need for consistency or predictability, or a low risk of serious judicial error), the costs of minimalism will outweigh its benefits.[38] With this caveat, I want to suggest here that the DR account of adjudicative authority provides strong general support for the practice (if only the presumptive practice) of judicial minimalism.[39]

Samuel Alito in place of O'Connor (with Anthony Kennedy now the Court's swing vote), would pursue a similarly minimalist approach. *See* Christopher J. Peters, *Under-the-Table Overruling*, 54 Wayne L. Rev. 1067 (2008) [hereinafter Peters, *Under-the-Table Overruling*]. That notion is now being challenged, however, by the Roberts Court's recent willingness directly to overrule precedent, even when doing so is not strictly necessary to resolve a case. *See* Citizens United v. Fed. Election Comm'n, 120 S. Ct. 876, 913 (2010) (overruling precedent to hold that restrictions on corporate spending in federal elections, imposed by the so-called McCain-Feingold statute, were unconstitutional). The Court could have decided *Citizens United* without directly overruling prior case law, by (for example) holding "that Citizens United was not the sort of group to which the McCain-Feingold law was meant to apply, or that the law did not mean to address 90-minute documentaries, or that video-on-demand technologies were not regulated by the law." *See* Adam Liptak, *Justices, 5–4, Reject Corporate Campaign Spending Limit*, N.Y. Times, Jan. 22, 2010, at A1, *available at* 2010 WLNR 1385136.

36. *See, e.g.*, Alexander M. Bickel, The Least Dangerous Branch: The Supreme Court at the Bar of Politics (2d ed. Yale Univ. Press 1986) (1962); Sunstein, One Case at a Time, *supra* note 35. For a comparison between Sunstein's and Bickel's versions of minimalism, see Christopher J. Peters & Neal Devins, *Alexander Bickel and the New Judicial Minimalism*, in The Judiciary and American Democracy 45 (Kenneth D. Ward & Cecilia R. Castillo eds., 2005).

37. *See* Sunstein, One Case at a Time, *supra* note 35. Sunstein also notes that minimalist decisions can promote the achievement of consensus on a multimember court. *See* Cass R. Sunstein, Legal Reasoning and Political Conflict 35–61 (1996).

38. *See* Sunstein, One Case at a Time, *supra* note 35, at 19–23, 57–60.

39. What follows is a considerably shortened version of the arguments in Christopher J. Peters, *Assessing the New Judicial Minimalism*, 100 Colum. L. Rev. 1454, 1513–21 (2000).

Recall that the primary authority of adjudication, on the adversary, common-law model, flows from this fact: The most direct impact of a judicial decision typically falls only on those who either have participated in the decision or share crucial interests with a participant. This source of authority is threatened by judicial "maximalism"—an attempt to lay down broad rules when deciding cases—because maximalism risks divorcing the impact of a decision from the factual context in which the decision is rendered (and thus from the litigant interests that stem from that context).

Suppose, for example, that the Court in the Michigan affirmative-action lawsuits had laid down a broad rule: An interest in racial diversity always justifies consideration of race in government decisionmaking. (In fact the Michigan decisions were substantially narrower than this: The Court held that diversity in higher education was a compelling government interest, but one that could only be pursued by a holistic process considering race along with many other factors, not a procedure that assigns fixed value to an applicant's race.[40]) A rule this broad would have applied, in meaningfully binding ways, in contexts notably distinct from law school and university admissions: in military recruiting, in government hiring and contracting outside higher education, and in the assignment of students in public primary and secondary schools, for example.[41]

And yet, broad as the participation was in the Michigan cases, it was not broad enough to encompass meaningful roles for those who might be injured by affirmative action in any of these very different contexts. None of the intervening parties or *amici* in either case, for example, were primary- or secondary-school students (or their parents) opposed to race-based school or classroom assignments. Thus no participant in the cases had much of an incentive to argue that, say, consideration of race in primary or secondary education is less warranted than in higher education (perhaps on the ground that young children are less likely to have unique race-influence perspectives than college and professional students, or because it is less important in primary and secondary schools to foment the kind of vigorous classroom exchanges that diversity permits). And yet a broad ruling along the lines sketched above would have foreclosed these kinds of arguments in subsequent cases.[42] As a result, subsequent litigants or

---

40. *See Grutter,* 539 U.S. at 325, 336–37; *Gratz,* 539 U.S. at 266.

41. In fact the Court subsequently declined to apply *Grutter's* rationale to allow race-conscious pupil assignments in public schools. *See* Parents Involved in Cmty. Sch. v. Seattle Sch. Dist. No. 1, 551 U.S. 701, 725 (2007). In doing so, a plurality of the Court suggested that *Grutter's* holding that diversity is a compelling state interest is limited to the context of higher education—a suggestion that, in my view, reads *Grutter* too narrowly. *See* Peters, *Under-the-Table Overruling, supra* note 35, at 1070–71.

42. To be precise, such a broad ruling would have *purported* to foreclose these distinguishing arguments in future cases. Subsequent courts can be quite creative in undermining broad rulings by finding distinctions where none seem to exist. The history of Supreme Court abortion decisions following *Roe v. Wade,* 410 U.S. 113 (1973), in which

potential litigants would have been bound to a result that neither they nor their interest representatives helped to make.

It is tempting to think that this problem with broad rulings can be addressed by allowing for correspondingly broader participation in the process of generating them. But there are three reasons to think this is not so. First is the obvious problem, alluded to in the previous section, of unwieldiness: At some point a lawsuit will become too broadly participatory for a court to manage. Second is the familiar problem of indeterminate legal rules: Like a legislature, a court will be unable to predict every circumstance in which its broadly stated rule might apply, and so the court could not invite the participation of everyone who might be bound by a rule, even if it somehow could oversee the procedural Frankenstein's monster that would result.

Third, the expansion of participation in the judicial creation of a broad rule seems unlikely to compensate, at least not completely, for the mismatch between the rule's breadth and the factual context from which it is born. Suppose the court in the Michigan affirmative-action lawsuits had allowed the intervention of parents opposed to race-based assignments of their children in public schools. Because no policy of race-based public-school assignments was at issue in those cases (which involved race-conscious university and law school admissions), the implications of the court's potential ruling for such a policy would be only dimly perceived, both by the parties and by the court. The actual Michigan cases involved enormous amounts of evidence relevant primarily or solely in the higher-education context: testimony about law-school classroom dynamics, statistical evidence of racial disparities in admissions-test scores and high school or undergraduate grade-point averages, and so on. Without similar evidence from the very different contexts of primary and secondary education, it is difficult to see how a court decision directly applying in those contexts could claim much competence, participation or no. (And of course allowing the intervenors to present evidence relevant primarily to *those* contexts—and, *a fortiori*, allowing other intervenors to present evidence relevant to other contexts—would threaten to push the managerial capacity of the court beyond its breaking point.)

The *ad hocery* of the common-law method, it turns out, does more than cabin the binding effects of a court decision to similarly situated parties; it also contributes to judicial competence by giving the court and the litigants a concrete set

---

the Court gradually whittled away at what had seemed, in *Roe*, to be a fairly broad rule-like decision, illustrates this possibility rather dramatically. *See, e.g.,* Maher v. Roe, 432 U.S. 464, 474 (1977) (stating that *Roe v. Wade* implied "no limitation on the authority of a State to make a value judgment favoring child-birth over abortion, and to implement that judgment by the allocation of public funds"); Harris v. McRae, 448 U.S. 297 (1980) (upholding the Hyde Amendment's provision which reimbursed states in the Medicaid program for costs of abortions performed only where the life of the mother was placed in danger if the fetus was carried to term).

of facts to focus on, "the flesh and blood of an actual case," in Alexander Bickel's phrase.[43] Justiciability doctrines, which limit a court's ability to decide issues not arising from actual extant controversies, might be understood as a reflection of this fact.[44] So might a presumption in favor of minimalism—of avoiding unnecessarily broad rulings in deciding public-law (and for that matter other sorts of) cases.

5. FROM DEMOCRATIC ADJUDICATION TO CONSTITUTIONALISM

I've argued that adjudication can be democratic, in two senses. Adjudication can apply democratically enacted legal rules in particular circumstances, thus enhancing the dispute-resolving authority of majoritarian democracy. And in doing so, adjudication can itself incorporate meaningfully democratic elements of participation and fairness.

In contemporary America, however—and increasingly in other parts of the world—the acid test of adjudication's democratic credentials occurs in the context of constitutional law. American constitutionalism requires that courts sometimes refuse to apply democratically enacted laws—indeed declare their invalidity—in the name of exceptionally indeterminate legal rules enacted many generations ago. Many have wondered whether the seemingly antidemocratic implication of this process—the "countermajoritarian difficulty" of constitutional judicial review—overrides whatever good it might be thought to achieve.

In this book's final two chapters, I offer an argument, based in the DR account of law, for the authoritativeness of constitutional judicial review. I contend that constitutional law can serve as a reasonably accurate procedure for preventing malfunctions in democratic authority and resolving disputes about that authority.

---

43. BICKEL, *supra* note 36, at 26.

44. On this possibility, see R. L. Brilmayer, *Judicial Review, Justiciability and the Limits of the Common Law Method*, 57 B.U. L. REV. 807 (1977); Lea Brilmayer, *The Jurisprudence of Article III: Perspectives on the "Case or Controversy" Requirement*, 93 HARV. L. REV. 297 (1979); Christopher J. Peters, *Adjudication as Representation*, 97 COLUM. L. REV. 312, 420–30 (1997).

7. LAW VS. DEMOCRACY?

1. THE COUNTERMAJORITARIAN DIFFICULTY

I've argued that the Dispute-Resolution (DR) account endorses majoritarian democracy as a way to generate legal rules, and participatory, common-law adjudication as a way to apply those rules. But in the United States, and increasingly in other parts of the world, courts sometimes apply legal rules *against* majoritarian democracy. Americans expect their government to adhere to a written Constitution—a charter, originally adopted more than 200 years ago and amended periodically since, that establishes the structure and powers of the national government, regulates the federal relationship between the national and various state governments, and lists certain individual "rights" that government must respect. And Americans recognize the authority of the Supreme Court—a judicial body consisting of nonelective judges who can serve for life—to render binding interpretations of the Constitution's (often highly indeterminate) general rules.

Constitutional law and judicial review are often said to create a "countermajoritarian difficulty"—a clash between the broadly participatory, presumptively majoritarian mechanisms of democracy and the entrenched, often archaic democracy-constraining rules of constitutional law as enforced by an elite cadre of politically unaccountable judges.[1] And the DR account, at first blush, seems only to make the countermajoritarian difficulty more difficult. The DR account holds out legal rules as the authoritative product of democratic processes, and adjudication as a sort of second-best means to authoritatively apply legal rules (given the impossibility of using the full-dress democratic process to do so). But constitutional law seems to invert this hierarchy; it seems to give

---

1. The term "counter-majoritarian difficulty" was coined in mid-century by the highly influential constitutional theorist Alexander Bickel. *See* ALEXANDER M. BICKEL, THE LEAST DANGEROUS BRANCH: THE SUPREME COURT AT THE BAR OF POLITICS (2d ed. Yale Univ. Press 1986) (1962). The term has since become synonymous with worries about the democratic legitimacy of judicial review. *See generally* Barry Friedman, *The Birth of an Academic Obsession: The History of the Countermajoritarian Difficulty, Part Five*, 112 YALE L.J. 153 (2002). The "difficulty" applies not just to judicial review, however, but to constitutional law more generally. Even if binding interpretations of the Constitution were rendered by the political branches of government rather than the Court, those interpretations still would be *interpretations* of—attempts to understand and apply—legal norms laid down by previous generations, norms that cannot be changed by "the actual people of the here and now," in Bickel's phrase, through ordinary democratic processes. *See* BICKEL, *supra*, at 17.

extrademocratic legal rules priority over democracy, and semidemocratic adjudication a trump card against democratic politics. Constitutional law claims to resolve very important disputes by apparently nondemocratic means, and thus its authority, on the DR account, is rather saliently open to question.

I will argue in this chapter and the next that constitutional law, including judicial review, can in fact be authoritative on the DR account, and that the American practice of constitutional law in particular (though not exclusively) possesses general authority. The special authority of constitutional law lies in its capacity to mitigate partiality in the resolution of disputes about democracy itself. But that claim to authority would risk being swamped by a tide of antidemocratic entrenchment and elitism, were it not for the ability of constitutional law to respond in various ways to political and popular inputs. Authoritative constitutional law, I'll argue, ultimately is a balancing act between impartiality and competence, between fairness and participation, and (most fundamentally) between the authority of law and the moral imperative of the moment.

I begin by canvassing the most influential kinds of response that have been offered to the countermajoritarian difficulty. All of them have weaknesses; most of them have significant strengths that will inform the DR response I will offer. The chief advantage of the DR response over the others will be its capacity to unite the strengths of these rivals into a single compelling defense of constitutional law.

2. STRATEGIES FOR RESOLVING THE DIFFICULTY

The countermajoritarian difficulty has prompted four basic types of response from defenders of constitutional law and judicial review. There is what I will call a *substantive* response, which holds that certain fundamental values trump democratic processes and thus require extrademocratic protection from democracy. There is a *proceduralist* response, which denies that substantive values trump democracy but asserts that extrademocratic procedures are necessary to keep democracy itself in good working order. There is a *dualist* response, which holds that constitutional law is just another form of democracy, one with special authority as compared to its "ordinary" form. And there is a *reductionist* response, which asserts that constitutional law is simply part of ordinary democratic politics.

A. The Substantive Strategy

A long tradition in American constitutional theory holds that democracy, when push comes to shove, must yield to certain substantive values, such as equality or justice. On this view, it is all well and good to subject garden-variety disputes to democratic politics; but on fundamental matters of equality or justice, what is democratic must give way to what is right. Constitutional law, this approach holds, trumps democracy because (and to the extent that) it protects fundamental substantive values from impairment by the democratic process.

This view, which has affinities with John Locke's notion of natural rights,[2] fairly can be attributed to many if not all of the American Founders[3]—and in particular to James Madison and Alexander Hamilton, the principal authors of the *Federalist Papers*, which proved to be the most influential and enduring defense of the Constitution of 1789. The Declaration of Independence, of course, opened its indictment of the British Crown by invoking the "unalienable rights" of men, and the Federalists worried that unfettered democratic government would threaten those rights just as an abusive monarchy had. They therefore

---

2. The straightforward view that government exists to protect natural rights, and that a government's failure to do so justifies replacing that government, often is attributed to Locke. *See, e.g.,* RANDY E. BARNETT, RESTORING THE LOST CONSTITUTION: THE PRESUMPTION OF LIBERTY 70–71, 75, 325–27 (2004); GORDON S. WOOD, THE CREATION OF THE AMERICAN REPUBLIC, 1776–1787, at 282–304 (1969). There is, however, a somewhat more nuanced plausible reading of Locke's understanding about the relationship between natural rights and government, a reading that centers on the procedures of dispute resolution rather than the substance of natural rights. Locke emphasized that a pregovernmental state of nature was insufficient, not just to protect natural rights, but to resolve disputes about the content and application of natural rights. In Chapter 9 of the *Second Treatise*, Locke listed, among the "many things wanting" in the state of nature

> First,. . . an *establish'd*, settled, known *Law*, received and allowed by common consent to be the Standard of Right and Wrong, and the common measure to decide all Controversies between them.
>
> Secondly,. . . a *known and indifferent* Judge, with Authority to determine all differences according to established Law.
>
> Thirdly,. . . *Power* to back and support the Sentence when right, and *to give* it due *Execution*.

JOHN LOCKE, *Second Treatise of Government, in* TWO TREATISES OF GOVERNMENT 395, §§ 124–26, at 396–97 (Peter Laslett ed., 1960) (emphasis in original). The problem with the state of nature, for Locke, was not simply (or even primarily) that people would viciously violate the rights of others, but rather that people, "being biased by their Interest, as well as ignorant for want of study," will do so innocently. *See id.* § 124, at 396. Recall from the discussion in Chapter 4 that Locke's rejection of Hobbesian absolutism turned on his recognition that a Hobbesian monarch would himself be biased by self-interest and thus ultimately would fail as an "indifferent judge" of society's disputes. The "long train of abuses" that would, for Locke, spark a justified revolution can be understood, not as a series of clear monarchical violations of the dictates of natural law, but as a collection of instances in which the monarch displays his partiality by taking his own side in disputes about what natural law requires. *See id.* § 225, at 463. Locke, in other words, might be understood as advocating government (and critiquing absolutist government) not on the ground that some agreed set of natural rights must be protected, but for the reason that disputes about natural rights cannot acceptably be resolved without (reasonably competent, reasonably impartial) government.

3. *See* BARNETT, *supra* note 2, at 70–71, 75; WOOD, *supra* note 2, at 282–304.

extolled the proposed Constitution, with its multiple layers and divisions of government (including its independent judiciary), in part for its capacity to protect individual and minority rights from the "passions" and "interests" of the majority.[4] The addition of the Bill of Rights in 1791 was a concession to those who believed (among other things) that individual and minority rights would not sufficiently be guarded by the structural features of the original Constitution.[5]

We can take the American Founders' understanding of natural rights, as exemplified in the Declaration and in the *Federalist Papers*, as a paradigmatic example of a substantive approach to the countermajoritarian difficulty. The Declaration, paraphrasing Locke, understood the purpose of government itself as the preservation of certain "unalienable" natural rights (including "Life, Liberty,

---

4. For example, in *Federalist No. 10*, Madison rebutted objections to the relatively powerful central government the Constitution would create by arguing that a large republic can "control[] [the] effects" of "factions"—groups "of citizens, whether amounting to a majority or a minority of the whole, who are united and actuated by some common impulse of passion, or of interest, adverse to the rights of other citizens, or to the permanent and aggregate interests of the community." THE FEDERALIST No. 10, at 122, 125, 128 (James Madison) (Isaac Kramnick ed., 1987) [hereinafter Madison, FEDERALIST No. 10].

Madison reemphasized the point in *Federalist No. 51*, arguing that the Constitution's combination of vertical division of powers (between the states and the national government) and horizontal separation of powers (at the national level) would create "a double security. . . to the rights of the people. . . . [T]he society itself will be broken into so many parts, interests, and classes of citizens, that the rights of individuals, or of the minority, will be in little danger from interested combinations of the majority." THE FEDERALIST No. 51, at 318, 321 (James Madison) (Isaac Kramnick ed., 1987) [hereinafter Madison, FEDERALIST No. 51].

In *Federalist No. 78*, Hamilton explained the (relatively) politically independent judiciary created by Article III in part as a way "to guard the Constitution and the rights of individuals from the effects of those ill humors which the arts of designing men, or the influence of particular conjunctures, sometimes disseminate among the people themselves, and which. . . have a tendency. . . to occasion dangerous innovations in the government, and serious oppressions of the minor party in the community." THE FEDERALIST No. 78, at 436, 440 (Alexander Hamilton) (Isaac Kramnick ed., 1987).

5. *See* Centinel, Letter to the Editor, *Centinel I*, PHILADELPHIA INDEPENDENT GAZETTEER, Oct. 5, 1787, *reprinted in* 2 THE COMPLETE ANTI-FEDERALIST, 136, 142–43 (Herbert J. Storing ed., 1981) ("The framers of [the proposed Constitution] have made no provision for the *liberty of the press*, that grand *palladium of freedom*, and *scourge of tyrants*; but observed a total silence on that head.") (emphasis in original) (authorship attributed to Samuel Bryan); Brutus, Letter to the Editor, *Brutus II*, NEW YORK JOURNAL, Nov. 1, 1787, *reprinted in* 2 THE COMPLETE ANTI-FEDERALIST, *supra*, at 372, 373 ("[I]n forming a government on its true principles, the foundation should be laid. . . by expressly reserving to the people such of their essential natural rights, as are not necessary to be parted with.") (authorship attributed to Robert Yates). *See also* James Madison, Speech in Congress (June 8, 1789), *available at* http://www.constitution.org/jm/17890608_removal.htm (introducing the Bill of Rights and acknowledging Anti-Federalist objections).

and the pursuit of Happiness"). On this understanding, government vitiates its raison d'être if it violates these natural rights, and thus mechanisms to prevent government from violating rights are justified, even necessary. Democracy itself might be, or consist of, precisely such mechanisms; it might be better than other forms of government (such as Hobbesian absolutism) at the task of protecting natural rights. But to the extent democracy is imperfect at this task, it must be constrained by nondemocratic means: structural devices like those defended in the *Federalist Papers* (federalism, the separation of powers, an independent judiciary), and perhaps a written Bill of Rights. The constraint of democracy by constitutional law (on this view) is justifiable because constitutional law holds democracy to its purpose, namely the protection of natural rights. The countermajoritarian difficulty is no difficulty at all: The very purpose of democracy requires that the majority be countered where fundamental rights are at stake.

This substantive justification of constitutional law finds contemporary expression, among many other places, in Ronald Dworkin's account of constitutionalism and judicial review. Dworkin's "constitutional conception of democracy" holds that "government [is] subject to conditions. . . of equal status for all citizens."[6] Some of those conditions are essentially procedural: They relate to the terms on which citizens can participate in government. But many of them are substantive in the same sense as the Declaration's "unalienable rights": They specify what individual citizens may demand of the community or what the community may not demand of its citizens. According to Dworkin, one "democratic condition" is a condition of equality: "[T]he political process. . . must express. . . equal concern for the interests of all its members."[7] Another is a condition of liberty or autonomy, or what Dworkin calls "moral independence": The community must respect "an individual's own responsibility to decide for himself what life to live given the resources and opportunities that. . . collective decisions leave to him."[8] These values are, perhaps not accidentally, redolent of the Declaration's avowal that "all men are created equal," endowed with the rights to "Life, Liberty, and the pursuit of Happiness"; they are prepolitical values, values whose advancement is, on Dworkin's view as in the Declaration's, the very point of democratic government. Constitutional law, for Dworkin as for many of the Founders, is a codification of these values against encroachment by the form of government that is supposed to protect them.[9]

---

6. Ronald Dworkin, Freedom's Law: The Moral Reading of the American Constitution 17 (1996).

7. *Id.* at 25.

8. *Id.* at 26.

9. Dworkin glosses his substantive understanding of constitutionalism with proceduralist rhetoric, describing his "constitutional conception" as a superior version of democracy itself. *See id.* at 15–19. Dworkin is of course entitled to apply the label "democracy" to

These substantive approaches attempt to resolve the countermajoritarian difficulty by prioritizing constitutional law—as the entrenched protection of prepolitical rights or other values—over the procedures of majoritarian democracy. And it should be readily apparent that such approaches are anathema on the DR account, for the same reason that outcome-based accounts of authority are problematic more generally: They rely on content-dependent reasons for obedience. People disagree about the existence and content of prepolitical rights, and it is precisely those disagreements that legal authority, including the authority of both democratic legislation and constitutional law, is (on the DR account) supposed to avoid or resolve. The countermajoritarian difficulty is a tension between two alternative methods of resolving disputes about rights; that choice cannot turn on the question of which side of a dispute is correct.

Imagine, for example, a public disagreement over whether people have a right of what Dworkin might call "moral independence"—or what the Founders would call "liberty and the pursuit of happiness"—to engage in consensual sexual relations with others of the same sex. The countermajoritarian difficulty poses the question of which set of procedures—the majoritarian democratic process or judicial interpretation of a written Constitution—is capable of resolving this dispute most acceptably. The answer cannot be that whichever procedures resolve this particular dispute *correctly*—by getting the normatively right answer—are the procedures that should be used. "[T]he design of a decision-procedure must be independent of the particular disagreement it is supposed to settle," Jeremy Waldron reminds us; "it is no good if it simply reignites it."[10]

The DR account, of course, is built on the plausibility of endorsing procedures on the ground that their results will be generally perceived as reasonably correct over the long run. But that is not what substantive approaches like Dworkin's assert with respect to constitutional law. Dworkin and other substantive theorists hold that the Constitution is authoritative because (and to the extent that) it protects certain values from the democratic process, that is, because it picks the correct side in particular disputes over values. Substantive approaches

---

whatever set of arrangements or values he likes; but for our purposes Dworkin's maneuver is merely semantic. Recall that the understanding of "democracy" I outlined in Chapter 4 is a procedural one, in the sense of John Rawls's "imperfect procedural justice": It values democratic procedures as a way to generate, over time, results that are generally perceived as reasonably accurate. But it does not value democracy as a way to generate *particular* results. (On the distinction between purely substantive, or outcome-based, accounts of procedure and accounts of "imperfect procedural justice," see the discussion in Chapter 3, section 2.) Dworkin's "constitutional conception of democracy" is substantive, not procedural, in this latter sense: Dworkin values democracy as a way to generate particular results, namely the advancement of his "democratic conditions" of equal concern and moral independence.

10. Jeremy Waldron, *The Core of the Case Against Judicial Review*, 115 YALE L.J. 1346, 1373 (2006) [hereinafter Waldron, *Core Case*].

to the countermajoritarian difficulty thus beg the very questions that create the need for democracy and, arguably, constitutional law in the first place.

B. The Proceduralist Strategy

A more recent tradition, and ultimately a far more promising one, attempts to dissolve the countermajoritarian difficulty by envisioning constitutional law not as a constraint on democracy, but as simply the rules of the democratic game, designed to make democracy more fair and participatory. This procedural approach has roots as far back as *McCulloch v. Maryland*, the 1819 decision in which the Supreme Court held, among other things, that the state of Maryland could not constitutionally impose a tax on the federally chartered Bank of the United States.[11] Writing for the Court, Chief Justice John Marshall noted that a state tax on the federal Bank would amount to a tax on citizens of other states who could not vote in Maryland—a literal example of "taxation without representation." Marshall thus used constitutional law to enforce the democratic principle of fair participation in binding decisions. So understood, the Constitution was not so much a constraint on the democratic process in the state of Maryland as a guarantor of democratic safeguards in the politics of the nation as a whole.

The watershed moment for procedural approaches to constitutional law, however, did not arrive until 120 years after *McCulloch*, with the famous "Footnote Four" of Justice Harlan Fiske Stone's 1938 opinion for the Court in *United States v. Carolene Products Co.*[12] The *Carolene Products* decision continued the New Deal Court's recently discovered policy of deference to the political branches on matters of economic regulation, a policy that reversed roughly three decades of occasionally aggressive judicial use of the Constitution's Commerce and Due Process Clauses to invalidate Progressive-era legislation. As the Court committed itself to staying out of economic affairs, however, it simultaneously began to sense the need to intervene more forcefully in other controversial areas, particularly on matters involving political participation and social equality.[13]

---

11. McCulloch v. Maryland, 17 U.S. 316 (1819).

12. United States v. Carolene Products Co., 304 U.S. 144, 152 n.4 (1938).

13. In a series of cases beginning during the First World War, the Court had addressed First Amendment challenges to laws criminalizing speech against the war or the draft and, later, speech espousing socialist or communist ideology. Most of these decisions upheld convictions, but from them emerged a rhetorically powerful series of opinions (mostly dissents) in which Justices Oliver Wendell Holmes and Louis Brandeis articulated a free-market theory of the Free Speech Clause, one advocating tolerance of dissenting viewpoints (and owing much to the ideas of John Stuart Mill). *See* Whitney v. California, 274 U.S. 357, 372, 377 (1927) (Brandeis, J., concurring); Gitlow v. New York, 268 U.S. 652, 672 (1925) (Holmes, J., dissenting); Schenck v. United States, 249 U.S. 47 (1919); Abrams v. United States, 250 U.S. 616, 624, 630 (1919) (Holmes, J., dissenting). *Cf.* JOHN STUART MILL, *On Liberty, in* UTILITARIANISM, ON LIBERTY, AND CONSIDERATIONS ON REPRESENTATIVE GOVERNMENT 69, 83–123 (H. B. Acton ed., 1972) (1859).

In *Carolene*, the Court attempted to accommodate these competing impulses: judicial deference to politics in economic matters on the one hand, aggressive judicial enforcement of political and egalitarian rights on the other. The *Carolene* Court, upholding a federal prohibition on so-called "filled milk," declared that it would not invalidate "regulatory legislation affecting ordinary commercial transactions... unless... it is of such character as to preclude the assumption that it rests upon some rational basis."[14] But it qualified this "rational basis" test in a lengthy footnote—Footnote Four—suggesting that "more exacting judicial scrutiny" might be appropriate in two types of circumstance: where "legislation... restricts those political processes which can ordinarily be expected to bring about repeal of undesirable legislation," and where "prejudice against discrete and insular minorities... tends seriously to curtail the operation of those political processes ordinarily to be relied upon to protect minorities."[15]

Footnote Four implies a procedural account of constitutional rights, by which judicial enforcement of rights prevents or cures defects in the democratic process itself rather than simply trumping democratic outcomes with results the Court prefers. One way the democratic process might go wrong is if those

---

While the Holmes/Brandeis approach would not be accepted, more or less fully, by the Court for another thirty years (see *Brandenburg v. Ohio*, 395 U.S. 444 (1969)), the Court in 1938, when *Carolene Products* was decided, must have grasped the possibility that the Free Speech Clause might be applied relatively aggressively to protect dissident speech. Indeed, during the succeeding two terms the Court used the Clause to strike down a city ordinance prohibiting the distribution of leaflets on the public streets and sidewalks, see *Schneider v. New Jersey*, 308 U.S. 147 (1939), and to reverse the disturbing-the-peace conviction of a Jehovah's Witness who played an anti-Catholic phonograph record on a street corner, see *Cantwell v. Connecticut*, 310 U.S. 296, 308 (1940).

The *Carolene* Court also stood on the cusp of the revolution in Equal Protection jurisprudence that eventually produced *Brown v. Board of Education* and outlawed Jim Crow. Later in the same term the Court would hold, in *Missouri ex rel. Gaines v. Canada*, 305 U.S. 337 (1938), that a state could not maintain its all-white public law school by paying for black citizens to attend school in neighboring states. This chink in the armor of the "separate but equal" doctrine—the principle, embodied in *Plessy v. Ferguson*, 163 U.S. 537 (1896), that equal protection was satisfied so long as racially segregated public facilities are materially equivalent—would be widened in subsequent decisions before the armor eventually fell away entirely in *Brown*. *See* Sipuel v. Bd. of Regents, 332 U.S. 631 (1948) (reaffirming *Gaines*); Sweatt v. Painter, 339 U.S. 629 (1950) (holding that a new blacks-only public law school was not materially equivalent to the established whites-only school); McLaurin v. Oklahoma State Regents, 339 U.S. 637 (1950) (holding that the isolation of black students within a formally "integrated" graduate school violated equal protection).

14. *Carolene Products*, 304 U.S. at 152.

15. *Id.* at 152 n.4. Footnote Four also suggested a third category of case, irrelevant for our purposes here, in which "[t]here may be a narrower scope for operation of the presumption of constitutionality": cases in which "legislation appears on its face to be within a specific prohibition of the Constitution, such as those of the first ten Amendments." *Id.*

holding temporary power—a momentary political majority, or elected officials currently in office—rig the system to entrench that power and prevent others from legitimately taking or sharing it. A democratically elected government, for example, might decide to prosecute dissenters for speaking against government policies, thus depriving voters of information and arguments critical of those policies and increasing the chance that the government will retain power at the next election. Constitutional law targeted at preventing these abuses—a judicially enforced guarantee of freedom of political speech, for instance—would ensure that democratic mechanisms work properly, allowing meaningful citizen participation by maintaining the flow of information and opinion upon which participation can be based. It would be strange to think of constitutional law, used this way, as contradicting or overriding democratic decisions; constitutional law, rather, would be a means of making sure that political decisions truly are democratic.

Another way the democratic process might go wrong is if irrational prejudice or bias leads to the formation of artificial political minority groups. As we saw in Chapter 4, democratic majorities and minorities typically are in flux, in two related senses. First, political majorities and minorities coalesce around particular issues or sets of issues, and thus a minority with respect to one issue may be a majority with respect to other issues. Second, even with respect to particular issues, political majorities and minorities often change over time, as dominant social attitudes about those issues evolve.

Suppose, however, that a certain subset of the population shares some non-political characteristic—race, say, or religion or gender—that triggers irrational negative bias on the part of others; and suppose members of that group also (thanks perhaps to the long-term effects of that bias) tend to share certain political interests and viewpoints. The existence of the irrational bias might prevent those political interests and viewpoints from having a fair hearing in the political process. The interest of African Americans in more funding for inner-city schools, for example, might be discounted by others precisely because of its association with African Americans, a group subject to pervasive racial prejudice. A minority religious group's argument for an exemption for its practices from generally applicable laws—say, an exception to the drug laws for the sacramental use of peyote by Native Americans—might fall on deaf ears thanks to the majority's religious bias against its proponents.

But constitutional provisions aimed at protecting "discrete and insular minorities" from the effects of majority animosity—a guarantee that the laws will provide "equal protection," for example, or a prohibition against laws targeting particular religions or religious practices—might force democracy back on its track, preventing the formation of discrete and insular minorities and limiting their significance if they form. Again, constitutional law viewed this way seems less like a trump on majoritarian democracy and more like a corrective against democratic pathologies.

This Footnote Four approach—later expanded and popularized by constitutional theorist John Hart Ely[16]—seeks to evade the countermajoritarian difficulty, not by prioritizing rights over democracy as the substantive approach does, but by conceiving of constitutional rights as elements of a properly functioning democratic system. The approach sees judges as mechanics, armed with the tools of constitutional doctrine and charged with keeping the machinery of democracy humming. An invalidation of a statute on constitutional grounds, this approach holds, is not so much a rebuke of the machine itself as a jolt designed to nudge the machine back into working order, a good whack with the judicial wrench.

The Footnote Four proceduralist strategy has much in common with the DR approach I will outline below. But for our purposes it has two important limitations, both of which flow from a failure to fully appreciate the connection between legal authority and the resolution of disputes. First, the proceduralist account of democratic malfunctions envisions a rather narrow scope for constitutional law. Footnote Four, and Ely's subsequent elucidation of it, focus somewhat myopically on the danger that irrational bias against "discrete and insular minorities" will taint the democratic process. As I will explain, however, democracy can malfunction whenever a majority (or even a well-organized minority) becomes partial with respect to a particular issue—whenever the majority is "united and actuated by some common impulse of passion, or of interest," in Madison's famous phrase.[17] As Madison's description suggests (and as a reading of *Federalist No. 10* makes quite clear), a majority united by self-interest can be every bit as partial as a majority united by irrational bias. By spotlighting the role of bias in politics, however, Footnote Four and Ely emphasize the risk of majority "passion" and ignore the danger of majority "interest." Thus they underestimate the value of constitutional law in preventing and remediating self-interested abuses of power by the majority—a function, not coincidentally, that has often been performed in the American system by the Due Process Clause, whose scope the *Carolene Products* Court was attempting to curtail.

Second, and more fundamentally, Footnote Four proceduralism is insufficiently attentive to questions of process. As espoused by Ely and the *Carolene Products* Court, proceduralism is, somewhat counterintuitively, concerned primarily with the substance, or content, of constitutional law—with the kinds of disputes that should be removed from ordinary democratic politics. But Footnote Four proceduralism pays precious little attention to the questions of how those disputes, once removed, should then be resolved, and of why constitutional means of resolving them are superior to ordinary democratic ones.

---

16. *See* JOHN HART ELY, DEMOCRACY AND DISTRUST: A THEORY OF JUDICIAL REVIEW (1980).

17. Madison, FEDERALIST NO. 10, *supra* note 4, at 123.

Consider two manifestations of this inattentiveness. The first and most glaring is proceduralism's lack of an explanation for the constitutional text itself, and for the process that generated the text. Proceduralism holds that courts should closely scrutinize political decisions that tend to entrench those in power or that reflect, or promote, bias against discrete and insular minorities. But why should courts be bound by textual provisions, particularly centuries-old textual provisions, in doing so? The project of tethering democracy-reinforcing judicial decisions to the language of an eighteenth- or nineteenth-century clause seems at best gratuitous on a proceduralist theory, and at worst affirmatively obstructionist. The fact that a collection of eighteenth-century politicians chose a particular verbal formula—"freedom of speech, or of the press"—hardly seems relevant to the question of how best to protect political participation and fairness under contemporary conditions. The constitutional text, and indeed the efforts of the constitutional Framers generally, appear to be little more than annoying distractions to a Footnote Four proceduralist (which is why Ely dismisses the significance of the text with the epithet "clause-bound interpretivism"[18]).

A second aspect of the paradoxical proceduralist inattention to process is a decidedly shallow appreciation of courts themselves and of the constitutional tasks they are asked to perform. In defending constitutional courts as referees of democracy, Ely contrasts the relative political independence of judges with the interest-driven processes of ordinary politics;[19] but he pays almost no mind to the procedures of constitutional adjudication themselves. As a result, he tends to lose sight of the fact that constitutional courts are not simply "calling balls and strikes," to use a recent and inapt metaphor,[20] but are in fact attempting to resolve difficult and contentious disputes. For example, since the mid-1970s the Supreme Court has struggled with the First Amendment validity of laws regulating spending in connection with political campaigns.[21] Opponents of regulation generally argue that it stifles the communication of political information and opinion, thus frustrating a core purpose of the Free Speech Clause; proponents

---

18. Ely entitled Chapter 2 of *Democracy and Distrust* "The Impossibility of a Clause-Bound Interpretivism." *See* ELY, *supra* note 16, at 11.

19. *See id.* at 101–04,106–07, 151–52.

20. Chief Justice John Roberts opined at his confirmation hearing that "[j]udges are like umpires. Umpires don't make the rules, they apply them. They make sure everybody plays by the rules, but it is a limited role. Nobody ever went to a ball game to see the umpire." *Confirmation Hearing on the Nomination of John G. Roberts, Jr. to Be Chief Justice of the United States: Hearing Before the S. Comm. on the Judiciary*, 109th Cong. 55 (2005) (statement of John G. Roberts, Jr., Nominee to be Chief Justice of the United States).

21. *See, e.g.*, Buckley v. Valeo, 424 U.S. 1 (1976); First Nat'l Bank of Boston v. Bellotti, 435 U.S. 765 (1978); Austin v. Michigan Chamber of Commerce, 494 U.S. 652 (1990); McConnell v. Fed. Election Comm'n, 540 U.S. 93 (2003); Fed. Election Comm'n v. Wisconsin Right to Life, 551 U.S. 449 (2007); Citizens United v. Fed. Election Comm'n, 130 S.Ct. 876 (2010).

generally argue that it mitigates distortions in the marketplace of ideas by which wealthier speakers are disproportionately able to communicate their views. This is a genuine and important disagreement, and its difficulty is not diminished by the fact that it involves the procedures of democracy rather than some purely "substantive" concern. But Ely does not explain why the process of adjudication is a better way to resolve these disagreements than the process of politics; instead he naively offers proceduralism as a way to prevent judges from imposing their own values on the rest of us.[22]

The DR approach I will offer here draws heavily on the Footnote Four/Ely strategy, in particular by justifying constitutional law as a response to predictable kinds of defects in the democratic process. But the DR approach pays closer attention than the proceduralist strategy to the actual procedures of both constitutional law and ordinary democracy. It explains typical democratic defects as failures of impartiality, and it describes in some detail how a written constitution and judicial review can avoid or remediate those failures. It thus offers an account of constitutional process as well as constitutional doctrine.

C. Dualist Strategies

A third influential family of approaches to the countermajoritarian difficulty holds that constitutional law is, in essence, simply another form of democracy. According to these *dualist* strategies, constitutional law, while not undemocratic, trumps ordinary democratic politics—either because constitutional law is better than ordinary democracy at deciding issues of "principle" or "values," or simply because its procedures are more democratically legitimate than everyday democracy.

(i) **Bickelian Dualism** Alexander Bickel's defense of judicial review was a progenitor of one type of dualist approach. Bickel distinguished between "expediency" on the one hand and "principle" on the other—between "immediate results" and "enduring general values."[23] Citizens of a democracy, Bickel suggested, are likely to value both halves of this dichotomy; they are likely to want favorable immediate results but also to care about enduring values, and thus they are likely to want to act, as a collective governing body, in ways that properly balance the former with the latter. But the procedures of the ordinary "political marketplace"— elections, lawmaking by representative legislatures, and enforcement by an elected executive, where "the pressure for immediate results is strong enough and emotions ride high"—tend to ignore enduring values in the pursuit of expediency.[24] A different set of procedures, therefore, might be necessary in

---

22. For Ely's rejection of judicial value-imposition—and thus his implicit argument that proceduralism offers a meaningful alternative—see ELY, *supra* note 16, at 43–72 (chapter 3).

23. BICKEL, *supra* note 1, at 24–27.

24. *Id.* at 25.

order to supply the "principle" side of the equation. And (Bickel suggested), constitutional review by judges, who "have. . . the leisure, the training, and the insulation to follow the ways of the scholar in pursuing the ends of government," and who "are concerned with the flesh and blood of an actual case," can be defended as just such a necessary set of procedures for articulating enduring values.[25]

The recent work of Christopher Eisgruber offers a more fully developed Bickelian account of constitutionalism and judicial review.[26] Like Bickel, Eisgruber distinguishes between two kinds of substantive democratic goals, which Eisgruber calls "values" ("views about how [people] ought to behave," about matters of "moral duty") and "interests" ("views about what [people] want or desire").[27] Values and interests sometimes conflict with each other, and "[w]hen such conflicts occur, people commonly believe they ought to subordinate their interests to their values."[28]

Constitutionalism and judicial review, Eisgruber argues, are institutional strategies for subordinating interests to values in the realm of democratic politics. Ordinary majoritarian politics is likely to do a poor job of this, for a number of related reasons. It might not distinguish issues of values or principle from issues of mere self-interest, and when it does it might tend to prioritize the latter over the former. And in addressing matters of value, ordinary majoritarian politics is likely to "merely serve the majority" rather than "respond to the. . . opinions of all the people."[29]

By contrast (Eisgruber contends), a relatively obdurate constitution identifies certain topics of dispute that are not subject to ordinary politics. In doing so, it tags those topics as matters of value, not merely of interest, thus increasing the likelihood that they will be resolved through serious public deliberation; and it makes it more difficult for temporary political majorities to consolidate their power (and entrench their own views on matters of value) against the minority. Trusting the development of constitutional law to the process of judicial review, moreover, enhances the probability that issues of value will be treated as such, resolved according to "the right kind of reasons—reasons of moral principle rather than self-interest"—but also in a way that credibly can be claimed to "speak on behalf of the people."[30] Judges (in the American federal system) are, thanks to their lifetime tenure, relatively "disinterested" with respect

---

25. *Id.* at 25–26.
26. *See* CHRISTOPHER L. EISGRUBER, CONSTITUTIONAL SELF-GOVERNMENT (2001). The description of Eisgruber's account as "Bickelian" is mine, not Eisgruber's; in fact Eisgruber cites Bickel only once in his book. *See id.* at 225 n.50.
27. *Id.* at 5, 53.
28. *Id.* at 53.
29. *Id.* at 19.
30. *Id.* at 55, 3.

to politics and thus free to decide based on genuine moral convictions rather than estimations of short-term political gain. Their authority to resolve issues alone or in small groups, and their obligation to defend those resolutions publicly, encourages judges to take moral responsibility for their decisions. And yet the political process by which they are appointed ensures that judicial decisions, over time, tend to hew closely enough to mainstream public opinion that the judges can claim to represent the people in their decisionmaking.[31]

The Bickel/Eisgruber defense of constitutional law shares with substantive accounts (like Dworkin's) a belief in the priority of "principle" or "values" over mere "expediency" or "self-interest" and a distrust of the capacity of regular majoritarian politics to enforce that priority. Where Bickelian dualism differs from substantive approaches, however, is in its refusal to endorse any particular set of sanctified, prepolitical substantive values. The point of constitutional law on the Bickelian account is not to entrench any particular collection of values against democracy, but rather to identify, prioritize, and enforce whatever set of values a democratic community chooses to recognize. Constitutionalism and judicial review are, for Bickel and Eisgruber, simply means of holding the democratic "people" to its (democratic) commitment to values, even (indeed especially) where momentary exigencies make it difficult to fulfill that commitment. The democratic "people" are Ulysses; constitutional law is Ulysses tied to the mast.

(ii) Problems with Bickelian Dualism Like Footnote Four proceduralism, Bickelian dualism sees constitutional law as a response to certain shortcomings of ordinary democracy. In fact Bickel and Eisgruber improve upon proceduralism in one key respect: They offer a procedural account of constitutional law itself, one that attempts to explain how constitutional courts can decide some issues better than ordinary democracy can. The device Bickelian dualism employs to that end, however—the supposed distinction between matters of "value" or "principle" on the one hand and matters of "interest" or "expediency" on the other—turns out to be inadequate to the task.

The first difficulty with the distinction is that it seems likely to be substantively controversial. As Eisgruber acknowledges, a distinction in kind between "values" and "interests" does not exactly operate at the level of undeniable moral truism—a reasonable person might well reject its validity.[32] And someone who rejects the distinction will, by virtue of her skepticism, lack any good reason to accept the authority of constitutional law to resolve (what she believes to be) nonexistent issues of "principle." The Bickelian account fails to justify the exercise of constitutional authority over such a person, just as substantive accounts

31. See id. at 46–78 (chapter 2).
32. See id. at 55 ("Of course, people might believe none of this. They might believe that moral positions are nothing more than tastes which people happen to have. . . . But I think that most Americans do, in fact, believe that one should have moral reasons for taking moral positions, and that it is productive to discuss these reasons.").

fail to justify constitutional authority over someone who disagrees with the particular constitutional values being enforced. Bickelian dualism is an improvement over substantive strategies in that it abstracts away from disputes about particular results; but its "values/interests" dichotomy might not be abstract enough to avoid collapsing into content-dependence and thus failing as an account of constitutional authority.

A second, related problem is that the "values/interests" distinction, even if it is widely accepted in theory, is so vague as to invite frequent controversy in practice. Consider, for example, the problem of how to balance civil liberties with national security during a struggle against international terrorism. Which side of this balance represents "values" or "principle" and which side represents "interests" or "expediency"? The "expedient" imperative to keep people safe might also be understood as an enduring command of "principle"; the "value" of protecting civil liberties might be dismissed as simply a matter of convenience or of narrow "interests." One person's "principle" is another's "expediency," and there is no readily apparent algorithm for distinguishing the former from the latter. Of course, such boundary-line issues probably will haunt any strategy that attempts to demarcate different spheres of authority—the DR account will be no exception; but the "values/interests" or "principle/expediency" distinction seems indeterminate to a striking degree.

A third problem, one that flows to some extent from the first two, is the shallowness of the narrative of constitutional process offered by Bickelian dualism. True, that narrative is an improvement on Footnote Four proceduralism, which justifies constitutional judicial review principally on the ground that it is *not* ordinary democratic politics. Bickelian dualism at least describes certain features of constitutional courts—the relative political independence of judges, the professional norms associated with legal argument—that might generate more accuracy than politics can with respect to some issues. But the Bickel/Eisgruber model of constitutional procedure, like the values/interests distinction to which it responds, remains notably undertheorized. The question for constitutional procedure is not simply whether it performs better than ordinary politics according to certain metrics, but whether its existence improves overall accuracy as compared to a purely democratic system. And Bickelian dualism gives us precious little sense of what the answer to this query might be, or even of how to go about answering it. Are the gains in "principle" from constitutional judicial review likely to outweigh the costs in terms of "expediency"? Bickel and Eisgruber cannot say—in part because their treatment of constitutional procedure itself is relatively superficial, and in part because (again) the standards of "principle" and "expediency" are so vague as to defy measurement.

Finally, there is the difficulty that Bickelian dualism, like Footnote Four proceduralism, seems to give short shrift to the constitutional text and the process of its creation. Bickel and Eisgruber focus on the supposed procedural advantages of courts in identifying and enforcing values or principles, but they fail to explain why courts should feel themselves bound by the constitutional text in the process of doing so. Why should the centuries-old text be a better source of enduring values than the judges themselves, or for that matter the political process upon which the judges are intruding? As with Ely, the text for Bickel and Eisgruber seems little more than an annoyance.

The DR account I will offer here accepts the Bickelian notion that there is something procedurally special about constitutional judicial review that justifies its existence. It improves on the Bickelian strategy in two ways, however. First, it rejects the problematic "values/interests" or "principle/expediency" distinction as the basis for constitutional authority. Constitutional authority, I'll argue, is not issue-dependent in this sense; it does not depend on the normative status or weight of the matter being decided. It is, rather, *dispute*-dependent; it exists as a relatively impartial way to resolve disputes that otherwise would be tainted by democratic self-judging. Second, the DR account explains in sufficient detail what exactly is advantageous about constitutional process (including both judicial review and the enactment of an original text)—how it is that these procedures can avoid or remediate democracy's self-judging problems.

(iii) Ackerman's "Dualist Democracy" Bickelian dualism, however, is not the only type of dualist strategy. There is another brand of dualism that avoids some of the Bickelian shortcomings: the "dualist democracy" offered by Bruce Ackerman.[33] Like Bickel and Eisgruber, Ackerman distinguishes between different institutional expressions of democracy: an everyday "normal politics" and a separate track, which Ackerman calls "higher lawmaking." Higher lawmaking occurs during periodic "constitutional moments"—really constitutional phases— in which proponents "convince an extraordinary number of their fellow citizens" to support an initiative, opponents have "a fair opportunity to organize" against the initiative, and "a majority of. . . Americans [become convinced] to support [the] initiative as its merits are discussed, time and again, in. . . deliberative fora."[34] Often—but not always—these episodes of higher lawmaking result in one or more foundational constitutional amendments, as during the Framing itself and in the immediate aftermath of the Civil War; sometimes they amend the Constitution functionally (by means of "transformational judicial opinions") if not formally, as during the New Deal.

Ackerman asserts that the special characteristics of higher lawmaking give it priority over the results of "normal politics," which is simply the run-of-the-mill process of representative government in which elected officials make policy and

---

33. The canonical statement of Ackerman's theory appears in 1 BRUCE ACKERMAN, WE THE PEOPLE: FOUNDATIONS (1991) [hereinafter ACKERMAN, FOUNDATIONS]. *See also* 2 BRUCE ACKERMAN, WE THE PEOPLE: TRANSFORMATIONS (1998).

34. ACKERMAN, FOUNDATIONS, *supra* note 33, at 6.

periodically stand to account by means of regular elections. And Ackerman defends judicial review as necessary to preserve the superauthoritative results of higher lawmaking against backsliding during periods of normal politics. Ackerman's dualism differs from the Bickelian version, however, in that Ackerman's hierarchy of higher lawmaking over normal politics is not (at least not openly) driven by the premise that there are some issues (matters of "values" or "principle") that the former can decide better than the latter can. Ackerman prioritizes the "rare occasions" of higher lawmaking, not because they are likely to generate more-accurate resolutions of certain types of questions, but because they (and they alone) "earn[] the special recognition accorded the outcomes of mobilized deliberation made in the name of We the People."[35] It is the procedural pedigree of the results of higher lawmaking that confers its special status, not the subject matter to which it applies. If this understanding is right, then Ackerman's brand of dualism can avoid the difficulties of controversy and indeterminacy that plague the "values/interests" or "principle/expediency" distinction. It also, not incidentally, can explain the role of text in constitutional decisionmaking in a way that neither Bickelian dualism nor Footnote Four proceduralism can.

(iv) Problems with Ackerman's Dualism In fact, however, Ackerman's dualism is ambiguous in a number of respects that are crucial to its consistency with a DR account of legal authority. At the core of the difficulty is the question whether Ackerman's account is entirely process-based and noninstrumental or rather outcome-based and instrumental, at least in part.

Dualist democracy as an instrumental theory. We can get at this difficulty by probing more deeply into Ackerman's reasons for prioritizing higher lawmaking over normal politics. One plausible type of reason (the most plausible, in fact) is instrumental: Ackerman might believe that higher lawmaking produces (or tends to produce) better decisions than normal politics can. If this premise applies only to certain kinds of decisions—if, for example, Ackerman believes that higher lawmaking is better than normal politics at deciding issues of principle— then Ackerman's account is really a version of Bickelian dualism, and it is subject to most of the shortcomings of Bickel's approach canvassed above. But let us suppose that Ackerman's account, unlike Bickel's and Eisgruber's, does not in fact rely on a distinction between principle and expediency or some similar dichotomy between types of normative issues. (Nothing in Ackerman's articulation of his account suggests reliance on such a distinction.)

If Ackerman's dualism is not based on a dichotomy between different types of normative decisions, it might nonetheless be a more general kind of instrumental account: Ackerman might believe that higher lawmaking produces (or tends to produce) better decisions across the board, on most or all types of

---

35. *Id.* at 7.

questions, than normal politics does. We should recognize by now that a case-specific outcome-based account along these lines will run smack into the Encroachment Flaw: If Ackerman's assertion is that normal politics should defer to higher lawmaking in a given case because, in that case, higher lawmaking is more likely to have generated the correct result, it is a variety of Epistemic-Guidance (EG) account of authority and, as such, fails to provide a strong reason for normal politics to defer in cases of disagreement. But of course Ackerman's theory might instead be systemically instrumental in the same sense as the DR account of authority—it might assert, not that higher lawmaking is more likely to get it right in every case, but that it is entitled to deference on the ground that it is reasonably likely to get it right over the run of cases.

Understood this way, however—as a claim about the general systemic accuracy of higher lawmaking versus normal politics—Ackermanian dualism becomes deeply unpersuasive. It is true that one tempting reason to be skeptical of such a claim turns out to be unfounded. We might initially think that Ackerman's broad instrumental claim, if true, proves too much: If higher lawmaking (i.e., constitutional law) is a better way to make most or all decisions than ordinary democratic politics, why should we bother with ordinary politics at all? Why not simply subject every decision, or at least every reasonably important one, to the constitutional process?

There is a two-part response to this objection (although the first part suggests a more trenchant objection, which I explore below). First, deciding every important question by means of higher lawmaking—making every legislative moment a "constitutional moment"—would be prohibitively cumbersome and time-consuming. An Ackermanian "constitutional moment" features a complex series of proposals, mobilizations, deliberations, reactions, and (ultimately) canonical legal codifications, the whole of which takes considerable time, effort, and collective expense to complete.[36] Relying on that process for the bulk of a society's lawmaking would be impractical in the extreme; efficiency imperatives therefore impose natural limits on the scope of constitutional law.

As I discuss below, this efficiency rejoinder opens the door to another worry about Ackermanian dualism, namely that its potential instrumental advantages are confined to the work product of constitutional moments themselves—a potentially crippling limitation, given the inevitably substantial interpretive role of subsequent courts. But there is a related rejoinder as well: Higher lawmaking as Ackerman envisions it would, if used as the primary or only source of legislation within a system, give disproportionate power to political minorities. It is one thing to claim, as Ackerman might be understood as claiming, that the results of supermajoritarian consensus, where they exist, deserve priority over the results of simple majoritarian politics. It is something else entirely to claim

---

36. Ackerman describes the process in detail in chapter 10. *Id.* at 266–94 (chapter 10).

that every political decision, or at least every important one, should be subjected to the kind of supermajoritarian process Ackerman attributes to constitutional moments. A supermajority requirement gives a minority, perhaps a relatively small minority, the power to block legislation; the exercise of this power (or the threat of its exercise, for the purpose of bending the legislation in the minority's favor) operates not as democracy, but as a sort of oligarchy. Systematic supermajoritarianism thus undercuts the evenhanded participatoriness that gives democracy its claim to reasonable accuracy.

The Ackermanian response to the "baby with the bathwater" objection—that is, to the worry that the priority of higher lawmaking implies the worthlessness of ordinary democratic politics—therefore is, in essence, that the perfect is the enemy of the good. Where higher lawmaking actually succeeds—where its supermajority requirement and other hurdles are overcome—then its progeny has a strong claim to accuracy and thus to priority over the results of normal politics. But higher lawmaking is entitled to no such priority where it fails; its failure does not preclude ordinary politics from filling the gap, any more than the absence of ordinary legislation precludes unregulated private activity. To rely on higher lawmaking—that is, on constitutional law—for the bulk of a society's legislative output would be, in essence, to preclude legislation through ordinary politics in the absence of constitutional law on an issue, and that, in addition to being prohibitively inefficient, would give way too much power to political minorities.

If we understand Ackerman's dualism in broad instrumental terms, then, we cannot reject it on the ground that it proves too much. But we may be able to reject it on the ground that it proves too little. There are two closely related arguments here, the first of which hearkens back to the discussion of indeterminacy in Chapter 5.

Recall from that discussion that legal rules inevitably are indeterminate to some extent. The frequency and degree of indeterminacy in the case of constitutional rules are likely to be especially great; constitutions typically are intended to last for a long time, and so their Framers tend to draft their provisions in relatively broad, open-ended language that can be applied in a myriad of unforeseen circumstances. This certainly is true of many provisions in the U.S. Constitution; consider the vague guarantees of "freedom of speech" in the First Amendment, of "due process of law" in the Fifth and Fourteenth Amendments, and of "equal protection of the laws" in the Fourteenth Amendment. And the relative textual indeterminacy of constitutional provisions makes more work for courts and other *ex post* interpreters, who must specify a provision's meaning as applied to the facts of a great many cases unforeseen by the constitutional Framers.

If Ackerman's dualist theory is in fact an instrumental one, however, then his case for the greater accuracy of higher lawmaking rests on the character, not of the process of judicial interpretation of constitutional provisions, but of the framing of those provisions themselves—or, in cases where a "constitutional moment" generates *de facto* but not formal constitutional amendment (such as the New Deal), of the struggles leading to "transformative judicial opinions" that innovatively interpret existing provisions.[37] Ackerman's is a theory about the special authority of those "rare occasions" involving "mobilized deliberation made in the name of We the People,"[38] occasions (again, really phases or intervals) featuring a complex series of procedural steps. It is plausible to think that the extraordinarily deliberative, dynamic, supermajoritarian character of these "constitutional moments" gives them special accuracy in deciding important political questions. But it is much less plausible to imagine that garden-variety judicial review—decision by a small cadre of unelected judges (albeit following a process that is, as I'll explain in Chapter 8, meaningfully and broadly participatory in a number of respects)—possesses the same kind or degree of special accuracy.

And yet the endemic indeterminacy of written constitutional provisions means that a large percentage of actual on-the-ground constitutional decision-making—including virtually the entire business of judging the constitutional validity of actual statutes or other government actions—will be performed, not by the full-dress process of Ackerman's higher lawmaking, but by the considerably less-imposing means of everyday judicial review. The premise that normal politics should yield to higher lawmaking thus does not necessarily, or even very plausibly, lead to the conclusion that normal politics should give way to the specific, highly contingent interpretations of extremely indeterminate higher law that are rendered by unelected judges.

The first reason to be skeptical of Ackermanian dualism as a claim about relative systemic accuracy, then, is that the procedural conditions that would make such a claim persuasive will not actually exist, or will exist only in traces, in most instances of constitutional decisionmaking. The second reason is closely related to the first: It is simply that higher lawmaking's claim to special accuracy seems likely to fade with the passage of time.

Let us assume away the first reason as best we can by considering a relatively determinate constitutional provision—say, the requirement in Article II of the U.S. Constitution that a person "have attained to the Age of thirty five Years" in order to be eligible for the office of President. Suppose a majority of Americans, in the 2012 election cycle, favors electing a thirty-three-year-old as President. Does the relative accuracy of the process of framing and ratifying Article II in the late 1780s give the minimum-age requirement a plausible claim of authority over the popular majority in 2012?

The argument seems problematic at best. Even if we assume that the obvious defects in the 1780s ratification process—its total exclusion of women and

---

37. *Id.* at 107–08. Ackerman explains this process of higher lawmaking without formal constitutional amendment in chapters 5 and 6. *Id.* at 105–30 (chapter 5); 131–64 (chapter 6).

38. *Id.* at 7.

near-total exclusion of nonwhites and nonproperty owners—were not enough to overcome the benefits of the dynamic, deliberative, supermajoritarian character of that process, the fact remains that ratification occurred more than 220 years ago. Life expectancies are much longer now; the regular duties of the President have been refined to a much greater degree of detail; people's expectations of leadership may well have altered a good deal over the past two centuries. In short, a simple majority in 2012 might seem (to that majority) every bit as likely as, perhaps more likely than, a supermajority in 1789 to render a good decision regarding the minimum age for a President. The accuracy-generating advantages of the higher lawmaking process, plausible as they may be if we ignore the factor of time, become less and less plausible as time marches on.

So: If we give Ackermanian dualism its most plausible understanding—as an instrumental theory holding that constitutional law ("higher lawmaking") is generally more accurate than normal politics—it loses traction where the rubber of high theory meets the road of practical necessity. No society could (or would want to) rely on constitutional moments for most or all of its lawmaking; that would be impossibly cumbersome and would in any event give minorities too much power. But if constitutional moments are relatively rare, the legal rules they generate—in the form of constitutions, constitutional amendments, or "transformative" judicial decisions—will of necessity be quite indeterminate. High indeterminacy in constitutional rules will require that courts be given substantial authority to interpret and apply those rules in particular cases; and this will mean that the bulk of constitutional law will in fact be attributable to the everyday work of elite, relatively unaccountable judges rather than to supermajoritarian constitutional moments. As a constitutional moment fades more distantly into the past, moreover, its own authority as a specially accurate procedure is likely to fade along with it. The upshot is that the instrumental reading of dualist democracy becomes, in any real democratic system, considerably less than compelling.

Dualist democracy as a noninstrumental theory. But what if we conceive of Ackerman's brand of dualism in noninstrumental rather than instrumental terms? What if we understand Ackerman as claiming, not that higher lawmaking is a better (more accurate) way to generate important political decisions, but simply that it is more legitimate than normal politics without regard to the quality of the decisions it generates? This would be a purely process-based theory of constitutional authority.

We got a sense in Chapters 2 and 3 of the nature of the core challenge facing any purely process-based account of legal authority. Such an account must plausibly explain what it is, aside from the quality of the results a process produces or tends to produce, that creates a strong moral reason to defer to that process. As we saw in those chapters, the most plausible basis of such an account appears to be consent; but Ackerman's dualist theory of constitutional democracy cannot reasonably be interpreted as turning on consent in any of its forms.

A noninstrumental reading of Ackerman thus faces a substantial handicap from the very beginning.

One implication of that handicap is the difficulty in imagining what in particular it might be about the processes of higher lawmaking (aside from their results) that would confer authority upon them. But we need not resolve this puzzle in order to expose the shortcomings of dualist democracy as a noninstrumental theory. Those shortcomings mirror the weaknesses of the instrumental version of the theory. First, whatever are those features of higher lawmaking that give it a special claim to procedural legitimacy, surely they are diluted when higher law is strained through the medium of judicial review. Ackerman describes higher lawmaking as lawmaking "by the American people," in contrast to normal politics, which is lawmaking "by their government."[39] While the processes of a constitutional moment might plausibly be understood as an action of "the People" themselves, the same can hardly be said for subsequent judicial interpretations of the products of such a moment. And as we have seen, there is no way around giving substantial authority to courts or some other institution to interpret inevitably vague constitutional provisions.

Second, the legitimating features of the higher lawmaking process (whatever they are) are themselves likely to lose their potency—relative to the features of normal politics—over time. The People who act more-or-less directly through higher lawmaking (however they may do that) are the People of a particular time and place; as that time fades further into the past, those People are likely to have less and less in common with Bickel's "people of the here and now." There are theories by which we might envision the corporate People of the framing and the corporate People of the here and now as the same People,[40] but it is difficult to articulate a convincing process-based account of why a supermajoritarian consensus that occurred 150 or 200 years ago is more legitimately binding than a majoritarian consensus that exists today. None of today's People participated in the framing or ratification of centuries-old constitutional provisions; and as the cultural gap between today's People and those who did participate grows wider with time, it becomes more and more difficult to imagine that the interests of many of today's People were well represented in the framing and ratification process.

It is possible, though it seems unlikely, that there is a persuasive process-based explanation of why a current democratic majority should consider itself bound by unelected judges' interpretations of constitutional provisions laid

---

39. *Id.* at 6.

40. See, for example, the creative theory offered in JED RUBENFELD, FREEDOM AND TIME: A THEORY OF CONSTITUTIONAL SELF-GOVERNMENT (2001). For a powerful argument against such an approach (which does not, however, mention Rubenfeld's theory in particular), see JEREMY WALDRON, LAW AND DISAGREEMENT 255–81 (1999) [hereinafter WALDRON, LAW AND DISAGREEMENT].

down by long-ago supermajorities. But such an explanation, if it exists, is far from obvious. As things stand, a noninstrumental understanding of Ackerman's dualist democracy appears subject to essentially the same shortcomings as an instrumental understanding.

Rescuing Ackerman's dualism. The difficulties with Ackerman's version of dualism flow from his premise, largely implicit, that higher lawmaking is procedurally superior to ordinary democracy (albeit practicable only at infrequent "constitutional moments"). Even if that is so, it fails to explain why the authority of constitutional law does not diminish with time, or why the decisions of constitutional courts should carry the same weight as the efforts of constitutional Framers.

The DR account of constitutional law will not share that premise. The DR account begins with the assumption that ordinary democracy is, generally speaking, the most accurate (and thus the most authoritative) way to resolve disputes about the prospective content of the law. The role played by constitutional law on the DR account is not that of an extraordinary, idealized version of democracy that occasionally appears to set regular democracy straight, like an Olympian god descending to walk for a while among mortals. Its role, rather, is simply that of a backstop: Constitutional law steps in to resolve disputes where some salient flaw renders ordinary democracy incapable of doing so. On the DR account, therefore, what matters is not whether constitutional procedures can always live up to a "higher lawmaking" ideal, but whether constitutional procedures typically can resolve those disputes more accurately than ordinary democracy can. I will suggest in this chapter and the next that constitutional process, considered as a whole, generally is capable of meeting that challenge.

D. The Reductionist Strategy

A fourth prominent response to the countermajoritarian difficulty attempts to deny or downplay the existence of a meaningful difference between constitutional law and ordinary democratic politics. There is a critical version of this strategy, which holds in essence that constitutional adjudication is simply politics in disguise and thus lacks the legitimacy of democratic politics in its more overt forms (which legitimacy some of these same critics, incidentally, also question).[41] My interest here is in the use of this approach, which we might label *reductionism*, to defend constitutional law and judicial review. Reductionists argue that the procedures of constitutional law are infused with political elements, and subject to political constraints, to such an extent that they are in effect part of the system of ordinary democratic politics and thus are not substantially countermajoritarian at all. Reductionists emphasize such factors as the

---

41. *See, e.g.,* DUNCAN KENNEDY, A CRITIQUE OF ADJUDICATION (Fin de siècle) (1997); Girardeau A. Spann, *Pure Politics,* 88 MICH. L. REV. 1971 (1990).

political appointments process for federal judges; Congress's power to control the budget, size, jurisdiction, and procedure of the federal courts; and the need for political officials and lower-court or state-court judges to implement judicial decisions. These features of constitutional decisionmaking, they contend, strongly limit judges' typical willingness or ability to reach constitutional results that stray far from the American political mainstream. Reductionists back up this claim by pointing to the historical record, which suggests that constitutional doctrine eventually, if not immediately, tends to "follow the election returns," to paraphrase Mr. Dooley.[42]

The purest examples of reductionist theory come from positive political science, many practitioners of which tend to view the Supreme Court as just another political institution, albeit an idiosyncratic one.[43] In the legal academy, semireductionist theorists like Neal Devins, Louis Fisher, and Barry Friedman take a more nuanced view, emphasizing the presence of "dialogue" between the judiciary and the political branches and asserting that constitutional doctrine tends, in the long run, to reflect input from both directions.[44] These semireductionists agree with the political scientists, however, that the Supreme Court's constitutional decisionmaking ultimately is constrained by popular and political forces, not the other way around.

There is, as I'll argue in the next chapter, considerable and important truth in the reductionist insight. As a defense of constitutional law and judicial review, however, it suffers from two complementary shortcomings. First, as a normative matter it treads perilously close to critique; for it fails to stake out a strong distinctive role for constitutional law and thus a persuasive justification for it. However closely the Court follows the election returns, surely it almost always lags behind the elected branches themselves in this regard—begging the question why we need the Court or the Constitution at all, if what they provide is just a less-efficient form of ordinary majoritarian democracy. One might venture an explanation that turns on the advantages of divided power or of a relatively nonpopulist brake to promote deliberation and prevent sudden fluctuations in

---

42. *See* PETER FINLEY DUNNE, MR. DOOLEY'S OPINIONS 26 (1901) ("[N]o matter whether th' constitution follows th' flag or not, th' supreme coort follows th' iliction returns.").

43. The patron saint of reductionism is the political scientist Robert Dahl. *See* Robert A. Dahl, *Decisionmaking in a Democracy: The Supreme Court as a National Policy Maker*, 6 J. PUB. L. 279 (1957). Other key works in this vein are David Adamany, *Legitimacy, Realigning Elections, and the Supreme Court*, 1973 WISC. L. REV. 790 (1973), and Richard Funston, *The Supreme Court and Critical Elections*, 69 AM. POL. SCI. REV. 795 (1975).

44. *See, e.g.*, NEAL DEVINS & LOUIS FISHER, THE DEMOCRATIC CONSTITUTION (2004); NEAL DEVINS, SHAPING CONSTITUTIONAL VALUES: ELECTED GOVERNMENT, THE SUPREME COURT, AND THE ABORTION DEBATE (1996); LOUIS FISHER, CONSTITUTIONAL DIALOGUES: INTERPRETATION AS A POLITICAL PROCESS (1988); BARRY FRIEDMAN, THE WILL OF THE PEOPLE: HOW PUBLIC OPINION HAS INFLUENCED THE SUPREME COURT AND SHAPED THE MEANING OF THE CONSTITUTION (2009).

the system, but the idea of the Court as a sort of backup Senate hardly seems sufficient to justify the enterprise. In any event, it utterly fails to make sense of the Constitution itself, which can only be interpreted as an attempt, not simply to slow the pace with which the election returns are implemented, but to impose real limits on what the election returns can accomplish.

This last point suggests the second major shortcoming of the reductionist defense, namely that as an interpretation of American constitutional practice it is noticeably thin. As I'll suggest in the next chapter, the relationship between the election returns and the constitutional doctrine generated by the Court is considerably more complicated than one of cause and effect. To be fair, theorists I've labeled as "reductionists" almost never claim a simple cause-and-effect connection. But for reductionism to work as a normative defense of constitutional law, it must give short shrift to two central features of American constitutionalism. The first, just mentioned, is the existence of the Constitution itself, which—regardless of how it is implemented—clearly represents an effort to constrain ordinary democracy. To envision constitutional law as simply a subset of democratic politics thus is to deny any significance to the fact that the Constitution exists.

The second feature, following closely on the first, is the fact that the Court frequently interprets the Constitution in ways that are widely unpopular, obstructive of the immediate goals of the political branches, or both. There are many well-known examples here, from the Court's holding in 1793 that the states are not immune from damages suits in federal court,[45] to its *Dred Scott* decision essentially forbidding Congress to compromise on the issue of slavery in the territories,[46] to its long string of decisions invalidating popular Progressive-era and New Deal economic regulations,[47] to its 1967 ruling striking down

---

45. *See* Chisholm v. Georgia, 2 U.S. (2 Dall.) 419 (1793). The decision in *Chisholm* was overturned by the ratification of the Eleventh Amendment in 1795.

46. *See* Scott v. Sandford, 60 U.S. (19 How.) 393 (1857).

47. *See, e.g.*, United States v. E.C. Knight Co., 156 U.S. 1 (1895) (applying the Commerce Clause to prevent the application of the Sherman Antitrust Act to a combination of sugar refineries); Lochner v. New York, 198 U.S. 45 (1905) (applying the Due Process Clause to invalidate a state regulation of the working hours of bakery employees); Hammer v. Dagenhart, 247 U.S. 251 (1918) (applying the Commerce Clause to invalidate a federal prohibition on the interstate sale of goods produced by child labor); Adkins v. Children's Hosp., 261 U.S. 525 (1923) (applying the Due Process Clause to invalidate minimum-wage regulations in the District of Columbia); A.L.A. Schechter Poultry Corp. v. United States, 295 U.S. 495 (1935) (applying the Commerce Clause and general separation of powers principles to prevent the president from issuing "codes of fair competition" to regulate prices and trade practices in the poultry industry); Carter v. Carter Coal Co., 298 U.S. 238 (1936) (applying the Commerce Clause to prevent Congress from regulating labor standards and wages in the coal industry).

antimiscegenation laws,[48] to its 2010 holding that corporations can spend freely in election campaigns.[49] In each of these areas (with the exception of campaign finance, which is still very much in flux), the Court's current doctrine coincides with broad popular opinion. On some issues, however (e.g., state sovereign immunity, slavery), it took one or more constitutional amendments to accomplish this;[50] in other cases (e.g., economic regulation) the Court came around only after a long period of sustained political movement in a particular direction.[51] And in some instances (e.g., antimiscegenation laws) it appears to be the public's opinion that has evolved to match the Court's, not the other way around.

As these examples show, there is some significant functional substance to American constitutional law that transcends, and sometimes confounds, the workings of normal democratic politics. At the very least, constitutional law and judicial review "may clog the administration" and "convulse the society," as Madison said of minority factions.[52] And sometimes they might affirmatively change the course of societal values. These effects cannot be explained away by classifying constitutional law as simply a subset of politics; if they are to be justified, they will require something substantially more robust.

3. WALDRON'S CHALLENGE

The DR account rejects outright the substantive response to the countermajoritarian difficulty, and it can patch the significant holes in the proceduralist,

---

48. *See* Loving v. Virginia, 388 U.S. 1 (1967). Some commentators have noted the unpopularity of the Court's decision in *Loving. See* David R. Stras & Ryan W. Scott, *Retaining Life Tenure: The Case for a "Golden Parachute,"* 83 WASH. U. L.Q. 1397, 1430–31 (2005) (noting that *Loving v. Virginia* "encountered fierce resistance when decided"); Kevin Noble Maillard, *The Color of Testamentary Freedom,* 62 SMU L. REV. 1783, 1793–94 (2009) (pointing out that even though *Loving v. Virginia* declared antimiscegenation laws unconstitutional in 1967, South Carolina's prohibition on interracial marriage was "in its books until 1999").

49. *See* Citizens United v. Fed. Election Comm'n, 130 S. Ct. 876 (2010). An ABC News/*Washington Post* poll conducted shortly after the decision suggested that roughly 80 percent of Americans opposed it, with broad agreement across the political spectrum. *See* Dan Eggen, *Poll: Large Majority Opposes Supreme Court's Decision on Campaign Financing,* WASHINGTON POST, Feb. 17, 2010, http://www.washingtonpost.com/wp-dyn/content/article/2010/02/17/AR2010021701151.html?sid=ST2010021702073.

50. *See* U.S. CONST. amend. XI (denying federal jurisdiction over suits against states by citizens of other states or foreign nations); amend. XIII (outlawing slavery); amend. XIV, §1 (giving citizenship to former slaves and guaranteeing them due process, equal protection, and the "privileges" and "immunities" of citizenship).

51. For an excellent narrative of the Court's longstanding resistance, and ultimate capitulation, to the Progressive Era and New Deal tide of economic regulation, see FRIEDMAN, *supra* note 44, at 167–236 (chapters 6–7).

52. Madison, FEDERALIST NO. 10, *supra* note 4, at 125.

dualist, and reductionist responses. I want to set up the DR approach to constitutional law by first describing the most articulate contemporary statement of
the countermajoritarian difficulty, which belongs to Jeremy Waldron.

Waldron's critique of constitutional law follows two tracks, only one of which
will be my central focus here. Waldron's first line of attack (and, one senses,
the approach he thinks most important) is, in his phrase, "process-based":
Waldron argues that noninstrumental considerations—reasons of what John
Rawls called "pure procedural justice"[53]—favor decisionmaking by majoritarian
democracy over decisionmaking by supermajoritarian constitutional procedures
supplemented by elitist judicial review. Waldron's theory of legal authority
(including constitutional authority) is a type of DR account: He believes law
must be justified, if at all, as a response to the problem of disagreement.[54]
Waldron's account, however, turns primarily on what he believes to be the inherent value of procedure—on the supposed capacity of a decision-procedure to
generate strong reasons for obedience to its results, quite apart from the quality
or nature of those results themselves. Such "process-based" reasons, Waldron
notes, would (assuming they exist) fulfill the requirement that legal authority be
justified only by reference to content-independent considerations; process-based
reasons are types of content-independent reasons.[55] And Waldron asserts that
fair participation among equals is a procedural feature capable of generating
process-based reasons to obey the procedure's results—that is, of clothing those
results with legal authority.[56] But, Waldron argues, majoritarian democracy is
far more fairly and equally participatory than countermajoritarian constitutional
law and judicial review. Process-based considerations therefore favor ordinary
democracy over constitutional law.[57]

There is cause to be skeptical of this process-based attack. As I suggested in
Chapter 3, it is difficult to discern just what inherent value—value without any
regard to outcomes—that is capable of supporting legal authority might lurk
within features of a procedure. The most plausible candidate as a procedural
feature that can generate process-based reasons for obedience appears to be the

---

53. JOHN RAWLS, A THEORY OF JUSTICE 86 (1971) ("By contrast, pure procedural justice
obtains when there is no independent criterion for the right result: instead there is a
correct or fair procedure such that the outcome is likewise correct or fair, whatever it is,
provided that the procedure has been properly followed.").

54. This is the central theme of Waldron's book *Law and Disagreement. See generally*
WALDRON, LAW AND DISAGREEMENT, *supra* note 40; *see also* Waldron, *Core Case, supra* note
10, at 1371–76.

55. *See* WALDRON, LAW AND DISAGREEMENT, *supra* note 40, at 232–54 (chapter 11);
Waldron, *Core Case, supra* note 10, at 1371–73, 1375.

56. *See* WALDRON, LAW AND DISAGREEMENT, *supra* note 40, at 232–54 (chapter 11);
Waldron, *Core Case, supra* note 10, at 1386–89.

57. *See* WALDRON, LAW AND DISAGREEMENT, *supra* note 40, at 232–54 (chapter 11);
Waldron, *Core Case, supra* note 10, at 1386–95.

kind of fair and equal participation that Waldron cites, but it is much easier to understand the value of participation in the instrumental, outcome-based terms I outlined in Chapter 3. Without some reference to outcomes, it's hard to see why people ought to care about procedure at all, at least in the ways necessary to generate legal authority. And even if we take participation to be a purely process-based value, majoritarian democracy does not have a monopoly on fair participation, as the discussion of adjudication in Chapter 5 suggests.

I will focus here, however, on Waldron's second line of attack, which seeks to undermine the "outcome-based" or instrumental defense of constitutional law and judicial review. As I noted in Chapter 3, Waldron accepts the possibility that legal authority, on a DR account, might derive from a certain kind of "outcome-based" reason, one that turns not on the substance of any particular result generated by a procedure, but rather on the procedure's tendency, over the run of cases, to generate good results.[58] This is the type of reason to which I've been referring as one of procedural *accuracy* (what Rawls calls a matter of "imperfect procedural justice"[59]). Waldron considers some prominent arguments that constitutional judicial review is more accurate, on questions of individual rights, than ordinary democracy and finds them all wanting. In response to points offered by Bickel and others, he asserts that by the time constitutional cases reach the Supreme Court or other high-level constitutional tribunals, their original basis in concrete facts has become obscure and their issues tend to be presented in a form that is at least as abstract as those the legislature decides.[60] Waldron also contends that the presence of a canonical constitutional text tends to "distract" courts, and others, from substantive arguments about rights, and that judicial attentiveness to matters of constitutional "principle" thus often misses the point, focusing on interpreting archaic language or divining the "original intent" of its authors rather than the underlying normative issues themselves.[61] His conclusion is that there is little or no reason to believe that

---

58. *See* Waldron, *Core Case, supra* note 10, at 1373–74.

59. RAWLS, *supra* note 53, at 85–86.

60. *See* Waldron, *Core Case, supra* note 10, at 1379–80. Although Waldron does not expressly cite Bickel, he can be understood as responding to an argument in favor of judicial review presented in BICKEL, *supra* note 1, at 26:

> Another advantage that courts have is that questions of principle never carry the same aspect for them as they did for the legislature or the executive. Statutes, after all, deal typically with abstract or dimly foreseen problems. The courts are concerned with the flesh and blood of an actual case. This tends to modify, perhaps to lengthen, everyone's view. It also provides an extremely salutary proving ground for abstractions; it is conducive, in a phrase of Holmes, to thinking things, not words, and thus to the evolution of principle by a process that tests as it creates.

61. *See* Waldron, *Core Case, supra* note 10, at 1380–86. These points too can be understood as responses to the defenses of constitutional law and judicial review offered by the likes of Bickel and Eisgruber.

constitutional law and judicial review are more-accurate ways to identify and enforce rights than the procedures of ordinary democracy.

In what follows, I will have relatively little to say about Waldron's specific points of comparison between judicial review and democratic legislation.[62] Waldron's outcome-based arguments turn on considerations of what I've called *competence*: Waldron offers reasons to think judicial review is no more competent (and perhaps less so) than democratic legislation in resolving disputes about rights. My own outcome-based case for constitutional law and judicial review, by contrast, will be based mostly on considerations of *impartiality*, an ingredient of procedural accuracy that Waldron largely ignores.[63] I will argue that constitutional law and judicial review, despite their flaws, are necessary responses to the problem of partiality that inevitably crops up when democracy is asked to resolve fundamental disagreements about itself. Some of the features of which Waldron complains—particularly the focus on divining principles from archaic texts—turn out, I'll contend, to play a central role in the relative impartiality of constitutional law. And I will suggest that American-style constitutional adjudication can be acceptably competent, too—in ways that, not incidentally, bring it into closer contact than Waldron acknowledges with the workings of ordinary democracy that he rightly admires.

4. CONSTITUTING DEMOCRACY

To begin a response to Waldron's statement of the countermajoritarian difficulty, let us assume that the alternative to constitutional law and judicial review is to rely solely or primarily on democracy in the general form outlined in Chapter 4. As I argued in that chapter, democratic government derives its authority from the three central features of broad participation, majority rule, and regular elections; so let's assume that the alternative to submitting some issues for constitutional resolution—the "majoritarian" end of the countermajoritarian difficulty—is to resolve them by a democratic process that includes these features.

Note, however, that rather open-ended, even aspirational concepts like "broad participation," "majority rule," and "regular elections" are not by themselves sufficient actually to operationalize democratic government. Before we can have

---

62. Some arguments I made in Christopher J. Peters, *Assessing the New Judicial Minimalism*, 100 COLUM. L. REV. 1454, 1492–1513 (2000), suggest there is more to be said for judicial review in these respects than Waldron allows.

63. I suspect Waldron largely ignores the question of impartiality because his own allegiance is to a purely process-based or noninstrumental account of legal authority. *See* WALDRON, LAW AND DISAGREEMENT, *supra* note 40, at 249–54 (arguing against an instrumental account of the right of participation).

a working democracy, we will need to mold these general ideas into concrete forms—legislatures, electoral systems, methods of enacting, enforcing, and interpreting laws, and so on. Democracy (however defined) presupposes certain procedures and institutions—"the people [cannot] magically speak for themselves unfettered by institutions or procedures," as Christopher Eisgruber (citing Stephen Holmes) puts it[64]—and those procedures and institutions cannot operate or even exist, at least not for long, without relatively stable rules to govern them. Constitutional law in some form thus seems necessary to democracy in the same way that rules of grammar are necessary for speech (or, to revisit an example from Chapter 2, that rules of the road are necessary for driving): It "set[s] out the rules by which political discussion will occur," as Cass Sunstein notes.[65]

At a basic, literally *constitutive* level, then, constitutional law is not only consistent with democracy but essential to it. The existence and functioning of anything we can call "democracy" depend on the existence of constitutive rules. They also depend on a certain degree of obduracy in those rules. Like the rules of driving or of grammar, constitutive rules would fail to perform their function—namely to establish and facilitate some activity, such as democracy—if participants in that activity spent most of their time debating the rules themselves. If the activity is to succeed, the understanding among most of the participants must be that its constitutive rules should be presumptively resistant to sudden change. Waldron's democratic premises thus depend to some extent on the presence of what can fairly be called constitutional law—a set of rules, or norms, that establish the democratic process, are relatively fixed and stable, and thus constrain the process they have established.

Waldron, for one, appears to accept roughly this degree of constitutional law. His critique assumes "a broadly democratic political system with universal adult suffrage" that includes "a representative legislature, to which elections are held on a fair and regular basis."[66] (In fact Waldron makes a few more-robust assumptions as well, including bicameralism and a committee structure in the legislature and the existence of political parties.[67]) "None of this is meant to be

---

64. EISGRUBER, *supra* note 26, at 12 (citing STEPHEN HOLMES, PASSIONS AND CONSTRAINTS 167–69 (1995)).

65. CASS R. SUNSTEIN, DESIGNING DEMOCRACY: WHAT CONSTITUTIONS DO 98 (2001).

66. Waldron, *Core Case*, *supra* note 10, at 1361.

67. Here is Waldron's full statement of his assumptions about the democratic process in question:

I assume that the society we are considering is a democratic society and that, like most in the modern Western world, it has struggled through various forms of monarchy, tyranny, dictatorship, or colonial domination to a situation in which its laws are made and its public policies are set by the people and their representatives working through elective institutions. This society has a broadly democratic political system

controversial," Waldron asserts; these assumptions merely "pick[] out the way in which democratic legislatures usually operate."[68]

Note, too, that the need for constitutive democratic rules presupposes the need for some extrademocratic institutions and procedures that will create those rules. Constitutive rules bring democracy into existence; those rules cannot themselves be fashioned using (as yet nonexistent) democratic procedures. This is not to say that the mechanisms for generating constitutive rules cannot *be* democratic, in the sense of being broadly participatory, utilizing majority rule, and so on; the point is simply that the democratic system that will be constituted by the rules cannot, by definition, be the system that creates the rules constituting it. Constitutive rules must be generated by some mechanism that preexists, and thus is external to, the institutions and procedures of democratic government they make possible.

And note, finally, that the function of rules, including constitutive rules, requires mechanisms to interpret and apply those rules to particular cases. (This was of course a central theme of Chapter 5.) I will argue below that those mechanisms too must be in some meaningful way external to the democratic system whose constitution they are interpreting. For now the point is only that some standing apparatus for interpreting and applying constitutive rules must exist in a functioning democracy.

We have, then, a sort of bare-bones case for constitutional law, one that is implicit in the very idea of democratic government. Constitutional law at some level is necessary simply to constitute democracy, to bring it into existence and give it form. Constitutional lawmaking procedures—procedures separate from the democracy being constituted—are required to carry out this genesis, and standing procedures are required to interpret and apply the constitutive rules of democracy going forward.

---

with universal adult suffrage, and it has a representative legislature, to which elections are held on a fair and regular basis. I assume that this legislature is a large deliberative body, accustomed to dealing with difficult issues, including important issues of justice and social policy. The legislators deliberate and vote on public issues, and the procedures for lawmaking are elaborate and responsible, and incorporate various safeguards, such as bicameralism, robust committee scrutiny, and multiple levels of consideration, debate, and voting. I assume that these processes connect both formally (through public hearings and consultation procedures) and informally with wider debates in the society. Members of the legislature think of themselves as representatives, in a variety of ways, sometimes making the interests and opinions of their constituents key to their participation, sometimes thinking more in terms of virtual representation of interests and opinions throughout the society as a whole. I assume too that there are political parties, and that legislators' party affiliations are key to their taking a view that ranges more broadly than the interests and opinions of their immediate constituents.

Id. (citations omitted).

68. *Id.*

All of this, I take it, is unobjectionable to Waldron and most other critics of constitutional law. The problem for Waldron and others arises once we move beyond basic constitutive rules and begin using constitutional law as a way to *constrain* rather than simply constitute democracy. Of course democratic institutions and procedures require rules to bring them into existence, and of course those rules will constrain in the sense of defining those institutions and procedures—in the same way the rules of grammar constrain the activity of speech. The crisis, for Waldron and other critics, appears when constitutional law is used not to constrain how democracy works, but rather to constrain *what democracy does*. The fact that rules of grammar necessarily constrain the process of speech does not justify separate rules that constrain what can be said—what topics are off limits, what topics must be discussed, and so on. It is these sub-stance-constraining rules—which Waldron describes, in shorthand, as constitu-tional *rights*[69]—that create the countermajoritarian difficulty.

It turns out, however, that the need to define (and thus to constrain) how democracy works is a rather broad imperative indeed—so broad, in fact, that often the line between how democracy works and what democracy does becomes blurred beyond recognition.

5. RESOLVING DISPUTES ABOUT DEMOCRACY

The problem, in a nutshell, is that there is plenty of room for disagreement about what exactly the institutions and procedures of democracy should look like and whether, in any given instance, they are functioning correctly. Those disagreements will have to be avoided, mitigated, or resolved in most cases in order for democracy to function, that is, to generate laws and other decisions that are generally recognized as authoritative. But the institutions and procedures of democracy themselves—the things people may disagree about—are unlikely to be capable of resolving those disagreements authoritatively. A more expansive role thus begins to emerge for constitutional law—a role including not just the establishment of basic constitutive rules, but also the expansion of those rules to avoid disagreements about democratic authority, the interpretation and enforce-ment of those rules in a way that constrains the institutions they define, and the resolution of disputes about whether the rules are being followed in any given instance.

---

69. *See generally id.*; WALDRON, LAW AND DISAGREEMENT, *supra* note 40, at 209–312 *seriatim.*

A. The Possibility of Democratic Dysfunction

We can begin to grasp this broader dispute-resolving function of constitutional law by recognizing the possibility that one or more of the features that makes democracy relatively accurate will be missing, or malfunctioning, in a particular instance.

Consider the two basic types of democratic dysfunction identified in Footnote Four of the *Carolene Products* decision and elucidated by John Hart Ely. The first is legislation that "restricts. . . political processes," thus artificially entrenching those currently holding power (the "ins," as Ely calls them).[70] A paradigmatic example is the Sedition Act of 1798, which outlawed, among other things, conspiracies "to oppose any measure or measures of the government of the United States" and the knowing publication of "any false, scandalous and malicious writing. . . against the government of the United States. . . with intent to defame the said government."[71] The Sedition Act made much antigovernment speech and opposition political activity punishable as a crime, thus protecting incumbent government officials from criticism and insulating them artificially against the possibility of removal at the next election. Had the Act remained in force—thankfully it was allowed by the incoming Republican Congress to expire in 1801—it might well have disrupted the normal cycling function of democracy, the process (discussed in Chapter 4) by which regular elections can launder the effects of occasional partiality. It also, and as a result, might have concentrated political power in a group of like-minded officials, frustrating the partiality-atomizing function of broad participation and majority rule and compromising the competence that normally flows from diversity. The Act, in short, threatened to undermine many of the qualities that give democracy its authority.

The other type of dysfunction identified by Footnote Four and Ely is legislation that reflects, or perpetrates, "prejudice against discrete and insular minorities" who can't get a fair shake in the democratic process.[72] Here the classic (tragic) examples are the mandatory school segregation and other Jim Crow laws common in the American South during the first half of the twentieth century. Those laws, born of a shared conviction on the part of most southern whites that blacks were inferior, had the effect of isolating blacks, ensuring that their inability to participate fully in democratic politics would continue indefinitely. Again both the impartiality and the competence of democracy were compromised: impartiality, because the white majority acted (and entrenched its power to act) as a self-interested faction on issues relating to race; and competence, because the benefits of broad-based and diverse decisionmaking were lost as a result. For all intents and purposes, southern blacks during Jim Crow

---

70. *See Carolene Products,* 304 U.S. at 152 n.4; ELY, *supra* note 16, at 103, 105–34.
71. Sedition Act of 1787, ch. 74, 1 Stat. 596 (1798) (expired 1801).
72. *See Carolene Products,* 304 U.S. at 152 n.4; ELY, *supra* note 16, at 135–79.

(like South African blacks during apartheid) were not citizens of a democracy; they were subjects of a white oligarchy.

These examples are relatively extreme and, in a reasonably well-functioning modern democracy, relatively uncommon. But they demonstrate that dysfunction *can* occur even in democratic systems. As Waldron notes, "[n]o decision-procedure"—democracy included—"will be perfect."[73] And the mere *possibility* of democratic dysfunction also raises the possibility—indeed the inevitability—of reasonable disputes about whether, in any given case, such a breakdown has occurred.

B. The Inevitability of Democratic Disputes

Imagine that a small postcolonial country—Carolenia—establishes basic democratic procedures and institutions along the lines sketched in Chapter 4, featuring regular elections, broad participation, and majority rule. And suppose the newly formed legislature of Carolenia enacts a statute substantially similar to the Sedition Act. A citizen of Carolenia (we can call him Quentin) believes the legislation represents a democratic dysfunction, a failure of the reasonable competence and impartiality that give democracy its authority. But suppose there are reasonable arguments on the other side of the question: At the time the Carolenian Sedition Act is adopted, Carolenia is under threat of invasion by a hostile foreign power with many agents and sympathizers within Carolenia itself, and many Carolenian citizens believe the law is justifiable as a temporary response to this serious danger.

Notice that what we now have is a *dispute* among the citizens of Carolenia about the existence of democratic authority. Quentin (and others of like mind) believe the Carolenian version of the Sedition Act is an abomination, an utter failure of democratic process that, as a result, lacks democratic authority; they believe, moreover, that the democratic authority of the Carolenian government as a whole is put at risk by the artificial entrenchment the statute threatens to create. But other Carolenians disagree; some think Quentin's complaints about the statute's supposed threat to democratic authority are overblown, while others recognize the threat but think it is outweighed by pressing requirements of national security. There is, then, a reasonable, good-faith dispute over whether the sedition statute in fact embodies a form of democratic dysfunction.

So long as democratic dysfunction is possible, disagreements like this one inevitably will arise in a democratic society. People will disagree, reasonably and in good faith, about what constitutes a malfunction or breakdown in democratic authority; and they will disagree about whether, and when, malfunctions can be tolerated in the name of other important goals. Indeed—and this is an important point—this phenomenon of prevalent disagreement inevitably will extend

---

73. Waldron, *Core Case, supra* note 10, at 1372.

beyond the question of democratic breakdowns to the constitutive features of democracy itself. People will disagree not just about whether democracy has failed in some particular instance, but more generally, about what democracy even is and what it entails. They will disagree about what constitutes reasonable democratic impartiality and competence, and thus reasonable democratic accuracy. They will disagree about how "broad" democratic participation must be, about the applications of and exceptions to majority rule, and about whether elections are sufficiently "regular." And they will disagree about the likely factual consequences of particular legislation or other government actions for democratic authority. These many manifestations of democratic disagreement will be unavoidable products of the Rawlsian "burdens of judgment," discussed in Chapter 2, that the members of any liberal society will face.[74]

As Waldron notes with respect to disputes about rights,[75] the lion's share of these disagreements must be resolved peacefully if a democratic society is to function. Legislatures and other institutions of democracy cannot operate for long without knowing *how* they are to operate and what kinds of laws they may enact. A society cannot remain a society amidst pervasive uncertainty about the legitimacy of its laws and the duty of its members to obey them.

The question then becomes what sort of institutions and procedures are best able to resolve these (inevitable) democratic disagreements in a way that is acceptable to the disputants. And there is good reason to think the answer is *not* the very institutions and procedures that are themselves the subjects of dispute.

C. The Partiality of Democratic Self-Judging

To see why, suppose someone suggests to Quentin, our dissenting Carolenian citizen, that he take his concerns about the sedition legislation to the Carolenian legislature itself, petitioning the body to repeal the statute on the ground that it entrenches incumbents and thus undermines democratic authority. Quentin might quite reasonably object that the very institution that enacted the questionable statute is unlikely to be an impartial arbiter of its democratic propriety. He might worry that the members of the legislature—who, after all, stand to benefit personally from continued enforcement of the statute—would not provide a truly impartial hearing for his complaint.

The problem Quentin faces is akin to one of the chief reasons a community like Carolenia might choose democracy over autocracy or oligarchy in the first place. People with their own strong interests in an issue are unsuitable to impartially resolve disputes about that issue; judges should not decide cases that affect their pocketbooks, jurors should not vote on the fate of friends and

---

74. RAWLS, *supra* note 53, at 54–58.
75. *See* Waldron, *Core Case, supra* note 10, at 1368–69.

relatives, and so on. As we've seen, the principle *nemo iudex in sua causa*—no one should serve as judge of his own case—is a central tenet of acceptable dispute resolution. An autocrat or small collection of oligarchs often will be self-interested in the issues they must decide, thus posing an obvious threat to the *nemo iudex* principle. Of course, democratic citizens often are self-interested as well; but, as we saw in Chapter 4, democracy's technique of blending each citizen's (potentially self-interested) vote on an equal basis with every other citizen's (potentially self-interested) vote tends to launder that partiality, to mitigate the force of each individual's self-interest by atomizing it among that of many others. This stands in contrast to autocracy or oligarchy, in which the likelihood of some shared self-interest on the part of those in power—a single individual or small group of them—becomes proportionately higher.

With respect to challenges to its own power, a democratic legislature is, or at least is quite likely to be, a self-interested oligarchy. Legislators, like other human beings, are inclined to look sympathetically on measures that would extend or preserve their own authority; perhaps more to the point, the rest of us are unlikely to trust legislators (as human beings) to assess those measures impartially. "If men were angels," Madison reminded us, "no government would be necessary";[76] nor must we assume that legislators are devils in order to distrust their judgment on questions of their own power. As Ely puts it, "[p]erspective is critical, and one whose continued authority depends on the silencing of other voices may well *in all good faith* be able to convince himself" that doing so is justified on appropriate grounds.[77]

Notice that the threat to legitimate authority here is not that the legislature is an oligarchy in the sense of being an elite subset of the citizenry as a whole. The problem, rather, is that the legislature is an oligarchy in the sense that its members share the same interest in an issue they have the power to decide. We trust democratic legislatures (elitist though they may be) to resolve most policy issues because we know there is likely to be a cacophony of interests, and thus of voices, regarding such issues in the body—and in the larger community the body represents. Self-interest on one side is balanced by self-interest on the other; the result, if things work well, is a lively debate that generates an outcome better than any side on its own could have produced. But the legislature's

---

76. Madison, FEDERALIST No. 10, *supra* note 4, at 319.

77. ELY, *supra* note 16, at 107 (emphasis in original). And remember that worries about the good faith of legislators, or of members of a voting majority of citizens, do not contradict our standing assumption that legal subjects will act as good-faith moral reasoners in deciding whether to obey the law. Legislators and voting citizens are not (in those capacities) legal *subjects*; they are rather legal *officials*, deciding how to exercise (or to claim to exercise) legal authority, not whether to obey it. (But legislators and voting citizens *are* legal subjects with respect to the commands of laws that purport to govern them *in their capacities* as legal officials—that is, with respect to constitutional law.)

interest in retaining power is likely to be monolithic, or nearly so. Some members may pursue that interest purposefully, others may allow it to sway them subconsciously, but most are likely to be moved by it somehow.

Note, too, that the crucial question is at least as much one of perception as of reality. The appeal of democracy (on the DR account) is not merely that is likely to be more competent and impartial than the alternatives, but that it is—mostly as a function of these real advantages—more likely to be widely *perceived* as competent and impartial. Acceptable dispute resolution depends ultimately upon people's beliefs about the procedure to which they are submitting. So the issue, with respect to democratic self-judging, is not whether any given set of legislators at any given time is capable of remaining objective and neutral on questions respecting their own power. The issue is whether a democratic citizenry is likely to accept, as reasonably impartial, a system in which democratic legislatures routinely have final authority to decide those questions. And the principle *nemo iudex in sua causa* strongly suggests that the answer might well be no.

D. The Promise of Constitutional Dispute Resolution

If disputes about democratic authority inevitably will arise (as both the possibility of democratic dysfunction and the indeterminacy of concepts like "democracy" ensure), a democratic community will have to develop means for resolving them acceptably. But there is good reason to think the institutions that are the subjects of these disputes—legislatures and other units of ordinary democratic government—will be saliently partial, or will be seen to be so, and thus will not be suited to the task. A democratic community therefore will have cause to submit these democratic disputes to institutions and procedures that are meaningfully external to democracy—separate from and independent of the institutions and procedures whose authority is at stake—and thus relatively impartial with respect to the issues being resolved.

The idea here is familiar from chapters 3, 5, and 6; it is the notion of a neutral third party to serve as a reasonably impartial arbiter of disagreements. We can now begin to grasp a central justification of the "countermajoritarian" nature of constitutional law, and in particular of a constitutional *process* that includes judicial review. Constitutionalism in the American mode assigns important decisions about democratic authority to relatively politically unaccountable judges. This comparative unaccountability is precisely the thing that Waldron and many other critics of judicial review find most offensive. On the emerging DR account of constitutional law and process, however, the relative political independence of judges—their externality with respect to democratic politics— is at the core of their justification, of their *raison d'être*. The political insularity of constitutional judges gives them an impartiality with respect to democratic disputes that more-accountable democratic decisionmakers—those whose authority is in dispute—saliently lack.

In Chapter 8, I will back up this admittedly rather cursory assertion with a more extensive narrative of judicial impartiality. And I will combine that narrative with another one that is equally important: an account of how constitutional adjudication, in addition to being relatively (and crucially) impartial, also can be reasonably competent as a way to resolve disputes about democratic authority. (Remember that impartiality can't stand alone as a marker of systemic accuracy; competence is required too.) The point for now is a rather general one, namely that the inevitability of democratic disputes, and the obvious partiality of ordinary democratic institutions as a way to resolve those disputes, sets the stage for some relatively apolitical, external mechanism for settling them.

E. The Advantages of Constitutional Rules

We have now the bare-bones outline of a case for extrademocratic dispute resolution in a democratic community. But constitutional law typically consists of more than simply ad hoc acts of *ex post* dispute resolution by courts; it consists also of constitutional *rules*, of a body of legal doctrine to which the community adheres (or tries to) even absent an active dispute, and which constitutional courts apply (or try to) to disputes when they arise. By now the existence of constitutional rules should be no mystery, for their advantages in a number of respects have already been made clear.

Recall, first of all, the need for some relatively obdurate constitutive rules establishing the basic institutions and procedures of a democracy. Democracy cannot get up and running, and keep itself running, without reasonably stable understandings of the fundamental institutions and procedures of which it consists. Even critics of constitutionalism like Waldron rarely object to the existence of a set of baseline constitutive rules for democratic government to follow (and thus for courts, as relatively impartial arbiters of democratic authority, to enforce).

Note, however, that the need for constitutive democratic rules is simply a special case of the more general argument for legal rules advanced in Chapter 4. Legal rules, generally speaking, are advantageous—and, in a complex modern society, probably necessary—because they reduce the incidence and costs of *ex post* disputes about what should be done. They accomplish this by stating ahead of time, with some measure of determinacy, the consequences of particular actions. In the constitutional context, constitutive democratic rules bring relative determinacy to the structure of democratic government, thus reducing the incidence and costs of disputes about that structure, disputes that would prevent democratic government from functioning if they were too frequent or costly. Of course, as we saw in Chapter 5 and earlier in the present chapter, legal rules can never be perfectly determinate, and thus disputes about their application inevitably will arise. This seems even more likely to be true of constitutive democratic rules, which, if they truly are to be confined to a relatively foundational level, will tend to be exceptionally open-ended and vague. I will have more to say on this point in Chapter 8. But even relatively open-ended rules can provide some determinacy and thus serve a valuable dispute-mitigating function.

Notice, too, that (as we saw in Chapter 5) legal rules, including constitutive democratic rules, can serve another important purpose as well: They can constrain the discretion of *ex post* dispute-resolvers such as courts. A judge who attempts, in good faith, actually to *apply* a constitutive rule to a dispute about democratic authority is not, to that extent, simply imposing her own views or preferences on the matter. If we are tempted to worry about the unintended consequences of ceding important decisional authority to politically unaccountable judges—and how can we not have some concern on this front?—the presence of constitutional rules, and of a strong judicial ethic of interpreting them faithfully, may ease our fears somewhat.

Given all that rules can do, it is important, as Chapter 5 explained, that they be generated by a process that is itself reasonably accurate, that is, reasonably competent and impartial. I will have much to say in the next chapter about the American-style process of generating constitutional rules. For present purposes, the crucial point in this regard is as follows: Just as the institutions of ordinary democracy are, thanks to their salient partiality, inapt at resolving ad hoc disputes about their own authority, so they are likely to be ill-suited to establishing general legal rules defining and governing that authority. The same element of self-judging rears its ugly head in the latter context as in the former. There will, then, be good reason for a democratic society to establish some process for creating constitutive and other constitutional rules that is meaningfully external to the processes of ordinary democracy those rules will govern.

There is an important caveat here, though. The perspective of someone—a person, a government official, a legislature or other decisionmaking body—seeking to define what its own authority will be in future cases may well be crucially distinct from the perspective taken by that same actor trying to assess its own authority in an immediately pressing case. It may be easier for Ulysses, anticipating his encounter with the Sirens, to lay down ahead of time a rule requiring that he be tied to the mast than for Ulysses to resist the Sirens' song while it dances around in his ears. (This is precisely the point of the rule.) To borrow a slightly different trope, a group of people deciding on rules from behind what John Rawls called a "veil of ignorance"—that is, without knowing precisely how they will be affected by the rules they are adopting—may be a more reliable decisionmaker than the same group deciding how to act *ex post*, with knowledge of precisely how the decision will affect them.[78] Distance can bring ignorance

---

78. *See* RAWLS, *supra* note 53, at 11–22.

and thus relative partiality. And so it might be the case that *nemo iudex in sua causa* will be of less concern when legislatures or other democratic institutions lay down rules to define or constrain their authority in the future, than when they attempt to judge the existence or scope of their authority on some particular, immediate occasion. In fact, as I'll explain in Chapter 8, the constitutional rulemaking process on the American model incorporates the input of the democratic institutions whose authority is in question; but it tends to do so by using the passage of time to simulate Rawls's veil of ignorance and thus to promote relative impartiality.

There is, then, a plausible case for the establishment, not just of an external means to adjudicate disputes about democratic authority, but also of constitutional rules that can be applied in those disputes. There is a case as well for the creation of those rules by a process that is meaningfully external to the democratic institutions and procedures they will govern.

And, finally, there is a case for expanding the scope of constitutional rules beyond the merely constitutive. Disputes about democratic authority, remember, will not be limited to clearly constitutive matters like the structure and basic responsibilities of government institutions. Disputes also will go to the kinds of issues identified in Footnote Four—issues like whether those in power are attempting to entrench that power in a way that frustrates democratic authority, or whether a political majority is behaving as a faction with respect to a minority. There will be good reason to liquidate ahead of time as many of these disputes as possible, too, by means of legal rules.

Suppose, for example, that the citizens of our imaginary nascent democracy, Carolenia, want to reduce the threat of the kind of factional entrenchment embodied in the Sedition Act. Now they might hope that the constitutive rules they've put into place—rules providing for things like separation of powers, perhaps, and specifying regular intervals for elections—will be enough to do the trick; but the example of the Sedition Act (which occurred, after all, against a democratic backdrop featuring these and other structural safeguards against entrenchment) will suggest otherwise. So the citizens of Carolenia might take the additional step of adopting a rule that forbids the government to punish citizens for engaging in political speech (a rule that might even be phrased as a guaranteed "right" of free speech). Such a rule would not be strictly constitutive in the sense of creating basic democratic institutions and procedures. It would, rather, take the form of an external constraint on the democratic institutions and procedures that have been constituted—a limit on what democracy may do, not just one of the rules allowing democracy to exist in the first place. The purpose of such a constraining rule would be prophylactic: It would be to prevent the occurrence of a certain identifiable form of democratic dysfunction.

Suppose the citizens of Carolenia also want to avoid the emergence of laws motivated by (and tending to perpetuate) irrational majoritarian prejudice, like the Jim Crow laws in the American South. Here again, they might be tempted to hope that the structural features of the government they are constituting (separation of powers, federalism, and so on) will alone prevent such a malfunction from occurring; but history will suggest otherwise. So they might, again, adopt prophylactic rules imposing external constraints on what the democratic process can do: a rule, for example, that requires the government to afford "the equal protection of the laws" to every one of its citizens.

Constitutional law, in other words, might well consist of both constitutive and prophylactic rules. The constitutive rules would define the basic institutions and procedures of democratic government (a bicameral legislature, for example, or a system of separated powers or of federalism); the prophylactic rules would constrain those institutions and procedures in ways designed to prevent certain predictable types of democratic malfunctions (perhaps by guaranteeing "rights" of free speech or equal protection). Of course, the constitutive rules themselves also would serve a prophylactic function: By defining democracy in a certain way, they would represent attempts, not just to get democratic institutions up and running, but to design those institutions so as to maximize their authority-generating features (their impartiality, their competence) and minimize the risk that those features will break down.

These constitutive and prophylactic rules—constitutional *law*—and the extrademocratic means for creating and interpreting them—constitutional *process*—will of course constrain the ordinary mechanisms of democratic government. They could hardly constitute democracy, or prevent democratic malfunctions, or impartially resolve disputes about democratic authority if they were not constraining in this sense. At the same time, though, to describe them as "countermajoritarian"— or at least as counter*democratic*—would be to shortchange the extent to which constitutional law and process are necessary in order for democracy to serve its assigned function, namely to produce authoritative general laws.

In the next section of this chapter, I will explore in a bit more detail the types of democratic dysfunction that constitutive and prophylactic constitutional rules might be designed to avoid. (I will suggest that the list proffered by Footnote Four and Ely, while immensely insightful, is somewhat incomplete.) Then, in Chapter 8, I will describe how constitutional process—the means of creating constitutional rules and applying them to disputes—can avoid the partiality problem that afflicts ordinary democratic institutions while still retaining much that is meaningfully democratic.

6. DEMOCRATIC MALFUNCTIONS (AND CONSTITUTIONAL RESPONSES)

Recall from Chapter 4 that democratic authority rests, according to the DR account, on three basic properties of democratic government. Broad participation brings competence in the form of diversity, deliberation, and aggregation of viewpoints and interests. Majority rule minimizes partiality by balancing each potentially partial vote against many other votes. And regular elections, by allowing democracy periodically to revisit its decisions, reduce the impact of partial decisionmaking over time and promote competence through trial and error.

Malfunctions in democratic authority occur when one or more of these properties is substantially compromised. I will suggest here that this is likely to happen in two basic categories of circumstance. The first involves the potential for divergence between the interests of the democratic citizens themselves and those of their elected or appointed representatives in government: Government officials may seek to use their delegated power to enlarge or entrench that power. The second category involves the danger of majority (or, in some cases, well-organized minority) factions: Groups of citizens with the capacity to control public policy might find themselves united by a common bias or self-interest. Either of these circumstances can vitiate democratic authority by frustrating one or more of the three crucial components of democratic accuracy, and constitutional law and process are means of preventing this from happening.

A. Agency Failure

One type of democratic malfunction is *agency failure*: Government officials might use their positions to augment or entrench their own power without regard to (and possibly in opposition to) the interests of the public.

We have already seen an example (at least an arguable one) of agency failure: the Sedition Act of 1798, discussed above, which made it a federal crime "to oppose any measure or measures of the government of the United States" or to knowingly publish "any false, scandalous and malicious writing. . . against the government of the United States. . . with intent to defame the said government." By restricting speech that opposed them or their policies, Congress and the President (who was, ironically, our old acquaintance John Adams, advocate of "a government of laws and not of men") made it more difficult to unseat them at the next election, thus entrenching their own power and frustrating the normal cyclical pattern of democratic politics. The Sedition Act therefore disabled the typical capacity of democracy to launder partiality and promote trial-and-error competence through repeated election cycles. This in turn threatened to shift political power from the democratic majority to an elite cadre of incumbent public officials. The resulting quasi oligarchy, by concentrating power in a relative few, would have amplified the potential partiality in each individual's decisionmaking and diluted the competence advantages of broad participation.

Fortunately this parade of horribles did not come to pass as a result of the actual Sedition Act; the Federalists nonetheless lost both Congress and the Presidency in the 1800 elections, and the new Republican-controlled Congress allowed the Act to lapse in 1801. And in fact there is reason to suppose that Adams and the Federalist Congress adopted the Act, not as a way to punish political opponents and entrench their own power, but out of real (if overblown) fear that French *agents provocateurs* would foment domestic unrest. But the democracy-disrupting danger of legislation like the Sedition Act is readily apparent. So too, as we've seen, is the unsuitability of the democratic branches themselves to assess this danger. Reasonable minds can differ (and did) on the propriety of the Sedition Act, but the President and Congress themselves, as saliently self-interested parties, could hardly be trusted to resolve the dispute impartially. (The fact that the Federalists, whatever their motives for adopting the Act, used it primarily to prosecute their political enemies only underscores this point.[79])

Constitutional law can manage the risk of agency failure through constitutive and prophylactic rules that regulate the agent-principal relationship between democratic officials and the citizenry they are supposed to serve. The regulation might be direct—for example, a provision for regular elections or a prohibition on laws restricting political speech. It might also be indirect: division of power among different groups of officials who are selected, evaluated, and controlled by the citizenry in different ways, for example, thus allowing "[a]mbition. . . to counteract ambition."[80] Such means of "oblig[ing]" the government "to control itself"[81] are familiar in other agency contexts within modern law—in the law of corporations, for example, where officers and directors owe legally regulated fiduciary duties to shareholders, and in the law of professional responsibility, where experts like lawyers and doctors owe duties to clients and patients.

As Ely documented,[82] a large portion of American constitutional doctrine in fact can be understood as a series of hedges against the risk of agency failure. Articles I and II impose specific limits on the terms of office of elected representatives, thus requiring regular elections. The rights of speech, petition, and assembly guaranteed by the First Amendment limit incumbents' ability to insulate themselves from political challenges. Article I, § 5 requires each House of Congress to "keep a Journal of its Proceedings," thus enhancing the public's capacity to monitor what its representatives are doing. The system of separation of powers, combined with a bicameral legislature and including staggered terms of office and different means of selection for members of the various branches,

---

79. For an account of the events surrounding the adoption, enforcement, and eventual abandonment of the Sedition Act, with particular attention to the free-speech issues involved, see GEOFFREY R. STONE, PERILOUS TIMES: FREE SPEECH IN WARTIME: FROM THE SEDITION ACT OF 1798 TO THE WAR ON TERRORISM 15–78 (2004).

80. Madison, FEDERALIST No. 51, *supra* note 4, at 319.

81. *Id.*

82. *See* ELY, *supra* note 16, at 105–34.

258 A MATTER OF DISPUTE

greatly increases the transaction costs involved in the entrenchment of official power. The federal structure of the government has a similar effect.[83]

B. Majority (and Well-Organized Minority) Factions

A second kind of democratic malfunction is the development of *majority factions*: political majorities "united and actuated by some common impulse of passion, or of interest," in Madison's famous description.[84] Like official partiality, the development of a majority faction frustrates the atomizing function of democracy, concentrating a single type of partiality to the point where it dominates political decisionmaking on certain issues. The dominance of partiality in a majority faction also is likely to undercut the "many minds" benefits of democracy for decisionmaking competence. And sometimes majority factions (like factions of self-interested officials) can artificially expand or entrench their own power, disabling the usual cycling property of democracy.

We have already discussed an example of majority factionalism as well: the school-segregation and other Jim Crow laws endemic in the American South for nearly a century following the Civil War. The white majority population in each of the southern states, united by a shared racism and distrust toward the black minority, elected like-minded representatives who enacted these segregationist measures in an attempt to isolate and subjugate the black minority.

Note that the chief democratic malfunction embodied in Jim Crow, from the perspective of the DR account, was not the racist substance of the segregationist laws (although to the extent those laws had the effect of entrenching the white majority's power, that constituted a democratic failure too; more on this point below). The central problem was again one of partiality. Like the self-interested Congress and President who adopted the Sedition Act, the white southern majority was not a reasonably impartial judge on issues involving relations or allocation of resources between the two racial groups. This partiality problem risks being obscured by what are, to our modern sensibilities, obviously racist and inappropriate laws. But imagine a proposed law implicating race that is not so saliently venal: perhaps a bill requiring that affirmative action be used to remedy the inadequate representation of members of the black minority in public universities and employment. The partiality problem would remain with respect to such a proposal. If the members of the white majority share racist views, that majority hardly could be a reasonably impartial judge on the wisdom of the proposed law, any more than the members of Congress could impartially judge the wisdom of the Sedition Act.

---

83. The Framers were quite explicit about their belief that dividing power would reduce the risk of agency failure. *See, e.g.*, Madison, FEDERALIST NO. 51, *supra* note 4, at 321 (describing the combination of separated national powers and federalism as "a double security... to the rights of the people").

84. Madison, FEDERALIST NO. 10, *supra* note 4, at 123.

Note, too, that the partiality problem with Jim Crow laws was not simply a function of the fact that some individual members of the political majority voted based on racist views. As Madison recognized, and as I discussed in Chapter 4, individual or majority partiality can, in a democratic polity of reasonably large size, be cleansed by the votes of others in any given election and by a succession of elections over time; "relief" for such minority factions "is supplied by the republican principle, which enables the majority to defeat its sinister views by regular vote."[85] The democratic dysfunction of Jim Crow was the fact that the *same* source of salient partiality—a racist disdain for or distrust of members of the black minority—was shared by a majority of the citizens in the South. On matters relating to race, the southern white majority acted in essence like a Hobbesian autocrat, motivated by a single dominant set of biases and interests. It was this element of a majority acting as a single entity with respect to the minority that created the partiality problem by frustrating the usual atomizing properties of democracy.

(i) The Nature(s) of Majority Partiality Of course, majorities always in some sense "act as a single entity" in voting by majority rule: Their members come together and speak with a single voice on whatever is the issue at hand. What makes examples like Jim Crow problematic from the perspective of democratic authority—examples of majority *factions* in Madison's sense—is that the white majority shares a common source of *partiality*, a common "passion" or "interest" that deforms its judgment on certain issues. In fact this partiality might assume one or both of two distinct but related forms.[86]

Partiality as substantive prejudice. Racist partiality might take the form of pre-judgment (literally "prejudice") regarding *issues* relating to race—for example, a firm conviction that racial segregation is justified or necessary. The essence of this type of partiality is a resistance, a relative imperviousness, to the kinds of evidence and arguments that normally would be offered and considered in deciding such issues. A majority whose members share this kind of resistance is distinct from an ordinary majority that happens, after attending to the facts and arguments on either side, to reach the same conclusion on an issue involving race. Its substantive prejudice serves as the "common impulse of passion, or of interest" that makes the majority a faction.

Note, by the way, that we can recognize this prejudice as a type of partiality without taking a position in legitimate debates about issues involving race.

---

85. Madison, FEDERALIST No. 10, *supra* note 4, at 125.

86. Justice Antonin Scalia, in an interesting discussion in his opinion for the Court in *Republican Party of Minnesota v. White*, 536 U.S. 765 (2002), drew a similar distinction between different possible meanings of the concept of judicial "impartiality." Impartiality, Justice Scalia speculated, might mean "the lack of bias for or against either party to the proceeding." Or it might mean a "lack of preconception in favor of or against a particular legal view." *Id.* at 775–78.

We might reasonably disagree on the propriety of affirmative action—even on the propriety of racial segregation—while still acknowledging that a person or group that is impervious to facts and arguments on those issues is insufficiently impartial to authoritatively resolve our disagreement.

And note, relatedly and importantly, that this type of prejudice need not be the product of a belief, like that in racial superiority, that most of us are likely to consider irrational. Prejudice might be motivated by "interest" as well as "passion." Consider, for example, the prodairy legislation enacted in many states during the first half of the twentieth century, such as laws prohibiting the sale of margarine.[87] In passing these laws, political majorities in the dairy-heavy states might well have prejudged the issue of whether the sale of margarine should be permitted—not out of some irrational bias against margarine producers, but out of simple pecuniary self-interest. As Madison and his fellows understood, the ego as well as the id might render a person, or a group of people with similar interests, impervious to evidence and reasoned arguments.

Partiality as personal bias. The majority partiality behind Jim Crow–style laws might instead—or in addition—assume a related but subtly different form: It might amount to an animosity against a particular *person* or *group* of people, one that prevents the decisionmaker from treating that person or group fairly in the decision process. Members of the southern white majority might have supported racial segregation or opposed affirmative action, not because (at least not only because) they had formed relatively immutable views on the substance of those issues, but because they had a desire to harm members of the black minority or an ingrained resistance to taking their views and interests seriously. The adjudicative analogue here would be a judge or juror who has a strong preexisting dislike for one of the litigants.

This sort of interpersonal animosity seems to be what the Footnote Four Court had primarily in mind in worrying about "prejudice against discrete and insular minorities," and it (rather than the kind of substantive prejudgment discussed above) is the focus of Ely's elaboration of this Footnote Four concern.[88] As with substantive prejudgment, though, the concern with racial or other types of interpersonal animosity is, from the DR perspective, chiefly a concern about the sanctity of the procedure, not about controversial substantive outcomes. We need not take a position on substantive questions of racial merit—or, to invoke a more current and thus still-controversial topic, on substantive questions regarding the morality of sexual orientation—to agree that a decisionmaker who

---

87. For a narrative of dairy-industry influence in legislation during the early twentieth century, see Geoffrey Miller, *Public Choice at the Dawn of the Special Interest State: The Story of Butter and Margarine*, 77 CAL. L. REV. 83 (1989).

88. *See* ELY, *supra* note 16, at 135–79 (chapter 6).

harbors an active animosity toward members of the relevant minority group cannot impartially resolve those issues.[89]

The malfunction of majority factions. More generally, a focus on "discrete and insular minorities" tends to obscure the possibility of majority factions united by self-interest instead of, or in addition to, irrational bias based upon race or some other arguably irrelevant characteristic. A majority faction is problematic even if its animating impulse is indisputably logical—a desire to protect its members from economic competition, for example. Where the majority (or, as we'll see below, the minority) that holds political power shares the same self-interest, however rational, it lacks the capacity to impartially judge policy questions implicating that interest. The resulting democratic breakdown goes deeper than the (often arguable) presence of some unfounded psychological animosity—a fact neglected in Ely's elucidation of Footnote Four proceduralism.

If a majority shares one or both of these types of partiality—substantive prejudgment of an issue or psychological animosity toward members of the minority—it thus lacks the typical authority of democratic government to resolve relevant disputes. The fact that a majority shares the same impulse of partiality blocks the usual capacity of democracy to atomize the partiality of individual voters. And the fact that the impulse is one of partiality—a prejudgment or bias rather than a joint conclusion based on evidence and arguments—separates a majority faction, and thus a democratic malfunction, from the ordinary phenomena of majority rule.

(ii) Minority Factions While Madison and his colleagues focused many of their considerable faculties on the problem of majority factions, they discounted the danger of minority factions, which may "clog the administration" and "convulse the society" but, Madison confidently asserted, would "be unable to

---

89. This realization—that animosity toward a group with an interest in an issue destroys impartiality, regardless of which resolution of the issue is proper—probably motivated the Supreme Court's reliance on the concept of animosity in deciding at least one recent case involving the rights of homosexuals. In *Romer v. Evans,* 517 U.S. 620 (1996), the Court held that a Colorado constitutional amendment excluding homosexuals from antidiscrimination laws could not survive "rational basis" scrutiny under the Equal Protection Clause because it was "born of animosity toward" homosexuals. *Id.* at 634–35. In rejecting "a bare. . . desire to harm a politically unpopular group" as a legitimate governmental interest, the *Romer* Court drew on earlier equal protection decisions involving discrimination against "hippies" (*U.S. Dept. of Agriculture v. Moreno,* 413 U.S. 528 (1973)) and people with mental disabilities (*City of Cleburne v. Cleburne Living Center, Inc.,* 473 U.S. 432 (1985)). *Id.* Shades of this reasoning also appeared in the Court's decision invalidating a Texas prohibition of same-sex sodomy under the Due Process Clause. *See* Lawrence v. Texas, 539 U.S. 558, 574–75 (2003) (citing *Romer*'s anti-animosity principle). Justice O'Connor relied explicitly on that rationale in concurring in *Lawrence* on equal protection grounds. *See id.* at 579–82 (O'Connor, J., concurring). *See also infra* note 112 and accompanying text.

execute and mask [their] violence under the forms of the Constitution."[90] This confidence has turned out to be misplaced. As the modern field of public-choice theory—an intersection of political science and economics—has demonstrated, well-motivated, well-organized minority interest groups often succeed in extracting "rents" from the democratic political process: legislation that benefits their interests without a corresponding benefit to (and often at the expense of) the interests of the broader public.[91]

Consider a refinement of the prodairy legislation example. Suppose a majority of the voters in a state would prefer to have a choice between butter and margarine, a less-expensive butter alternative, while voters affiliated with the dairy industry—a minority—want, out of self-interest, to exclude margarine from the market. Each dairy-industry voter—a dairy worker, a dairy owner or major investor, a supplier of goods or services to the dairy industry—is likely to have a relatively strong interest in excluding margarine, namely that the possible alternative—a market shift toward margarine—will greatly impact each dairy voter's bottom line. This creates a powerful incentive for dairy voters to devote resources to the cause of excluding margarine and to other prodairy efforts. The most efficient way to do that might involve forming an industry organization that can lobby the state legislature, make targeted campaign contributions, and the like. And if the dairy industry is relatively small, the costs of organizing such a group will be relatively minimal. In contrast, any given member of the dairy-consuming public is unlikely to have a particularly strong interest in preserving the choice between butter and margarine; the marginal benefit of such a choice (and the marginal detriment of its loss) in the life of each consumer will not be worth the substantial investment of resources necessary to preserve (or avoid) it. The costs of organizing the huge, diffuse mass of the dairy-consuming public, moreover, into an effective political action organization will be quite high.

As these dynamics interact, the likely result will be the rise of the dairy industry as a politically powerful minority interest group with the capacity to extract "rents"—favorable legislation—from the political process in the state, including

---

90. Madison, FEDERALIST No. 10, *supra* note 4, at 125.

91. Classic studies of minority interest-group influence in democratic politics include ARTHUR F. BENTLEY, THE PROCESS OF GOVERNMENT: A STUDY OF SOCIAL PRESSURES (1908); E. E. SCHATTSCHNEIDER, POLITICS, PRESSURES, AND THE TARIFF (1935); DAVID B. TRUMAN, THE GOVERNMENTAL PROCESS: POLITICAL INTERESTS AND PUBLIC OPINION (1951); EARL LATHAM, THE GROUP BASIS OF POLITICS: NOTES FOR A THEORY (1952); ROBERT A. DAHL, WHO GOVERNS? DEMOCRACY AND POWER IN AN AMERICAN CITY (1961); and KAY LEHMAN SCHLOZMAN & JOHN T. TIERNEY, ORGANIZED INTERESTS AND AMERICAN DEMOCRACY (1986). The conventional economic theory explaining minority political influence was first articulated in MANCUR OLSON, THE LOGIC OF COLLECTIVE ACTION: PUBLIC GOODS AND THE THEORY OF GROUPS (1965). A good critical overview of interest-group theory can be found in DANIEL A. FARBER & PHILIP P. FRICKEY, LAW AND PUBLIC CHOICE: A CRITICAL INTRODUCTION 12–37 (1991).

a law taxing or prohibiting the sale of margarine. Legislators and other officials, for their part, will have strong incentives to do the dairy industry's bidding, thanks to that industry's well-organized lobbying and campaign-contribution efforts. And while legislators will not want to alienate the majority of voters who control their reelection, they will understand that the margarine issue matters relatively little to any individual (nondairy) voter and thus is relatively unlikely to influence many (nondairy) votes. The legislature, then, may well agree to enact prodairy, anticonsumer laws, including a tax or a ban on margarine, thanks to a rational calculation that the costs of displeasing the well-organized dairy industry will exceed the costs of displeasing the diffuse, disorganized majority of consumer-voters.[92]

Public-choice theory thus demonstrates that the problem of factions can combine with a sort of agency failure to allow minority interest groups to dictate public policy under certain conditions. This phenomenon is even more troubling on a DR account of democracy than the problem of majority factions. Empirically, the problem of rent-seeking minority factions appears substantially more likely to occur than the problem of majority factions: While the combination of a majority into a singly-motivated group probably will be infrequent in a large, diverse polity, the size and diversity of a polity actually is likely to enhance the effectiveness of minority interest groups by making it less likely that a diffuse majority will combine to offer resistance. And normatively, the possibility that policy issues will be determined by a self-interested or otherwise partial minority undercuts the impartiality and competence advantages of democracy even more than the danger of majority factions does.

(iii) Factional Entrenchment As Footnote Four proceduralism recognizes, the possibility that a faction, majority or minority, will assume legislative power in a democracy raises the further danger of *factional entrenchment*: The faction may attempt to enact legislation that would have the effect of entrenching its power. Consider the following examples, loosely based on real cases:

- A state's rural majority, predicting that the population will continue to shift toward urban areas, amends the state's constitution to establish legislative districts of roughly equal geographic size and provide for the election of one representative from each district, resulting in increasing proportional overrepresentation of rural voters.[93]

---

92. This hypothetical is based on the actual rise of the dairy industry as a powerful force in state and, eventually, national politics in the late nineteenth and early twentieth centuries. The rise is documented in Miller, *supra* note 87.

93. This is a simplified version of the state apportionment schemes struck down by the Supreme Court in *Gray v. Sanders*, 372 U.S. 368 (1963), and *Reynolds v. Sims*, 377 U.S. 533 (1964).

- A state legislature controlled by one political party redraws, or "gerry-manders," its electoral districts along demographic lines to disadvantage the opposing party.[94]
- A state's white majority institutes a "poll tax" and a literacy test as requirements for voting in state elections, both of which disproportionately prevent voting by blacks and other racial and ethnic minorities.[95]

In these cases, as with cases of agency failure, the democratic malfunction consists in the artificial entrenchment of current majorities by impeding the ability of minority groups to gain influence through democratic elections. And, as in the case of the Sedition Act, the majority in power, because of its self-interest or bias—that is, because of its status as a faction—is unqualified to

---

94. There is a long and sordid history of gerrymandering in the United States. The term "gerrymander" itself derives from a districting bill signed by Massachusetts governor Elbridge Gerry in 1812, which heavily favored Gerry's own Democratic-Republican party and included a district whose shape resembled that of a salamander. *See* Davis v. Bandemer, 478 U.S. 109, 164 & n.3 (1986) (Powell, J., concurring in part and dissenting in part). In *Gomillion v. Lightfoot*, 364 U.S. 339 (1960), the Supreme Court held that Alabama's redrawing of the Tuskegee city boundaries to form a 28-sided figure that excluded almost all black voters violated the Equal Protection Clause. In *League of United Latin Am. Citizens v. Perry*, 548 U.S. 399 (2006), the Court dismissed on procedural grounds most of an equal-protection challenge to Texas's redrawing of federal congressional districts, the result of which strongly favored the Republican party, which controlled the state legislature and held the governorship during the redistricting process.

95. After ratification in 1870 of the Fifteenth Amendment, which protected the right to vote of newly freed slaves, many southern states adopted poll taxes with "grandfather clauses" exempting citizens eligible to vote before slavery was abolished (i.e., white citizens). *See* 2 A. Leon Higginbotham, Jr., Shades of Freedom: Racial Politics and Presumptions of the American Legal Process 172–74 (1996); *see also* South Carolina v. Katzenbach, 383 U.S. 301, 310–14 (1966). Many of the same states later added literacy requirements, as did some northern states with large immigrant populations. *See* Higginbotham, *supra*, at 178–79; *Katzenbach*, 383 U.S. at 312. The combined effect of poll taxes and literacy tests disenfranchised large portions of the southern black population until well into the mid-twentieth century. *See* Higginbotham, *supra*, at 178–79. In 1964 the Twenty-Fourth Amendment, which banned poll taxes in federal elections, was ratified, and in 1966 the Supreme Court invalidated poll taxes in state elections as violations of equal protection. *See* Harper v. Virginia Bd. of Elections, 383 U.S. 663 (1966). The Voting Rights Act of 1965 effectively eliminated the use of literacy tests; its validity was upheld by the Supreme Court in *South Carolina v. Katzenbach, supra*, and *Katzenbach v. Morgan*, 384 U.S. 641 (1966).Recently some voting-rights advocates have argued that state voter-identification requirements amount to a functional poll tax by effectively limiting access to the polls by many impoverished citizens. In 2008, the Supreme Court rejected a facial equal-protection challenge to Indiana's voter-identification requirement, although the Court left open the possibility that such requirements might be challenged by individual voters who could establish harm. *See* Crawford v. Marion County Election Bd., 128 S.Ct. 1610, 1621–23 (2008).

impartially balance the competing considerations and assess the wisdom of the policies.

(iv) Constitutional Inoculation Against Factionalism A democratic community might develop constitutional legal rules designed to frustrate the formation of majority or powerful minority factions, by dividing the instrumentalities of power among different institutions, for example. (The American Constitution accomplishes this through separation of national powers, bicameralism, and federalism.) It might also seek to block or limit the power of factions when they do form, by requiring that laws be justifiable by reference to broad public interest and forbidding or strongly discouraging legislation that turns on race, religion, or other common markers of bias. (American due-process and equal-protection doctrine serve these functions by requiring that virtually every law meet a rationality requirement[96] and that laws employing "suspect" or "quasi-suspect" classifications—race, ethnicity, national origin, or gender—be subjected to heightened judicial scrutiny.[97] First Amendment doctrine similarly

---

96. "Rational basis" scrutiny under both the Due Process and Equal Protection Clauses requires that the government demonstrate a "rational relationship" between the law at issue and some "legitimate" objective. Most laws survive rational-basis scrutiny. *See, e.g.,* United States v. Carolene Products Co., 304 U.S. 144 (1938) (upholding a federal prohibition on the shipment of "filled milk" against a due process challenge despite obvious special-interest influence); Williamson v. Lee Optical, 348 U.S. 483 (1955) (upholding a state law requiring prescriptions for duplicating lenses against both due process and equal protection challenges); *see also* Geoffrey Miller, *The True Story of Carolene Products*, 1987 Sup. Ct. Rev. 397 (portraying the Filled Milk Act as the product of special-interest rent-seeking) [hereinafter Miller, *Carolene Products*]. Some do not survive it, however. *See* sources cited *supra* note 89.

97. "Strict scrutiny" under due process and equal protection requires the government to demonstrate that a law is "narrowly tailored" to serve a "compelling" objective. Equal protection strict scrutiny is triggered by laws that discriminate based on race, ethnicity, or national origin; due process strict scrutiny is triggered by laws that infringe some "fundamental interest." Most laws fail strict scrutiny. *See, e.g.,* Gratz v. Bollinger, 539 U.S. 244 (2003) (holding that a public university's program of affirmative action in admissions was insufficiently narrowly tailored to survive strict scrutiny under the Equal Protection Clause); Troxel v. Granville, 530 U.S. 57 (2000) (holding that a state law allowing visitation by nonparents in "the best interest of the child" lacked a compelling interest and thus failed strict scrutiny under the Due Process Clause). Some survive it, however. *See* Grutter v. Bollinger, 539 U.S. 306 (2003) (upholding a public law school's program of affirmative action in admissions as sufficiently narrowly tailored to survive strict scrutiny under the Equal Protection Clause).

The Court also has identified another form of heightened scrutiny under the Equal Protection Clause, typically referred to as "intermediate scrutiny," which requires the government to demonstrate that a law is "substantially related" to an "important" government interest. Intermediate scrutiny so far has been limited to laws that classify based on gender, and the results have been mixed, although most gender classifications have been struck down. *See, e.g.,* Craig v. Boren, 429 U.S. 190 (1976) (applying intermediate scrutiny to invalidate an Oklahoma law prohibiting males but not females to purchase 3.2 percent

requires special justification for laws that hinge on religion.[98]) And it might regulate the terms of political participation in a way that discourages majority entrenchment (through, for example, provisions for regular elections, guarantees that members of minority groups can vote and hold office,[99] and strong protections for political speech[100]).

---

beer at age eighteen); United States v. Virginia, 518 U.S. 515 (1996) (applying intermediate scrutiny to invalidate a Virginia policy of excluding women from its state military college); *but see* Nguyen v. INS, 533 U.S. 53 (2001) (applying intermediate scrutiny to uphold immigration rules favoring mothers over fathers).

98. *See* Church of Lukumi Babalu Aye v. City of Hialeah, 508 U.S. 520 (1993) (invalidating a city's ban on the slaughtering of animals on the ground that it was intended to prohibit the practices of the Santeria religion).

99. While the original Constitution was notably silent on the question of who could vote, six subsequent amendments had the direct or indirect effect of expanding the franchise. The Fifteenth Amendment (ratified in 1870) prohibited impairment of the right to vote "on account of race, color, or previous condition of servitude." U.S. CONST. amend. XV, § 1. The Seventeenth Amendment (ratified in 1913) replaced the original scheme of Senate appointments by the state legislatures with a system of direct popular election. *Id.* amend. XVII. The Nineteenth Amendment (1920) gave women the vote. *Id.* amend. XIX. The Twenty-Third Amendment (1961) assigned presidential Electors to the District of Columbia, thus effectively allowing D.C. residents to vote in presidential elections (though they still have no voting representatives in Congress). *Id.* amend. XXIII. The Twenty-Fourth Amendment (1964) eliminated use of the poll tax in federal elections, removing a powerful tool for disenfranchising the poor and especially African Americans; the Supreme Court quickly extended its principle to state and local elections. *Id.* amend. XXIV; *see also* Harper v. Virginia State Bd. of Elections, 383 U.S. 663 (1966) (invalidating a state poll tax on equal protection grounds). And the Twenty-Sixth Amendment (1971) effectively lowered the minimum voting age in both federal and state elections to a uniform eighteen years. U.S. CONST. amend. XXVI.

Article VI expressly bars "religious Test[s]" as requirements for federal office. U.S. CONST. art. VI. There is little doubt that state and local religious tests are banned by virtue of the Free Exercise and Establishment Clauses of the First Amendment, or that the Equal Protection Clause subjects discrimination among citizens for purposes of voting or holding office to strict scrutiny. *See* McDaniel v. Paty, 435 U.S. 618 (1978) (holding a state constitutional provision which prohibited ministers or priests from serving in the legislature violated the Free Exercise Clause of the First Amendment as applied to the states by the Fourteenth Amendment); Hill v. Stone, 421 U.S. 289 (1975) (striking down a state provision limiting the right to vote in city bond issue elections to persons who had "rendered" property for taxation as a violation of the Equal Protection Clause); Kramer v. Union Free Sch. Dist., 395 U.S. 621 (1969) (invalidating under strict scrutiny a state requirement that voters in school district elections either own or lease taxable real property within the relevant district or have children attending the local public schools); *Harper*, 383 U.S. 663 (1966) (invalidating under strict scrutiny a state poll tax); *cf.* Sugarman v. Dougall, 413 U.S. 634 (1973) (invalidating under strict scrutiny a state law prohibiting noncitizens from holding low-level civil-service positions).

100. Since at least the 1960s, the Court fairly consistently has used the Free Speech Clause of the First Amendment to protect expression that communicates a political

7. WHITHER "SUBSTANTIVE" CONSTITUTIONAL RIGHTS?
(THE *ROE V. WADE* PROBLEM)

The defense of constitutional law and process that I've outlined here, and will continue in the next chapter, resembles the Footnote Four/John Hart Ely approach in a crucial respect: Both approaches turn on the notions that ordinary democracy often suffers from certain kinds of flaws, and that constitutional law and process are reasonable responses to those problems. I will have a bit more to say in Chapter 8 about the relationship between my DR approach and Footnote Four proceduralism. For the moment, however, I want to address a worry that might seem to undermine any justification of constitutional law as a response to democratic dysfunction. The worry is that some elements that seem important to the actual practice of American constitutional law cannot be explained by such an account.

The paradigmatic object of this worry is the body of doctrine known as "substantive due process." The Due Process Clause—really two clauses, one in the Fifth Amendment that applies to the federal government, the other in the Fourteenth Amendment that applies to the states—prohibits deprivation of "life, liberty, or property, without due process of law." For more than a century the Supreme Court has interpreted the Clause to impose substantive limits on government's authority to deprive someone of her life, liberty, or property, limits that apply without regard to the process by which government effectuates the deprivation.[101] Prior to the New Deal, the Court used this "substantive due process" doctrine primarily to constrain the government's ability to regulate

---

message. *See, e.g.,* New York Times v. Sullivan, 376 U.S. 254 (1964) (requiring that public officials demonstrate "actual malice" to recover for defamation); Brandenburg v. Ohio, 395 U.S. 444 (1969) (requiring government to meet a stringent test before regulating speech on the ground that it might incite violence); Cohen v. California, 403 U.S. 15 (1971) (invalidating a conviction for disturbing the peace of a defendant who wore a jacket reading "Fuck the Draft" in a courthouse); Buckley v. Valeo, 424 U.S. 1 (1976) (applying strict scrutiny to laws regulating political campaign expenditures); Texas v. Johnson, 491 U.S. 397 (1989) (applying strict scrutiny to invalidate a state law prohibiting burning the U.S. flag); R.A.V. v. City of St. Paul, 505 U.S. 377 (1992) (applying strict scrutiny to content-based bans on "fighting words" that carry certain messages); *but see* United States v. O'Brien, 391 U.S. 367 (1968) (applying intermediate scrutiny to uphold a statute criminalizing the destruction of draft-registration cards as applied to a defendant who publicly burned his card in protest).

101. The Court's first "substantive" use of the Due Process Clause occurred in *Dred Scott v. Sandford,* 60 U.S. (19 How.) 393 (1857), where it suggested that Congress's attempt to ban slavery in parts of the territories deprived slaveowners of their property without due process of law.

economic interactions.[102] The Court abandoned that approach in the 1930s,[103] but it now protects certain "fundamental" noneconomic rights—"privacy," reproductive choice, sexual "autonomy"—under the banner of substantive due process.[104]

The account of constitutional law I'm offering here is intended to be interpretive—to fit reasonably, if not always perfectly, our actual practices of constitutional law and procedure. If the account fails to justify substantive due process, its claim to a reasonably good fit might thereby be diminished. And there is indeed reason to think that the DR account cannot fully explain substantive due process.

Consider *Roe v. Wade*, which is probably the best known (and certainly the most controversial) substantive due process decision. In *Roe*, the Court held that a "right of privacy" is "founded in the. . . concept of personal liberty" protected by the Due Process Clause and "encompass[es] a woman's decision whether or not to terminate her pregnancy."[105] The Court seemed to treat this privacy right, and its reproductive-choice component, as staking out an area of activity that is immune from government regulation, a sphere into which even democratic procedures cannot intrude. (This view parallels those the Court has taken in other substantive due process cases involving activities like making labor contracts[106] and engaging in private, consensual sex.[107])

But it is far from obvious how a constitutional rule protecting individual privacy or choice from government intrusion serves the sort of constitutive or

---

102. *See, e.g.*, Adkins v. Children's Hosp., 261 U.S. 525 (1923) (using due process to invalidate a state law requiring minimum wages for women); Lochner v. New York, 198 U.S. 45 (1905) (using due process to invalidate a state limitation on the working hours of bakers).

103. *See, e.g.*, United States v. Carolene Products Co., 304 U.S. 144 (1938) (upholding against a due process challenge a federal prohibition on the shipment of "filled milk" in interstate commerce); West Coast Hotel Co. v. Parrish, 300 U.S. 379 (1937) (overruling *Adkins* to uphold a minimum wage for women); Nebbia v. New York, 291 U.S. 502 (1934) (upholding price controls for milk against a due process challenge).

104. *See, e.g.*, Griswold v. Connecticut, 381 U.S. 479 (1965) (invalidating a law criminalizing the use of contraception by married couples as violating a right of "privacy" gleaned from "penumbras" emanating from several provisions of the Bill of Rights); *id.* at 499–501 (Harlan, J., concurring) (concurring in the judgment on substantive due process grounds); Roe v. Wade, 410 U.S. 113 (1973) (invalidating state laws prohibiting abortion as violating the "liberty" component of substantive due process); Lawrence v. Texas, 539 U.S. 558 (2003) (invalidating a state law criminalizing same-sex sodomy as violating a right to "autonomy" protected by substantive due process).

105. *Roe*, 401 U.S. at 153.

106. *See, e.g.*, *Lochner*, 198 U.S. at 45.

107. *See, e.g.*, *Griswold*, 381 U.S. at 479; *Lawrence*, 539 U.S. at 558. Although the majority opinion in *Griswold* did not expressly rely on the Due Process Clause, I think it is fair to treat the case as involving substantive due process, for reasons I explain in note 112, *infra*.

prophylactic function that drives constitutional law on the DR account. To pro-hibit government from regulating abortion is not to constitute the basic institu-tions and procedures of democracy. Nor does such a prohibition seem directed at preventing agency failure, factionalism, or some other type of democratic breakdown (in contrast to, say, a prohibition on government regulation of politi-cal speech). More broadly, it is hard to see how a debate about whether the govern-ment should regulate abortion qualifies as a dispute about democratic authority in the appropriate sense. The prochoice claim, at least as the *Roe* Court seemed to understand it, is not a claim that one of the key ingredients of democratic authority—broad participation, regular elections, majority rule—is missing or malfunctioning. Instead it is a claim that those ingredients, functioning prop-erly, have generated a morally wrong or harmful law. This is a claim about the substance of the legislation, not the authority of the process that enacted it; and it is precisely these kinds of substantive disagreements that ordinary democ-racy is designed to resolve acceptably.

If we understand substantive due process as the *Roe* Court did, then—as a position in a debate about substantive political morality, not about legal authority—then the doctrine has no apparent place in a DR account of constitu-tional law. But in fact it might be possible to understand much of substantive due process in other than purely substantive terms. Consider the doctrine's first sig-nificant incarnation, as a means to protect laissez-faire economic values during the first third of the twentieth century.[108] This "economic" due process was unjus-tifiable, and ultimately a failure, to the extent it attempted to use the instrumen-talities of constitutional law simply to impose one side of a substantive dispute. But economic due process had one redeeming feature: It made it more difficult for minority factions to extract rents from the political process.[109] In order to preserve an economic regulation from a due process challenge, the government had to convince the court that the legislation clearly benefited a broad spectrum of the public or, if it seemed to benefit only a subset of the public, that the benefited group had some special need for protection. Purely rent-seeking legis-lation typically had trouble clearing these hurdles. Supposedly "substantive" due

---

108. *See* sources cited *supra* note 102.

109. As David Bernstein points out, the statutory provisions at issue in *Lochner*—limitations on the working hours of bakery employees—can be understood as the prod-ucts of rent-seeking by politically powerful large bakeries and bakery unions, at the expense of less-powerful smaller bakeries and nonunionized (and largely immigrant) bakery workers and of disorganized consumers. *See* David E. Bernstein, *The Story of* Lochner v. New York: *Impediment to the Growth of the Regulatory State, in* CONSTITUTIONAL LAW STORIES 326, 328–35 (Michael C. Dorf ed., 2004). If this view is accurate, then the Court's close scrutiny of that and similar laws often had the effect of frustrating such rent-seeking behavior—and the Court's abandonment of close scrutiny during the New Deal had the opposite effect. For a rent-seeking account of the Filled Milk Act upheld in *Carolene Products*, a central New Deal decision, *see* Miller, *Carolene Products, supra* note 96.

process, in other words, served a sanguinary procedural function, one that fits into the DR account offered here: It limited the influence of minority factions. (The Court's ultimate rejection of economic due process—really its dilution in the form of a "rational basis" test for economic regulation—might be understood as a strategic calculation that the doctrine's substantive costs (in the form of judicial value-imposition) outweighed its procedural benefits (in the form of mitigation of special-interest influence).)

We might similarly understand much of modern "privacy"-based substantive due process as in fact serving DR-related procedural functions. Constitutional protection of an abortion right, for example, has the effect of eliminating or reducing a significant barrier to women's full and fair participation in democratic politics, namely the responsibilities of bearing and raising children, which, for a variety of reasons (some biological, some sociological), tend to devolve solely or predominantly on women.[110] The right to use contraceptives might be justified on similar grounds.[111] Constitutional protection of a right to same-sex intimacy might be necessary to counteract the work of factions, majority or minority, animated by personal bias against homosexuals or substantive prejudice (perhaps religiously inspired) with respect to the relevant issues. In this regard, the decision in *Lawrence v. Texas*, in which the Court used due process to invalidate a Texas law criminalizing same-sex sodomy, would be analogous to the requirement that economic regulations be rationally related to a legitimate governmental interest: In both contexts, the worry is that factions will legislate based on their own parochial interests or values rather than considerations of the broader public good.[112]

---

110. This is the central insight of a number of recent scholarly attempts to "rewrite" *Roe* as an equal-protection decision. *See, e.g.,* WHAT ROE V. WADE SHOULD HAVE SAID 31, 42–45 (Jack M. Balkin ed., 2005) ("opinion" of Jack M. Balkin); *id.* at 63, 63–82 ("opinion" of Reva B. Siegel). Hints of it also appear in the Court's *Casey* decision upholding the "central holding" of *Roe. See* Planned Parenthood v. Casey, 505 U.S. 833, 835 (1992) ("The ability of women to participate equally in the economic and social life of the Nation has been facilitated by their ability to control their reproductive lives.").

111. *See generally Griswold*, 381 U.S. at 485–86. In fact Justice William O. Douglas's opinion for the Court in *Griswold* expressly eschewed reliance on substantive due process in favor of a theory involving "penumbras" of privacy emanating from a number of provisions of the Bill of Rights. *See id.* at 481–82. Only the concurrences of Justices John Marshall Harlan and Byron White relied explicitly on substantive due process. *See id.* at 500, 503–04 (Harlan, J., concurring) (White, J., concurring). By virtue of its precedential influence in subsequent substantive due process cases, however, *Griswold* is now almost universally considered a *de facto* substantive due process decision. *See, e.g.,* Roe v. Wade, 410 U.S. 113, 129,155 (1973); Bowers v. Hardwick, 478 U.S. 186, 190–91 (1986); Washington v. Glucksberg, 521 U.S. 702, 720 (1997); *Casey*, 505 U.S. at 848–49; *Lawrence*, 539 U.S. at 564–66.

112. This way of understanding *Lawrence* illuminates the majority's caginess in that decision regarding the level of scrutiny it was applying. Much of Justice Anthony Kennedy's

On the other hand, not every aspect of contemporary substantive due process doctrine is comfortably justifiable on procedural grounds. In its 2000 decision in *Troxel v. Granville*, the Court invalidated a state law allowing "[a]ny person" to petition a court for the right of visitation of a minor child and requiring the court to order visitation in "the best interest of the child"; the Court invoked the "fundamental liberty interest[]" of parents "in the care, custody, and control of their children."[113] There certainly is a process-related danger in allowing the state to dictate a uniform educational program for every child; homogeny in education threatens subsequent homogeny in political views, thus compromising the central democratic advantage of broad political participation. And in fact the *Troxel* Court relied heavily on earlier decisions invalidating state bans on private-school education and the teaching of foreign languages.[114] But the decision in *Troxel* itself seems hard to interpret as an expression of this procedural concern. Allowing a court to grant visitation rights to nonparents without special deference to the parents' wishes poses no evident threat of rigid official indoctrination of uniform beliefs; nor is there reason to think that the law in question reflected some systemic bias against particular groups or prejudice with respect to the relevant issues.

---

opinion for the Court was devoted to undermining the Court's earlier holding in *Bowers v. Hardwick*, 478 U.S. 186 (1986), that same-sex intimacy was not a "fundamental right" and thus was undeserving of strict scrutiny pursuant to the Due Process Clause. *See Lawrence*, 539 U.S. at 567–68. But the *Lawrence* Court never actually declared that a "fundamental right" was involved in that case and thus never overtly applied strict scrutiny; instead it held that the Texas statute involved "furthers no legitimate state interest," thus employing the language of "rational basis" scrutiny. *See id.* at 578.

Justice Kennedy's opinion also made a point of citing *Romer v. Evans*, 517 U.S. 620 (1996), in which the Court had held that a Colorado ban on laws protecting homosexuals against discrimination was motivated by "animosity" toward homosexuals and thus could not survive rational-basis scrutiny under the Equal Protection Clause. *See id.* at 574–76. If we interpret *Lawrence* (and perhaps *Romer*) as responses to the problem of faction, the Court's use of rational-basis scrutiny to invalidate the laws in question—sometimes called "rational basis review with teeth"—makes some sense. On this view, the problem in *Lawrence* and *Romer* was that the political process had been compromised by bias against a particular minority group or prejudice with respect to the issues involved, in a way analogous to rent-seeking by economically motivated special interests.

113. Troxel v. Granville, 530 U.S. 57, 60, 65 (2000).

114. *See* Pierce v. Soc'y of Sisters, 268 U.S. 510 (1925) (invalidating a state law requiring that children be educated in public schools); Meyer v. Nebraska, 262 U.S. 390 (1923) (invalidating a state law prohibiting the teaching of foreign languages to children). We might classify *Brown v. Board of Education* as a response to similar concerns, except that enforced racial segregation in public schools fosters not homogeneity, but rather a sense of inferiority in students of the minority race and of superiority in students of the majority race (and thus a preordained partiality in the political process in which those students eventually will take part).

At bottom, though, it seems unlikely that the prominence of substantive due process doctrine in contemporary American constitutional law poses a dire threat to the DR account as an interpretation of our actual practice. If we fetishize the "substance" in substantive due process, viewing the doctrine as involving nothing more than judicial choices among controversial substantive values, then the doctrine will seem at odds with the DR approach. Typically, however, the doctrine need not be understood this way; much or most of it is consistent with the notion of constitutional law as a hedge against breakdowns in democratic authority. Of course, this is not to say that the content of substantive due process is somehow immune to reasonable disagreement. Obviously people disagree strongly about matters like abortion and gay rights; the point is that there is reason to think these disagreements cannot always be resolved acceptably using ordinary democracy alone.

8. FROM LAW TO PROCESS

I've argued here that constitutional authority can be justified as a way of preventing democratic malfunctions and of resolving disputes about democratic authority. A huge part of this account, however, has to do with process; at bottom, constitutional authority is justified, if at all, as the result of a procedure, or a series of procedures, that avoids the salient partiality problems that sometimes afflict ordinary democratic politics. But those procedures are part of an overall system that includes ordinary politics; and their justification depends on their capacity, not just to avoid occasional democratic partiality, but to do so in a way that does as little damage as possible to the other accuracy-promoting virtues that democracy embodies.

In the next (and final) chapter, I argue that the processes of American constitutional law—of framing, interpreting, and implementing constitutional rules—generally do an acceptable job of balancing externality from politics with responsiveness to it, and thus of accommodating reasonable impartiality with reasonable competence. American constitutional process, I'll contend, avoids the self-judging pathologies of democratic politics while ultimately honoring the primacy of democracy as a source of authoritative legal rules.

8. CONSTITUTIONAL PROCESS

The Dispute-Resolution (DR) account of constitutional authority depends in part on the substance of constitutional law—on the notion that constitutional doctrine can establish the basic elements of democracy and prevent them, as well as rules can do, from malfunctioning. But it depends at least as much on the procedure of constitutional law—on the idea that this doctrine can be created, interpreted, and applied by mechanisms that are more accurate, on the whole, than ordinary democracy itself for those purposes.

This chapter is about constitutional process, understood in this way. I will suggest here that the American model of constitutional process, writ large, is reasonably accurate as a way to manage the kinds of disputes with which constitutional law is properly concerned: disputes about the substance of constitutive and prophylactic democratic rules, and about whether democracy possesses authority in any particular instance. American constitutional process, I'll argue, can be seen as accurate along two dimensions, both of which should be fairly familiar by now. Compared to ordinary democracy, it is relatively *impartial*, precisely because it is generally *external* to ordinary democracy and the disputes that consume it. At the same time, our constitutional process retains significant indicia of democratic *competence*, principally because it manages to be *responsive* to ordinary democratic politics in a variety of ways despite its general externality to it.

I also will devote some time in this chapter to a special discussion of a perennial topic of debate within both the theory and the practice of American constitutional law, namely methodologies of constitutional interpretation. The DR account has something valuable to add to this debate, I think. It can illuminate both the appeal of formalist methodologies like originalism and textualism and their drawbacks (fatal ones, it turns out). At the same time, the DR account can underscore the need for *some* interpretive methodology, that is, for some methodology that qualifies as truly *interpretive*—as a good-faith attempt to apply existing constitutional norms, rather than simply to make up new ones. The latter is, in essence, what constitutional pragmatism recommends, and for reasons foreshadowed in Chapter 6, the DR account rejects pragmatism as a judicial philosophy in constitutional cases.

What the account supports instead is a version of the interpretive approach outlined in Chapter 5: a methodology that constrains judges to honoring the linguistic intent behind the constitutional text and implementing the best justification of the rule that text expresses. And the DR account also gives us a perspective on the difficult subject of constitutional precedent, supporting the notion that some acts of constitutional interpretation can take on, over time, authority akin to that of the constitutional text itself.

1. EXTERNALITY AND IMPARTIALITY

The dispute-resolution impetus behind constitutional law, we will recall from Chapter 7, is as follows. A democratic society will need to establish basic rules constituting its governing institutions and procedures in a way that takes advantage of the democratic procedural virtues outlined in Chapter 4. But democratic institutions and procedures—and thus democratic authority—are, inevitably, subject to malfunctions; no decision-procedure is perfect. The possibility of malfunction will, inevitably, generate disputes about whether democratic has, in any given instance, broken down. (Indeed, the inherent indeterminacy of concepts like "democracy," and of democratic virtues like broad participation, regular elections, and majority rule, will itself lead to inevitable disputes.) Some authoritative means of resolving these disputes will be required; but the institutions and procedures whose authority is at issue will be saliently partial and thus ill-suited to the task. A democratic society therefore will have reason to establish extrademocratic procedures for resolving democratic disputes. And it will have reason to make those disputes less frequent and less costly by means of *ex ante* legal rules—not just constitutive rules, but also prophylactic rules designed to prevent predictable sorts of malfunctions. There will be reason to establish extrademocratic mechanisms for generating those rules, too.

So: A key ingredient of a constitutional dispute-resolution procedure is what we might call *externality*. Constitutional processes (of *ex post* adjudication and of *ex ante* rulemaking) must be separate and apart, to a meaningful extent, from the procedures and institutions of ordinary democracy whose authority they will determine. This externality is necessary for the impartiality that justifies constitutional law in the first place.

It turns out that the things that are most familiar about constitutional law on the American model—and that are most roundly criticized about it—are precisely the things that give constitutional process its externality. The framework of American constitutional law consists of general rules created by distant generations with, in many respects, little in common with present-day Americans. The rules these Framers created are codified in a frequently inscrutable text whose interpretation occupies current generations, sometimes at the expense of direct engagement with the political and moral issues to which the text relates. And the chief agents of interpretation are elite professionals with little political accountability to the society their interpretations bind.

These are the most controversial aspects of American constitutional law. On the DR account, they also happen to be its most essential ingredients.

A. "The Dead Hand of the Past"
Although the precise sense in which the past matters to American constitutional process, and the degree to which it matters, are hotly contested—more on this later in the chapter—few deny that the past does matter in some important way.

The primary rules of constitutional law are embodied in the documentary text, and the most important provisions of that text were created roughly one and a half or two centuries ago. In some respects this seems the most troublesome aspect of constitutional law; for to be ruled, however loosely, by past generations is to be ruled to that extent not only by people other than ourselves, but by people so chronologically distant from us that we seem to have little in common with them. We cannot participate in the past; if the past rules us, it seems to do so with a dead hand, a judgment we have no power to influence. What could be less democratic than this?

Given that historiocracy is central both to American constitutional practice and to democracy-inspired worries about it, one would think it also would be central in some way to most defenses of constitutional law. But it is not, as we saw in the previous chapter. Substantive defenses care nothing for the past; they justify constitutional law by the results it generates, not by its pedigree. Footnote Four proceduralism and Bickelian dualism are indifferent to the past at best; they value the special role of courts in constitutional decisionmaking, and it is far from clear whether or how that role is aided by the need to interpret and implement something prior generations have done. The past is affirmatively threatening to reductionism, which values (or at least tolerates) constitutional law for its general consistency with evolving majoritarian preferences—evolving, that is, away from those of the generation that framed the document. Even Bruce Ackerman's brand of dualism, which celebrates the moments at which constitutional text is created, celebrates them despite the fact that they occurred in the past, not because of it. As I suggested in Chapter 7, the magic of Ackerman's constitutional moments—whatever is special about the process that creates the text—seems likely to fade with time, as those moments become more distant from "the actual people of the here and now."[1]

There is, of course, an unavoidable element of historiocracy in the notion of constitutive rules, which must be to some extent obdurate in order to function well.[2] Here again, though, it is not the rules' origin in the past that is their essential quality; what is important is simply their resistance to change. Constitutive rules could function just as well, *as* constitutive rules, whether they were established two centuries ago or only yesterday—so long as we're reasonably certain they will not change tomorrow. The property of obduracy tends to coincide with the property of antiquity, but they are not quite the same thing. And in any event, as we saw in the previous chapter, the basic constitutive function cannot

---

1. This is, again, Bickel's phrase. *See* ALEXANDER M. BICKEL, THE LEAST DANGEROUS BRANCH: THE SUPREME COURT AT THE BAR OF POLITICS 17 (2d ed. Yale Univ. Press 1986) (1962).

2. As Jeremy Waldron puts it, "Change the conventions of spelling [too often], and the Vice President may be unable to keep up." JEREMY WALDRON, DEMOCRACY AND DISAGREEMENT 277 (1999) [hereinafter WALDRON, DEMOCRACY AND DISAGREEMENT].

justify anything close to the full panoply of American constitutional practice. American constitutional law often does more than lay down the rules of democratic grammar; it purports to constrain what may be said using those rules.

We might attempt to defend this archaic element of constitutional practice using the idea of precommitment. As we saw in Chapter 2, a Kantian notion of autonomy turns on the capacity of the individual to govern herself, including laying down rules for herself that she then must follow (this is, literally, what "autonomy" means). If I want to lose weight, I might commit myself to following a strict diet and a regular exercise regimen. On those occasions when I am tempted to eat a big lunch or skip my workout, I might adhere to these commitments on the ground that doing so will advance my overall weight-loss plan. If I doubt my will power, I might establish enforcement mechanisms in advance—daily appointments with a dictatorial personal trainer, perhaps. One could hardly say that I am somehow sacrificing my autonomy by following my earlier commitments; instead this seems like "the epitome of self-government," as Jeremy Waldron acknowledges.[3]

Perhaps the same concept of precommitment can work, on a social scale, to justify the historiocratic quality of constitutional law. The people of a community, like an individual, might find it useful to make plans to which they then must adhere; they might decide that the cause of their own self-government, literally their democracy, would best be served by committing to the social analogue of a diet-and-exercise regimen (an imperative to treat each other with equal concern and respect, say), and they too might establish enforcement mechanisms—perhaps written constitutional principles and a politically insular court to enforce them against future lapses of will. Constitutional law thus might be understood to further democratic self-government rather than to impede it.

Notice, first of all, that this precommitment approach, like Ackerman's notion of constitutional moments or the need for constitutive rules, does not seem to justify historiocracy in itself. The authoritative force of an act of precommitment, if it has one, flows from the fact that the relevant actor—an autonomous individual or democratic community—has willingly engaged in that act as a means of carrying out its plans for self-development. The fact that the act of precommitment occurred in the past is, while inevitable, also incidental. Indeed, as with Ackermanian constitutional moments (and, arguably, with constitutive rules), the further into the past an act of precommitment took place, the weaker its normative force seems likely to be. The passage of time increases the likelihood that priorities will change and previous plans will come to seem foolish. I will say more on this point below.

Still, if the precommitment approach does not directly justify historiocracy, at least it seems inevitably to imply it. Since we experience the movement of time

---

3. *Id.* at 259.

in only one direction, keeping our commitments requires us to look to the past. But, as Jeremy Waldron has shown, the idea of precommitment ultimately disappoints as an attempt to explain constitutional authority.[4] Part of the problem tracks back to the failure of consensualist theories of legal authority discussed in Chapter 2. The idea of constitutional law as precommitment supposes an identity between the society that makes the commitment and the society that is bound by it. An actor, including a society, can further its autonomy by committing *itself* to follow a regimen and then following it; but autonomy is frustrated when the entity bound by the "commitment" is distinct from the entity that made it. And it is far from clear why we, "the actual people of the here and now," ought to think of ourselves as exactly the same "people" that established the rules of constitutional law 150 or 200 years ago.

This difficulty is not unique to the idea of collective precommitment. Individuals might become, in a sense, different people over time; Mel Brooks's 2000-Year-Old Man might not think of himself as the same person in year 2000 that he was in year 20. But the problem is exacerbated in the societal context, where even the biological identities of the actors disappear and are replaced over time. It is not just that the customs and mores and entire ways of life of Americans now differ vastly from those of Americans in 1787 or 1868; it's that the actual *Americans* now are, physically, different people from the Americans who existed then. No American alive now actually participated in the act of precommitment (if that's what it was) embodied in the ratification of the original Constitution in 1788, or of the Bill of Rights in 1791, or of the Fourteenth Amendment in 1868. The hand of the past, in this sense, truly is *dead*, and it is difficult to understand why we should think that the stroke of its pen was an act of precommitment by *us*, the living.

But suppose we can theorize around this identity problem (perhaps by invoking Edmund Burke's rhetorically compelling, if analytically mysterious, notion that generations of men must somehow "link with [one] another" to avoid becoming "little better than the flies of a summer"[5]). The precommitment approach suffers from another problem: Without some additional normative force besides the fact of a precommitment, the approach fails Aristotle's Challenge. To adhere to a commitment made by oneself at an earlier time is to acknowledge the authority of that commitment, and thus of one's earlier self. But why should I now, at time T, recognize the authority of myself in the past, at time T-n? Suppose that at time T-n, I made a commitment to exercise for an hour every day. Now, at time T, I am convinced that my time today would be better spent finishing my book manuscript. Why should I adhere to my earlier commitment when I now believe the result of doing so would be suboptimal?

---

4. *See id.* at 255–81.

5. Edmund Burke, Reflections on the Revolution in France 192–93 (L. G. Mitchell ed., Oxford Univ. Press 1993) (1790).

Perhaps I was then, at time *T-n*, in a better position than I am now, at time *T*, to make a good decision about how to behave now. (The metaphor here is Ulysses deciding, before encountering the Sirens, to tie himself to the mast, knowing that his faculties will be distorted once he hears the Sirens' song.) This is a version of the Epistemic-Guidance (EG) account of authority; it holds that I at time *T* have strong reason to adhere to the commitment I made at time *T-n* because I was more likely at *T-n* than I am at *T* to know how best to act. And of course it suffers from the same defect, the Encroachment Flaw, that afflicts all EG accounts. My belief now, at *T*, that the best thing for me to do is to work on my manuscript contradicts the commitment I made then, at *T-n*, and thus undermines my reason for thinking that I was then, at *T-n*, epistemically authoritative.

But perhaps my reason for adhering to my precommitment is simply that I recognize the value of precommitments to my autonomy: I know that I cannot truly govern myself without the capacity to make and keep commitments, and thus I see value in adhering to my commitments even in circumstances in which those commitments seem to produce suboptimal results. The obstacle to this view is the Problem of Exceptions. I may indeed believe that adhering to my commitments generally is the right thing to do; but I will recognize that there are exceptions, circumstances in which keeping a precommitment would be the wrong course of action. And I may well determine that the circumstance I face now, at time *T*, in choosing between exercising and finishing my book manuscript, is precisely such an exception. It can hardly be the right thing to do to keep a precommitment when doing so would produce the wrong results.

Even if we can overcome the generational identity problem, then, the idea of constitutional law as precommitment is, without more, deeply problematic. A political community will, like an individual, have reason to question the authority of its past self over its present self. In cases where the community is strongly convinced of the right thing to do, the fact that its past self thought otherwise is unlikely to provide a powerful counterargument.

Just as it does with legal authority generally, the DR account provides the crucial extra ingredient that justifies the historiocratic authority of constitutional law. The DR account sees the issue, not just as whether a political community at time *T* must defer to the judgment of the political community at time *T-n*, but as how best to resolve disputes within the political community at time *T* about how to act. This is where the analogy between individual and collective choice begins to fray at the edges: It is difficult to conceive of an individual disagreeing with herself in any meaningful way about how to act at time *T* and thus deferring to a decision she made at time *T-n* as a way of resolving the disagreement. (Granted, it is not impossible to imagine this; a person at time *T* might be confused or uncertain about how to act and thus might defer to her more-certain commitment at time *T-n* as a way to resolve the confusion.) It is natural, however, to think of a group of people—a political community, like the contemporary

United States—disagreeing among themselves about how to act at time *T*. The DR account holds that legal authority can be justified as a way of avoiding, mitigating, or resolving precisely this kind of social disagreement. And so that account might explain the community's deference, at *T*, to a decision it made at *T-n*—if that deference is a way to resolve disputes about how the community should act at *T*.

Why should the community at time *T* believe that deferring to rules that it (or some predecessor) laid down at time *T-n* can resolve its disputes about how to act? This is where the account of constitutional authority outlined in the previous chapter comes in. That account holds that some disputed issues—including issues involving the substance of rules designed to avoid democratic malfunctions—cannot be resolved by ordinary democratic politics with sufficient impartiality. What is needed to resolve them is a procedure that is external to ordinary democratic politics—and that is precisely what the historiocratic element of constitutional process can provide. A decision made in the past, at *T-n*, is a decision not made in the present, at *T*; a decision made by past generations is a decision not made by the current political process. A constitutional rule laid down 150 or 200 years ago by a generation of "Framers" thus is a rule that is external to today's democratic politics; and to resolve current disputes about democratic authority by reference to such an archaic rule is to resolve it in a way that, thanks to that externality, is relatively impartial.

The basic idea here—that disconnection from a dispute implies relative impartiality with respect to that dispute—is an applied version of John Rawls's famous heuristic of a "veil of ignorance."[6] In order to discern the best principles of justice, Rawls asked us to imagine what would be agreed to by institutional planners who know they will live in the society they are designing but do not know precisely what their place in that society will be. The resulting principles, Rawls suggested, would be reliable precisely because they would be untainted by their authors' knowledge of how they personally would fare pursuant to them. In the terminology of the DR account, the "veil of ignorance" serves as an ideally impartial way to generate basic principles of justice.

The process of framing a constitution obviously is an imperfect version of the veil of ignorance. The American Framers were designing a constitution not just for future generations, but also for themselves, and of course they could not claim any special impartiality with respect to the contemporary controversies that would be settled by their efforts. And while their circumstances were very different from our own, many of the central issues they faced—the role of religion in a democratic society, for example, or the balance between accountability and energy in the executive department—are, at a moderate level of specificity, the same issues we face today. In this sense, the Framers' partiality with

---

6. *See* John Rawls, A Theory of Justice 11–22 (1971).

respect to their own issues transposes to a sort of partiality with respect to our own. (This phenomenon suggests one reason—although I think not the only reason, and perhaps not even the primary one—why modern-day political conservatives tend to favor a methodology of constitutional interpretation that hews closely to the Framers' views. To the extent the Framers' 150- or 200-year-old views can be identified and applied to current controversies, those views tend, for obvious reasons, to appeal to today's conservatives.)

Imperfect though it is, reliance upon rules laid down by the Framers transfers some measure of decisionmaking authority from the saliently partial process of contemporary democratic politics to a process of archaic democratic politics that is, thanks to its chronological remove, somewhat less partial. And note that the further we move in time away from the Framing generation, the more external—and thus the more impartial—the Framing becomes with respect to current controversies. In this way the property of antiquity assumes, on the DR account, an affirmatively valuable role in the creation of constitutional authority. Our obsession with the constitutional past is revealed as fundamental to the function of constitutional law, not accidental, embarrassing, or downright detrimental as on the classic accounts.

Of course, externality, and the impartiality that comes with it, cannot be the only things that matter in constitutional process; otherwise we would gladly submit our constitutional disputes to institutions that are more external still, like the United Nations. (The recent furor over the Supreme Court's occasional citation of foreign and international law in constitutional cases confirms the unacceptability of such a strategy.)[7] Competence matters, too, and competence depends on some degree of responsiveness to popular and political inputs, as I will explain below. For present purposes, the point is simply this: The need for impartiality that the DR account reveals can explain the historiocratic element of American constitutional law in a way that the classic defenses cannot.

---

7. In *Lawrence v. Texas*, 539 U.S. 558, 572–73, 576–77 (2003), Justice Anthony Kennedy's opinion for the Court cited foreign statutes and decisions in support of its invalidation of a state law prohibiting same-sex sodomy; in *Roper v. Simmons*, 543 U.S. 551, 576–78 (2005), Kennedy's opinion for the Court cited a U.N. convention and legislation in other nations in holding that capital punishment is unconstitutional for juvenile offenders. Conservatives in Congress responded by introducing legislation purporting to prohibit federal courts from "rely[ing] upon any. . . law. . . [or] judicial decision. . . of any foreign state or international organization or agency" in interpreting the federal Constitution. Constitution Restoration Act of 2005, S. 520, 109th Cong. § 201 (2005). The legislation went nowhere, but the political outcry was significant. *See* Jeffery Toobin, *Swing Shift: How Anthony Kennedy's Passion for Foreign Law Could Change the Supreme Court*, THE NEW YORKER, Sept. 12, 2005, at 42–51.

B. The Text

Americans are used to the idea of following written laws, and so the binding nature of the constitutional text in our practice is perhaps less controversial than the fact that the text was, in the most important instances, authored many generations ago. But critics of constitutional law often focus on the text as an especially troublesome aspect of the enterprise. Waldron, for example, objects that American constitutional law tends to focus on the "canonical form of words" in which provisions happen to be expressed, at the expense of a direct engagement with the underlying rights and other principles at stake.[8] Courts and other interpreters, he worries, "tend to be distracted in their arguments about rights by side arguments about how a text like the Bill of Rights is best approached by judges."[9] The presence of a canonical text tends, on this view, to obfuscate rather than elucidate the important issues.

Here too, the classic defenses of constitutional law hardly provide a powerful rejoinder to Waldron's critique. Whether the text is a help or a hindrance on a substantive approach like Dworkin's depends entirely on whether the text can be read to protect the "correct" principles. A Footnote Four proceduralist can only be distracted by the happenstance of the text in pursuing a more fair democratic process; excessive attention to the text leads, in John Hart Ely's words, to "a clause-bound interpretivism."[10] Bickelian dualism hinges on judges' capacity "to follow the ways of the scholar in pursuing the ends of government" (Alexander Bickel),[11] on "the independence that comes with life tenure" (Christopher Eisgruber)[12]—neither of which has anything obvious to do with the task of interpreting a text. And the text, like resort to the history of its framing, typically stands in opposition to the reductionist project of bringing constitutional law in line with trends in majority opinion. Only Ackerman's dualist approach locates affirmative value in the constitutional text, which embodies the "higher law" made during a "constitutional moment"; but even Ackerman is compelled to downplay the significance of text in insisting that some constitutional moments— the New Deal, for example—can revolutionize the Constitution's meaning without altering its language one iota.[13]

---

8. Jeremy Waldron, *The Core of the Case Against Judicial Review*, 115 YALE L.J. 1346, 1381 (2006) [hereinafter Waldron, *Core Case*].

9. *Id.*

10. *See* JOHN HART ELY, DEMOCRACY AND DISTRUST: A THEORY OF JUDICIAL REVIEW 11 (1980).

11. BICKEL, *supra* note 1, at 25–26.

12. CHRISTOPHER L. EISGRUBER, CONSTITUTIONAL SELF-GOVERNMENT 58 (2001).

13. *See* 1 BRUCE ACKERMAN, WE THE PEOPLE: FOUNDATIONS 119 (1991) ("Roosevelt and the New Deal Congress had not chosen to codify their new constitutional principles by enacting a few formal amendments, of the sort contemplated by Article Five. Instead, the President and Congress left it to the Justices themselves to codify the New Deal revolution in a series of transformative judicial opinions. . . .").

The DR account, in contrast, can explain the centrality of the documentary text to American constitutional practice. The text communicates constitutional rules, and as we saw in Chapter 4, general rules can assist in resolving particular disputes by eliminating some issues that the disputants otherwise might fight about. Disputes about democratic authority—about whether a given law or other product of ordinary democracy is authoritative or rather reflects some fatal malfunction—can be resolved more easily if the applicable normative standards have been settled, or at least partly settled, in advance. By communicating the fundamental ground rules of democratic authority, the constitutional text therefore can narrow the scope of disputes, allowing the parties to focus on the facts and equities of the particular case rather than first principles. Of course a written text is not strictly necessary to serve this function (and indeed writing rules down cannot avoid disputes over their meaning in particular cases, as Chapter 4 demonstrated). But a written text is likely to serve this dispute-narrowing objective better than other conceivable ways of communicating rules (oral tradition, for example).

As we also saw in Chapter 4, rules, including written rules, can be the subjects of dispute as well as the remedy for it. Disputing parties will not accept the text's contribution to resolving their disagreement unless they view the substance of that contribution as authoritative. Textual rules, like all purportedly authoritative rules, must be the products of a procedure that is, *ex ante*, reasonably accurate in order to help resolve, *ex post*, particular disputes to which they are relevant. This means (among other things) that the process of generating a textual rule must be suitably impartial; and in the context of constitutional law, it means the process must be meaningfully external to the process of ordinary democratic politics that will be governed by its rules. This is where the past comes in: The constitutional text is the product of an archaic act of Framing which is, by virtue of its antiquity, independent of contemporary politics and thus relatively impartial with respect to it. The historiocratic nature of the Framing promotes the impartiality of constitutional rules, while the text allows those externally generated rules to be understood and applied in contemporary disputes.

C. Judicial Review

As troubling as the historiocracy and textualism of American constitutional practice are to many critics, by far its most controversial feature is judicial review. The reason for this is simple: Modern commentators recognize that history and text are vastly indeterminate in their exposition of constitutional rules (more on these points below) and that judicial interpretation of those rules therefore is the heart of the enterprise. Given the wide discretion that judges typically possess in determining what, on a particular set of facts, the Constitution means, the fact that judges are *judges*—nonelective (in the federal system), lifetime-tenured, and thus relatively unaccountable through political means—presents an obvious challenge in an ostensibly democratic system. As Waldron puts the point:

> The system of legislative elections is not perfect . . ., but it is evidently supe-
> rior as a matter of democracy and democratic values to the indirect and lim-
> ited basis of democratic legitimacy for the judiciary. Legislators are regularly
> accountable to their constituents and they behave as though their electoral
> credentials were important in relation to the overall ethos of their participa-
> tion in political decisionmaking. None of this is true of Justices.[14]

As I suggested in Chapter 5, and as I will elaborate later in this chapter, American-style adjudication—including (perhaps especially) in constitutional cases—embodies more in the way of "democratic values" than Waldron perhaps gives it credit for. My task at the moment, however, is to defend precisely that aspect of judicial review that Waldron and others find most offensive: its relative insulation from the institutions and procedures of ordinary democratic politics. The grounds of that defense should be evident by now: Judicial review consti-tutes a meaningfully external, and thus relatively impartial, mechanism for the application of general constitutional rules to particular democratic disputes.

Justifying judicial review based on the fact of (relative) judicial independence is of course nothing new. Alexander Hamilton famously made judicial indepen-dence the centerpiece of his defense, in *Federalist No. 78*, of Article III's provi-sion for tenure of judicial service "during good Behaviour."[15] Hamilton's professed confidence in absolute judicial impartiality ("The judiciary. . . may truly be said to have neither FORCE nor WILL but merely judgment"[16]) seems naïve to us now; it is silly to think that judges somehow can entirely divorce themselves from their predilections when they decide cases. But Hamilton, ever the realist, almost certainly recognized the hyperbole in his description. His deeper point went not to judicial objectivity, but to judicial independence from the political branches: If judges held their offices "by a temporary commission," with the power to reappoint them "committed either to the executive or to the legislature[,] there would be a danger of improper complaisance to the branch which possessed it."[17] Judicial independence from the political branches, and indeed from "the people themselves. . . whenever a momentary inclination happens to lay hold of a majority" of them[18]—independence, that is, from the processes of ordinary democratic politics—was necessary for Hamilton, not because independent judges magically attain perfect objectivity, but because

---

14. Waldron, *Core Case*, *supra* note 8, at 1391.
15. U.S. CONST. art. III, § 1; *see* THE FEDERALIST No. 78, at 436 (Alexander Hamilton) (Isaac Kramnick ed., 1987) [hereinafter Hamilton, FEDERALIST No. 78].
16. Hamilton, FEDERALIST No. 78, *supra* note 15, at 437.
17. *Id.* at 441.
18. *Id.* at 440.

independent judges are for that reason *external* judges, relatively untethered to the system whose authority they must assess and thus relatively impartial when that authority is questioned.

The advantage of judicial review on the DR account, then, is its potential for externality and thus for impartiality with respect to ordinary politics. The relative lack of accountability of which Waldron and other critics complain is precisely the feature that justifies judicial review. This suggests, on the one hand, that realist-inspired critiques of judicial review miss the mark, at least if their target is understood to be the practice of judicial review itself. Mark Tushnet, for example, has argued that, since politically liberal judges tend to reach politically liberal results and politically conservative judges tend to reach politically conservative ones, we might as well "take the Constitution away" from the judges and allow its meaning to be fought out in the political arena.[19] This view owes much to the "attitudinal model" of judicial behavior developed by political scientists, which holds that the primary determinant of judicial decisions is the "attitudes" or ideology of the judges making them.[20] As Waldron summarizes the argument: "If it is simply preferences versus preferences, or attitudes versus attitudes. . . then surely the only thing to do. . . is to let the numbers count"—that is, to implement the attitudes of the political majority.[21]

This critique contains a large component of factual truth; it seems undeniable that judges' political and moral "attitudes" do indeed influence their decisions, although the degree of this influence is open to considerable empirical debate.[22] And as a way to evaluate particular judicial decisions, particular judges,

---

19. *See generally* MARK V. TUSHNET, TAKING THE CONSTITUTION AWAY FROM THE COURTS 54–56 (1999).

20. *See* JEFFREY A. SEGAL & HAROLD J. SPAETH, THE SUPREME COURT AND THE ATTITUDINAL MODEL (1993); JEFFREY A. SEGAL & HAROLD J. SPAETH, THE SUPREME COURT AND THE ATTITUDINAL MODEL REVISITED (2002).

21. WALDRON, DEMOCRACY AND DISAGREEMENT, *supra* note 2, at 184. I have quoted Waldron somewhat out of context here; he is referring not simply to the idea that judges' "attitudes" determine their decisions, but to the argument that, if there is no moral objectivity—if "moral and political views are merely matters of attitude"—then the only fair way to resolve political and moral disputes is to allow the majority of the community to do so. *Id.* Waldron, as a moral realist—that is, a believer in objective morality—rejects this particular argument against judicial review. *See id.* (Note, by the way, the important distinction between "moral realism," which is the view that morality has actual objective content, and American "legal realism," which is the view that judicial decisions are not significantly constrained by preexisting legal rules (and which often is coupled with the "attitudinal" model of judicial behavior).)

22. *See, e.g.,* Thomas J. Miles & Cass R. Sunstein, *The New Legal Realism,* 75 U. CHI. L. REV. 831 (2008) (summarizing recent research on the determinants of judicial decisions); Brian Z. Tamanaha, *The Distorting Slant in Quantitative Studies of Judging,* 50 B.C. L. REV. 685 (2009) (arguing that quantitative studies overstate the degree to which judicial ideology determines decisions).

or particular courts, the critique is of course useful: We can criticize Judge A on the ground that her politics play too large a role in her decisionmaking, or (if we believe politics *always* plays a large role) on the ground that her politics, and thus her decisions, are too far to the left or to the right. But the critique misses the point of judicial review *as an institution*. That point is not to remove personal ideology from constitutional decisionmaking; the point is to remove constitutional decisionmaking from ordinary politics. Constitutional law is a response to the problem that political institutions and actors typically will be strongly self-interested in the question of their own authority, and thus strongly partial in resolving disputes about that authority. Externalizing constitutional decisions from those self-interested political institutions and actors—by assigning it to a process that depends upon rules made by previous generations, embodied in a text, and interpreted by politically insular judges—is a way to mitigate this partiality problem. It is not, and should not purport to be, a way to filter all ideology from the process.

The realist critique of judicial review does, however, highlight again the fact that externality from ordinary politics cannot be the only measure of constitutional authority. As applied to judicial review, this truth has two dimensions. First (and as the realists point out), judges may typically escape the particular kind of partiality that affects the political process—an inherent bias in favor of the authority of that process—but surely they have all sorts of other biases that they cannot completely evade. Conservative judges are partial toward politically conservative results, liberal justices toward politically liberal ones, and so on. A system of constitutional decisionmaking in which judges have unfettered power to impose their views on the rest of us would be so far from democracy as to be facially unacceptable; it would be scarcely better than a version of Hobbesian absolutism. Some meaningful constraints must be imposed on constitutional judges, then, for the system to claim authority.

Second, as we saw in Chapter 3, even a completely impartial system would not be sufficiently accurate without some degree of competence. Perhaps more to the point, a community will not accept a dispute-resolution process as accurate unless the community perceives that the process is reasonably competent. And it seems highly unlikely that Americans would acknowledge the general accuracy of judicial review, or of the constitutional process as a whole, if the process were entirely disconnected from the substantive values of the American mainstream. A Supreme Court whose constitutional decisions persistently deviate from what most Americans believe is right is a Court whose authority is likely, in the long term, to wear thin. Meaningful externality to politics therefore cannot imply a hermetic seal between judicial review and public opinion.

These observations suggest that constitutional externality to politics must be balanced with constitutional responsiveness to politics if the result is to be a generally authoritative process. Constitutional process must be meaningfully external to politics, but it cannot be entirely so. I argue below that popular and political influences seep into constitutional process from a number of sources, promoting medium- to long-term responsiveness while still preserving the distance necessary for relative impartiality.

2. RESPONSIVENESS AND COMPETENCE

As we saw in the previous chapter and above, most of the classic defenses of constitutional law celebrate its externality from ordinary politics. Aside from reductionism, however, which is the salient exception to this tendency, the classic approaches tend to ignore, even to be flummoxed by, the extent to which constitutional law is responsive to political and popular influence. The critics, for their part, typically question constitutional law precisely because of its externality; they too overlook its responsiveness.

I will contend here that American constitutional law is politically responsive along three distinct dimensions, each of which serves in its own way to tether constitutional doctrine to mainstream American understandings, thus promoting a general belief in constitutional competence and cabining the inevitable partiality of judges. Two of these dimensions are familiar from the classic defenses, and I will touch on them only briefly here. As Ackerman and others have emphasized, the process of framing the constitutional text typically has been extraordinarily participatory and deliberative, creating a wellspring of perceived competence that, despite our increasing chronological distance from those "constitutional moments," has not yet run dry. And as reductionist theorists have noted, the political dynamics of American constitutional law—the extent to which ordinary politics determines who will make constitutional decisions and whether and how those decisions will be implemented—seems, in the long run, to bring constitutional doctrine into line, more or less, with the election returns (although there is much nuance to be acknowledged in this respect).

The third dimension of constitutional responsiveness has been only dimly perceived in the classic theories, and I will spend most of my time on it in this section. This is the degree to which the process of American constitutional adjudication itself typically incorporates diverse popular and political participation. We got a sense in Chapter 5 of the participatory quality of adversary adjudication, and here I will expand that discussion to focus on the special nature of participation in constitutional and other important public-law cases.

A. The Framing(s)

Recall from Chapter 3 that accuracy is only partly a procedural value; it is concerned ultimately with results, albeit results in a general, systemic sense, not on a case-by-case basis. Disputants initially might accept a procedure to resolve their disputes on grounds primarily, even exclusively, of its impartiality, its neutrality with respect to the disputants themselves and their substantive positions in the dispute. Over time, though, it would be foolish for a disputant to continue to adhere to a procedure that has, by her lights, consistently generated substantively poor results—even if she continues to believe in the impartiality of that procedure. A procedure's competence—more to the point, the impression of its competence among those who will be bound by it—is every bit as important as its impartiality to its long-term authority.

I've argued that constitutional law is justified, as an alternative to ordinary democracy, mostly by its comparative impartiality with respect to questions of democracy's own authority. But we cannot neglect the competence side of the equation. A constitutional process that is, compared to ordinary democracy, relatively impartial but also relatively incompetent might not be worth the candle. And one obvious difficulty in this respect is that American constitutional law appears to have originated in a Framing act performed more than 200 years ago by "rich white men,"[23] "arrogantly self-satisfied Anglo-chauvinist[s]," "gentlemen in funny clothes" who seem to have "no more intimate connection to our [current] political identity than Martians."[24] Why should Americans today attribute any competence whatsoever to the deliberations of these distant ancestors—why should we think they somehow had the capacity to speak, through their archaic rules, to our distinctive modern problems? The very externality of the Framing process seems to weigh heavily against its relevance and thus its competence.

There is a reasonably satisfactory answer to these questions, I think, and it comes in two complementary parts. The first part is the fact that the Framing, while chronologically and culturally distant from today's America, was nonetheless an extraordinarily participatory and deliberative act, even (in some ways especially) by modern standards. The Framing thus can claim a good deal of democratic competence despite its undeniable flaws. And these qualities of special participation and deliberation have been repeated, for the most part, in the subsequent mini-Framings instantiated by periodic constitutional amendments.

The second part of the answer is that the Framers, to paraphrase John Marshall, did not forget that it was a *constitution* they were creating.[25] They recognized the limits of their own competence, and so, on most of the crucial issues, they drafted constitutional rules not as detailed, rigid prescriptions but as relatively abstract, flexible principles. In doing so, the Framers gave us the ben-

---

23. AKHIL REED AMAR, AMERICA'S CONSTITUTION: A BIOGRAPHY 14 (2005). Amar is engaging in self-conscious caricature here; an important thesis of his book is that the Framing of the original Constitution was in fact extraordinarily participatory by the standards of the time.

24. ACKERMAN, *supra* note 13, at 166. Ackerman too is rhetorically exaggerating a stereotype with which he largely disagrees.

25. *See* McCulloch v. Maryland, 17 U.S. (4 Wheat.) 316, 407 (1819) ("In considering this question, then, we must never forget that it is a *constitution* we are expounding.").

efit of their collective wisdom on the core values of democratic government—on its "great outlines," in Marshall's words—while leaving us free to fill in the "minor ingredients" for ourselves.[26]

(i) Superdemocracy The adoption of the original American Constitution between 1787 and 1790 was, as constitutional historian Akhil Amar writes, "the most democratic deed the world had ever seen" in the late eighteenth century.[27] It included an "extraordinarily extended and exclusive ratification process"[28] that followed "the widest imaginable participation rules."[29] The constitutional text was hammered out in Philadelphia during the summer of 1787 by delegates from twelve of the thirteen existing states[30] and then submitted, pursuant to its own Article VII, to specially assembled popular conventions in each state for approval. Those conventions

> aim[ed] to represent "the People" in a particularly emphatic way—more directly than ordinary legislatures. Taking their cue from the Preamble's bold "We the People" language, several states waived standard voting restrictions and allowed a uniquely broad class of citizens to vote for ratification-convention delegates. For instance, New York temporarily set aside its usual property qualifications and, for the first time in its history, invited all free adult male citizens to vote. Also, states generally allowed an especially broad group of Americans to serve as ratifying-convention delegates. . . . All told, eight states elected convention delegates under special rules that were more populist and less property-focused than normal, and two others followed standing rules that let virtually all taxpaying adult male citizens to vote.[31]

Of course, women and slaves were excluded from participation in the Framing process, a reflection of the dominant attitudes of even the more enlightened inhabitants of late-eighteenth-century America. (Amar attributes the exclusion in part to the fact that women and slaves did not take up arms in collective self-defense, a commonly understood prerequisite to citizenship in the political theory of the day.[32]) The process was far from ideally participatory, but it nonetheless was remarkably so—more participatory than the normal mode of representative democracy in most of the states, and easily participatory enough to rebut any casual charge of elitism, even by modern standards.

---

26. *Id.*

27. AMAR, *supra* note 23, at 5.

28. *Id.* at 7.

29. *Id.* at 18. They were "[t]he widest rules imaginable *in the eighteenth century*, of course." *Id.* (emphasis added).

30. Rhode Island was the nonconformist exception. It also was the last of the original thirteen states to ratify the Constitution, in 1790.

31. AMAR, *supra* note 23, at 7 (citations omitted).

32. *See id.* at 19.

Popular participation in the ratification process was unusual in other ways as well. State legislatures were, and still are, elected to conduct the ongoing business of government, encompassing a variety of issues from the momentous to the mundane and doing so over a period, typically, of two or more years between elections. But the ratifying conventions of 1787–1790 were focused on a single question—whether to adopt the new Constitution—and on the tightly connected body of particular issues that question invoked. Much more than was (or is) typically the case, voters for convention delegates were voting for *ideas,* not primarily for people. The results in each state thus reflected a highly atypical degree of popular attention to a particular set of problems regarding democratic government.

The Framing was, moreover, a supermajoritarian affair. Votes in each state convention were subject to simple majority rule, but Article VII of the Constitution, which governed the document's own ratification, required approval by conventions in nine of the thirteen states before the instrument could take effect (and made it binding only "between the States so ratifying" the document).[33] The consequence was to require something reasonably close to the assent of a supermajority of voting citizens. For reasons we've touched on already, supermajority rule is an antidemocratic way to run the day-to-day business of government; it has the effect of narrowing effective participation, not broadening it, by giving a veto to a minority. But supermajority rule is only problematic in this sense when it fails to materialize. A measure that actually earns supermajority approval is the product of broader effective participation than a measure approved by a simple majority. And so the fact that the original Constitution was approved by something approximating a supermajority of American citizens (again, admittedly with women and slaves excluded) between 1787 and 1790 bespeaks an extraordinary level of effective participation in the process.

The Framing thus can be understood as a supermajoritarian act of popular assent to a relatively focused collection of governing principles. But the idea of "popular assent" is still too thin a conception of what actually occurred in the process. The actual voting by citizens in each state took place only after an extended and intense series of deliberations, first by the drafters of the text at the Philadelphia convention, then by defenders and detractors of the text in the public forum; the final votes of each state convention followed yet further deliberations in those conventions themselves. Although the debates of the Philadelphia convention were kept secret (precisely to promote open and honest deliberation among the delegates),[34] the public and the state-convention delegates

---

33. *See* U.S. Const. art. VII.

34. An official journal of the convention's proceedings was kept, but it was not made public until Congress ordered its publication in 1818. The notes of a number of convention participants, most notably James Madison, were published gradually thereafter. For an account of the publication history of records of the Philadelphia convention, see

had ample access to competing views in the form of essays and speeches by prominent proponents and opponents of ratification. (The *Federalist Papers*, of course, were foremost among these.)[35] Within the ratifying conventions, debates often were protracted (and the final votes often correspondingly close).[36] The modern reader perusing the surviving elements of each of these debates—in the Philadelphia convention, in speeches and the press, and in the state ratification conventions—is likely to be struck by the fact that their quality (if not always their tone) is exceedingly and almost uniformly high. The antagonists were articulate, learned, dedicated men (albeit all *men*) who regularly and directly engaged one another on fundamental issues of political theory. There is very little in their deliberations that is trivial or obtuse, and almost nothing that is casual or careless. As Michael Meyerson has written, "the ratification conflict was waged on an intellectual plane that is difficult to imagine today."[37]

The extraordinary breadth of participation in the original Framing; the fact that the delegates to the state conventions were elected directly by the citizenry for the sole purpose of deliberating and voting on the proposed Constitution; and the large quantity and high quality of the public and political debates leading to ratification combine to suggest a process with a legitimate claim to a special degree of democratic competence. Ackerman takes the Framing as his template of "higher lawmaking," with its successive phases: "signaling" (convincing a majority to view the issues involved with more gravity than ordinary politics allows), "proposal" (offering specific steps for reform), "mobilized popular deliberation" (testing these proposals against conservative resistance in a repeated, sustained way), and "legal codification" (giving the proposals status as

---

Max Farrand, *Introduction* to 1 THE RECORDS OF THE FEDERAL CONVENTION OF 1787, at xi, xi–xxv (Max Farrand ed., rev. ed. 1966). Farrand's three-volume *Records*, along with a more-recently published *Supplement*, remains the definitive collection of official and first-hand accounts of the deliberations at the convention.

35. *See generally* Isaac Kramnick, *Editor's Introduction* to THE FEDERALIST PAPERS 11, 36–40 (Isaac Kramnick ed., 1987); MICHAEL I. MEYERSON, LIBERTY'S BLUEPRINT: HOW MADISON AND HAMILTON WROTE THE FEDERALIST PAPERS, DEFINED THE CONSTITUTION, AND MADE DEMOCRACY SAFE FOR THE WORLD 75–108 (2008).

For a collection of published essays, speeches, private letters, and excerpts from state-convention debates relating to ratification, see 1 THE DEBATE ON THE CONSTITUTION: FEDERALIST AND ANTIFEDERALIST SPEECHES, ARTICLES, AND LETTERS DURING THE STRUGGLE OVER RATIFICATION (Bernard Bailyn ed., 1993) [hereinafter 1 DEBATE ON THE CONSTITUTION]; 2 THE DEBATE ON THE CONSTITUTION: FEDERALIST AND ANTIFEDERALIST SPEECHES, ARTICLES, AND LETTERS DURING THE STRUGGLE OVER RATIFICATION (Bernard Bailyn ed., 1993) [hereinafter 2 DEBATE ON THE CONSTITUTION].

36. For excerpts from many of these debates, see 1 DEBATE ON THE CONSTITUTION, *supra* note 35, at 789–945; 2 DEBATE ON THE CONSTITUTION, *supra* note 35, at 575–917.

37. MEYERSON, *supra* note 35, at ix.

binding law).[38] Ackerman argues, convincingly, that the most significant amendments to the original Constitution were the products of similarly super-democratic processes: the addition of the Bill of Rights in 1791 (which is best understood as part of the original Framing)[39] and of the Reconstruction Amendments between 1865 and 1870.[40] The Constitution's Article V, after all, specifies a formal amendment process that, like the Framing itself, is superma-joritarian and thus almost inevitably highly deliberative.[41]

But a large part of Ackerman's point is that the Constitution's formal amend-ment procedures are, in a real sense, irrelevant: Extraordinary elements of par-ticipation and deliberation have to exist for dramatic constitutional change to occur, and when they exist the technical legal prerequisites for that change are more or less superfluous. The Framing itself was an illegal act if assessed by the law ostensibly in force when it happened; the Reconstruction Amendments were, at the very least, procedurally irregular.[42] Ackerman, in fact, considers the New Deal to be a period of "higher lawmaking" despite its failure to generate any formal amendments, on the ground that it matches his four-step template of a "constitutional moment."[43]

We need not agree with all the details of Ackerman's analysis to accept its basic thrust: The most important provisions of the Constitution's documentary text have resulted from periods of exceptional and sustained participatory deliberation. The Framing moments have been characterized, in this sense, not by a rejection of democracy but by a wholesale embrace of it. If strong indica-tions of competence, and thus powerful strains of authority, flow from the deliberation and broad participation typically found in democratic government, then they flow in at least that degree from the same features of constitutional lawmaking.

(ii) The "Great Outlines" of the Constitutional Text But what were the Framing generations deliberating about? Decidedly not, as John Marshall put it, "a legal code"—a collection of detailed rules for how the government they were creating would operate.[44] The problem with such an approach would not simply have

---

38. *See* ACKERMAN, *supra* note 13, at 266–94.

39. *See id.* at 40.

40. *See id.* at 40, 44–47, 81–86.

41. In order for the Constitution to be amended pursuant to Article V, two-thirds majorities in each house of Congress first must approve an amendment; it then must be ratified by the legislatures of, or conventions in, three-fourths of the states. *See* U.S. CONST. art. V.

42. On the illegality of the original Framing, see ACKERMAN, *supra* note 13, at 41–42, 173–75. On the procedural irregularity of the Reconstruction Amendments, see *id.* at 42, 44–47.

43. *See id.* at 40, 47–50, 103–04, 105–30.

44. McCulloch v. Maryland, 17 U.S. (4 Wheat.) 316, 407 (1819).

been the one Marshall identified in *McCulloch v. Maryland*: that a detail-laden document, in its "prolixity. . ., could scarcely be embraced by the human mind. It would probably never be understood by the public."⁴⁵ The larger difficulty would have been one not of comprehensibility, but of competence: The more the Framers had attempted to resolve particular disputes preemptively by drafting exhaustive legal rules, the more quickly their competence to do so would have run dry. As the Framing generations well knew, they lacked the capacity to foresee even a small fraction of the infinite variety of disputes about democracy that might arise in the future. And as the wisest among them surely understood, any attempt to prescribe detailed rules governing issues that they *could* anticipate risked being treated with increasing skepticism by each successive generation. The presumptive competence of the Framing process would quickly be outweighed, in the minds of later Americans, by the growing chronological distance between the world as the Framers knew it and the world each subsequent generation faced.

It is no accident, therefore, that most of the important provisions of the Constitution's text are expressed in relatively abstract, open-textured language. The document uses strikingly nebulous phrases—"legislative Powers," "[t]he executive Power," "[t]he judicial Power"—to describe the functions of the three branches of the government it creates.⁴⁶ The categories of things that government is empowered to accomplish are, in many cases, identified using similarly indeterminate language: to "collect taxes. . . to. . . provide for the general Welfare"; to "regulate Commerce. . . among the several States"; to "enforce, by appropriate legislation, the provisions of" the Fourteenth Amendment; to "make all Laws which shall be necessary and proper for carrying into Execution" its other powers.⁴⁷ And of course there are the Constitution's important individual-rights provisions, which guarantee such imprecise concepts as "the free exercise" of religion, "the freedom of speech," "due process of law," and "the equal protection of the laws."⁴⁸

This is not to say that the constitutional text lacks relatively specific provisions. Many of these were the products of negotiated compromises among the Framers, like Article I's infamous Three-Fifths Clause, which apportioned representation in the House by awarding slave states the equivalent of 60 percent of a free person for each (nonvoting) slave, or the equally infamous Migration or Importation Clause, which protected the slave trade until 1808.⁴⁹ (Both of these were extracted by the South in exchange for allowing the national government

---

45. *Id.*
46. *See,* respectively, U.S. CONST. art. I; art. II, § 1, cl. 1; art. III, § 1.
47. *See,* respectively, *id.* art. I, § 8, cls. 1, 3; amend. XIV, § 5; art. I, § 8, cl. 18.
48. *See,* respectively, *id.* amend. I; amend. V; amend. XIV, §1.
49. *See,* respectively, *id.* art. I, § 2, cl. 3; art. I, § 9, cl. 1.

to regulate commerce;[50] neither remains in force today.[51]) Many others reflect the need to draw more-or-less arbitrary lines in order to establish the basic ground rules of governmental institutions, such as the maximum number of constituents per Representative (30,000) and the particular numerical requirements to override presidential vetoes or propose constitutional amendments (two-thirds in each chamber) and to ratify those amendments (three-fourths of the states).[52]

It is fair to say, however, that most of these comparatively determinate textual provisions reflect judgments that are relatively noncontingent on chronological or factual happenstance. Thirty thousand may or may not make sense as the maximum number of constituents per Representative, but that is not a question whose answer seems likely to change radically over time or with subtle differences in facts. By contrast, the question of what constitutes "due process of law" (for example) seems relatively contingent in both these senses: Its answer depends heavily on the facts of the particular case, and how it is answered seems likely to evolve from generation to generation. On these types of question—large issues of political morality concerning liberty, equality, due process, freedom of religion and expression, and the like—the constitutional language is notably skeletal, both in the sense of providing a core framework and in the sense of leaving considerable flesh to be added to its bare bones.

The result is a balance, struck at the various moments of Framing, between superdemocratic consensus on the one hand and the need for continuing flexibility on the other. We, "the actual people of the here and now" in Bickel's phrase, can respect the judgments of the Framers—can attribute significant competence to those judgments—by virtue of the extraordinarily participatory and deliberative processes by which the text was framed. And, while that respect seems likely to fade with the increasing distance of time, we can recognize that the issues the Framers actually decided tend to be foundational ones of principle, not matters of transitory detail. The Framers, through their exceptionally participatory and deliberative process, determined that freedom of speech and of religion, due process of law, equal protection, separation of powers, federalism, and the like are fundamental values of an authoritative democracy. Those values, for the most part, seem universal enough to evade historical contingency; there is little reason to think the Framers' judgments with respect to them have

---

50. *See* Joseph J. Ellis, Founding Brothers: The Revolutionary Generation 94 (2001) (describing the "Sectional Compromise" by which the northern states agreed to protect slavery in return for the southern states' agreement to allow Congress to regulate commerce by simple majority vote).

51. The Migration or Importation Clause died a natural death when it expired in 1808; the Three-Fifths Clause was rendered meaningless by the Thirteenth Amendment, which prohibited slavery, and expressly superseded by Section 2 of the Fourteenth Amendment.

52. *See*, respectively, U.S. Const. art. I, § 2, cl. 3; art. I, § 7, cl. 2; art. V.

become suspect with the passage of time. We ourselves may endorse or reject them, but if we do reject them it will not be on the ground that the Framers' understandings about free expression, equality, divided government, and the like are irredeemably archaic.

As this line of reasoning suggests, there is a crucial difference, in terms of competence, between the Framers' enshrinement of foundational general principles of democracy and their judgments regarding particular implications of those principles. The Framers' endorsement, in 1868, of the principle of racial equality is one thing; the views of many of them that equality allowed for enforced racial segregation in schools and other public institutions is quite another. I will have more to say in this regard when I discuss interpretive methodologies later in this chapter. For now, the basic point is that the extraordinarily democratic nature of the Framing processes, combined with the typically skeletal nature of the text those processes framed, stake a claim to competence that remains compelling many generations later.

B. The Political Dynamics of American Constitutional Law[53]

The "great outlines" of the Constitution's text leave much interpretive work to be done, even more so than typical legal rules. As we've seen—and as most of the classic defenses of constitutional law emphasize—the process by which this interpretation occurs is not one of ordinary democratic politics: Constitutional interpretation is spearheaded by nonelective, life-tenured judges who are, for those reasons, insulated from political influence. The result is a measure of impartiality. But the phenomenon is one of insulation, not hermetic isolation. Popular and political influences bleed into the system from a number of sources and in a number of ways. This is inevitable; it also is necessary for the system to project competence, as it must to perform its dispute-resolving function.

In this section I will canvass the main sources of outside political and popular influence on the process of constitutional interpretation—sources, that is, that originate from outside the process of constitutional adjudication itself. (In the next section I will describe the role of popular and political influences within the adjudicative process.) Those sources fall into four general categories. Politics and popular opinion shape interpretation through the process of making judicial appointments; through overt political threats against judicial hegemony; through the need for other actors to implement judicial decisions (and thus the

---

53. With respect, and apologies, to Louis Fisher and Neal Devins, whose ground-breaking textbook *Political Dynamics of Constitutional Law*, along with their other work (both collectively and individually), has greatly influenced the summary that follows. *See* LOUIS FISHER & NEAL DEVINS, POLITICAL DYNAMICS OF CONSTITUTIONAL LAW (3d ed. 2001).

opportunity for them to resist doing so); and through the natural desire of judges to avoid criticism and earn respect for their actions.

(i) Judicial Appointments The most obvious (and arguably the most contro-versial) avenue of political and popular influence in courts' interpretation of the Constitution is the process of appointing judges to the bench. Pursuant to Article II, federal judges are nominated by the President, a popularly elected official, and must be confirmed by the Senate, which similarly is comprised of popularly elected officials.[54] This process, historically, has occurred on average about every two and a half years.[55] This means that the public, through their elected officials, are able to participate in choosing an average of four justices every decade—nearly half of the current nine-member Court.

Does the appointments process have a meaningful effect on the course of the Court's constitutional decisionmaking? In a basic sense the answer clearly is yes: Replacing old justices with new ones can alter the Court's voting lineup on key constitutional issues, causing shifts in doctrine. This has occurred demon-strably on many occasions over the Court's history,[56] most recently (as of this writing) during the 2009 term, when Justice Samuel Alito's vote was sufficient to overturn a campaign-finance precedent decided just seven years earlier by a majority that included Justice Sandra Day O'Connor, whom Alito replaced.[57] Of course, the fact that justices disagree with, and sometimes vote differently from, their predecessors does not establish the existence of external popular or political influence on those votes. But the nature of the appointments process strongly suggests such an influence.

There is, first of all, simply the fact that judicial nominations are products of politics which are, in turn, products of their times. The justices appointed by Ronald Reagan during the 1980s and by George W. Bush between 2000 and 2008 are, it seems safe to say, substantially more ideologically conservative than those appointed by fellow Republicans Richard Nixon and Gerald Ford in the early and mid-1970s. (We need only glance at the careers of John Paul Stevens, appointed by Ford in 1975 and, at his retirement in 2010, arguably the Court's most liberal member; or of Harry Blackmun, appointed by Nixon in 1970 and firmly situated within the Court's left wing when he stepped down in 1994.)

---

54. *See* U.S. CONST. art. I, § 2, cl. 2.

55. *See* BARRY FRIEDMAN, THE WILL OF THE PEOPLE: HOW PUBLIC OPINION HAS INFLUENCED THE SUPREME COURT AND SHAPED THE MEANING OF THE CONSTITUTION 374 (2009).

56. For some cases in point, see NEAL DEVINS, SHAPING CONSTITUTIONAL VALUES: ELECTED GOVERNMENT, THE SUPREME COURT, AND THE ABORTION DEBATE 25–27 (1996).

57. *See* Citizens United v. Fed. Election Comm'n, 130 S.Ct. 876 (2010) (overruling *McConnell v. Fed. Election Comm'n*, 540 U.S. 93 (2003)). The replacement of Justice O'Connor with Justice Alito also has produced a number of "underrulings" of recent prec-edents—decisions that effectively eviscerate a precedent without formally overruling it. *See* Christopher J. Peters, *Under-the-Table Overruling*, 54 WAYNE L. REV. 1067 (2008).

This simply reflects the changing tenor of the times: The nation as a whole became more conservative in the 1980s (and probably remains so today) than it had been in the 1960s and 1970s. When the public elects a conservative President and a Senate that is conservative enough to approve his or her nominees, the result is likely to be conservative justices and, over time, more-conservative constitutional doctrine. Elections have consequences, not just for legislation but for Supreme Court doctrine as well.

Nor are the makeup of the Court, and the direction of constitutional doctrine, exactly afterthoughts in contemporary American politics. Presidential candidates now routinely make anticipated judicial appointments a centerpiece of their campaigns,[58] and Supreme Court confirmation fights are just that—hotly contested battles for which Congress, the White House, the political parties, and myriad interest groups gird themselves well ahead of time and which they join fervently.[59] This process focuses public attention on the importance of an institution, the Court, whose members do not campaign for reelection and whose deliberations are not televised on C-SPAN. That attention in turn encourages the President to consider public opinion in making his or her nomination and the Senators to consider it in voting to confirm or reject. It puts the justices on notice that their work is subject to public and political scrutiny, and it exposes them firsthand, through Senators' questioning and media coverage, to the issues the public finds important. To some extent, the process also forces prospective justices to commit themselves publicly to constitutional values, albeit relatively abstract ones like a respect for precedent or to the existence of unenumerated constitutional rights.[60]

---

58. *See* Gregory J. Sullivan, *Balancing the Judiciary*, THE TIMES, TRENTON N.J., May 16, 2008, at A9, *available at* 2008 WLNR 9290705 (discussing statements by candidates George W. Bush and John McCain regarding the type of judges they would appoint); Elisabeth Bumiller, *McCain Assures Conservatives of His Stance on Judges*, N.Y. TIMES, May 7, 2008, at A22, *available at* 2008 WLNR 8497277 (discussing McCain's promises to appoint "judicial conservatives"); Peter Baker & Jeff Zeleny, *Souter's Exit to Give Obama First Opening*, N.Y. TIMES, May 2, 2009, *available at* 2009 WLNR 8333124 (noting Barack Obama's campaign remark that he would look for judges "who hopefully have a sense of what real-world folks are going through").

59. *See, e.g.*, JEFFREY TOOBIN, THE NINE: INSIDE THE SECRET WORLD OF THE SUPREME COURT 311–16 (2007) (describing the fight over Justice Alito's nomination); FRIEDMAN, *supra* note 55, at 368–69 (describing the same); TOOBIN, *supra*, at 273–83 (describing the considerably milder process of Chief Justice Roberts's confirmation); ROBERT H. BORK, THE TEMPTING OF AMERICA: THE POLITICAL SEDUCTION OF THE LAW 267–349 (1991) (chronicling, and bemoaning, the failed nomination of the author to the Supreme Court in 1987); STEPHEN CARTER, THE CONFIRMATION MESS: CLEANING UP THE FEDERAL APPOINTMENTS PROCESS (1994) (describing, and lamenting, the increasingly politicized nature of judicial nominations generally post-Bork).

60. For examples of nominees professing their respect for constitutional *stare decisis* during Senate hearings, see Ruth Marcus, *Regard for Precedent Will Be Critical Issue; Study*

By making public opinion relevant to the choice of judges, the political appointments process allows that opinion to influence the constitutional decisions made by the Court (and not just those of the Supreme Court, but those of lower federal courts as well, whose judges must undergo the same confirmation process, though usually with less scrutiny). Note, however, the typically gradual nature of this influence. While judicial departures from the Court have been, historically, relatively frequent, the average tenure of a justice on the Court has been relatively long and, with life expectancy increasing, is now on the order of a generation.[61] This usually makes for a significant delay between major shifts in public attitudes and major changes in constitutional doctrine.

When the Court is closely divided between conservatives and liberals, as it is at this writing, a single replaced justice can make a relatively large difference relatively quickly, as Samuel Alito's replacement of Sandra Day O'Connor appears to be doing. But the apparent suddenness of such doctrinal swings masks the slow, deliberate, fits-and-starts process of which they are the culmination. Republican Presidents occupied the White House for all but twelve of the forty years between 1969 and 2009; during that span they appointed twelve new justices and three Chief Justices to the Democrats' two and zero, respectively. The current Court's move to the right is simply the continuation of a gradual shift that began more than four decades ago. If the election of a Democrat to the White House in 2008 signals the beginning of a long-term swing back to the left in American political mores—certainly a debatable prospect, but let us indulge it for the moment—it is likely to take a similarly long time for the Court to catch up. Given the age of most of the conservative justices on the current Court—Antonin Scalia and Anthony Kennedy, both born in 1936, are senior to

---

Lists 31 Areas of Bork's Disagreement, WASH. POST, Sept. 15, 1987, § 1, at A9; Ronald J. Ostrow & David Lauter, Bork Assures Senators He Respects Precedent; Testifies He Was Acting as "Theorist" in Criticizing High Court Decisions; Unsure on Abortion Issue, L.A. TIMES, Sept. 16, 1987, pt. 1, at 1; Roberts Fields Senators' Queries for Second Day, CNN, Sept. 14, 2005, http://www.cnn.com/2005/POLITICS/09/13/roberts.hearings/index.html; Adam Liptak, Court in Transition: The Hearings; Issues and (Possible) Answers: A Primer on the Alito Hearings, N.Y. TIMES, Jan. 9, 2006, at A1, available at http://query.nytimes.com/gst/fullpage.html?res=9C0CE5DA1F30F93AA35752C0A9609C8B63; Court in Transition: "When a Precedent Is Reaffirmed, That Strengthens the Precedent," N.Y. TIMES, Jan. 11, 2006, § A, at 26, available at 2006 WLNR 566586.

On the Senate's ability to extract commitments from judicial nominees more generally, see DEVINS, supra note 56, at 27–28 (citing Stephen J. Wermeil, Confirming the Constitution: The Role of the Senate Judiciary Committee, 57 L. & CONTEMP. PROB. 121 (1993)).

61. See Steven C. Calabresi & James Lindgren, Term Limits for the Supreme Court: Life Tenure Reconsidered, 29 HARV. J.L. & PUB. POL'Y 769, 777–80 (2006) (citing data showing that the average tenure on the Court increased dramatically from 14.9 years between 1789 and 1970 to 26.1 years after 1970).

the next-youngest conservative justice (Clarence Thomas) by more than a decade—President Barack Obama is at least as likely to replace existing liberal justices with new ones (as he did in nominating Sonia Sotomayor to replace David Souter and Elena Kagan to replace Stevens) as to replace conservatives with liberals. And of course the President's appointments choices are cabined by what is possible in the Senate, where even the minority party can block nominations using the filibuster. Only a sustained movement to the left in American politics, with a succession of relatively liberal presidencies and strong liberal majorities in the Senate, will bring the Court back to the left along with it.

The appointments process thus promotes a sort of attenuated responsiveness by the Court to public opinion, serving (to borrow Barry Friedman's evocative image) as a kind of bungee cord by which the Court's jurisprudence is tethered to mainstream values.[62] Significant long-term movements in opinion will, eventually, drag the Court behind them, but typically there is a delay before the elasticity kicks in. By the same token, if the Court gets too far out ahead of the public (as may have occurred with the Warren Court's more aggressive criminal procedure and desegregation opinions during the 1960s), the bungee cord will, eventually, pull the Court back toward the center. The political nature of judicial appointments prevents the Court from wandering too far from majority attitudes, but it does not close the crucial gap between constitutional interpretation and everyday politics.

(ii) Political Threats The appointments process is a blunt instrument of political and popular influence on the Court, not only because it typically takes so long to make real inroads on the Court's doctrine, but also because justices have a habit of allowing their views to evolve (or perhaps to be revealed) once they're on the bench. I mentioned above the cases of John Paul Stevens and Harry Blackmun, both Nixon appointees who became two of the Court's most liberal members (although it's possible that the rest of the Court moved as much to the right during their tenure as they moved to the left). Perhaps the most famous examples are Earl Warren and William Brennan, whom Dwight Eisenhower appointed and who became, to Ike's regret, champions of the left.[63]

But there are other avenues of influence as well. The political branches wield some direct power over the Court, at least in theory, through their control

---

62. *See* FRIEDMAN, *supra* note 55, at 373.

63. While Eisenhower often is quoted as saying his appointment of Warren was "the biggest damn-fool mistake I ever made," the quote itself appears to be apocryphal. Brennan's biographer Kim Eisler, however, reports that Eisenhower once told Justice Harold Burton that his appointments of Warren and Brennan were both "big mistakes." *See* Kim Eisler, Letter to the Editor, *Eisenhower's "Mistakes,"* N.Y. TIMES, July 28, 1997, http://www.nytimes.com/1997/07/28/opinion/l-eisenhower-s-mistakes-336475.html? pagewanted=1. (Kim Eisler is the author of *A Justice for All: Justice William J. Brennan, Jr. and the Decisions that Transformed America*).

of the Court's size, jurisdiction, and finances. Article III of the Constitution requires that there be "one supreme Court" with power to decide "Cases arising under. . . this Constitution," but it does not specify crucial details like how many justices the Court must have and how often it should convene, and it subjects the Court's appellate jurisdiction to "such Exceptions, and. . . such Regulations as the Congress shall make." Congress, then—with the concurrence of the President—can enlarge or shrink the Court (so long as it does not divest any sitting justice of tenure), control its schedule, and decide what kinds of cases it will hear (although this latter power is not unlimited). And Congress has the power to impeach federal judges, including Supreme Court justices, for failing to exhibit the "good Behaviour" required by Article III.

Congress has in fact employed (or threatened to employ) most of these devices over the years, sometimes for the clear purpose of influencing the Court's decisions and, sometimes, with that apparent effect. In 1801, the outgoing Federalist majority in Congress passed a statute creating sixteen new circuit judgeships—all of which would be filled by Federalists—and reducing the Supreme Court's membership from six to five, probably with the intent of denying incoming Republican President Thomas Jefferson an anticipated appointment. In 1802, promptly after taking office, the new Republican majority repealed the statute—and canceled the Supreme Court's next term in order to delay a ruling on the constitutionality of the repeal.[64] When the Court reconvened in 1803, a chastened Supreme Court, under the leadership of the Federalist Chief Justice John Marshall, appeased the Republicans by declining to order that a Federalist justice of the peace, appointed at the eleventh hour by the lame-duck Adams administration, be given his commission. (Marshall deftly turned lemons into lemonade when he claimed in that same decision—the now-famous *Marbury v. Madison*—the judicial power to exercise constitutional review of congressional enactments.)[65]

The same period saw the use of the impeachment power as a political weapon against the judiciary. In 1803, Jefferson and the Republican Congress succeeded in impeaching and removing from office the Federalist district judge John Pickering; the charges of drunkenness and *ultra vires* conduct were fully warranted, but the *in terrorem* effect remained.[66] Then, in 1804, the House voted articles of impeachment against Samuel Chase, a controversial Federalist colleague of Marshall's on the Supreme Court, accusing Chase of partisan conduct in presiding over treason and sedition prosecutions. The Senate ultimately acquitted Chase, but the message had been sent: Federalists assumed the Pickering and Chase impeachments were the start of a broader Republican campaign against Federalist judges, and Marshall went so far as to suggest surrendering

---

64. *See* FRIEDMAN, *supra* note 55, at 48–59.

65. *See generally id.* at 58–64; Marbury v. Madison, 5 U.S. (1 Cranch) 137 (1803).

66. *See* FRIEDMAN, *supra* note 55, at 60.

the power of judicial review in return for job security.[67] Constitutional historian Barry Friedman interprets Chase's ultimate acquittal as the result of a tacit agreement by which judges would refrain from overt partisanship on the bench in return for Congress's renunciation of the impeachment power as a means to control judicial decisions.[68] And indeed no Supreme Court justice has been impeached since Chase, although politically tinged attempts have been made, including one led by then-Representative Gerald R. Ford against William O. Douglas in 1970 (which failed).[69] The thirteen lower-level federal judicial impeachments since then have involved financial, sexual, or other personal misconduct rather than political partisanship.[70] But the impeachment threat lingers, sometimes bubbling to the surface in the wake of particularly controversial judicial rulings.[71]

Congress's power to control the size of the Court has been employed more than once in circumstances that suggest an attempt to influence the Court's decisions (or future Presidents' ability to shape the Court, which amounts to the same thing). The Federalists' effort to reduce the Court's membership by one in 1801 was an example; another was Congress's reduction of the Court's size from ten to seven members in 1866, most likely in an effort to prevent President Andrew Johnson from appointing anti-Reconstruction justices.[72] The best-known example, of course, was Franklin Roosevelt's proposed "Court-packing" plan of

---

67. See id. at 64–71.

68. See id. at 68–71.

69. See Adam Liptak, The End of an Era, for Court and Nation, N.Y. Times, Apr. 9, 2010, http://www.nytimes.com/2010/04/10/us/politics/10judge.html?hp=&pagewanted=print (referencing Ford's attempt to impeach Douglas); see also James F. Simon, Independent Journey: The Life of William O. Douglas 391–411 (1980) (detailing the attempted impeachment of Douglas). The attack on Douglas closely followed the resignation of Associate Justice Abe Fortas amidst a scandal involving his financial dealings. See Friedman, supra note 55, at 277; Laura Kalman, Abe Fortas: A Biography 359–70 (1990).

70. See generally Louis Fisher, Constitutional Dialogues: Interpretation as Political Process 145–46 (1988) (describing the circumstances of a number of federal judicial impeachments).

71. See, for example, the hints floated by then-House majority leader Tom Delay following the refusal, by the Supreme Court and lower courts, to halt the removal of feeding tubes from a brain-dead Florida woman named Terri Schiavo. Delay called for an investigation of the judges' conduct and was quoted as saying, "We set up the courts. We can unset the courts. . . . The time will come for the men responsible for this to answer for their behavior." Delay never uttered the word "impeachment," but the threat seemed clear. See Adam Cohen, Psst. . . Justice Scalia. . . You're an Activist Judge, Too, N.Y. Times, Apr. 19, 2005, http://www.nytimes.com/2005/04/19/opinion/19tue3.html?_r=1&scp=1& sq=scalia%20tom%20delay%20schiavo&st=cse; John Files, From Chicago Judge, a Plea for Safety and Softer Words, N.Y. Times, May 19, 2005, http://www.nytimes.com/2005/05/19/ politics/19courts.html?scp=1&sq=files%20delay%20cornyn%20lefkow&st=cse.

72. See Fisher, supra note 70, at 124.

1937, which would have added a new justice to the Court for every sitting justice over age seventy. The proposed legislation would have given Roosevelt six new appointments, virtually ensuring preservation of the New Deal programs that the existing nine-member Court had routinely been striking down. The Court-packing legislation itself ultimately failed, but not before a key swing voter on the Court, Justice Owen Roberts, cast several important votes in favor of New Deal programs, followed shortly by the retirement of one of the Court's anti–New Deal "Four Horseman," Willis Van Devanter. The Court's rulings moved accordingly to the left, a "switch in time" that may have "saved nine."[73]

Probably the most direct avenue of congressional influence on judicial decisionmaking is Congress's ability to limit the issues the Court decides, through its Article III powers to make "Exceptions" to and "Regulations" of the Court's appellate jurisdiction and to "ordain and establish" "inferior Courts." Congress has used this power successfully on a number of key occasions and unsuccessfully on others; members of Congress have threatened to use it much more often. In 1868, over Andrew Johnson's veto, Congress repealed the Court's appellate jurisdiction to hear *habeas corpus* appeals after the Court had already heard arguments in such a case. The Court unanimously upheld the validity of the repeal statute. Three years later, however, the Court struck down a similar statute as a violation of the separation of powers.[74] As constitutional scholars Louis Fisher and Neal Devins put it, these decisions "leave the question of political controls over Court jurisdiction in a shadowy realm" that "is principally about policy and political prudence, not constitutionality."[75] The murkiness of that realm has encouraged the frequent (and almost always unsuccessful) introduction of jurisdiction-stripping legislation over the years, including (to cite just a few examples) attempts to prevent the Court from hearing cases involving the First Amendment rights of accused communists during the McCarthy Era; involving the rights of criminal suspects during the 1950s and 1960s; involving school busing, school prayer, and abortion during the 1970s and 1980s; and, more recently, involving public religious displays and the use of the words "under God" in the Pledge of Allegiance.[76]

---

73. *See generally* FRIEDMAN, *supra* note 55, at 212–36 (describing the Court-packing plan and events surrounding it). As for whether the "switch in time" was motivated by fear of the Court-packing plan, Friedman finds the evidence ambiguous, but thinks the important point is that the public at the time understood the Court's reversal of course as a response to public opinion. *See id.* at 229–34.

74. *See* Ex parte McCardle, 74 U.S. (7 Wall.) 506 (1868); United States v. Klein, 80 U.S. (13 Wall.) 128 (1871); *see generally* FISHER & DEVINS, *supra* note 53, at 42–43.

75. FISHER & DEVINS, *supra* note 53, at 43.

76. An example of this latter type of proposal is Senate Bill 520, introduced in the 109th Congress in March 2005, which would have removed the federal courts' jurisdiction over "any matter to the extent that relief is sought against an entity [or officer or agent] of Federal, State, or local government,. . . concerning that entity's, officer's, or agent's

One recent jurisdiction-stripping attempt that actually became law (for a time) was Congress's 2006 denial of *habeas corpus* to detainees at the Guantánamo Bay facility in favor of a system of military tribunals with limited rights of appeal. By a five-to-four vote, the Supreme Court invalidated the statute on the ground that it functionally suspended *habeas corpus* in violation of the Suspension Clause of Article I, § 9.[77]

And then there is Congress's control over the federal purse and, with it, the salaries of federal judges. The drafters of Article III, sensitive to the potential *in terrorem* effect of Congressional power over judicial pay, prohibited Congress from "diminish[ing]" the salaries of federal judges "during their Continuance in Office." But Congress could achieve similar results by simply refusing to raise salaries to keep pace with inflation, or by denying financial support to the judiciary in other ways (for example, by refusing to provide sufficient funds for judicial staff). In fact, members of the judiciary have long complained of inadequate compensation and bare-bones funding,[78] and although there is little reason to suspect that Congress has purposefully used these tools to influence judicial doctrine, the potential (and thus the threat) always exists.

The prevalence of these external political threats to judicial independence leads Barry Friedman to conclude that "[i]f. . . history shows anything, it is that when judicial decisions wander far from what the public will tolerate, bad things happen to the Court and the justices."[79] Friedman may be exaggerating a bit; such threats usually remain merely threats, and the instances in which they demonstrably have affected the Court's decisionmaking are few and far between. What the record suggests is that these control techniques comprise another thread in Friedman's "bungee cord" loosely tying the Court's doctrine to mainstream public opinion. Reprisal against the Court is a politically costly proposition

---

acknowledgment of God as the sovereign source of law, liberty, or government." Constitution Restoration Act of 2005, S. 520, 109th Cong. § 1260 (2005). The other examples listed here are described in FISHER & DEVINS, *supra* note 53, at 42–46.

77. The Suspension Clause provides: "The Privilege of the Writ of Habeas Corpus shall not be suspended, unless when in Cases of Rebellion or Invasion the public Safety may require it." U.S. CONST. art. I, § 9, cl. 2. The government made no attempt to argue that the triggering conditions for suspension of the writ had been met; instead it argued that the Guantánamo detainees were not protected by the Clause or, in the alternative, that the writ had not effectively been suspended. *See* Boumediene v. Bush, 128 S.Ct. 2229 (2008).

78. *See* Robert Barnes, *Supreme Court Chief Justice Roberts Opts Not to Ask Congress to Raise Judicial Salaries*, WASH. POST, Jan. 1, 2010, http://www.washingtonpost.com/wp-dyn/content/article/2009/12/31/AR2009123102599.html ("Roberts abandoned the decades-old practice of history lessons and philosophical lectures accompanying the call for bigger salaries that have become standard for the Year-End Report on the Federal Judiciary.").

79. FRIEDMAN, *supra* note 55, at 375.

for Congress and the President, not to be used lightly; it becomes a realistic option only when the political stakes are especially high, as during the partisan battles of the early Republic or the aftermath of the Civil War, or when there is widespread agreement that the Court has in fact strayed too far from public opinion, as during the New Deal. Threats of reprisal therefore appear to serve, not to give the political branches *de facto* control over the Court's decision-making, but rather to rein in the Court when its decisions edge toward the extreme or when it threatens to take sides in a dire political controversy. Political threats constrain the Court at the margins—a meaningful constraint, to be sure, but far from sufficient to transform judicial decisionmaking into a branch of ordinary politics.

(iii) Implementation and Resistance Courts, as Hamilton noted, possess the powers neither of sword nor purse; whether they exercise "will" as opposed to "judgment," clearly they lack the capacity to exert much in the way of "force."[80] It is, then, up to other governmental actors—federal and state political officials and state and lower federal-court judges—to enforce the decisions and doctrines the Court announces. The Court's knowledge that others must enforce its decisions drives it to make those decisions enforceable—understandable, and tolerable, to the lower-court judges and political officials who must interpret and obey them. Enthusiastic (or at least stoic) implementation of Court decisions sometimes causes the Court to push even harder in subsequent cases; reluctant implementation or resistance can cause the Court to draw back, even to reverse itself. And even if implementation of the Court's decisions has little or no effect on the formal course of legal doctrine, obviously it can influence that doctrine in a *de facto* sense, adjusting how it is applied on the ground.

The best-known example of the implementation of a Supreme Court decision becoming an issue unto itself is the "massive resistance" in the South to the Court's desegregation ruling in *Brown v. Board of Education*. Resistance in the wake of *Brown* affected the course of constitutional doctrine in a number of interesting ways. Preemptively, the prospect of southern opposition moderated the content of the Court's ruling: Fearing widespread resistance (a concern encouraged by the school districts' own lawyers during oral argument[81]), the Court equivocally ordered in its second *Brown* ruling that desegregation commence with "all deliberate speed."[82] When the anticipated resistance materialized, the Court mostly kept its hands off school desegregation for the next decade,

---

80. *See* Hamilton, FEDERALIST No. 78, *supra* note 15, at 437.

81. *See* FRIEDMAN, *supra* note 55, at 246–47 (quoting statements of attorney S. Emory Rogers that southerners "would not send our white children to the Negro schools" even if ordered to do so).

82. *See* Brown v. Bd. of Educ., 349 U.S. 294, 301 (1955) (*Brown II*). *See generally* FRIEDMAN, *supra* 55, at 244–48 (interpreting the "all deliberate speed" language as an anticipatory response to southern resistance to *Brown*).

leaving it to lower federal courts to work out the implications (and take most of the heat) of the *Brown* doctrine.[83] Counterintuitively, the South's resistance backfired when Congress, tiring of the many (and increasingly violent) instances of open defiance of federal law, overcame a southern filibuster to enact the Civil Rights Act of 1964, which (among other things) authorized the Justice Department to litigate for school desegregation and used the power of the federal purse to prohibit discrimination in local school systems.[84] The backing of Congress in turn emboldened the Court, which reentered the school desegregation arena with a series of decisive orders, declaring in one case that "[t]he time for mere 'deliberate speed' has run out."[85] But the newly aggressive judicial attitude toward desegregation itself produced a backlash: The expansion of desegregation remedies to northern cities, and in particular the increasing use of mandatory busing as a judicially ordered remedy for segregation (endorsed by the Court in 1971), triggered widespread popular and political condemnation, including by President Nixon (who made busing a campaign issue), and the Court quickly retreated from controversial segregation remedies.[86]

The path of the Court's school desegregation decisions suggests that the Court, in fashioning constitutional doctrine, both anticipates and responds to the reception given that doctrine by nonjudicial officials. This is so not merely with respect to the content of that doctrine, but also with respect to its form. As Devins and Fisher note, the Court "generally announces broad guidelines" for the application of constitutional provisions: "'undue burden' for abortion; 'compelling governmental interest,' 'narrowly tailored,' and 'all deliberate speed' for desegregation; and 'prurient' for obscene material." The result—almost certainly an intended one—is to leave it "up to elected officials and juries"—and

---

83. *See* Neal Devins & Louis Fisher, The Democratic Constitution 156 (2004) [hereinafter Democratic Constitution] ("From 1954 to 1964, the Court's only foray into school desegregation was its Little Rock decision."). That decision, in *Cooper v. Aaron*, 358 U.S. 1 (1958), was a direct response to open refusal by state and local officials to obey a district court's desegregation order; it was handed down only after President Eisenhower had ordered federal troops into Little Rock to enforce the order. *See* Democratic Constitution, *supra*, at 155–56; Friedman, *supra* note 55, at 247–48.

84. *See* Democratic Constitution, *supra* note 83, at 157; Friedman, *supra* note 55, at 248–49.

85. Griffin v. County Sch. Bd., 377 U.S. 218, 234 (1964). *See generally* Friedman, *supra* note 55, at 249–50 (describing the Court's emboldened reaction to the Civil Rights Act); Democratic Constitution, *supra* note 83, at 157–58 (describing the same).

86. *See* Democratic Constitution, *supra* note 83, at 159–61. The Court's endorsement of busing as a remedy came in *Swann v. Charlotte-Mecklenburg*, 402 U.S. 1 (1971). In *Milliken v. Bradley*, 433 U.S. 267 (1977), the Court declined to approve a segregation remedy that would have bused children from the overwhelmingly white school districts of Detroit's suburbs to its urban schools and vice versa. In 1991, the Court "issued several decisions signaling the end of court-ordered desegregation." Democratic Constitution, *supra* note 83, at 161 (citing *Bd. of Educ. v. Dowell*, 498 U.S. 237 (1991)).

lower-court judges—"to translate those general principles. . . and apply them to particular cases. The Court defines the edges; nonjudicial actors" (and lesser judicial ones) "fill in the important middle."[87] Relatively open-textured judicial doctrine thus serves a purpose similar to the relatively open-textured constitutional provisions that doctrine interprets: It allows for the flexibility to meet unforeseen circumstances and even, within bounds, to change course.

Finally, the real-world impact of the Court's constitutional doctrine can be profoundly affected by nonjudicial actors even when the Court does not intend it (and indeed may not be aware of it). Consider that fact that, twenty years after the Court ruled that officially sponsored prayer in public schools was unconstitutional, authorities in many districts continued the practice;[88] or the fact that Congress continued to place "legislative veto" provisions in statutes even after the Court declared that the practice violated the separation of powers.[89] Where most of those affected by a policy—in the case of school prayer, teachers, students, and parents in conservative rural districts; in the case of the legislative veto, members of Congress and officials of federal agencies—do not feel especially aggrieved by that policy, it might continue through "the sheer force of inertia," to quote Louis Fisher,[90] despite the Court's once having struck it down. This sort of passive resistance (or perhaps passive indifference) can shape the actual contours of constitutional doctrine in a way that the Court has little opportunity to control. If no one is willing to bring a lawsuit to stop an unconstitutional policy, after all, the Court cannot order that it be stopped.

(iv) Popular Opinion And then there is the simple fact that Supreme Court justices are human beings, most of whom, we can assume, dislike being shouted at and called names and enjoy being praised. While many Supreme Court decisions, even on constitutional issues, go relatively unnoticed by the public at large, many others trigger *causes célèbres*, sometimes to an extent the Court itself could not have foreseen. Consider the angry reaction across a broad spectrum of political viewpoints to the Court's seemingly workmanlike 2005 decision in *Kelo v. City of New London*, which upheld a city's use of the eminent domain power to forcibly purchase residents' homes and transfer them to private developers.[91] Despite the fact that the Court in *Kelo* actually exercised judicial restraint by declining to overrule a political decision, the ruling sparked howls of judicial activism and *ad hominem* attacks on the justices; one furious activist convinced Justice David Souter's home town of Weare, New Hampshire, to vote on whether

87. Democratic Constitution, *supra* note 83, at 232.

88. *See* Fisher, *supra* note 70, at 222. The decision in question was *Engel v. Vitale*, 370 U.S. 421 (1962).

89. *See* Fisher, *supra* note 70, at 225. The decision in question was *INS v. Chadha*, 462 U.S. 919 (1983).

90. Fisher, *supra* note 70, at 222.

91. *See* Kelo v. City of New London, 545 U.S. 469 (2005).

to condemn Souter's farm and transform it into the "Lost Liberty Hotel." (The measure was defeated, but it received almost 30 percent of the vote.)[92] The public response to the Court's 2010 decision invalidating restrictions on corporate campaign spending, while not as vehement, has been at least as uniformly negative.[93]

It is difficult to believe that the justices somehow can completely tune out popular reaction to their decisions. It is just as unlikely that the justices can avoid thinking about how they will be remembered by posterity. Pity the soul of poor Justice Henry Billings Brown, who today is best remembered for authoring the 1896 opinion in *Plessy v. Ferguson* that endorsed the "separate but equal" doctrine, or that of his colleague Rufus Wheeler Peckham, who wrote the now universally condemned opinion in *Lochner v. New York* that elevated laissez-faire economics to the status of constitutional necessity.[94] (And compare the legacy of the first Justice John Marshall Harlan, now widely admired in large part because he dissented in both cases.) Judges who end up on the wrong side of history are forgotten at best, mocked or vilified at worst; judges who anticipate the tide of the times, and perhaps help it along a little—John Marshall, who championed judicial review and the expansion of federal power during the early years of the Republic; Oliver Wendell Holmes, whose dissenting views on economic regulation and free speech came to be accepted as the doctrine of the Court; Earl Warren, whose leadership on controversial subjects like civil rights and criminal procedure has shaped the law in those areas to this day—are elevated to the pantheon of the Court's greatest jurists.

Supreme Court justices are not radicals; the appointments process rules out radicalism. As the products of a relatively elite profession (the law) and, typically, of comparatively privileged backgrounds, they are not ordinary Joes or Jills, exactly (although Justice Clarence Thomas is said to attend NASCAR races[95]); but there is every reason to think that they perceive, if sometimes a bit dimly, the content of mainstream public opinion, and that they would rather be favored than condemned by it. And their tinge of elitism seems likely, if anything, to engender special concern about what their places in history will turn out to be. This basic human desire to be admired might well be one of the strongest

---

92. For an account of the public reaction to the *Kelo* decision, see Toobin, *supra* note 59, at 305–08.

93. The decision is *Citizens United v. Fed. Election Comm'n*, 130 S. Ct. 876 (2010). Polls taken shortly after the decision suggested that four out of five Americans opposed it. *See* Dan Eggen, *Poll: Large Majority Opposes Supreme Court's Decision on Campaign Financing*, Washington Post, Feb. 17, 2010, http://www.washingtonpost.com/wp-dyn/content/article/2010/02/17/AR2010021701151.html?sid=ST2010021702073.

94. *See* Lochner v. New York, 198 U.S. 45 (1905); Plessy v. Ferguson, 163 U.S. 537 (1896).

95. *See* Toobin, *supra* note 59, at 99.

threads tethering the Court's constitutional doctrine, over time, to the values of the American majority.

(v) "The Opinion of the Age" These many political and popular restraints force responsiveness in the Court's constitutional doctrine: That doctrine must track majoritarian opinion over time. As Justice Robert Jackson frankly noted in 1953, "[t]he practical play of the forces of politics is such that judicial power has often delayed but never permanently defeated the persistent will of a substantial majority."[96] Political responsiveness in turn promotes the impression of competence, and it tempers the risk that the justices will act partially, using constitutional law as nothing more than a vessel for their own private ideas of right and wrong. But do these outside political influences push constitutional doctrine too far in the direction of ordinary politics? Will the Court simply "write [the Constitution] the way the majority wants," as Justice Antonin Scalia fears?[97]

There is plenty of evidence that, in the American system, constitutional doctrine remains apart from everyday politics, coinciding with majority opinion over the long run but not necessarily in the near term. The Court regularly issues constitutional decisions that are widely unpopular, sometimes cleaving public opinion in two (as with the *Dred Scott* decision in 1857,[98] the *Brown* decision in 1954, and the *Roe* decision in 1973), sometimes alienating a sizeable majority of the public (as with *Loving v. Virginia* in 1967,[99] *Kelo* in 2005, and the *Citizens United* campaign-finance decision in 2010). Just as telling is the fact that the Court on occasion has resisted the trends of popular opinion on important issues for extended periods of time, thus "delay[ing] the persistent will of a substantial majority," in Justice Jackson's words, before finally capitulating. This is what occurred during the Progressive Era and the early New Deal, before the "switch in time," and it may be happening again as I write, with the Court's vigorous (but until now largely unnoticed) protection of corporate interests bracing for the impacts of a new wave of economic interventionism by the federal government and a rising tide of populism.[100] These holdout periods are an inevitable part of a system in which turnover among the justices is gradual; the justices of

---

96. *See* FISHER, *supra* note 70, at 138 (quoting Jackson).

97. Antonin Scalia, *Common-Law Courts in a Civil-Law System: The Role of United States Federal Courts in Interpreting the Constitution and Laws*, in A MATTER OF INTERPRETATION: FEDERAL COURTS AND THE LAW 3, 47 (Amy Gutmann ed., 1997).

98. *See* Scott v. Sandford, 60 U.S. (19 How.) 393 (1857) (invalidating the Missouri Compromise and holding that former slaves cannot be citizens).

99. *See* Loving v. Virginia, 388 U.S. 1 (1967) (invalidating laws prohibiting interracial marriage).

100. On the Court's recent string of probusiness decisions, see FRIEDMAN, *supra* note 55, at 377–78 (citing Jeffrey Rosen, *Supreme Court Inc.*, N.Y. TIMES MAG., March 15, 2008, at 38). To the list we should add the Court's recent decision in the *Citizens United* case. *See supra* note 93 and accompanying text.

an earlier political era, their views made conservative by the passage of time, lag behind the faster-moving attitudes of everyday politics.[101]

There also is the fact that influence flows in both directions—to the Court from politics and public opinion, but also to politics and public opinion from the Court. Exhibit A of this phenomenon is the process, well documented by Barry Friedman, of public acceptance of the practice of judicial review itself—a practice fashioned by the Court over time, if not quite from whole cloth, then from available scraps of original intent, opportunity, and necessity.[102] The Court enjoys a relatively high level of public confidence from year to year, by some measures more confidence than the other institutions of government[103]—a reservoir of good will that has allowed it to overcome, time and again, the momentary crises of ill-received or divisive decisions.[104] The public's endorsement of judicial review and esteem for the Court has meant that instances of outright

---

101. *See* FISHER, *supra* note 70, at 201 ("The judiciary is most likely to be out of step with Congress or the President during periods of electoral or partisan realignment, when the country is undergoing sharp shifts in political directions while the courts retain the orientation of an age gone by.").

102. Friedman's book *The Will of the People* is an excellent historical narrative of this process. *See* FRIEDMAN, *supra* note 55; *see also* BICKEL, *supra* note 1, at 14–16 (describing the "moral approval" bestowed on judicial review over time).

103. In annual Harris polls asking about public "confidence" in "people in charge of running" various institutions from 1979 through 2004, the Court received ratings of "a great deal of confidence"—the highest rating—from between 23 percent of the respondents (in 1991) and 42 percent of the respondents (in 1999). By comparison, the high-confidence ratings of "the White House" varied from a low of 13 percent in 1995 (during Bill Clinton's first term) to a high of 50 percent in 2002 (following the September 11 attacks) and fell below the Court's during most years. Respondents consistently rated "Congress" and the "Executive branch of the Federal Government" well below the Court; Congress's high-confidence ratings ranged from a low of 8 percent in 1994 to a high of 28 percent in 1984, while those of the executive branch ranged between 9 percent (in 1995) to 33 percent (in 2002). *See* BUREAU OF JUSTICE STATISTICS, SOURCEBOOK OF CRIMINAL JUSTICE STATISTICS 2003, at 112 (2003), *available at* http://www.albany.edu/sourcebook/ pdf/t29.pdf. Surveys by the Pew Research Center for the People & the Press between June 2005 and February 2010 show the Court's "favorable" rating ranging between a high of 72 percent in January 2007 to lows of 57 percent in July 2007 and June 2005. The "favorable" rating of Congress during the same period ranged from a high of 53 percent in January 2007 to a low of 37 percent in August 2009. The Pew survey does not ask for favorability ratings of the presidency, inquiring instead about job approval with respect to each holder of the office. *See* THE PEW RESEARCH CTR. FOR THE PEOPLE & THE PRESS, MIDTERM ELECTION CHALLENGES FOR BOTH PARTIES: OBAMA'S RATINGS ARE FLAT, WALL STREET'S ARE ABYSMAL 1 (Feb. 12, 2010), http://people-press.org/reports/pdf/589.pdf.

104. *See* James L. Gibson et al., *Measuring Attitudes Toward the United States Supreme Court*, 47 AM. J. POL. SCI. 354 (2003) (finding a consistently high level of public confidence in the Court that is relatively unaffected by perceptions of individual decisions); *see also* FRIEDMAN, *supra* note 55, at 379 (noting the existence of "diffuse support" for the

resistance to the Court's decisions have been relatively rare, especially among federal officials. During the height of the Watergate scandal, Richard Nixon obeyed the Court's order to turn over incriminating tapes of his Oval Office conversations, apparently calculating that overt defiance of the Court would be worse for his political fortunes than revealing the tapes' contents.[105] (He may have been wrong, but there is no way of knowing.) The George W. Bush administration might have made a similar calculus in acceding, however grudgingly, to the Court's string of rulings against its policies for detaining "enemy combatants" and terrorism suspects.[106] Public respect for the Court thus often translates to political respect for the Court's rulings. And the content of those rulings probably is capable of moving public opinion to some degree; the now universal reverence for the *Brown* decision—despite the massive resistance it initially provoked—suggests as much.[107]

The politics-law interaction, as the more sophisticated semireductionist theorists recognize, thus probably resembles a dialogue more than a judicial lecture on the one hand or a series of political threats on the other.[108] And, like most ongoing dialogues, it takes time to produce measurable results. The Court does not simply jump to it when the majority yells loudly enough; Justice Scalia's fear is in this sense overblown. Instead the Court listens to what the

---

Court—"the idea that there is enough institutional support for the Court that people will tolerate a certain amount of deviation, a number of decisions they dislike").

105. *See* United States v. Nixon, 418 U.S. 683 (1974); *see also* DEMOCRATIC CONSTITUTION, *supra* note 83, at 223–24 (noting that "[p]ublic opinion strongly supported the Court's authority to compel President Nixon to release the Watergate tapes").

106. Those rulings include *Rasul v. Bush*, 542 U.S. 466 (2004), holding that *habeas corpus* jurisdiction extended via statute to detainees at Guantánamo Bay; *Hamdi v. Rumsfeld*, 542 U.S. 507 (2004), holding that U.S. citizens cannot be detained as "enemy combatants" on U.S. soil without access to a neutral tribunal to assess their status; *Hamdan v. Rumsfeld*, 548 U.S. 557 (2006), holding that the use of military commissions to try Guantánamo detainees was unlawful without congressional authorization; and *Boumediene v. Bush*, 553 U.S. 723 (2008), holding that a congressionally mandated procedure for trying Guantánamo detainees by military commissions unconstitutionally deprived them of the right to *habeas corpus*.

107. While there is relatively little reliable empirical data on the influence of Court decisions on public opinion, some studies suggest that the fact that the Court has reached a certain decision tends to increase public agreement with the substance of that decision over time, and that Court decisions can have both positive and negative effects on the attitudes of various segments of the public with respect to the underlying issues. *See, e.g.,* Charles H. Franklin & Liane C. Kosaki, *Republican Schoolmaster: The U.S. Supreme Court, Public Opinion, and Abortion*, 83 AM. POL. SCI. REV. 751 (1989). In his book *Shaping Constitutional Values*, Neal Devins makes a convincing case that the Court's *Roe v. Wade* decision "ignited a constructive constitutional dialogue." *See* DEVINS, *supra* note 56, at 5.

108. For elaborations of this dialogic understanding, see FRIEDMAN, *supra* note 55; DEVINS, *supra* note 56; FISHER, *supra* note 70; DEMOCRATIC CONSTITUTION, *supra* note 83.

majority has to say, sometimes agreeing, sometimes retorting, with the result that over time the Court's doctrine and majority attitudes tend to coincide. The crucial distinction, as the future president Woodrow Wilson wrote in 1908, is between "the opinion of the moment and the opinion of the age."[109] The former is the fare of ordinary politics, the latter of constitutional process.

C. Participatory Constitutional Adjudication

In Chapter 5, I argued that adversary adjudication can claim some democratic authority of its own, even apart from its function of implementing democratically enacted rules. Like majoritarian democracy, adversary adjudication can be meaningfully participatory, a feature (or rather a collection of features) that fosters both its competence and its impartiality. And I suggested in Chapter 6 that in circumstances where adjudication will have a broad contemporaneous impact, as it will in most public-law cases, its direct authority can be preserved by broadening its participatory scope in a corresponding fashion.

I want to build on these points here by illustrating the ways in which constitutional adjudication can, in the American system, be broadly and meaningfully participatory, and thus can be understood to possess both reasonable competence and reasonable judicial impartiality despite its relative insulation from the regular democratic process. I will use as my case study two companion decisions rendered by the Supreme Court in 2003, both of which I mentioned briefly in Chapter 6. The cases are *Grutter v. Bollinger* and *Gratz v. Bollinger*, the lawsuits challenging the constitutionality of the University of Michigan's affirmative-action admissions policies.[110]

In *Grutter*, the plaintiff, a white woman named Barbara Grutter who had been denied admission to the University of Michigan Law School, sued the university, the law school, and several university and law school officials alleging that the law school's race-conscious admissions policy violated the Equal Protection Clause. In *Gratz*, two white applicants denied admission to the university's undergraduate program, Jennifer Gratz and Patrick Hamacher, sued the university alleging that its policy of race-consciousness in undergraduate admissions similarly violated equal protection.[111]

---

109. WOODROW WILSON, CONSTITUTIONAL GOVERNMENT IN THE UNITED STATES 172 (1908). I owe my awareness of this quotation to Barry Friedman. *See* FRIEDMAN, *supra* note 55, at 382.

110. *See* Grutter v. Bollinger, 539 U.S. 306 (2003) (challenging the law school's admissions program); Gratz v. Bollinger, 539 U.S. 244 (2003) (challenging the university's undergraduate admissions program).

111. The plaintiffs in both cases also alleged that the respective policies violated Title VI of the 1964 Civil Rights Act, 42 U.S.C. § 2000d, which prohibits race discrimination by an educational institution that accepts federal funds. I will focus here only on the constitutional questions presented to the Court.

The affirmative action policies followed in the law school and the university's undergraduate program were—crucially, as it turned out—different in their particulars. The undergraduate program at issue in *Gratz*—known as the College of Literature, Science, and the Arts, or LSA—assigned applicants a numerical score of up to 150 points based upon high school GPA, standardized test scores, and a number of other "softer" variables. Pursuant to the LSA admissions policy, an applicant who was a member of one of several specified minority groups automatically received 20 of the 100 points necessary to guarantee admission.

By contrast, the law school policy challenged in *Grutter* considered an applicant's minority status as a "plus" factor in his or her favor but did not assign that factor any specific quantitative weight. Indeed, the law school's admissions process, unlike the LSA process, did not use a numerical score system at all, although an applicant's "index" score (the combination of his or her undergraduate GPA and LSAT score) was the dominant variable in most admissions decisions. Statistical testimony at trial established that the law school's use of race as a "plus" factor gave minority applicants a significantly greater chance of admission than nonminority applicants with similar index scores.

Both the law school and the LSA defended their consideration of race in admissions as necessary to promote racial "diversity" among their respective student bodies. Faculty and administrators in both programs testified that a "critical mass" of minority students among the student body was necessary to ensure a level of racial diversity sufficient to meaningfully enhance the educational experience.

The *Grutter* and *Gratz* lawsuits both were filed in 1997 in the U.S. District Court for the Eastern District of Michigan, but the cases were assigned to different judges. In *Gratz*, the district court held, on summary judgment, that the LSA had established "a compelling governmental interest in the educational benefits that flow from a racially and ethnically diverse student body"[112] and that its use of race as a factor in its admissions process was narrowly tailored to serve that interest. The district court thus upheld the LSA's admissions policy as constitutionally valid. In *Grutter*, following a bench trial, the district court held as a matter of law that the law school's stated interest in racial and ethnic diversity was not a compelling governmental interest and that, in any case, its use of race as a "plus" factor in admissions was not narrowly tailored to serve that interest; it thus struck down the law school policy.[113]

Both decisions were appealed to the U.S. Court of Appeals for the Sixth Circuit, and both ultimately were argued before an *en banc* court. In May 2002, the Sixth Circuit issued a decision in *Grutter* reversing the district court's holding that the law school's admissions policy was unconstitutional. The vote

---

112. Gratz v. Bollinger, 122 F. Supp. 2d 811, 819 (E.D. Mich. 2000).
113. Grutter v. Bollinger, 137 F. Supp. 2d 821 (E.D. Mich. 2001).

on the *en banc* court was five to four.[114] In December 2002, the Supreme Court granted certiorari to review the case. At the same time the Court granted certiorari in the *Gratz* case, which had not yet been decided by the Sixth Circuit.

The Supreme Court heard oral argument in both cases on April 1, 2003[115] and rendered its decisions in June 2003. In *Grutter*, a five-to-four majority of the Court upheld the law school's affirmative action policy, with Justice O'Connor writing the majority opinion and Chief Justice William Rehnquist and Justices Kennedy, Scalia, and Thomas dissenting. In *Gratz*, a six-to-three majority struck down the LSA's policy, with Chief Justice Rehnquist writing the majority opinion and Justices Ruth Bader Ginsberg, Souter, and Stevens dissenting.

Grutter and *Gratz* (to which I occasionally will refer collectively as "the Michigan cases") illustrate the extent to which American constitutional adjudication is a meaningfully participatory enterprise, that is, a process driven in large part by the contributory efforts of affected parties. More subtly, the cases demonstrate the nuanced interplay between judges and other actors in the process, a dynamic that can both inform and constrain the judges' decisionmaking.

(i) The Centrality of Dispute Resolution In the Michigan cases, as in high-profile constitutional cases more generally, it is easy to overlook the basic point that neither case would have seen the inside of a courtroom without the presence of an active dispute that needed resolving. The plaintiffs in *Grutter* and *Gratz* claimed the university's policies had violated their legal rights to their detriment and sought remedies for that harm; the university denied that it had violated the plaintiffs' rights. The courts' initial *raison d'être* in each case, therefore, was to resolve an actual dispute between particular parties.

One implication of a court's primary function as a resolver of disputes is simply the fact that no court, not even the Supreme Court, can play the role of freelance problem-solver, wandering the earth looking for wrongs to right like the solitary lead character in the old TV series *Kung Fu*. Courts are not like legislatures in this respect; they must wait for the problems to come to them and then must take those problems as they find them.

Suppose, by way of contrast, that a majority of Congress decides that it opposes affirmative action. Congress can implement its preference by eradicating affirmative action in government hiring and contracting and prohibiting it to the wide range of institutions—universities, corporations, state governments—who receive funds from or do business with the federal government. (In states that

---

114. There were only nine active judges on the Sixth Circuit at the time *Grutter* was decided. As one judge noted in his *Grutter* concurrence, the court thus was "operating with only one-half of the active judges' positions filled." Grutter v. Bollinger, 288 F.3d 732, 772 (6th Cir. 2002) (Clay, J., concurring).

115. While most appellate lawyers, and many law professors, no doubt fantasize about arguing a case before the Supreme Court, I suspect that few of them would choose to do so on April Fool's Day.

allow for direct electoral amendments to their constitutions, a majority of the citizens could act on this preference, too, by banning government-sponsored affirmative action in that state. This is in fact precisely what happened in Michigan after *Grutter* and *Gratz* were decided.[116]) If a majority of Congress takes the opposite view, Congress can implement that preference broadly as well, by enacting requirements rather than prohibitions.

But the anti- or pro-affirmative action judge—even if she is a Supreme Court justice—can only invalidate or uphold affirmative action in the particular context of a case properly before her. The dispute-resolution function of a court generally limits that court, even in a constitutional case, to deciding the legal import of the facts with which the disputing parties have presented it. So the Supreme Court in the Michigan cases hardly could have declared whether diversity was a compelling interest in the contexts of, say, government contracting, or military promotions, or agency hiring; the Court was practically limited to the facts of the disputes before it, which involved higher education.

I use qualifiers like "practically" and "hardly" here because, of course, courts (particularly the Supreme Court) sometimes seek to lay down rules that transcend the particular facts of a given case, and often do lay down such rules whether they seek to do so or not. The prodiversity holding in *Grutter*, for instance, seems likely to have some impact beyond the specific topic of university admissions (or at least *seemed* likely to have such an impact before the Court, after a crucial change of personnel, substantially undercut *Grutter*'s reasoning in a subsequent case[117]). The point, though, is not that the Court never reaches out to decide issues not before it, but that the dispute-resolution function of a court carries with it fairly strong norms against doing so.

A corollary phenomenon is that the posture of dispute in which courts decide issues imposes practical obstacles to a judge who seeks to create a broader rule. Litigants who want their particular dispute to be resolved typically have incentives to present proofs and arguments relevant to that dispute, not to hypothetical disputes in which they have no stake. In *Grutter* and *Gratz*, for instance, both sides expended considerable resources developing statistical evidence regarding the effects of the particular policies being challenged and sociological evidence regarding the value of diversity in higher education. Such evidence has no application in noneducational contexts, and so the Court scarcely could have used it as the factual basis for a broader rule about the value of racial diversity.

---

116. In 2006, a majority of Michigan voters approved the so-called Michigan Civil Rights Initiative, a ballot measure that amended the Michigan state constitution to prohibit "preferential treatment. . . on the basis of race, sex, color, ethnicity, or national origin" in state government, including state universities. *See* MICH. CONST. art. I, § 26.

117. *See* Parents Involved in Cmty. Sch. v. Seattle Sch. Dist. No. 1, 555 U.S. 701 (2007) (invalidating race-conscious student assignment policies in public school districts as insufficiently narrowly tailored).

The relatively narrow incentives of the litigants as disputing parties imposed practical limits on the reasonable scope of the Court's ultimate holding.

The basic dispute-resolution function of courts, then, cabins the extent to which judges can implement their own political preferences, because it regulates both the occasions and the scope of judicial decisionmaking. It also fosters a certain type of responsiveness, one that is keyed to the interests and viewpoints of the parties before the Court. I should note here that the idea that courts are primarily dispute-resolvers is at the core of justiciability doctrine, particularly the Supreme Court's much-criticized contemporary doctrine of standing to sue. The injury-in-fact requirement of standing[118] can be understood as a way, albeit an imperfect one, of preventing courts from intervening to decide issues where there is no active dispute in need of resolution and thus no concrete factual matrix within which the court can embed its decision.[119]

(ii) The Breadth of Participation While the dispute-resolution function constrains court decisionmaking within the factual confines of particular disputes, increasingly permissive joinder rules and related devices allow anyone with a significant interest in the resolution of a dispute to participate, directly or by proxy, in the process of resolving it. Constitutional cases tend to have especially broad impacts, involving as they do the validation or invalidation of statutes, policies, and other government decisions that affect large numbers of people. It is appropriate, then, that modern procedural doctrines permit the representation of a wide spectrum of affected interests in the litigation of a constitutional challenge. *Grutter* and *Gratz* are salient cases in point.

Consider the broad spectrum of interests that were represented, more or less directly, in the process of deciding the Michigan cases:

The disputing parties themselves. It is an obvious but crucially important fact that the courts in the Michigan cases, like Anglo-American courts generally, went about their dispute-resolving tasks not unilaterally but multilaterally. Neither trial judge, upon receiving the pleadings, sequestered himself away to emerge later with some Delphic proclamation deciding the case. Instead each judge relied heavily upon the disputants—now litigants—themselves, through their lawyers, to present the factual proofs and submit the legal arguments upon which the judge ultimately would rely for his decision. The parties who would be most significantly affected by the court's decision—the disputants themselves—thus participated directly and meaningfully in the process of forming that decision.

Others who were situated similarly to the plaintiffs. The disputants themselves, however, were not the only parties with a stake in the Michigan cases. In any case with potential precedential impact, parties who are similarly situated to the

---

118. *See, e.g.,* Allen v. Wright, 468 U.S. 737 (1984).

119. For a more extensive argument along these lines, see Christopher J. Peters, *Adjudication as Representation*, 97 Colum. L. Rev. 312, 420–30 (1997).

litigants but not actually participating in the case are likely to be bound in some meaningful sense by the result. In the Michigan cases, however—as in many important public-law cases—the binding impact of a decision on absent parties was formalized through the class action device, as both cases were certified as plaintiff's class actions.[120] The resolution of a class action is binding on represented members of the class by means not merely of *stare decisis* but also of what lawyers call issue and claim preclusion: Represented class members, like the named litigants themselves, are directly prohibited from subsequently challenging that result in court.

With the extraordinary binding effect of a class action come extraordinary obligations on the part of the named class representatives and of the court. Before certifying a class, the court must find that the named representatives have claims that are typical of those of the class and will serve as fair and adequate representatives of the class.[121] For their part, the named representatives— Barbara Grutter in the case bearing her name, Jennifer Gratz and Patrick Hamacher in the *Gratz* case—assume a legal obligation to represent absent class members diligently and in good faith.

Each of the named plaintiffs in the Michigan cases thus litigated not only on his or her own behalf, as a party seeking to vindicate an interest in a dispute, but also as formal representatives of other similarly situated parties whose similar interests stood to be similarly affected, positively or negatively, by the court's ultimate resolution of the dispute.

Nonsimilarly situated parties who nonetheless might have been significantly affected by the outcome of the dispute. Even where a dispute brought before a court broadens into a class action, some parties with strong interests in that dispute might find themselves unrepresented by any of the active litigants. For example, consider the potential interest in the outcome of *Grutter* held by a current University of Michigan Law School student who thinks she benefits from racial diversity in the student body, or of a prospective minority applicant to the law school. A ruling in favor of the plaintiff in the case would harm both the current student's interest in continued racial diversity and the prospective minority applicant's interest in gaining admission. But the existing defendant in the case—the law school itself—might not have the strongest incentive to protect these interests. Suppose, for instance, that a showing of past intentional discrimination in admissions by the law school would be the most effective way to

---

120. In both cases the class mostly likely was certified pursuant to Rule 23(b)(2), which applies where

> the party opposing the class has acted or refused to act on grounds generally applicable to the class, thereby making appropriate final injunctive relief or corresponding declaratory relief with respect to the class as a whole. . . .

FED. R. CIV. P. 23(c).

121. *See* FED. R. CIV. P. 23(a).

justify the law school's current affirmative action plan.[122] The law school itself might be reluctant to make such a showing in its defense for fear of the ancillary legal consequences—lawsuits by rejected minority applicants, perhaps—that might result.

This line of reasoning underlies Federal Rule of Civil Procedure 24, which allows third parties to intervene in a lawsuit when they have an interest that might not adequately be protected by the existing litigants.[123] Rule 24 intervenors become full-fledged parties to the case, filing pleadings and motions, conducting discovery, participating in a trial, and binding themselves to the ultimate result to the same extent as the original parties. In each of the Michigan cases, the lower courts applied Rule 24 to allow intervention by large groups of interested parties (seventeen individuals and one organization in *Gratz*, forty-one individuals and three organizations in *Grutter*) consisting mostly of current or prospective students.

Other parties with an interest in the issues being litigated. As we saw in Chapter 5, most court cases, even those involving garden-variety private disputes, have the potential to affect a wide variety of interests in outward ripples from the litigants themselves. A slip-and-fall suit against a grocery store, for instance, might affect not only the injured plaintiff and the store's owner but also the plaintiff's family (who would benefit from any recovery), the store's employees (who might lose their jobs after a large judgment), the store's customers (who might benefit from greater attention to safety or, on the other hand, might suffer from the higher prices necessary to pay a judgment), and so on. And of course if the court deciding the slip-and-fall case establishes a new legal principle, other grocery store owners and their employees and customers, and other slip-and-fall victims and their families, will be affected when that principle is applied, through *stare decisis*, in subsequent cases.

We might usefully divide these ripple effects of a court decision into *precedential* and *ancillary* dimensions. A decision has precedential impact to the extent it establishes a legal norm that may subsequently be applied in similar cases through *stare decisis*, and thus may subsequently bind similarly situated litigants and people who change their behavior in order to avoid becoming litigants. If the grocery store slip-and-fall case produces, say, an expanded basis for premises liability, similarly situated store owners within the jurisdiction will find themselves precedentially bound by that principle.

In contrast, a decision has ancillary impact to the extent its effects fall on nonlitigants whose lives will be changed in a practical way by the decision, even though they may never litigate, or worry about litigating, the issues involved in the decision. If the grocery store is found liable in the slip-and-fall suit, its

---

122. In point of fact there was no evidence of past intentional discrimination introduced by any party in either of the Michigan cases.

123. *See* Fed. R. Civ. P. 24.

customers will be affected by having to pay higher prices to cover the costs of the judgment, even though few of them will ever find themselves involved in their own slip-and-fall lawsuits.

A distinguishing feature of constitutional adjudication is that both its precedential and its ancillary effects tend to be especially salient. *Grutter* and *Gratz* are cases in point. The precedential impact of a decision holding that racial diversity in higher education is not a compelling interest would have forced most institutions of higher education in the country, public and private,[124] to eliminate their race-conscious admissions programs; only schools able to demonstrate a history of intentional discrimination against racial minorities could have justified affirmative action as a remedial tool.[125] And if such a decision had resulted in fewer minorities being admitted to elite schools, as almost certainly would have been the case, its ancillary impact would have been quite broad indeed—falling upon minority applicants themselves; upon nonminority students denied significant opportunity to interact with minority classmates; upon instructors deprived of the rich classroom environment that can result from racial diversity; upon employers denied access to well-educated minority graduates; upon minority communities, denied leaders and role models; upon society as a whole, denied the benefits of diversity in its leadership ranks; and so on, extending outward in concentric circles.[126]

Some of these precedential and ancillary effects can be accounted for—and were accounted for in the Michigan cases—through the device of intervention,

---

124. The scope of such a decision would have extended to private schools through Title VI, which prohibits racial discrimination by schools receiving federal funds; the Supreme Court has interpreted Title VI to be coextensive with the Equal Protection Clause. *See* Alexander v. Choate, 469 U.S. 287, 293 (1985).

125. Supreme Court decisions prior to the Michigan cases had strongly suggested that the remediation of general societal discrimination, as opposed to specific intentional discrimination by the governmental unit in question or by private actors within that governmental unit's jurisdiction, is not a sufficiently compelling interest to justify affirmative action. *See* Adarand Constructors v. Pena, 515 U.S. 200 (1995); City of Richmond v. J.A. Croson Co., 488 U.S. 469 (1989); Regents of the Univ. of California v. Bakke, 438 U.S. 265 (1978).

126. I recognize that my illustration of the point here assumes the pro-affirmative action stance that I happen to share. The same point, however, can be illustrated by considering, from an anti-affirmative action viewpoint, the actual precedential and ancillary effects of the Court's holding in both Michigan cases that racial diversity in higher education is a compelling state interest. Most universities in the nation, public and private, now can (and undoubtedly will) continue to use race as a factor in admissions, thus reducing the chances that nonminority applicants like Barbara Grutter, Jennifer Gratz, and Patrick Hamacher will gain admission to the elite schools. The negative ripple effects of the decision might include a rising tide of nonminority resentment against affirmative action (and thus against its minority beneficiaries); the denial to employers and society as a whole of the services of well-educated nonminority graduates; and so on.

as I discussed above. But the further away from the metaphorical center of the lawsuit its ripple effects flow, the less likely it is that those who feel the effects will possess the level of interest that is legally required for intervention or, for that matter, that is practically necessary to justify the significant expenditure of resources that full-fledged intervention in a lawsuit entails.

Enter the concept of *amicus curiae*, which allows parties with an interest in the issues being litigated in a case to participate through the limited means of briefs and, sometimes, oral arguments.[127] The Michigan cases featured an astounding number of *amicus* briefs in both the Court of Appeals and the Supreme Court. By my count:

- In the Court of Appeals, fifteen different *amici* filed briefs in either the *Grutter* or *Gratz* case or both: twelve supporting the university and three supporting the plaintiffs.[128]
- In the Supreme Court, fully *ninety-one* different *amici* or coalitions of *amici* filed briefs in either *Grutter*, *Gratz*, or both: seventy supporting the university, seventeen supporting the plaintiffs, and four supporting neither party.[129]
- And the actual number of *amici* was even higher than this, as many of the *amicus* briefs were filed on behalf of multiple parties.

The range of interests represented by the *amici*, moreover, was quite diverse. The *amici* supporting the university included—to name only a few—the NAACP "Inc." Fund; the ACLU; the AFL-CIO; a group of "former high-ranking officers

---

127. The Supreme Court's rules encourage the filing of *amicus curiae* briefs that "bring[] to the attention of the Court relevant matter not already brought to its attention by the parties," and allow them with the unanimous consent of the parties or the permission of the Court. SUP. CT. R. 37.1–37.3. The Federal Rules of Appellate Procedure similarly allow the filing of *amicus* briefs in the Courts of Appeals by unanimous consent or leave of court. FED. R. APP. P. 29(a). Both sets of rules allow the federal or state governments to file *amicus* briefs without consent or leave of court. SUP. CT. R. 37.4; FED. R. APP. P. 29(a). Both sets of rules also allow *amici* to participate in oral argument by leave of court, SUP. CT. R. 28.7; FED. R. APP. P. 29(g); absent the consent of the party on whose side an *amicus* will argue, the Supreme Court grants leave "only in the most extraordinary circumstances," SUP. CT. R. 28.7.

128. All of these *amici* filed briefs in the *Grutter* case; two *amici* also filed briefs in the *Gratz* case. In addition to the seventeen total *amicus* briefs listed as "filed" on the Sixth Circuit dockets for either case, six briefs are listed as "tendered" but not "filed," which apparently means the court never gave formal permission for their filing. Of those tendered briefs, five supported the university; it is not clear from the docket which side was supported by the sixth brief.

129. This does not count the three *amicus* briefs filed in support of the petition for certiorari in one or the other case.

and civilian leaders of the Army, Navy, Air Force, and Marine Corps"[130]; more than twenty states and territories; various other law schools, colleges, universities, and administrators and faculty members thereof; members of Congress; a long list of major corporations; the governor of Michigan; a coalition of Indian tribes; the American Psychological Association and the American Sociological Association; groups of minority lawyers and law students; and the College Board. *Amici* on the other side included a number of conservative think-tanks and activist organizations such as the Cato Institute and the Center for Individual Freedom; various scholarly groups, including a coalition of anti-affirmative action law professors; the State of Florida and its governor, Jeb Bush; and the U.S. government as represented by the Solicitor General. (The Solicitor General also participated in the oral argument of both cases, in each case splitting time with the plaintiffs' counsel.)

It is worth taking special note of the presence of federal, state, and local governmental entities and officials as *amici* on both sides of the Michigan cases, a phenomenon facilitated by the Supreme Court rules and the Federal Rules of Appellate Procedure, which generally allow the federal and state governments (and, in the case of the Supreme Court rules, local governments) to file *amicus* briefs without consent of the parties or leave of court.[131] The *amicus* participation of government might be seen to broaden representation in the proceedings in a special way, as governments are directly politically accountable to their citizenry. If a majority of the citizens of Maryland, for example, object to their attorney general's having joined in an amicus brief supporting the Michigan cases, they can express their displeasure at the polls during the next election. The same goes for the citizens of the country generally if they object to the U.S. Solicitor General's participation in the case—at the behest of the President of whose administration he is a part—in support of the plaintiffs. Thus it is not stretching things too much to say that "the people" themselves were represented, through government *amici*, in the decision of the Michigan cases, as they are in many important constitutional decisions.

Of course, with ninety-one *amicus* briefs in the Supreme Court, it is difficult to believe that any justice—indeed, any justice's law clerk—could have read all of them. Most likely some *amicus* briefs—certainly the Solicitor General's brief, and possibly the briefs filed by advocacy groups well-known to the Court, like the Inc. Fund and the ACLU—do garner the close attention of the justices. But most probably go unread. Much of the point of *amicus* participation in high-profile cases like *Grutter* and *Gratz*, however, is simply the signal it sends to the Court about the likely impact (practical and political) of any decision it

---

130. *See* Consolidated Brief of Lt. Gen. Julius W. Becton, Jr. et al. as Amici Curiae in Support of Respondents at 1, Grutter v. Bollinger, 539 U.S. 306 (2003) (No. 02–241); Gratz v. Bollinger, 539 U.S. 244 (2003) (No. 02–516), 2003 WL 1787554.

131. *See supra* note 127.

might render. A quick survey of the list of *amici* in the Michigan cases would tell a justice generally what kinds of groups, and how many of them, are lining up on each side. In this way a justice can get a sense of the political consequences of her vote—a sense that might temper the justice's own political leanings about the result of the case. *Amicus* participation, in other words, can inject a strong element of broad-based democratic politics into constitutional adjudication.

Citizens represented by the governmental entities whose policies were being challenged. Finally, we need to keep in mind that the defendants in the Michigan cases were themselves government bodies and officials. The University of Michigan Board of Regents is a public body whose membership is determined by the citizens of Michigan in statewide elections. The Board of Regents in turn appoints the university president, who appoints the deans of the law school, the LSA, and the university's other units. The admissions policies being challenged in the Michigan cases thus were ultimately attributable to elected state government officials. In litigating the Michigan cases, then, the defendants were in a very real sense representing the people of the state of Michigan. The people of Michigan participated by proxy in the decision of the cases.[132]

As the Michigan cases illustrate, therefore, participation in the litigation of a major constitutional challenge can be very broad indeed. Such cases are not decided by judges isolated in ivory towers. They are decided, rather, by judges under pressure from—and able to draw upon the contributions of—a wide range of litigants and *amici* who represent a diversity of interests in the outcome of a case.

(iii) The Impact of Participation Of course, there is a difficulty lurking in a participatory model of adjudication, one that is perhaps exacerbated in controversial constitutional cases. The difficulty is simply that the presence of a lot of eager participants in cases like *Grutter* and *Gratz* need not guarantee that their participation will accomplish anything. How do we know litigant and *amicus* participation actually makes a difference to the outcome of a case? Why should we think that participation is in fact meaningful and not just an elaborate but ultimately empty display, a "splendid bauble" in John Marshall's dismissive phrase?[133]

---

132. Of course, not all of Michigan's citizens agreed with the university's race-conscious admissions policies. But this is a large part of the point: By exerting sufficient political pressure (down to replacing members of the Board of Regents at the next election), a majority of Michigan's citizens could have prevented the university from defending its policies in court, or for that matter could have revoked or changed the policies. The university's lawyers thus were acting on behalf of the public, not of some private interest.

133. This is how Marshall, in *McCulloch v. Maryland*, described the notion of a Constitution parsimoniously interpreted to narrowly confine Congress's powers. *See* McCulloch v. Maryland, 17 U.S. (4 Wheat.) 316, 421 (1819).

If we are not judges—and even, I suspect, if we are—we have to rely mostly on circumstantial evidence in trying to answer this question. Consider the following pieces of data in this regard:

Written opinions. One very basic but telling bit of evidence in support of the idea that participation is meaningful is the nearly universal American norm, carrying the force of law in many circumstances,[134] that a judge should explain a dispositive decision in a written opinion that addresses both the factual proofs and the legal arguments presented by the litigants. And the bigger and more important the case, the more extensive the paper trail of judicial opinions is likely to be.

The Michigan cases, for example, produced a total of twenty judicial opinions on the merits: one by the district judge in the *Grutter* case[135] and two by the district judge in *Gratz*;[136] four by Court of Appeals judges in the *Grutter* case[137] (the Sixth Circuit did not issue a decision in *Gratz*); and thirteen by Supreme Court justices, six in *Grutter* and seven in *Gratz*. Every judge with a say in the outcome of the cases either wrote or joined in an opinion explaining the grounds for his or her decision. In doing so the Michigan judges did not behave like Delphic oracles or Platonic Guardians; they behaved like accountable decision-makers whose decisions must be justified to others.

Oral argument. Lawyers for the litigants typically have the opportunity to present oral arguments prior to an appellate decision or a dispositive ruling by the trial court.[138] As anyone closely familiar with American adjudication is aware, oral "argument," especially at the appellate level, tends to consist primarily not

---

134. The Federal Rules of Civil Procedure, for example, require a district judge to file a written opinion stating her findings of fact and conclusions of law following a bench trial. *See* FED. R. CIV. P. 52.

135. *See* Grutter v. Bollinger, 137 F. Supp. 2d 821 (E.D. Mich. 2001).

136. *See* Gratz v. Bollinger, 122 F. Supp. 2d 811 (E.D. Mich. 2000) (addressing the university's defenses); Gratz v. Bollinger, 135 F. Supp. 2d 790 (E.D. Mich. 2001) (addressing the defendant-intervenors' defenses).

137. Seven Court of Appeals judges actually filed opinions in *Grutter*, but three of the opinions (a concurrence by Judge Moore and dissents by Judges Siler and Batchelder) went only to an unusual procedural issue presented in the case and not to the merits. *See* Grutter v. Bollinger, 288 F.3d 732, 752 (6th Cir. 2002) (Moore, J., concurring); *id.* at 815 (Siler, J., dissenting); *id.* at 815 (Batchelder, J., dissenting).

138. At the trial court level, the Federal Rules of Civil Procedure do not contain a general presumption in favor of oral argument on motions. Most local district court rules allow for oral argument, however. The Federal Rules of Appellate Procedure require oral argument "in every case unless a panel of three judges who have examined the briefs and record unanimously agrees that oral argument is unnecessary." FED. R. APP. P. 34(a)(2). The Supreme Court rules assume that oral argument will occur in every case for which the Court grants *certiorari*. *See* U.S. SUP. CT. R. 16.2 ("Whenever the Court grants a petition for a writ of certiorari. . . [t]he case then will be scheduled for briefing and oral argument.").

of a lawyer's recitation of a prepared line of reasoning but rather of questions from the bench and answers from counsel.[139] The arguments before the Supreme Court in the Michigan cases were no exception to this rule; they featured active questioning of attorneys on both sides (including of the Solicitor General arguing as *amicus* for the plaintiffs).[140] The trial courts in both cases also heard oral argument on the parties' cross motions for summary judgment,[141] and the Court of Appeals, sitting *en banc*, itself heard oral argument in both cases.[142]

Do oral arguments matter? *Grutter* and *Gratz* offer some evidence that they do. The justices refer several times in the Supreme Court opinions to statements made at oral argument.[143] More generally, appellate judges often claim that oral arguments can help resolve uncertainties, confusions, reservations, and the like that they may have after reading the briefs.[144]

Attention to the proofs. Even in constitutional cases presenting hotly contested legal issues, judges at least make a show of paying attention to the proofs presented by the litigants. Often the show is a very convincing one. Consider District Judge Bernard A. Friedman's opinion in the *Grutter* case.[145] The opinion consumes fifty-two pages of the *Federal Supplement Second* reporter. About twenty-three

---

139. The Supreme Court rules provide:

Oral argument should emphasize and clarify the written arguments in the briefs on the merits. Counsel should assume that all Justices have read the briefs before oral argument. Oral argument read from a prepared text is not favored.

U.S. Sup. Ct. R. 28.1.

140. *See* Transcript of Oral Argument, Grutter v. Bollinger, 539 U.S. 306 (2003) (No. 02–241), 2003 WL 1728613; Transcript of Oral Argument, Gratz v. Bollinger, 539 U.S. 244 (2003) (No. 02–516), 2003 WL 1728816.

141. *See* Grutter v. Bollinger, 137 F. Supp. 2d 821, 823 (E.D. Mich. 2001); *Gratz*, 122 F. Supp. 2d at 814. The *Grutter* court took the summary judgment motions under advisement and ultimately decided the merits after a trial, *see Grutter*, 137 F. Supp. 2d at 823, while the *Gratz* court decided the merits on summary judgment.

142. *See* Docket for the U.S. Court of Appeals for the Sixth Circuit, Grutter v. Bollinger (No. 01-1447); Docket for the U.S. Court of Appeals for the Sixth Circuit, Gratz v. Bollinger (No. 01-1438) (both available on Westlaw).

143. *See* Grutter v. Bollinger, 539 U.S. 306, 342–44 (2003); *id.* at 364–66 (Thomas, J., dissenting); Gratz v. Bollinger, 539 U.S. 244, 265–66, 272–74 (2003); *id.* at 283–89 (Stevens, J., concurring); *id.* at 291–93 (Souter, J., dissenting); *id.* at 302–03 (Ginsburg, J., dissenting).

144. *See* The Honorable Ruth Bader Ginsburg, *Remarks on Appellate Advocacy*, 50 S.C. L. Rev. 567, 569 (1999) ("Inquiries from the bench give counsel a chance to satisfy the court on matters the judges think significant, issues the judges might puzzle over in chambers, and resolve less satisfactorily without counsel's aid."); The Honorable Rhesa Hawkins Barksdale, *The Role of Civility in Appellate Advocacy*, 50 S.C. L. Rev. 573, 575 (1999) (remarking that in regard to oral argument "the court wants to test or challenge the strength or logic of positions advanced by counsel").

145. Grutter v. Bollinger, 127 F. Supp. 2d 821 (E.D. Mich. 2001).

of those pages consist of detailed, balanced, essentially nonevaluative summary of the proofs presented at trial, featuring voluminous cites to the trial transcript and many quotes from testimony and documentary evidence.[146]

Why did Judge Friedman devote so much time and energy to simply rehashing the evidence? Not to facilitate review on appeal: the Court of Appeals and Supreme Court had available to them full copies of the record, including the trial transcript, and Judge Friedman's actual findings of fact were summarized more pithily elsewhere in his opinion.[147] Not to assist lawyers and judges in assessing the precedential scope of his decision: Judge Friedman surely knew that his decision would be appealed and thus would have little or no precedential value (and again, in any case, he presented his actual findings of fact elsewhere in the opinion). The most likely explanation is that Judge Friedman simply wanted to demonstrate his attention to the proofs presented by the litigants; he wanted to show that he had carefully considered the evidence offered by both sides before making his decision.[148]

What is more, the proofs appear to matter. Judges, of course, say they matter: They purport to be basing their decisions on the evidence presented. And the Michigan cases give us a good indication that facts sometimes do make a difference. Justices O'Connor and Stephen Breyer switched sides, as it were, between the *Grutter* and *Gratz* cases, turning a five–four victory for the law school in *Grutter* into a six–three defeat for the LSA in *Gratz*. What accounts for the switch?

It can only be the factual differences between the two lawsuits. Justices O'Connor and Breyer agreed that obtaining the benefits of racial and ethnic diversity in higher education can serve as a compelling state interest sufficient to justify some race-consciousness in admissions.[149] That legal interest, of course, existed in both the *Grutter* and the *Gratz* cases. Justices O'Connor and Breyer voted to uphold the law school policy but not the LSA policy, however, on the factual ground that the former "provide[d] for a meaningful individualized review of applicants" while the latter did not.[150] For Justices O'Connor and Breyer, the law school's proof that its admissions policy included individualized review made the difference in the *Grutter* case, while the plaintiffs' proof that the

---

146. *See id.* at 825–39, 855–63.

147. *See id.* at 839–55, 863–72.

148. Really by *all* sides, as the defendant-intervenors themselves presented substantial evidence at trial. *See id.* at 855–63 (summarizing the intervenors' evidence).

149. Justice Breyer joined in Justice O'Connor's opinion for the Court in *Grutter* in which she held that diversity in education is a compelling government interest. *See* Grutter v. Bollinger, 539 U.S. 306, 326–34 (2003).

150. Gratz v. Bollinger, 539 U.S. 244, 276–78 (2003) (O'Connor, J., concurring, joined by Breyer, J.).

LSA policy did not include such individualized review made the difference in the *Gratz* case.

Responsiveness to the arguments. So the Michigan cases provide some evidence that judges, even in high-profile constitutional cases, pay attention to the parties' proofs. What about the parties' arguments regarding the legal consequences of those proofs? Litigants can hardly be said to be "participating" in the decision of a case if the judges who actually render the decision ignore their arguments in doing so.

It seems there are two complementary ways in which we might want a judge to be responsive to the arguments made by the litigants.[151] We might want the judge to base her ruling on the arguments actually made by the litigants on the winning side, not on arguments of her own contrivance. And we might want the judge to acknowledge the arguments made by the losing litigants and to explain the basis of her disagreement with them.

I suspect the Michigan cases are not unusual in the fact that the judges deciding them, from the district court to the Supreme Court, generally did pretty well, if not perfectly, at living up to both these ideals. Consider first the extent to which the various judges appear to have based their rulings on the arguments actually made by the winning litigants. There is no indication that any of the judges at any level went off-road, as it were, to decide issues not argued by the parties or to rely upon grounds the parties did not offer.[152] Of course, this kind of off-roading is likely to be relatively rare in precisely the highly visible constitutional lawsuits I am writing about here, because the issues typically will be

---

151. I use "litigants" here as shorthand for "the lawyers representing the litigants," which usually is a more accurate description of the people doing the actual proving and arguing.

152. No indication, that is, with one potential exception. Justice Stevens, joined by Justice Souter, dissented in the *Gratz* case on the grounds that the plaintiffs, who had enrolled and obtained degrees at other colleges after being denied admission to Michigan, lacked standing to seek prospective relief against the LSA admissions policy and were inadequate representatives of a class including current or future applicants. *See Gratz*, 539 U.S. at 282 (Stevens, J., dissenting, joined by Souter, J.). The issues of standing and representative adequacy apparently had not been raised or argued by the university or any other party, except that counsel for the plaintiffs had been asked about standing during the oral argument before the Court. *See* Transcript of Oral Argument, *Gratz*, 539 U.S. 244 (No. 02–516), 2003 WL 1728816.

I think we can see Justice Stevens's reliance on the unargued standing problem as an exception that proves the rule. The Court's precedent treats standing, and justiciability requirements generally, as aspects of federal subject-matter jurisdiction: Without them a federal court has no power to hear a case. *See, e.g.*, Allen v. Wright, 468 U.S. 737 (1984). The point of this is to preserve the dispute-resolving posture that animates participatory adjudication in the first place. Objections to justiciability, then, are a logical exception to the general principle that courts should limit themselves to responding to arguments proffered by the disputants themselves.

relatively well-defined (Is diversity a compelling interest or isn't it? Is the plan narrowly tailored or not?)[153] and the lawyering usually will be top-notch. If there is a reasonable argument to be made in a constitutional case that reaches the Supreme Court, somewhere along the line the appropriate party is likely to have made it.

In this regard, one benefit of *amici curiae* is that they sometimes are better suited than the litigants to making certain arguments. In the Michigan cases, the Supreme Court in fact seems at several points to have relied on arguments made by *amici* that only those *amici* were in a position to press. In her opinion for the *Grutter* majority, for example, Justice O'Connor cited *amicus* briefs filed by, respectively, a group of law school deans and a coalition of colleges for the point that a great many schools had designed their admissions programs to accord with Justice Lewis Powell's opinion in the 1978 *Bakke* case, which had suggested that diversity is a compelling interest and that consideration of race along with many other factors might be permissible.[154] The University of Michigan Law School, standing alone, could not have made this point so convincingly. Later, Justice O'Connor rested her holding that racial diversity is in fact a compelling interest in part on assertions by corporate and military *amici* of the importance of diversity in global business and in military training;[155] these too are arguments the law school by itself was not well-equipped to make.

What about the participation of the losing litigants? Obviously there is a sense in which the losing parties' participation was less "effective" than the winning parties'; after all, they lost. But of course it would be asking too much of participation to demand that both sides win. Our ambitions for responsiveness need to be more modest. We might think a judge owes each litigant not victory—that would be impossible—but rather acknowledgment and attention; she must listen in good faith even to the arguments of the party she ultimately rules against, and she must take those arguments into account in making her ruling.

Is there any indication that the various judges met this obligation in the *Grutter* and *Gratz* cases? I think the answer is yes (and again I have no reason to believe the Michigan cases are extraordinary in this respect). Without listing the instances in exhaustive detail,[156] suffice it to say that the district courts' opinions

---

153. The analytic framework in which the Michigan cases were argued and decided—strict scrutiny under the Equal Protection Clause, which requires the government to demonstrate that it has a compelling interest which its policy or decision, whatever it might be, is narrowly tailored to serve—has been well-established since *Bakke*, which held that even remedial race-consciousness by the government is subject to strict scrutiny. *See* cases cited *supra* note 125.

154. *See Grutter*, 539 U.S. at 322–24.

155. *See id.* at 330–34.

156. The curious or skeptical reader can locate examples himself or herself by downloading electronic versions of the district courts' opinions and searching for occurrences of words containing the roots "argu-" and "conten-"; those words frequently are used to

in both cases are replete with express references to the arguments of the losing litigants (the law school in *Grutter*, the plaintiffs in *Gratz*) and explanations of why the court rejects those arguments. The same practice appears with more subtlety in the Court of Appeals and Supreme Court opinions, where references to arguments of the other side tend to be directed to the judges or justices who adopted those arguments, not to the litigants that originally made them. (Again, I will not take up space with voluminous citations here.) But the basic phenomenon on appeal is the same as in the district courts, with the disagreeing judges serving as proxies for the disputing litigants whose views they represent. Indeed, the absorption of the losing litigants' contentions by dissenting judges or justices serves to emphasize the extent to which those contentions were given full voice and taken seriously.

Finally, the Michigan cases also provide a somewhat less common, but perhaps more salient, illustration of the phenomenon of a court's addressing a losing party's arguments. Recall that groups of individual students, would-be applicants, and pro-affirmative action groups were allowed to intervene as defendants in both cases. Their primary purpose for intervening was to offer two related justifications for the university's admissions policies that the university itself chose not to put forward: The intervenors argued that race-consciousness in the university's admissions was necessary to remediate both the effects of general racial discrimination in American society and the more specific discriminatory effects of the university's own policies.[157]

The relevant point here is that the courts at every level addressed the intervenors' contentions, meaning that the courts took those contentions seriously and responded to them in good faith. The district courts devoted the most attention to the intervenors' arguments, rejecting them in both cases but still giving substantial consideration to the intervenors' proofs and their legal positions.[158] The Court of Appeals in *Grutter* acknowledged the intervenors' position but declined to address its merits, having already upheld the law school's policy on a

---

describe reasoning with which the court disagrees, and they appear often in that context in both opinions.

157. *See* Grutter v. Bollinger, 137 F. Supp. 2d 821, 855–72 (E.D. Mich. 2001) (describing the *Grutter* intervenors' arguments); *Gratz v. Bollinger*, 135 F. Supp. 2d 790 (E.D. Mich. 2001) (describing the *Gratz* intervenors' arguments). It's fairly obvious why the university itself chose not to press this latter argument. As for the general remediation justification, no doubt it seemed to the university's lawyers—whose clients arguably had the most to lose, as it was their policies at stake—to be a likely loser under Supreme Court precedent. *See* cases cited *supra* note 125.

158. Judge Friedman in the *Grutter* case spent nearly seventeen reporter pages on the intervenors' arguments, *see Grutter*, 137 F. Supp. 2d at 855–72; Judge Patrick J. Duggan in *Gratz* wrote a separate twelve-page opinion addressing them.

diversity rationale.[159] The Supreme Court too addressed the argument, although it gave it shorter shrift than it perhaps deserved: In a *Gratz* footnote, the Court agreed with the district court "that respondent-intervenors 'failed to present any evidence that the discrimination alleged by them, or the continuing effects of such discrimination, was the real justification for the LSA's race-conscious admissions programs.'"[160] The Court did not address the intervenors' contentions in *Grutter*, presumably because (like the Court of Appeals) it upheld the law school's policy on diversity grounds.

(iv) Participation, Competence, Impartiality Participation, then, can be quite broad indeed in constitutional litigation, as the Michigan cases suggest. And participation can make a difference—it can actually help to shape the results.

From the perspective of the DR account of constitutional process, the participatory nature of constitutional adjudication is significant in two ways. First of all, participation promotes competent constitutional decisionmaking and, especially, the image of competent constitutional decisionmaking. Like broad participation in democratic politics, broad participation in adjudication can enhance competence by incorporating a diversity of viewpoints and facilitating deliberation—in the context of adjudication, really more like debate—among those viewpoints. Broad participation in constitutional adjudication also can promote competence (and the perception of it) by further tying the judicial process to the democratic process, acquainting courts with the real-world relevance of the issues they must decide and the spectrum and intensity of positions on those issues.

Second, participation promotes actual and perceived judicial impartiality. A principal danger of judicial review is that insulating the process from ordinary politics only trades one type of partiality for another: It removes constitutional law from the biases of majoritarian democracy, only to subject it to the biases of judges. Participatory adjudication cannot eliminate this risk, but it can mitigate it, as I think the foregoing discussion suggests. A judge who must respond to the arguments of both the winning and the losing parties is a judge whose discretion is to that extent constrained.

I want to elaborate briefly on this second point, to make clear what I am *not* claiming. I am not asserting that meaningful participation in constitutional adjudication somehow avoids bias, predisposition, or other types of partiality in judicial decisions. A participatory model of adjudication does not imply that because the litigants are allowed to present their proofs and arguments, all reasonable judges will be led inexorably to unanimous agreement about the outcome of a case. Constitutional questions tend to be extremely difficult ones,

---

159. *See* Grutter v. Bollinger, 288 F.3d 732, 739 n.4 (6th Cir. 2002). The Court of Appeals never rendered a decision in *Gratz*, as the Supreme Court granted *certiorari* before it could do so.

160. Gratz v. Bollinger, 539 U.S. 244, 257 n.9 (2003).

susceptible of more than one reasonable answer; that is why they are controversial, and why they make it to the Supreme Court. It would be surprising, and perhaps even disturbing, if reasonable people (including reasonable judges) did not differ on the answers to such questions. It would be equally surprising if a judge's larger set of political affiliations and ideological commitments did not contribute to her answers.

The significance of participation, rather, is that it forces a judge to engage with the viewpoints of an array of affected parties, and with the facts of a particular dispute, before deciding such issues. Judges must pay attention to the affected parties' proofs and arguments, must consider and respond to those proofs and arguments, and must be seen to be doing so. The hope is that this process will cause judges in close cases to keep an open mind. Participatory adjudication is frustrated, not when a judge ultimately decides in accordance with her preexisting political bent, but rather when the judge decides based *solely* on her preexisting bent, without any receptiveness whatsoever to the proofs and arguments. The enemy of participatory adjudication is judicial closed-mindedness, not judicial predisposition.

3. INTERPRETIVE METHODOLOGY

The institutional dynamics of American constitutional process thus strike a balance, sometimes a delicate one, between externality and responsiveness, and therefore between relative impartiality and reasonable competence. This balance, of course, ought to be nurtured by the methodology that American judges (and, sometimes, other actors) use to interpret constitutional rules.

The discussion to this point suggests why interpretation is especially important in the constitutional context. The American Framers, recognizing the limits of their competence to anticipate and authoritatively resolve the myriad specific disputes that would arise over the life of the Constitution, typically rendered constitutional norms in especially open-textured language. The textual expression of constitutional rules tends to be less determinate than the expressions of many other legal rules, particularly rules embodied in statutes. Constitutional rules therefore typically liquidate proportionally fewer disputes ahead of time, merely by virtue of their textual expression, than statutes do; a larger percentage of constitutional dispute resolution must be done *ex post*, by courts (and sometimes other interpreters) once a dispute already has arisen.

In Chapter 5, I outlined methodologies of statutory and common-law interpretation that employ the concepts of linguistic intention and justification. I will suggest below that this basic methodology is appropriate for the interpretation of constitutional rules as well. But first I want to explain why two alternative interpretive approaches, both of which find expression in currently popular methodologies of interpretation, do not work very well on a DR account of constitutional law.

A. The False Promise of Formalism

I introduced, and critiqued, formalist methodologies of legal interpretation in Chapter 5. Formalists attempt to eliminate or greatly reduce the need for *ex post* adjudication of normative disputes by relying on the text or the "original intent" behind a legal rule. The formalist hope is that the text or original intent will make a rule very determinate, giving potential disputants notice of how the rule will govern their conduct so disputes can be avoided or, if they arise nonetheless, can be resolved without much effort by a judge. Some formalists (what I called Default Formalists) go further and assert that where a legal rule is not determinate in one of these ways, it should be held *not* to apply to a dispute, thus preserving the status quo (and by doing so promoting another form of determinacy).

Formalism has proven especially attractive to many theorists and practitioners of constitutional interpretation,[161] and the discussion to this point suggests two very big reasons why. First, formalism promises significant externality in the process of constitutional interpretation: It suggests that judges can apply constitutional rules to particular cases in a way that relies little (if at all) on the judges' own creativity and mostly or entirely on decisions made by the constitutional Framers when they enacted those rules. Because, as we've seen, the Framing process occurred, in most cases, multiple generations ago, an interpretive methodology that simply implements decisions made at the Framing can lay claim to substantial impartiality with respect to the current disputes it is used to resolve. That impartiality can provide a strong justification for the countermajoritarian force of constitutional law and judicial review; it also can derail potential worries that judges themselves are simply implementing their own (partial) preferences when they decide constitutional cases.[162]

---

161. Among the most influential examples are Scalia, *supra* note 97; Antonin Scalia, *Originalism: The Lesser Evil,* 57 U. Cin. L. Rev. 849 (1989); and Bork, *supra* note 59.

162. The formalist's pursuit of both these goals is magnificently captured by Justice Scalia in the following passage from his dissent in *Planned Parenthood v. Casey,* the 1992 decision in which the Court declined to overrule *Roe v. Wade*:

> As long as this Court thought (and the people thought) that we Justices were doing essentially lawyers' work up here—reading text and discerning our society's traditional understanding of that text—the public pretty much left us alone. Texts and traditions are facts to study, not convictions to demonstrate about. But if in reality our process of constitutional adjudication consists primarily of making *value judgments.* . ., then a free and intelligent people's attitude towards us can be expected to be (*ought* to be) quite different. The people know that their value judgments are quite as good as those taught

This promise of formalism turns out to be false, for reasons canvassed in Chapter 5 that in fact apply with special force in the constitutional context. Before elucidating this claim, however, allow me to mention the second reason why constitutional formalism has been and remains quite popular, a reason that connects closely to the failings of the first reason. It happens that constitutional formalism, if it works (a big "if," as we'll see), tends to favor results preferred by contemporary political conservatives. The Framers, after all, lived generations ago, and particular social and political views that were mainstream then, even progressive, almost inevitably seem conservative (if not archaic) now. Many or most of the late-eighteenth-century Framers of the Eighth Amendment's Cruel and Unusual Punishments Clause, for example, probably accepted the validity of capital punishment, a position more likely to be favored today by political conservatives than by political liberals. Those same Framers probably did not, for the most part, contemplate that the concept of "liberty" protected by the Fifth Amendment's Due Process Clause would encompass the rights to abort a fetus or to engage in sexual conduct with a person of the same sex. If judges could mechanically implement decisions made by the Framers on these issues, the results almost certainly would coincide with those endorsed by conservatives in today's politics.

For this reason, there is a political valence to contemporary discussions of constitutional formalism that tends to obscure the question of its actual merits as an interpretive methodology. In fact the tilt of formalism is not entirely conservative; on some issues, such as the validity of affirmative action under the Equal Protection Clause and of regulations of commercial speech and campaign finance under the Free Speech Clause, a successful originalist methodology probably would generate results favored by modern-day progressives. In any event, however, I want to put aside the ideological dimensions of formalism and focus on whether, as a matter of principle, it actually can fulfill its apparent dispute-resolving promise.

That promise, again, is the promise of impartiality—of resolving contentious current issues by simply applying dictates handed down by the Framers, whose chronological distance from us makes their decisions relatively impartial with respect to our disputes. That promise is a false one, for two reasons. First, constitutional rules tend to be highly indeterminate—even more so than ordinary legal rules—and thus it rarely is possible for contemporary interpreters to apply them without exercising substantial interpretive creativity in doing so. And second, as I suggested above, those rules are especially indeterminate for

---

in any law school—maybe better. If, indeed, the "liberties" protected by the Constitution are. . . undefined and unbounded, then the people *should* demonstrate, to protest that we do not implement *their* values instead of *ours*. . . Value judgments, after all, should be voted on, not dictated.

505 U.S. 833, 1000–01 (1992) (Scalia, J. dissenting) (emphasis in original).

good reason: Their Framers knew they could not competently resolve ahead of time the infinite variety of specific disputes to which the rules might apply.

(i) Constitutional Indeterminacy Redux In Chapter 5, I canvassed the failings of formalism as a strategy for bringing determinacy to legal rules. Textualist formalism runs up against the frequently open-textured nature of legal rules, which itself is a product of the realities of the legislative process. Originalist formalism founders on the many conceptual and empirical obstacles to isolating and identifying some original intent or understanding that might bear on the issue to be resolved. A would-be formalist judge, supposedly engaged in the simple project of locating and applying a rule fabricated by the legislators, in fact inevitably finds herself exercising her own creativity at each turn—in choosing from among different plausible meanings of the rule's language, for example, or in deciding which of the many potential "legislators" had intentions that matter and which of their many potential mental states count as the relevant "intentions" or "understandings."

These challenges only grow larger in the constitutional context. As I explained earlier in this chapter, many constitutional rules are expressed using language that is notably abstract, phrases like "the equal protection of the laws" and "the legislative power." This problem with respect to determinacy, already significant, is exacerbated even further by the possibility that the core meanings of some constitutional words and phrases, adopted many generations ago, have changed over time. (The word "misdemeanors" in Article II's Presidential Impeachment Clause is an example; it originally meant "noncriminal misconduct" but has come to signify minor criminal acts.[163]) Textualist formalism therefore is an especially inapt tool for constitutional interpretation.

Originalism fares no better. Part of the problem here is that the broadly participatory process of constitutional creation and amendment expands the universe of potential "Framers"—individuals whose mental states "count" for originalist purposes—to an even less manageable size. Originalist interpretation of garden-variety statutes requires us to sort through various legislative coalitions, committees, and so forth in identifying the "legislators" whose intent or understanding we care about; originalist interpretation of constitutional provisions requires us to consider not only members of the Constitutional Convention (for the original Constitution) or the relevant Congress (for subsequent amendments), but also members of each state convention or legislature that ratified the text. Another part of the problem is that reliable evidence of the relevant mental states (whatever they are) of the relevant people (whoever they are) is likely to be more difficult to find when the lawmaking process took place many generations ago. And then there is the decreasing likelihood, as time goes by, that any

---

163. On the likely original meaning of the phrase "high Crimes and Misdemeanors," see AMAR, *supra* note 23, at 200–01.

particular issue faced by a modern-day interpreter will have been considered by the relevant Framers to the extent necessary to form the requisite mental state. (The clichéd but still telling example here is the fact that the Framers of the Fourth Amendment could not, in 1791, have considered how its prohibition of "unreasonable searches and seizures" would apply to the use of modern investigative technology like wiretaps, computer traces, infrared imaging, and so on.)

The endemic indeterminacy of constitutional rules thus dashes the formalist hope that latter-day interpreters can mechanically implement constitutional rules, leaving the hard part to the Framers and thereby remaining entirely above the contemporary political fray. If constitutional process is going to be meaningfully external to ordinary politics, it cannot rely entirely on the Framers and the rules they created for that externality; the interpretive process itself will have to be relatively external and impartial.[164]

---

164. I should deal briefly here with the most recent version of constitutional formalism, which is essentially an attempt to combine textualism and originalism. The tactic is to appeal, not to the original "intent" of some set of Framers, but rather to the original "meaning" (or "understanding") of the text from the perspective of the broader public at the time of its adoption. Justice Antonin Scalia, for example, looks for "the original meaning of the text, not what the draftsmen intended"—for "how the text of the Constitution was originally understood." Scalia, *supra* note 97, at 38. Robert Bork similarly looks to "the meaning understood at the time of the law's enactment," "what the public of that time would have understood the words to mean." BORK, *supra* note 59, at 144. The "original meaning" turn appears designed to avoid the many conceptual and empirical difficulties with the pursuit of what Bork calls "subjective intention." *See id.* It fails at this task, for the same reasons that earlier forms of textualism and originalism fail. Typically there is no reason to think that the language of a given constitutional provision would have been less open-textured from the perspective of "the public of that time" than it is to us now; nor is there any reason to think that "the public," any more than "the Framers," was a unified entity possessing a single coherent "understanding" of the text, or that the concept of "meaning" or "understanding" is any less vague than the concept of "intent."

And in fact we need not speculate about the failure of original-meaning formalism to bring determinacy to constitutional interpretation; we need only look to the numerous occasions on which new constitutional text has generated almost instant controversy regarding its meaning. In 1791, a mere three years after the Philadelphia Convention, Alexander Hamilton proposed the establishment of a Bank of the United States; the question of whether chartering a bank fell within Congress's constitutional powers was vigorously debated in Congress and among members of George Washington's cabinet and was not finally addressed by the Supreme Court until 1819. *See* MELVIN I. UROFSKY & PAUL FINKELMAN, A MARCH OF LIBERTY: A CONSTITUTIONAL HISTORY OF THE UNITED STATES, VOLUME I, at 132–34 (2d ed. 2002) (describing the debate over the Bank); *see also* McCulloch v. Maryland, 17 U.S. (4 Wheat.) 316 (1819) (upholding the constitutionality of a second Bank). A few years later, in 1789, Federalists and Republicans vehemently disagreed about whether the Alien and Sedition Acts violated the Free Speech and Free Press Clauses of the First Amendment, ratified only eight years earlier. *See* UROFSKY & FINKELMAN, *supra*, at 181–84 (describing the Acts and the fierce debate). Within fifteen years of the Fourteenth

(ii) Formalism vs. Responsiveness But things are even worse than that for constitutional formalism. Even in those relatively few cases where it succeeds in bringing reasonable determinacy, it purchases externality (and thus impartiality) at too high a price in responsiveness (and thus in competence). Consider the likely original understanding regarding the effects of the Fourteenth Amendment on school segregation. Although there is debate on the issue, the weight of the historical evidence suggests that most Framers of the Amendment believed, or would have believed if the question had been presented to them, that racially segregated public schools were perfectly consistent with the Amendment's guarantees of equal protection, due process, and the "privileges" and "immunities" of citizenship.[165] But it is nearly impossible to countenance that proposition today; more than fifty years after *Brown v. Board of Education,* the view that *de jure* segregation is repugnant to the Constitution has taken on the force of gospel. Roughly the same can be said for the views that government cannot forbid married couples to use contraceptives or punish innocently false statements about public officials, despite the likelihood that neither of these tenets is supported by an originalist methodology.[166] Originalist interpretations of the Constitution in these and other areas—assuming they could be made determinate—would produce results that contemporary generations, even most political conservatives among us, would find abhorrent.

A formalist might respond that contemporary attitudes in each of these areas could be reflected in legislation protecting the relevant rights (or in the absence of legislation infringing them); the lack of constitutional protection of the rights need not be decisive. I do not think this is an adequate response to the problem of constitutional obsolescence that successful formalism would present. For one thing, pockets of hyperconservative resistance to the rights

---

Amendment's ratification in 1868, the Supreme Court divided on such central issues as the meaning of its Privileges or Immunities Clause and whether Congress could use its power to "enforce" the Amendment to directly regulate private discrimination. *See* The Slaughter-House Cases, 83 U.S. (16 Wall.) 36 (1872) (narrowly interpreting the Privileges or Immunities Clause); The Civil Rights Cases, 109 U.S. 3 (1883) (holding that Congress's enforcement power did not justify direct regulation of private discrimination). These and other similar examples show the ubiquity of disagreement about the meaning of open-textured constitutional provisions even among the generations that framed them.

165. *See* Michael J. Klarman, *Brown, Originalism, and Constitutional Theory: A Response to Professor McConnell,* 81 Va. L. Rev. 1881 (1995) (arguing that the evidence suggests an original understanding that school segregation was consistent with the Amendment); Michael W. McConnell, *Originalism and the Desegregation Decisions,* 81 Va. L. Rev. 947 (1995) (arguing the opposing position).

166. The relevant Court decisions are *Griswold v. Connecticut,* 381 U.S. 479 (1965) (contraception), and *New York Times Co. v. Sullivan,* 376 U.S. 254 (1964) (innocently false statements about government officials).

could produce state or local legislation that would impair them, even if a strong national consensus existed in their favor.

Moreover, constitutional obsolescence affects government powers as well as individual rights. Congress's broad use of the Commerce Clause to regulate subjects ranging from private racial discrimination to marijuana growth for medicinal purposes, for example, almost certainly exceeds what most of the Framers would have countenanced; on a strictly originalist view of the Commerce Clause, the national majority, acting through Congress, would have substantially less power than it now does to enact its will.[167]

And finally—although admittedly this point is more speculative—it is my sense that most contemporary Americans believe not simply that values like racial equality and privacy should be respected and protected, but that they should have the status of constitutional rights—that is, that they should be enshrined via constitutional law as part of the nation's pantheon of core democratic values. If I am correct about this, then formalist interpretation, even if it would not deny protection for these rights, would nonetheless deny something essential about them *as* rights. Remember, in this regard, that the central importance of responsiveness is to affirm the competence of the constitutional process. A process that fails to protect rights and other values viewed by a broad consensus of Americans as essential to democracy is likely to be a process whose competence is generally questioned—even if those values themselves are protected by other means.

The likelihood that contemporary judgments will, over time, diverge ever more sharply from the Framers' judgments on particular issues is, again, what explains the Framers' use of relatively abstract language to express most constitutional rules. Constitutional formalism—the attempt to somehow glean determinacy from those open-textured phrases—is in this sense a betrayal of the one aspect of original intent of which we are most certain, namely the Framers' intent to craft relatively indeterminate rules. "Not the least characteristic of great statesmanship which the Framers manifested," Justice Felix Frankfurter once wrote, "was the extent to which they did not attempt to bind the future."[168] But this crucial aspect of constitutional process is entirely disregarded by formalists.

(iii) Constitutional Formalism as a Default Rule For similar reasons, Default Formalism is particularly inapt in the constitutional context. Default Formalism (we will recall from Chapter 5) is the view that, when formalist techniques fail

---

167. *See* Heart of Atlanta Motel v. United States, 379 U.S. 241 (1964) (upholding Congress's use of the Commerce power to prohibit private racial discrimination in places of public accommodation); Katzenbach v. McClung, 379 U.S. 294 (1964) (upholding the same); Gonzalez v. Raich, 545 U.S. 1 (2005) (upholding Congress's use of the Commerce power to criminalize the growth of marijuana for personal medicinal use).

168. Youngstown Sheet & Tube Co. v. Sawyer (*The Steel Seizure Case*), 343 U.S. 579, 596 (1952) (Frankfurter, J., concurring).

to identify a determinate meaning of a legal rule, the rule should be assumed not to apply at all to the situation at hand. The problem with Default Formalism as a general approach is that it leaves disputes to be "resolved" by the happenstance of the status quo, automatically awarding the victory to whichever disputant finds herself on top when the dispute reaches a court. There is nothing competent, or accurate more generally, about a system that relies on Default Formalism.

The same can be said for Default Constitutional Formalism, except that the situation there is, predictably, a whole lot worse. The typical indeterminacy of constitutional rules means that formalist techniques routinely, indeed endemically, will fail to generate results in particular cases. This in turn means that on a Default Formalist approach, very few constitutional cases actually would be resolved by constitutional law (resolved, that is, in the sense of being decided in part by reference to particular constitutional rules rather than to a general default rule that indeterminate rules do not apply). A body of law that is supposed to lay the ground rules of democracy and prevent democratic malfunctions would end up leaving the vast majority of democratic disputes to be resolved by democracy itself—precisely the result constitutional law exists to avoid.

Formalism needs a high rate of determinacy to survive as an interpretive strategy; but determinacy is precisely what is most lacking in constitutional rules. That lack of determinacy frustrates formalism's ability to deliver on its promise of true impartiality with respect to current democratic disputes. It also makes formalism deeply problematic as a default rule. And even on those occasions where formalism can provide determinacy, it does so at the expense of responsiveness and thus of competence. The meager and intermittent light shed by constitutional formalism simply is not worth the candle.

B. The Allure of Pragmatism[169]

At something like the opposite end of the interpretive spectrum from constitutional formalism is constitutional pragmatism, a version of the judicial pragmatism discussed in Chapter 6. A constitutional pragmatist believes judges in constitutional cases should strive to reach the morally best results, all things considered, and should feel themselves "bound" by constitutional rules only in a narrowly instrumental sense, as a means to achieving the all-things-considered best result. Of course, a judge adopting a DR approach is a "pragmatist" in a certain sense: She thinks that things will work out best, all things considered, if she and other judges recognize a *prima facie* duty to interpret and apply constitutional and other legal rules. (The central claim of this book is that we should all be pragmatists in this sense.) But the judicial pragmatism I considered in

---

169. With apologies to John Hart Ely, who titled the first chapter of *Democracy and Distrust* "The Allure of Interpretivism." *See* ELY, *supra* note 10, at 1.

Chapter 6, and its constitutional form that I will consider here, are pragmatist not in the sense of adopting a systemic strategy that includes strong presumptive respect for the authority of legal rules, but in a sense that denies that authority. Judicial (including constitutional) pragmatists decide, on more or less a case-by-case basis, whether attributing authority (or appearing to attribute authority) to a legal rule will produce an all-things-considered good result.

Now pragmatism is not really a methodology of *interpretation*, strictly speaking, in that its primary purpose is not to accurately apply existing legal rules to particular cases. And it must be said that thoroughgoing constitutional pragmatists are hard to find. Richard Posner, a prominent theorist and sitting federal judge, espouses pragmatism in his academic writing, but it seems doubtful that he practices it consistently in his judicial role, at least in the sense in which I understand the concept here.[170] The influential constitutional theorist who perhaps comes closest to pragmatism is John Hart Ely; as we've seen, constitutional rules for Ely seem largely incidental to the judicial project of policing the representative process. But even Ely does not advocate all-things-considered judgments in constitutional cases.

Nonetheless, a brief focus on constitutional pragmatism may be helpful here to demonstrate the extent to which its most appealing alternative, constitutional *interpretivism*—a good-faith attempt to apply existing constitutional rules, even indeterminate ones, to particular cases—is central to the DR account. As I explained in Chapter 6, pragmatism relies for the authority of judicial decisions entirely on the *primary* authority of the process—on the capacity of participatory adjudication to acceptably resolve disputes on an *ex post* basis.[171] This creates

---

170. Posner's most extensive defense of pragmatism in law appears in his book *Law, Pragmatism, and Democracy*. RICHARD A. POSNER, LAW, PRAGMATISM, AND DEMOCRACY (2003). But elsewhere Posner has emphasized the existence of role-based constraints on the judicial role. *See* RICHARD A. POSNER, HOW JUDGES THINK (2008); *see also A Conversation with Judge Richard Posner*, 58 DUKE L.J. 1807 (2009) (transcript of an interview with Posner). Judge Posner's judicial opinions are frequently cited by other federal judges, including those on the Supreme Court—an indication that he is at least perceived by other professionals as "playing by the rules." *See* Stephen J. Choi & G. Mitu Gulati, *Mr. Justice Posner? Unpacking the Statistics*, 61 N.Y.U. ANN. SURV. AM. L. 19 (2005).

171. To the extent, that is, that pragmatism relies on the concept of legal *authority* at all. It is possible to understand pragmatism as concerned solely with reaching substantively optimal results in particular cases, without regard even to the procedures by which those results are reached. As we saw in Chapter 2, a litigant who substantively disagrees with a pragmatist decision would not accept that decision's authority over her without some content-independent reason to do so. But perhaps pragmatist judges can rely simply on the law's coercion mechanisms to solve this problem; the content-independent reason for a losing litigant to accept the result would be that the sheriff or federal marshal will enforce that result at gunpoint if necessary. Or perhaps pragmatist judges can camouflage the pragmatic nature of their decisions behind the trappings of participatory adjudication and rule-based reasoning. Neither of these tactics seems likely to be successful as a way to

two categories of problems for the authority of pragmatic judicial decisions. The first is that those decisions lack whatever *derivative* authority comes from application of legal rules produced by a democratic legislative process. The second is that those decisions may be deficient even in their primary authority, because the absence of rules to guide adjudication threatens to make the litigants' participation less effective.

Both these shortcomings afflict constitutional pragmatism as well. A purely pragmatic process of constitutional adjudication lacks any true ties to the Framing, and thus it sacrifices an important source of externality from current democratic disputes and thus of impartiality with respect to those disputes. It also forgoes the competence of the superdemocratic Framing process. Purely pragmatic adjudication is all sail and no anchor, but the presence of an anchor— in the form of durable, externally imposed rules—is essential to the dispute-resolving authority of constitutional law.

Purely pragmatic adjudication also lacks much of the relative impartiality and competence that a fully participatory method of adjudication can provide. The absence of a requirement that judicial decisions be tethered, in a plausible fashion, to externally imposed rules removes a significant constraint on the judge's own partiality; the resulting decision becomes mostly or entirely a product of the judge's personal moral and political convictions. Where a judge is simply filling gaps in democratically enacted law—answering questions left unanswered by statutes—this phenomenon might not seem especially problematic; the judge's decision, after all, can be overturned by the full democratic process. But constitutional adjudication often trumps democracy rather than merely supplementing it; and it is difficult to see, from the perspective of accuracy, why the political or moral judgments of a single judge ought to overturn those of democratic politics. Pragmatic adjudication thus undercuts the case for having constitutional law in the first place.

And, as I suggested in Chapter 6, pragmatic adjudication risks diluting participation by keeping the litigants guessing about the true grounds of the decision they are trying to influence. If litigants argue from the rules while the judge will decide on other grounds, it's hard to see how their participation has been especially effective. And if the litigants know the judge will not decide based on rules, it may be quite difficult for them to anticipate the grounds upon which the judge actually will rely. Pragmatic judges thus might find themselves freed, not only of the tethers of constitutional rules themselves, but also of the need to respond meaningfully to the litigants' participatory efforts. This judicial freedom

---

induce general acceptance of pragmatist decisions over the long run. And in any event it seems that a conscientious and suitably modest pragmatist judge would, as a general matter, prefer participatory adjudication to her own isolated, unilateral decisionmaking as a way to determine what result would, in a given case, be best, all things considered.

may be a large part of the point of pragmatism—but it eviscerates the dispute-resolving authority of the process.

C. An Interpretivist Alternative

So constitutional formalism fails to deliver on its promise of determinacy, and where it happens to succeed it does so at too high a price to responsiveness. But at least formalism, by aspiring to perfect impartiality, makes some sense of the dispute-resolving purpose of constitutional law; constitutional pragmatism lacks even this virtue. What is required is an interpretive methodology that is, well, *interpretive*—an attempt actually to apply constitutional rules—but not naïvely mechanical.

The discussion of rule application in Chapter 5 provides a good framework for such an account. That discussion turned on two central ideas: *linguistic intention* and *justification*. Linguistic intention is the concept or concepts the rulemaker intended to communicate using the language of the rule, concepts that are made relatively determinate by the context in which the language is chosen and thus remain binding over time. Justification is the most normatively attractive explanation of why the rulemaker created the rule using that language, an explanation that depends in part upon facts about the language (e.g., positive and negative paradigm cases of its application), in part upon facts about the rule's adoption (e.g., the circumstances or problems to which the rule was responsive), and in part upon the interpreter's own judgment about the relative moral attractiveness of alternative reasonable explanations.

This version of interpretivism seems especially promising for constitutional law because it makes sense of the mixture of externality and responsiveness that characterizes that process. As I suggested in Chapter 5, deference to a rule's linguistic intention and respect for its justification both make it meaningfully possible to *apply* an indeterminate rule; as such, they allow some of the authority that flows from the rulemaking process to enhance the authority of the adjudicative process and thus of the resulting decision. In the constitutional context, this methodology—in pointed contrast to pragmatism—takes advantage of the externality, and thus the relative impartiality, of the Framing. In contrast to formalism, this approach latches onto those decisions made by the Framers whose competence is most likely to translate well to later generations: their decisions regarding open-ended concepts like liberty and equality, rather than their specific understandings of how those concepts would apply. And so, unlike formalism, the linguistic intention/justification approach allows room for interpreters, by adjusting the ways in which the Constitution's open-textured concepts apply, to respond over time to evolving public values.

My suggestion here—that a form of interpretivism focusing on linguistic intention and justification is appropriate on a DR account of constitutional process—is prescriptive in a sense that the rest of the discussion in this chapter, and indeed in this book, has not been. Interpretive methodology is a hotly contested aspect of current American constitutional practice: Different judges favor different methodologies, the same judges sometimes use different methodologies in different cases, different methodologies often are used to interpret the same constitutional provisions, and interpretive methodology itself sometimes is an explicit bone of contention among judges. So I cannot claim that American constitutional interpretation typically proceeds along the lines I'm advocating.

I do think it is reasonable to assert, however, that American constitutional law generally has developed in a manner that is consistent with this interpretive methodology. Very few extant constitutional doctrines make hash of the language in which the relevant provision is expressed. The oxymoronic doctrine of "substantive due process"—which Ely once compared to "green pastel redness"[172]—may be a counterexample; but if so it probably is an excusable compensation for the Court's questionable early decision to construe the Privileges or Immunities Clause narrowly.[173] The fact that the First Amendment's protection of "the freedom of speech, and of the press" has been extended to activities that are themselves neither speech nor press—spending on political campaigns, for example[174]—is at worst a limited exception and at best a reasonable interpretation of "speech" as a proxy for "expression" more generally. There may be other arguable counterexamples, but they are scarce. Contemporary constitutional doctrine, that is, generally respects the notion of linguistic intentions.

I think it generally respects the notion of justification as well. This is not to say that the Court has always relied upon a consistent set of justifications in interpreting each constitutional provision—far from it—or that the justifications supporting any given body of constitutional doctrine are coherent or internally consistent. It certainly is not to say that I always agree with the justifications upon which the Court seems to have relied. It is, rather, to suggest two points, neither of which is provable without starting another book but both of which, I think, will resonate with close observers of American constitutional jurisprudence. The first point is that the Court typically engages directly with the question of a provision's justification in interpreting that provision. Granted, the engagement is not always extensive and is very often unsatisfactory; granted, the Court often focuses more on the justifications of its own earlier decisions than on the justification of the underlying provision itself (more on this below);

---

172. ELY, *supra* note 10, at 18.

173. The decision in question is *The Slaughter-House Cases*, 83 U.S. (16 Wall.) 36 (1872). *See* ELY, *supra* note 10, at 22–30 (discussing *Slaughter-House* and the fate of the Privileges or Immunities Clause).

174. *See* Citizens United v. Fed. Election Comm'n, 130 S.Ct. 876 (2010); McConnell v. Fed. Election Comm'n, 510 U.S. 93 (2003); Buckley v. Valeo, 424 U.S. 1 (1976).

and granted, the justices often search for what I've called "justification" under other labels, like "purpose," "policy," and even "original intent." The process of trying to understand and implement some reasonable, normatively attractive explanation for a provision nonetheless is a familiar feature of American constitutional interpretation.

The second point is that, normative considerations aside, few if any current doctrines in American constitutional law lack some strong connection to the linguistic and social ingredients of justification: core examples of the relevant concepts, negative paradigms, and salient problems to which the Framers sought to respond. For example, the concerns obviously at the center of the Framers' decision to adopt the Free Speech Clause—primarily fears about government punishment or censorship of political speech—remain at the heart of free speech doctrine today. The same can be said about the concerns animating the Religion Clauses (forced state indoctrination of religious belief or compulsion of religious practice), the Equal Protection Clause (continued discrimination against freed black slaves and their descendants), the Commerce Clause (protectionist, conflicting, and otherwise inefficient local regulation), and most other provisions of the Constitution. The doctrine generally has remained tethered, however loosely, to the act taken by the Framers when they created the rules that doctrine is supposed to interpret.

Finally, it should be entirely noncontroversial to note that in many respects, current American constitutional doctrine has rejected as nonbinding the legal intentions of the Framers as opposed to their linguistic intentions. Here are some prominent examples, a few of which I also mentioned above: The rejection of school segregation (and "separate but equal" more generally) despite ample evidence that most of the Framers endorsed or at least tolerated it; the protection of various "privacy" rights—contraception, abortion, same-sex sexual conduct—despite the unlikelihood that many of the Framers would have countenanced such rights; the expansion of the freedom of speech to cover defamation, commercial speech, and campaign spending; and the use of the commerce power to regulate private racial discrimination, the growing of marijuana for private medicinal use, and other local activities. Despite frequent objections from professed formalists, American constitutional law has taken seriously the Framers' choice to phrase crucial constitutional provisions using flexible, open-textured language.

While the interpretivist methodology I've sketched here and in Chapter 5, then, is more than a bit aspirational—it clearly does not represent anything like a current consensus among judges, practitioners, and scholars—it also is far more than a fantasy. Its general features, I think, are recognizable to anyone familiar with our practice; it's only that some of those features are controversial. But there is another feature of our constitutional practice, one I've touched on only lightly to this point, that is both undeniably central to that practice and itself quite controversial. That feature is the Supreme Court's professed respect for its own prior constitutional decisions.

D. Constitutional Precedent

An important way in which the Court brings some measure of determinacy to necessarily open-textured constitutional rules is through the doctrine of *stare decisis*—the principle that the Court presumptively will adhere to its own prior decisions. I illustrated and provided a conceptual framework for *stare decisis* in Chapter 5, in discussing the common law. It turns out that the place of *stare decisis* in constitutional decisionmaking is especially controversial. This is in part because constitutional issues tend to be publicly and politically salient. Mostly, however, it is a product of the special consequences of *stare decisis* in the constitutional context. Hard as it is to overturn a garden-variety judicial decision elaborating the common law or interpreting a statute, it is orders of magnitude more difficult to overturn a Supreme Court decision interpreting the Constitution. Either the Constitution itself must be amended, an event that has occurred only twenty-seven times in the nation's history (ten of them all at once during the first few years of the republic); or the multifaceted and often messy political dynamics described earlier in this chapter must be allowed to work, a prospect that is as uncertain as formal amendment and often no less time-consuming.

This difficulty of overturning the Court's constitutional decisions by external means suggests two potentially competing implications. The first, emphasized by constitutional formalists, is that suboptimal (formalists would say "erroneous") constitutional decisions may linger for a very long time and perhaps even proliferate. If the Court misinterprets the Constitution in Case A (perhaps, on a formalist view, by misreading original intent), *stare decisis* threatens to replicate that misinterpretation in similar Case B, and perhaps to extend it in less-similar Case C. This is particularly grating to formalists, who see the Constitution as typically or always having a single rigid, fixed meaning that the Court might "get wrong." Formalists thus tend to be skeptical of, and sometimes downright opposed to, *stare decisis* in constitutional cases.[175] (The problem is perhaps not as great for nonformalists, who understand that most constitutional provisions are susceptible of multiple reasonable interpretations.) In this sense, *stare decisis* seems especially problematic in the constitutional context.

On the other hand—second—the difficulty of politically overturning constitutional decisions of the Court emphasizes the importance of *stare decisis* as an instrument of judicial constraint, or at least judicial self-restraint. With little chance of immediate correction by the political branches, it might seem as

---

175. Justice Scalia grudgingly accepts *stare decisis* as "not part of my originalist philosophy" but rather "a pragmatic exception to it." Antonin Scalia, *Response, in* A MATTER OF INTERPRETATION: FEDERAL COURTS AND THE LAW, *supra* note 97, at 129, 140 (emphasis in original). A few formalist scholars have rejected even this "pragmatic exception" to originalism. *See* Randy E. Barnett, *Trumping Precedent with Original Meaning: Not as Radical as It Sounds*, 22 CONST. COMMENT. 257 (2006); Gary Lawson, *The Constitutional Case Against Precedent*, 17 HARV. J.L. & PUB. POL'Y 23 (1994).

though the primary safeguard against the justices' bare imposition of their own preferences is the presumptive need to demonstrate some consistency with prior decisions. This constraining role takes on particular importance for nonformalists, precisely because, for them (I should say for *us*), the devices of text and original intent themselves provide so little constraint.[176]

The DR account has at least three valuable and interrelated things to say about constitutional precedent. The first is that the case for it is reasonably strong (and in fact closely matches a well-known justification of precedent offered by the Court itself). In its 1992 decision in *Planned Parenthood v. Casey*, which preserved the "essential holding" of *Roe v. Wade*, the Court offered an interesting reason for adhering to its own prior constitutional decisions: Failure to do so would undermine the Court's own authority. Much of that authority (the Court suggested) rests on a widespread public belief that the Court decides constitutional questions based on principle rather than expedience or mere politics. But frequent overruling of constitutional precedent, or overruling of especially controversial precedents, would threaten this belief. Thus the Court should avoid, or at least have very good countervailing reasons for, overruling constitutional precedents, particularly on highly controversial topics like abortion (and especially when there has been an intervening change in the Court's membership).[177]

There is an obvious affinity between the *Casey* justification of constitutional *stare decisis* and the DR account of constitutional process I have sketched in this and the previous chapter. I've argued that constitutional authority depends in part on the externality of the process with respect to ordinary politics. As the *Casey* rationale suggests, *stare decisis* might supply that externality—or at least evince it—where text and original intent cannot. A Court that adheres to a precedent decided a generation ago, after all, applies to that extent an externally imposed rule—a rule generated by an earlier Court that was not a party to current political controversies. The Court's adherence to precedent also suggests that its constitutional decisionmaking is more than mere imposition of the

---

176. It's worth remarking on another possible reason why formalists tend to dislike constitutional *stare decisis* and nonformalists tend to like it. As I suggested earlier in the chapter, constitutional formalism, on those rare occasions when it actually works to bring reasonable determinacy, also tends to produce results that contemporary political conservatives favor. This might in part explain why political conservatives—those who have considered the matter, anyway—usually are constitutional formalists (and why political liberals usually aren't). Political conservatives, it happens, also tend to dislike many of the constitutional decisions rendered between, roughly, 1935 and 1980 by the (relatively liberal) New Deal, Warren, and Burger Courts, with *Roe v. Wade* being Exhibit A. An anti-precedent stance thus makes sense for them (especially given that the current Court is dominated by conservatives); a proprecedent stands makes sense for liberals, for the same reason.

177. *See* Planned Parenthood v. Casey, 505 U.S. 833, 864–69 (1992).

justices' own preferences. In these ways, constitutional *stare decisis* can bolster impartiality and the impression of it—in contrast to frequent overruling, which suggests a Court that is just a creature of day-to-day politics.

But of course constitutional *stare decisis* cannot be an inexorable command; that would frustrate the necessary responsiveness of constitutional doctrine to long-term movement in public opinion. This is the second implication of the DR account: While the Court should be extremely reluctant to reverse course quickly, it must be willing to change course gradually. Constitutional *stare decisis* is at bottom a balancing act, one that is sensitive to many subtle issues and that lacks a magic formula with which to accommodate them. A full treatment—well beyond my ambition here—would have to consider things like the time that has passed since the precedential decision, the changes in the Court's membership during that time, the extent to which a precedent's reasoning has been undermined by other decisions, the degree and direction of change in political and popular attitudes, and the Court's own ability (or lack thereof) to assess these many factors. (This is in addition to the general dispute-resolving virtues of *stare decisis* suggested in Chapter 5—its capacity to enhance determinacy and thus reduce the likelihood and cost of *ex post* disputes—and to other potential virtues that have little or no dispute-resolving valence, such as reliance and efficiency.)

And there is a third potential implication of the DR account—the most tentative of the three, I'm afraid. The account provides support for the notion that some constitutional decisions acquire the status of "superprecedents"—decisions whose precedential force is much stronger than the usual presumption against overturning.[178] Recall the accuracy-related advantages of constitutional law on the DR account: It is meaningfully external to ordinary democratic politics (and thus relatively impartial with respect to challenges to democratic authority); and it is, at the same time, meaningfully responsive to political and public inputs over the medium to long term (and thus reasonably competent and perceived as such). Judicial review provides a measure of externality—judges are insulated from the push and pull of everyday politics—while also allowing for long-term responsiveness. The normal mode of judicial review, then, is to avoid too-frequent overrulings (thus preserving the appearance of externality) while allowing for occasional overrulings (thus maintaining responsiveness).

Some judicial interpretations of the Constitution, however—many of them, in fact—become entrenched rather than dislodged by political responsiveness over time. As we've seen, *Brown v. Board of Education* is the classic example of this phenomenon; deeply divisive when it was rendered, that decision was repeatedly reaffirmed by the Court, eventually bolstered by congressional legislation

---

178. For a brief overview and history of the concept of "superprecedents," see Jeffrey Rosen, *So, Do You Believe in "Superprecedent"?*, N.Y. Times, Oct. 30, 2005, http://www. nytimes.com/2005/10/30/weekinreview/30rosen.html.

(the 1964 Civil Rights Act), and now enjoys the status of a fixed star in our constitutional firmament. Other plausible "superprecedents" include *West Coast Hotel Co. v. Parrish* and its New Deal progeny, which rejected the notion that economic regulations are subject to heightened scrutiny under the Due Process Clause;[179] *NLRB v. Jones & Laughlin Steel Corp.* and subsequent decisions allowing Congress substantial regulatory authority under the Commerce Clause;[180] *Griswold v. Connecticut*, recognizing a constitutional right of personal "privacy";[181] and of course the ultimate superprecedent, *Marbury v. Madison*, in which the Court claimed for itself the power of judicial review.[182]

Superprecedents like *Marbury* and *Brown* acquire almost the status of mini-Framings. Because they are decisions rendered by Courts of prior generations, they are external to the democratic disputes of today. And the fact that they have been repeatedly endorsed over time, not just by the Court itself (although that is important) but also by the actions of the other branches, gives them the stamp of special competence, not unlike the supermajoritarian process necessary to frame the original Constitution and its amendments. This understanding, of course, resonates with Bruce Ackerman's position that "constitutional moments" can occur even without formal amendments, as during the New Deal (although the "superprecedent" idea is perhaps more retrospective that Ackerman's account, focusing on the entrenchment of a judicial decision over time rather than the operative political dynamics when the decision was rendered).[183]

Note that the concept of superprecedent has its limitations; not every longstanding decision amounts to a superprecedent. *Roe v. Wade*, for example, probably

---

179. *See* West Coast Hotel Co. v. Parrish, 300 U.S. 379 (1937) (upholding a minimum wage for women against a due process challenge); United States v. Carolene Prod. Co., 304 U.S. 144 (1938) (upholding a federal ban on the shipment of "filled milk" against a due process challenge).

180. *See* NLRB v. Jones & Laughlin Steel Corp, 301 U.S. 1 (1937) (upholding the application of the National Labor Relations Act to a steel company with interstate operations); United States v. Darby, 312 U.S. 100 (1941) (upholding a federal minimum wage as applied to the production of goods for interstate commerce); Wickard v. Filburn, 317 U.S. 111 (1942) (upholding a federal quota on wheat production for home use as having a substantial aggregate effect on interstate commerce).

181. 381 U.S. 479 (1965) (invalidating a state's prohibition on contraceptive use by married couples as violating a right of privacy).

182. 5 U.S. (1 Cranch) 137 (1803). Barry Friedman's book *The Will of the People* is in essence a two-century history of *Marbury*'s evolution into a superprecedent. *See* FRIEDMAN, *supra* note 55.

183. Was *Brown* part of a "constitutional moment"? Was *Griswold*? Was *Marbury*? Probably not on Ackerman's account, which requires a phased process of "signaling," "proposal," "mobilized popular deliberation," and "legal codification." *See* ACKERMAN, *supra* note 13, at 266–67. These decisions don't fit Ackerman's pattern, and yet it is difficult to dispute that each possesses an authority in our constitutional practice that is akin to that of formal amendments to the constitutional text.

cannot claim that status. It is true that *Roe* has not been overturned despite numerous opportunities for the Court to do so, and that its principles of reproductive autonomy and bodily integrity have found their way into other areas of the law. But many of the Court's "reaffirmances" of *Roe* have been grudging at best; the *Casey* decision itself only preserved the "essential holding" of *Roe* (that abortion is a protected right) while rejecting *Roe*'s trimester framework and upholding most of the restrictive provisions actually at issue in the case.[184] The Court itself, moreover, remains closely divided on the question of an abortion right, as does the public: While polls consistently show that a popular majority supports the basic right, that support is subject to numerous qualifications.[185] The status of *Roe* therefore falls short in crucial respects of the virtual untouchability of cases like *Brown* and *Griswold*.

Does the *Roe* example demonstrate that the notion of superprecedent is largely superfluous, applying only in circumstances where a precedent is unlikely to be challenged to begin with? The story of the Rehnquist Court's federalism revolution-that-wasn't suggests otherwise. Between 1995 and 2000, the Court rendered two decisions invalidating, for the first time since the mid-1930s, federal statutes on the ground that they exceeded Congress's power to regulate commerce.[186] While neither decision directly challenged the applicable New Deal and post–New Deal precedents, the general suspicion was that these decisions

---

184. *See* 505 U.S. 833, 846 (1992) (affirming the "essential holding" of *Roe*); *id.* at 873 ("We reject the trimester framework, which we do not consider to be part of the essential holding of Roe."); *id.* at 879–901 (upholding state-law provisions providing for "informed consent" and parental consent (with a judicial bypass) as prerequisites for abortions, holding that the "medical emergency" exception to these requirements was validly drawn, and upholding general provisions for recordkeeping relating to abortion procedures while invalidating a spousal notification provision).

185. *Casey* was a six-to-three decision; the Court's most recent abortion decision as of this writing, in *Gonzalez v. Carhart* (which upheld a federal ban on so-called "partial birth" abortion procedures), was a five-to-four decision, with Justice Anthony Kennedy, who joined the majority in *Casey*, writing the Court's opinion. *See* 550 U.S. 124 (2007). A 2005 Pew Center survey found that 65 percent of the Americans surveyed opposed completely overturning *Roe*, a result that is "in line with surveys conducted by Pew and the Gallup Organization dating back to 1989." *See* THE PEW RESEARCH CTR. FOR THE PEOPLE & THE PRESS, ABORTION, THE COURT AND THE PUBLIC: A PEW RESEARCH CENTER ANALYSIS 1 (Oct. 3, 2005), http://people-press.org/commentary/?analysisid=119. But only 35 percent of the respondents thought abortion should be "generally available"; 23 percent thought it should be "more limited," and 31 percent thought it should be illegal except in cases of rape or incest or to save the mother's life. *See id.*

186. *See* United States v. Lopez, 514 U.S. 549 (1995) (holding that a federal ban on gun possession in school zones exceeded Congress's authority to regulate commerce); United States v. Morrison, 529 U.S. 598 (2000) (holding that a federal law creating a private tort action for gender-motivated violence exceeded Congress's authority under both the Commerce Clause and the power to enforce the Fourteenth Amendment).

were the initial steps in a serious attempt, under the leadership of conservative Chief Justice William Rehnquist, to substantially rein in federal power and rediscover "states' rights."[187] But the anticipated revolution never happened; it ran smack into the wall of well-settled expectations and public acceptance that had gradually been erected over the preceding sixty years. The Court's decision in 2005 to uphold the application of federal drug laws to home-grown marijuana for medicinal use—despite its legality under the law of the relevant state—amounted to a white flag signaling that the federalism revolution was over.[188] Even a conservative majority appointed by a succession of Republican residents could not unseat the New Deal superprecedents.

The DR account suggests, on the whole, that constitutional precedent ought to correlate closely to the long-term evolution of public opinion: Precedent should reflect larger trends but should provide a bulwark against momentary political shifts. Constitutional decisions that have withstood, even been enhanced by, the test of time—the *Marburys*, *Browns*, and *Griswolds*—should for that reason become especially difficult to dislodge. Constitutional decisions that have failed that test (like *Plessy v. Ferguson*,[189] which endorsed the principle of "separate but equal," and *Lochner v. New York*,[190] which elevated laissez-faire economics to the level of a constitutional right) should eventually be overturned. But time is a crucial ingredient here: As the Court itself recognized in *Casey*, overturning recently decided precedents smacks not of responsiveness to evolving values but of simple politics.

4. THE COUNTERMAJORITARIAN DIFFICULTY: THE CLASSIC STRATEGIES REVISITED

I want to conclude by briefly revisiting the classic strategies for overcoming the countermajoritarian difficulty and summarizing the ways in which the DR account differs from each of them.

---

187. *See* FRIEDMAN, *supra* note 55, at 330–32 (describing the reaction to the Rehnquist Court's "federalism revolution").

188. *See* Gonzales v. Raich, 545 U.S. 1 (2005). The Court in the early 2000s also put the brakes on another aspect of its supposed federalism revolution—the imposition of strict limits on Congress's authority to "enforce" the Fourteenth Amendment by allowing private lawsuits against the states seeking damages under federal antidiscrimination laws. *See* Nevada Dep't of Human Res. v. Hibbs, 538 U.S. 721 (2003) (upholding the abrogation of state sovereign immunity from damages suits under the federal Family and Medical Leave Act); Tennessee v. Lane, 541 U.S. 509 (2004) (upholding the abrogation of state sovereign immunity under the Americans with Disabilities Act).

189. 163 U.S. 537 (1896).

190. 198 U.S. 45 (1905).

Of the substantive strategy there is little to say. The DR account departs radically from that approach, for it offers reasons to respect constitutional authority that do not turn on one's endorsement of particular results. Unlike the substantive strategy, the DR account is in fact a justification of the *authority* of constitutional law, not merely of some particular version of its content. So it provides a reason to accept that authority even when one finds the content disagreeable.

Footnote Four proceduralism, on the other hand, has much in common with the DR approach. Both emphasize the inadequacy of ordinary democratic politics as a way to resolve certain disputes about democratic authority; both offer constitutional law as a superior alternative. But the DR account is both broader and deeper than the version of proceduralism suggested by Footnote Four and elucidated by John Hart Ely. It is broader in that it understands constitutional law as a solution to more than just agency failure and irrational majority bias. Ely's theory focuses on the danger that democratic officials will seek to arbitrarily entrench their own power and on the phenomenon of prejudice against "discrete and insular minorities" within the political system. The DR account sees these problems as important, too. But the DR account recognizes that democratic politics can be unacceptably partial in other ways as well. Majority partiality can stem not just from irrational bias, but from perfectly rational self-interest (as Madison recognized long ago in *Federalist No. 10*). And—something Madison failed to appreciate—self-interested but well-organized minorities too can make the process unsuitably partial.

The DR account is deeper than Footnote Four proceduralism in that it explains core features of our constitutional practice—namely our fidelity to the text and our obsession with the Framing—that proceduralism largely ignores. Proceduralism rests on the relative insulation of the Court itself from the rough and tumble of ordinary politics—an important element, to be sure—but it has trouble explaining why the Court should see its mission as interpreting a centuries-old document rather than simply reaching the all-things-considered best democracy-promoting result. The DR account can make sense of this otherwise odd ritual by emphasizing the importance of externality to constitutional authority.

The various dualist strategies also resemble the DR account in important ways. Both Bickel's and Ackerman's varieties of dualism emphasize the nonuniform nature of democratic decisionmaking—the fact that processes, and results, can be meaningfully democratic without being the products of everyday majoritarian politics—and the DR account incorporates this insight as well. The dualism of Bickel and Eisgruber, however, relies on a distinction between "values" or "principles" and "interests" or "expediency" that is likely to be substantively controversial, if not generally then as applied in particular cases, and thus offers tenuous support for constitutional authority. The DR approach eschews this kind of substantive distinction, focusing instead on the potential for democracy to malfunction as a decisionmaking process. And like proceduralism, Bickelian dualism underappreciates the centrality of the text and, especially, of the Framing to American constitutional process, a shortcoming the DR account rectifies.

Ackerman's version of dualism, by contrast, almost fetishizes the Framing and similar "constitutional moments." The DR account shares Ackerman's appreciation for the superdemocratic character of the Framing process, but unlike Ackerman it offers a robust justification of the institution of judicial review. Ackerman's theory relegates judicial review to the task of preserving the products of constitutional moments and synthesizing them with each other—important work, but work that becomes less authoritative as the relevant moments fade further into the chronological distance. The DR account explains judicial review, not just as a way of translating the Framing, but as a sort of regulator valve that maintains appreciable externality from ordinary politics on the one hand while responding, over time, to popular and political inputs on the other.

In this latter sense, the DR account incorporates the reductionist message that constitutional doctrine tends, in the long run, to track the election returns. But the DR account emphatically denies that constitutional law is simply a political pig wearing legal lipstick. (To be fair, most legal academics with reductionist leanings also reject the extreme version of this claim.) The need to interpret a text, the sense of being beholden to history, and the typical (if not universal) judicial opacity to politics all are very real elements of American constitutional process. A pure form of reductionism ignores them, but they are central to the DR account.

Overall, the DR account of constitutional authority probably shares most in common with Ely's version of proceduralism; and in fact there would be nothing erroneous about classifying the DR account as a more deeply theorized version of Ely's approach. The two accounts are, I think, compatible; it is only that the DR account, unlike Ely's, traces the roots of constitutional authority back through the soil of democracy and, ultimately, of legality itself. It holds that constitutionalism and judicial review are simply manifestations of our more profound commitment to the use of legal processes to avoid or resolve substantive disputes.

EPILOGUE
The Limits of Law

On July 4, 1861, with the nation at war against itself, President Abraham Lincoln stood to address a special joint session of Congress. It was four months to the day since Lincoln had taken his oath of office; five months to the day since South Carolina and six other slave states had declared the formation of the Confederate States of America; and eighty-five years to the day since another band of rebels had, as Lincoln later would describe it, "brought forth . . . a new nation, conceived in liberty, and dedicated to the proposition that all men are created equal." Lincoln now intended to preserve that nation and uphold that proposition, with blood if need be.

But first he had some explaining to do. In April, after the clash at Fort Sumter, militiamen from Massachusetts, called to defend Washington, had been attacked by a mob in Baltimore. Fearing that Maryland would fall under secessionist control, thus isolating the capital, Lincoln had effectively declared martial law in the state, authorizing his military commanders to suspend the writ of *habeas corpus* along the railroad line between Philadelphia and Washington. The order was of questionable constitutionality. The Constitution authorizes the suspension of *habeas* "when in Cases of Rebellion or Invasion the public Safety may require it," but the placement of the Suspension Clause within Article I suggests the power in question belongs to Congress, not to the President. To make matters worse, Supreme Court Chief Justice Roger Taney (himself a slave-owning Marylander) had, in May, issued a *habeas* writ ordering the release of John Merryman, a Baltimore secessionist imprisoned at Fort McHenry. Acting at Lincoln's behest, the commanding general had ignored the order.

So Lincoln, when he stood before Congress on July 4, had suspended *habeas corpus* without congressional authorization and had directly disobeyed the order of a federal court. The body he was to address included no representatives from the seceding states—many of them had left Washington to join the provisional Confederate Congress, about to convene in Richmond—but it nonetheless contained many skeptics. As Lincoln himself put it, "the legality and propriety" of his actions had been "questioned," even by some unionists. And Lincoln needed Congress's loyal support, and the support of the northern states, to prosecute the war.

Lincoln's defense of his conduct before Congress was simple, honest, and— to twenty-first century ears used to hearing even the most egregious actions explained away with creative legalisms—quite remarkable. "[T]he attention of the country," Lincoln began by noting, "has been called to the proposition that one who is sworn to 'take care that the laws be faithfully executed'"—the duty imposed upon the President by Article II of the Constitution—"should not himself violate them." Consideration had "[o]f course . . . [been] given to the questions of power, and propriety" lurking beneath the *habeas* suspension. But the demands of law had given way to the requirements of necessity. "The whole of the laws which were required to be faithfully executed, were being resisted, and failing of execution, in nearly one-third of the States," Lincoln reminded Congress. "Must they be allowed to finally fail of execution, even had it been perfectly clear, that by the use of the means necessary to their execution, some single law . . . be violated? To state the question more directly, are all the laws, but one, to go unexecuted, and the government itself go to pieces, lest that one be violated?"

Lincoln's plea worked; Congress authorized funding for the war and, when Lincoln subsequently ordered the suspension of *habeas corpus* more broadly, Congress ratified his action. Perhaps more importantly for our purposes, Lincoln's conduct has stood the test of history. He is remembered in most quarters today as the Great Emancipator, the man chiefly responsible for preserving the Union, and one of a handful of truly great men to have occupied the office of the presidency. Of course, Lincoln himself paid a terrible price for having done what needed to be done. When John Wilkes Booth leaped from the presidential box at Ford's Theatre after lodging the fatal bullet in Lincoln's brain, he shouted "Sic semper tyrannis"—"Thus always to tyrants." Booth had been born and raised outside Baltimore, and to Marylanders with secessionist sympathies his violent action must have seemed a just measure of revenge.

* * *

This book has been about the rule of law—about law's capacity to motivate our reasoned obedience to its commands. But the story of Lincoln's July 4 address to Congress, and of the great national tragedy of which it was a part, is a story about the limits of law. As with many phenomena, a grasp of the essence of law leads eventually to a glimpse at its limitations.

I've argued here that the essence of law is the moral imperative to peacefully avoid or resolve disputes. Lincoln's example, however, reveals two important and related truths about that function.

The first is that the demands of law can never be, morally speaking, absolute. Sometimes the right thing to do—the *only* thing to do—is to disobey the law, lest all else "go to pieces," in Lincoln's phrase. Peaceful dispute resolution is morally important, and law's authority is a reflection of its great value. But there are other moral imperatives, too, and sometimes law must yield to them. In this crucial, unavoidable sense, Aristotle was right. And of course law itself can never tell us authoritatively when it should, for moral reasons, be disobeyed. The best that law can do is to provide us with strongly presumptive reasons—with something like a *prima facie* duty—to do what it tells us. We, like Lincoln, cannot somehow hide from our greater duty to measure law's demands against those of morality.

But—and here is a crucial lesson to learn from Lincoln—we *can* be honest about the choice between law and morality when we find ourselves facing it. In explaining his actions to Congress, Lincoln, himself a lawyer, refused to take refuge in lawyerly arguments about why what he had done really was perfectly legal, if only Congress would look at it the right way. Instead he granted the accusation that the "one" law had been violated, and he defended his conduct in moral terms, not in legal ones. In doing so, he threw himself upon the mercy of Congress, as it were; he indicated his willingness to accept the legal consequences of his moral judgments.

This is the only morally defensible attitude to take toward the law. The law speaks in absolutes—in the language of "shall" and "shall not" and "must"—not because it imposes absolute *moral* duties, but because it imposes absolute *legal* ones. The message the law sends to us is, not that we must never violate its commands, but that we will be punished if we do violate them. This message is morally valuable, because it forces us to think long and hard before we decide to break the law, to be as sure as we can be that breaking the law is the morally right thing to do. We must be willing to face the music for our actions—to suffer law's punishment in the name of a greater moral good. Lincoln was willing to do this, and that willingness—not his decision to break the law in the first place—is a large part of why he is admired by history. It is a lesson that all of us, including latter-day aspirants to Lincoln's mantle, would do well to heed.

And there is another important lesson, a more tragic one, to be learned from Lincoln and his times. The crisis to which Lincoln was forced to respond was the outbreak of a bloody conflict between two enemies with as much in common— linguistically, religiously, ethnically, historically, culturally—as any opposing sides in any war that ever has been. A single disagreement was so irreconcilable, so weighty as a matter of economics or of conscience (depending upon one's point of view), that it overrode, for the competing sides, every other moral imperative, including the fundamental Hobbesian desire to avoid violent conflict. Between late 1860 and the war's close in 1865, Americans in the North and Americans in the South could not agree on procedures—other than debate by cannon, musket, and bayonet—for resolving this fundamental dispute; they could not even agree that resolving the dispute somehow was preferable to killing and dying by the tens of thousands. They could not, in short, agree to law.

The lesson here is that law is limited not merely by morality, but also by reality. The possibility of law requires some basic social consensus that substantive commitments should be sacrificed to the cause of social order—which probably implies some basic social consensus about those substantive commitments themselves. And law requires consensus about the means by which substantive disagreements can, accurately and thus acceptably, be resolved. A society lacking one or both of these deep shared commitments is a society in which law, though morally desirable (even morally necessary), simply is not possible.

This is a lesson, not merely a lament, because social consensus itself is, like law, a product of decisions made and actions taken by human beings. And that fact itself has at least two implications as a matter of political morality. First, we ought to attend to the social prerequisites of effective law—to the development of common understandings on issues like toleration of difference, the fulfillment of basic human needs, and the reasonable allowance of individual autonomy—before we attempt to impose law, and in particular advanced legal structures like democracy and constitutionalism, upon societies that currently lack them. The absence of these elements of consensus, after all, may be the chief reason a society seems, to our eyes, to be lawless.

Second, we must keep our own societal house in order. We must respect the law, but we cannot rely on it to do everything for us. It matters that we share, at a very deep level and in a very abstract sense, certain fundamental moral values, and we must attend to those values, and to our consensus about them, rather than simply to the legal forms that reflect them. It matters also that we possess, and cultivate within ourselves, the disposition to resolve disputes agreeably—the inclination toward peace and thus away from moral absolutism. The road to a Hobbesian war of all against all, as our own Civil War demonstrates, is paved with social and cultural stones, not legal ones, and the path in the other direction must have a similar foundation. As Lincoln well understood, a house divided against itself cannot stand.

INDEX

A

absolutist legal authority, 35, 45
  as a consensualist account, 59
accuracy
  and competence, 75–78
  and the dispute-resolution (DR)
    account, 71–75
  and efficiency, 81–83
  and impartiality, 78–81
Ackerman, Bruce, 230–37
  "dualist democracy," 275, 281, 347–48
  higher lawmaking, 230–31
  in instrumental terms, 231–35
  in noninstrumental terms, 235–36
  shortcomings, 231–37
actual consent and legal authority, 49–52
Adams, John, 1
ad hoc decisionmaking, 5–7
ad hocery of common-law method,
  212–13
adjudication, democratic model of, 13,
  141–42, 155–87
  adversary system, 156–60, 169
  common-law method, 160–68, 181–86
  confinement by court decisions,
    160–61
  courts' function, 189
  Default Formalist view, 151–54
  ex post mechanisms, 154–55
  idea of interest representation, 166–67
  indeterminacy of legislative intent,
    146–51
  indeterminacy of text, 142–46
  and indeterminacy redux, 168–69
  indeterminate statute, 180n61
  inquisitorial system, 159
  legal positivism, 173–74
  legitimacy of representation, 165–66
  and linguistic intention, 174–76
  litigation-related tasks, 157–59
  Ninth and Tenth Amendments to the
    federal Constitution, 153, 154n15

overruling, 163n35
  participation and representation in,
    155–69
  perceived "participation gap" in, 162
  pragmatic, 337
  primary and derivative authority, 170–72
  reasonable accuracy, 169–70
  and statutory justification, 176–81
  textualism *vs* originalism, 142
adjudicative theory, 20–22
Adkins v Children's Hosp., 239n47, 268n102
adversary system of justice, 13, 156–60
affirmative action policies, 311, 313
al Qaeda, xiii
Alexander, Larry, 35n2, 64n47, 109n3
alternative dispute resolution (ADR)
  programs, 197, 199–201
American constitutionalism, 213, 239
American constitutional law, procedures
  of. *See* constitutional process
amicus curiae, 207, 318–20, 318n127, 325
analogizing, 164
analytic legal philosophy, 15–18. *See also*
  legal authority, problem of
  epistemic-guidance (EG) account, 18
Anglo-American law, 164, 184
  modern, 166
antidemocratic pathologies, 23
antimiscegenation laws, 240
aristocracy, 11n7
Aristotle, 3–4
  best government, 11
  challenge to legal authority, 33, 36, 38–39
  and the problem of exceptions, 3
  rule by virtuous men, 38
  vs Adams's rule-of-law ideal, 7–12, 39
  "attitudinal model" of judicial
    behavior, 284

B

Bakke case, 325
Bickel, Alexander, 22, 213